AMERICA-EUROPE

AMERICA-EUROPE

A Transatlantic Diary 1961-1989

The Civil Rights Movement in the U.S.A.
The European Integration
Questions of European Security
Space Travel and Exploration
Presidential Elections in the U.S.A.
The Immigration Experience
A Common World Civilization
The Atlantic Community

Klaus Lanzinger

Copyright © 2007 by Klaus Lanzinger.

Library of Congress Control Number: 2007904014
ISBN: Hardcover 978-1-4257-5664-2
       Softcover 978-1-4257-5663-5

All rights reserved. No part of this book may be reproduced or transmitted in any form or by any means, electronic or mechanical, including photocopying, recording, or by any information storage and retrieval system, without permission in writing from the copyright owner.

This book was printed in the United States of America.

English translation by the author of the original German text, "Amerika-Europa: Ein transatlantisches Tagebuch 1961-1989," which is accessible online at http://www.archives.nd.edu/kl/lnz.htm

Note: Comments added by the translator stand in brackets [Transl:].

To order additional copies of this book, contact:
Xlibris Corporation
1-888-795-4274
www.Xlibris.com
Orders@Xlibris.com

38926

CONTENTS

Foreword 11

Part I 1961-1971: Civil Rights Movement, Demonstrations, Space Travel And Exploration

    Section 1 19
    Section 2 47
    Section 3 74
    Section 4 115

Part II 1971-1979: The Decade of the Détente

    Section 5 155
    Section 6 194
    Section 7 239

Part III 1980-1989: The Breakthrough

    Section 8 287
    Section 9 324
    Section 10 354
    Section 11 393

Epilogue 435
Index of Names 449

To Aida,

My beloved spouse and unfailing companion
on our many travels

In gratitude to the University of Notre Dame, this Diary has been donated to the University of Notre Dame Archives. Without Notre Dame it could not have been written.

The years of the Berlin Wall 1961-1989 provided the time frame for the narrative. It was a critical period in the history of the West, when in response to an immense threat the Atlantic Alliance was formed.

The 55,000 BRT passenger ship *United States*, the second ship in the picture, lies docked at the Hudson River Pier in the Harbor of New York. The photo was taken from the roof garden of our hotel in Manhattan. It was the evening before we returned to Europe on board the *United States* the end of August, 1964.

"These ships are alive with the supreme ecstasy of the modern world, which is the voyage to America."

Thomas Wolfe, *Of Time and the River,* Chap. 102

FOREWORD

When America liberated Europe in 1945, it was the great unknown. What did we know of America? We knew very little, and the little we knew was a distorted picture. In hindsight it is very hard to imagine how compelling the need for knowledge about America was. I had experienced that development and was touched by it.

I was born in 1928 in the town of Wörgl, in the Lower Inn Valley of the Tyrol, Austria, where I also grew up. After graduating from the Realgymnasium* in Kufstein in 1948, I studied English Philology, History, and American Studies at the University of Innsbruck from 1948-52. In my second year of studies I received a Fulbright Scholarship that brought me for the academic year 1950-51 to Bowdoin College in Brunswick, Maine. Bowdoin is a New England Liberal Arts College with a rich tradition. Nathaniel Hawthorne and Henry Wadsworth Longfellow studied there from 1821-25. As I was given credit for my previous studies, I was able to graduate from Bowdoin College with a B.A. degree cum laude in June of 1951. The year at Bowdoin College was an eye-opener for me. From then on, the puzzle America has not let go of me anymore. In December of 1952 I obtained a Dr. of Philosophy (Ph.D.) with a dissertation on Nathaniel Hawthorne at the University of Innsbruck. Marriage and raising a family followed thereafter. My wife Aida, née Schüssl, comes from Vienna. Our two children, son Franz and daughter Christine, were born in 1955 and 1959 respectively in Innsbruck, Austria. Temporarily, I worked in the book selling and publishing business.

[Transl: *The Realgymnasium is generally assumed to be the equivalent of a high school plus two years of college.]

The chance to pursue an academic career offered itself in 1957 when I received the position of Research Assistant at the newly-founded Amerika-Institut of the University of Innsbruck. I became intensely preoccupied with American Studies, which at that time were still in their infancy. Especially valuable during my time as Research Assistant was the contact with the American Fulbright-guest professors who were interchangeably assigned to the Institute every year. For 1961 I received a grant from the Fulbright-Commission in Vienna that made it possible to spend a six month period of research in the United States. I was working at the time on a book project on the epic in the American novel with separate chapters on James Fenimore Cooper, Herman Melville, Frank Norris, and Thomas Wolfe. The University of Pennsylvania in Philadelphia granted me its "courtesy doctoral privileges" that gave me free access to its research facilities. The main reason for going to the University of Pennsylvania was Professor Robert E. Spiller who was one of the leading scholars in the area of American literature. Professor Spiller admitted me to his seminar and gave me helpful advice on how to carry out my research project. I could spend the summer months of 1961 at the Huntington Library in Pasadena, California. After my sojourn in the United States, an intense period of publication that comprised a number of articles on American literature followed. At the same time I was entrusted with the editorship of *Americana-Austriaca*, an American Studies series whose 5 volumes appeared from 1966-80 at the Wilhelm Braumüller Universitätsverlag in Vienna.

The unexpected turning point in my life occurred in the summer of 1962 when the University of Notre Dame in Indiana began a collaboration with the University of Innsbruck in order to establish a foreign studies program. I was put in charge of making the preparations for the establishment of the program. In doing so, an immediate close cooperation with the University of Notre Dame developed. After the preparatory work in Innsbruck had been finished, I was invited to come to Notre Dame as a Visiting Assistant Professor for the spring semester of 1964 to help with the preparation and selection of students for the program. This time my wife and I decided to travel together with our two children to America. We arrived in South Bend, Indiana, by the middle of January 1964. The Notre Dame Campus is located on the north end of the city. Notre Dame was founded by a French religious order in 1842.* Today the University of Notre Dame is regarded as one of the leading Catholic universities in North America. When I returned to Notre Dame as a Visiting Associate Professor in 1967, tenure was granted, i.e. permanent appointment as a faculty member of the University. The opportunity to teach at a well-known Catholic university in America made it much easier for me and my family to decide to emigrate. As a professor at Notre Dame I served several times as resident director of the Notre Dame Foreign Studies Program in Innsbruck. Consequently, our moving frequently between South Bend and Innsbruck led to a veritable transatlantic migration.

[Transl: * The University of Notre Dame was founded in 1842 by the Congregatio a Sancta Cruce (C.S.C.), or the Congregation of Holy Cross from Le Mans in France.]

How the Diary originated

The American journey of spring and summer 1961 initiated the practice of keeping a diary with observations on America in comparison to Europe. I first thought of an American diary concentrating on my American journeys of 1961 and 1964. Since there are no records available for the time in between, historical events of the years from 1962-64 and 1964-67 are briefly summarized. But from April 1967 on, the records continue uninterrupted until December 1989. They are not daily entries but such that were from time to time stimulated by travel experiences and important historical events. As a result, there are on the one hand gaps, and on the other a quick sequence of entries as the events required. Due to the frequent Atlantic crossings, the original American expanded to the present transatlantic diary. Changing residences every other year between America and Europe made it possible to reflect on and observe more thoroughly social and political conditions as well as different lifestyles on both sides of the Atlantic.

What was written down?

What I had written down at the time had surprised me and evoked my astonishment, while my attention remained concentrated on the following subjects: 1) The civil rights movement in the U.S.A.; 2) The European integration and questions of European security; 3) Space travel and exploration; and 4) The emerging common world civilization. Consciously, also my own immigration experience to the United States was recorded.

The Edition [ ]

After my retirement in 1997 I was able to attend to the diaries which had accumulated over four decades. The handwritten recordings had been stored away in cartons that were only opened again for the editorial work. I was often surprised myself about what had come to light. The editorial work lasted from the fall of 1997 to the spring of 2002. The original text was not changed in regard to its contents but only stylistically brushed up. Occasional sketchy entries on travels were brought on a coherent and readable form. Names, dates and historical events were checked on their accuracy through the reference sources listed below. Anything that was added through the editorial process stands in brackets [ ]. These include comments, supplements, biographical sketches, and connecting passages. The text has lost nothing of its immediacy to the historical event.

Indications of Place and Time

The place indicated is always the one where the entry was made. If no place is mentioned, then the immediately preceding place applies. This is mostly the case when sequences of events quickly follow one another. In order to maintain consistency, the dates of the entry in the original German text are given in German even if the entry was written in English.

[Transl: Throughout this translation all dates are consistently given in English.]

REFERENCE SOURCES

Names, biographies, historical events and dates have been checked on their accuracy through the following reference sources:

A) Encyclopedias, reference books

    Brockhaus Enzyklopaedie.
    Mannheim: F.A. Brockhaus, 19th rev. ed. 1986-1994. 24 vols.

    Collier's Encyclopedia.
    New York: P.F. Collier, rev. ed. 1996. 24 vols.

    The Encyclopedia Americana: International Edition.
    Danbury, Connecticut: Grolier Inc., rev. ed. 1999. 30 vols.

    Der Grosse Ploetz: Auszug aus der Geschichte.
    Freiburg: Verlag Ploetz, 1980.

B) Biographical reference works

    American National Biography.
    New York: Oxford University Press, 1999. 24 vols.

    [For biographies from American history up to 1900. Replaces the older *Dictionary of American Biography* (DAB) of 1926 and 1937.]

    Current Biography Yearbook.
    New York: H.W. Wilson Co., 1961-2000.

[There is a single volume available for each year.]

Deutsche Biographische Enzyklopaedie.
München: K.G. Saur, 1995-2000. 12 vols.

Who's Who in America.
New Providence, New Jersey: Marquis Who's Who, 2000.

Who's Who in the World.
New Providence, New Jersey: Marquis Who's Who, 2000.

[Single sources, especially books, newspapers and magazines are referred to in the text.]

PART I
1961-1971

Civil Rights Movement, Demonstrations, Space Travel and Exploration

Section 1: March 12, 1961-September 25, 1961
Historical Events 1962-64

Section 2: January 18, 1964-September 5, 1964
Historical Events 1964-67

Section 3: April 9, 1967-December 27, 1968

Section 4: January 14, 1969-July 23, 1971

SECTION 1

March 12, 1961-September 25, 1961

[As the beginning of my research at the University of Pennsylvania in Philadelphia had been scheduled for the middle of March 1961, I started my journey to the United States early in March. First I traveled by train on the Arlberg-Express from Innsbruck to Paris where I spent a few days. From there the regular boat train brought me from the Gare St-Lazare to Le Havre. I crossed the Atlantic on board the still fairly new 55,000 BRT passenger ship *United States*.]

[Transl: The *United States* was built in 1952. She was at the time the fastest passenger ship on the North Atlantic route. Crossing the Atlantic from Le Havre to New York took five days.]

New York, March 12, 1961

Coming back to New York, the city is more impressive than I remembered. After ten years, the aspects by which one sees the city have changed considerably. Today, New York gives the impression of being a world metropolis more than Paris. What comes to my special attention is the shift in the color line. Here whites and non-whites, Asians, Europeans, South Americans, and Africans meet in a matter of fact manner that is astonishing. Also the local colored population seems to mingle inconspicuously with whites. Anyway, demonstrations against segregation at the lunch-table that took place yesterday afternoon on Fifth Avenue did not make an impression either on colored people or whites.

New York, March 13, 1961

Trinity Church [On Broadway and Wall Street]

Trinity Church in Lower Manhattan (built ca. 1760) gives an idea of how the Financial District looked at the outset of its growth. Until late in the 19th century, houses there were not more than one or two stories high, whereas the skyline of Lower Manhattan now rises to dizzying heights. The Woolworth Building with its odd pseudo-gothic stucco exterior is an outstanding example of the old type of skyscrapers, while the new buildings on East 42nd Street set the pace for the modern line of architecture. The United Nations Building on the East River is the most impressive example of this new architectural design.

Brooklyn Bridge

To understand Walt Whitman and Thomas Wolfe one has to stand on the Brooklyn Bridge looking at the skyline to the right and watch the unceasing flow of traffic below.

Comment on the Brooklyn Bridge

[When the construction of the suspension bridge over the East River that connects Brooklyn with Manhattan was completed in 1883, it was regarded as a technological wonder. The Brooklyn Bridge as well as the Statue of Liberty, which was unveiled in 1886 on an island off Manhattan, is a symbol of America as the country of immigration. While the Statue of Liberty is more seen through the eyes of the world outside of America as a hopeful sign of the New World, the Brooklyn Bridge has been used in American literature as a manifold theme of historical significance. Already Walt Whitman in the second edition of *Leaves of Grass* (1856) had with "Crossing Brooklyn Ferry" sung of Manhattan and the stream of people who had crossed the East River before the Bridge was built. Hart Crane wrote the epic poem *The Bridge* (1930), in which he tried to find a synthesis of the American historical experience since Columbus. Thomas Wolfe who had lived in Brooklyn from 1931-35 treated his experience of the Bridge in his great novel *Of Time and the River* (1935). Finally, Arthur Miller wrote with *A View from the Bridge* (1955) an immigrant tragedy that is timelessly overarched by the Bridge. Significantly, Kafka began his novel *Amerika* (1912/1927) at the entrance to the harbor of New York with the Statue of Liberty—"die Statue der Freiheitsgöttin," around whose figure "die freien Lüfte wehten."]

Comment on the Street Gridiron of Manhattan

[The gridiron or rectangular network of streets of Manhattan makes it, as is well known, easy to find one's way in New York. This goes back to the New York city planning of 1811 whereby avenues were laid out running lengthwise and the streets in ascending numbers in rectangular position to them. Only Broadway meanders diagonally through the Peninsular. This rectangular design of the streets stands in sharp contrast to the maze of alleys of the historically grown cities in Europe.

But this gridiron has gained national significance beyond Manhattan and New York. The rectangular grid has virtually become the pattern for organizing space in America. Most cities have been laid out this way; county lines follow this pattern just as well. Also the border lines of states beyond the Mississippi are for the most part rectangular, a glance at a map will show. This rectilinear geometric pattern was practical, efficient, easily grasped, and it suited the American need for surveying and organizing space very well.]

[During my brief stay in New York I met at the Institute of International Education with the advisor who administered my grant from the Tona Shepherd Trust Fund. Immediately thereafter I went on to Philadelphia.]

Philadelphia, March 14, 1961

The natural friendliness and frankness in this country tend to relieve many of the mental frustrations and tensions that underlie official and unofficial encounters at home.

At a luncheon in the Franklin Inn Club I was reminded of the fact that, already at the time of the American Revolution, Philadelphia was the second largest city in the English speaking world. Only London was larger.

[When I arrived at the University of Pennsylvania, I was received with great friendliness by Professor Robert Spiller. Robert E. Spiller (1896-1988), Professor of English at the University of Pennsylvania, was one of the leading scholars in the area of American literature. He admitted me to his seminar and gave me helpful advice in carrying out my research project on the epic in the American novel. Immediately after my arrival, Professor Spiller introduced me into the Faculty Club, which was for me a new facility on the grounds of a university. The Faculty Club offered a reasonably-priced lunch; there was also a lounge with comfortable sitting and reading materials. In a relaxed atmosphere, it was possible to immediately strike up a conversation with colleagues. I saw a new world of an academic community that was common in America but at that time hardly existed in Europe. Professor Spiller also invited me to a luncheon in the Franklin Inn Club. The Franklin Inn Club, one of the oldest literary societies in America, met at that time in Rittenhouse Square in Philadelphia. It was for me an informative introduction to a refined urbane civilization that, since colonial times, had been cultivated in the cities along the East coast from Boston to Charleston.]

Philadelphia, March 20, 1961

Old Junk

This country has an incredible amount of old junk and debris just lying around; it is everywhere, on the streets, on sidewalks, in backyards. The country is overloaded with cars that usually end up in a junk yard.

Philadelphia, March 21, 1961

Unemployment

Unemployment causes serious problems. Although economists are inclined to see it as a natural fluctuation of the business cycle and thus regard it to some extent as a healthy cleansing of the economic process, it should be avoided for moral and human reasons. It is not so much hunger and want that confront the unemployed in this country but rather a sense of complete hopelessness and futility. They lose their self-respect and sense of personal integrity. The human values that are destroyed by putting someone out of work are the worst loss of all.

Migration to Northern Cities

It is interesting to note how the percentage of the colored population in Northern cities has increased in the last ten years. New York, Philadelphia, Wilmington, and Baltimore show an increase of almost 3 to 5%, while the rate in the South decreased. In these Northern cities the general impression is that of a completely mixed white and black population.

Philadelphia, March 27, 1961

Fire Alarm

There is something curious about Philadelphia that puzzles me: Every hour or so, one hears either a siren of a police car or a fire engine rushing through the streets. At this very moment a house is burning down next to where I live. Most houses here are too old and not properly maintained.

Philadelphia, April 1, 1961

Old Family Traditions

Particularly in a city like Philadelphia one becomes aware of old family traditions when one meets descendants of Benjamin Franklin or Nicholas Biddle as well as a goodly number of descendants of the signers of the Declaration of Independence. More than anything else, this reveals a continuity and stability of American history over the last two and a half centuries. Many European families of influence, mostly from the aristocracy, ceased to exist primarily because they were consumed by the series of revolutions and wars that mark European history during the same period.

Philadelphia, April 15, 1961

Flight into Space

Were it not for politics, all mankind would hail Gagarin's flight into space. The daring courage of the cosmonaut is most laudable, but the achievements of the mathematicians and engineers deserve equal acclaim.

[On April 12, 1961 the Soviet cosmonaut Yuri Gagarin (1934-1975) was launched into orbit around the planet earth. He was the first human being in space. That triggered a race between the Soviet Union and the U.S. for the control of space and space technology. It also intensified the arms race. NASA already trained astronauts for the flight into space. On February 20, 1962 John Glenn, Jr. (1921-) was the first American to orbit the earth. Glenn, like Lindbergh before him, was hailed as a national hero.]

Philadelphia, April 16, 1961

Had dinner tonight with Professor Arnold Toynbee at Professor Crawford's house in Germantown. The conversation centered on the recent space flight. Professor Toynbee mentioned that the flight into space is to some extent but another form of escapism. The troubles on earth will become more pressing, and something has to be done quickly in order to teach us to make mutual concessions so that we can live together in peace.

[The world-renowned British historian Arnold J. Toynbee (1889-1975) was a Visiting Professor at the University of Pennsylvania during the spring semester of 1961. He was honored with a doctorate honoris causa. William R. Crawford (1898-1976), Professor of Sociology at the University of Pennsylvania, was at the time President of the Philadelphia Council for International Visitors. Professor Crawford treated his guests from abroad with gracious hospitality. I am obliged for this information to the University Archives and Records Center of the University of Pennsylvania, letter of April 27, 1998.]

Philadelphia, April 20, 1961

Cuba

Cuba might become a second Hungary—what a dilemma for this hemisphere!

[After April 27, 1961 there was no doubt anymore that the Bay of Pigs invasion had failed. Cuban exiles had attempted to topple the Castro regime. President John F. Kennedy, just in office since January, had approved of the course of action taken by the Cuban exiles, but he did not support it with American military intervention. After the failure of the invasion, Castro's regime remained firm in its saddle. The communist Cuba was declared a Marxist-atheistic state. And, as Castro entered into an alliance with the Soviet Union, the Cold War was brought to America's doorstep. The communist Cuba has remained a thorn in the side of the United States for decades. It unleashed the largest stream of refugees in the Western hemisphere. In October 1962 the Cuban missile crisis brought the world to the brink of nuclear war.]

Philadelphia, May 7, 1961

The Americans are so concerned with the Russians that they seem to forget the rest of the world.

On the European imagination, the Susquehanna seems more like a brook, but if one sees it here, it is indeed as wide as the Danube.

Philadelphia, May 9, 1961

James Fenimore Cooper on American Society

It is surprising how many of Cooper's remarks about American society are still valid today. Every society in its early stages of growth seems to develop patterns of life that endure throughout its history. On this basis, differences between Europe and America throughout the 19th century up to the present day can be established with validity and meaningful insight.

[There are obvious similarities between the views of Cooper and the observations of Alexis de Tocqueville on American democracy.]

[By mid-May 1961 I followed an invitation of Professor and Mrs. Horace Montgomery to Athens, Georgia. Professor Montgomery from the University of Georgia had taught as Fulbright-guest professor at the Amerika-Institut of the University of Innsbruck during the winter semester of 1959-60. The acquaintance with the Montgomerys led to a lifelong friendly connection.]

May 12-20, 1961

First Impressions of the South

Southern thinking is still very much rooted in the era of the Civil War and its aftermath. Traveling through the Southern states, I realized what the Confederacy and Jefferson Davis meant to these people and how antagonistic the feelings against the North really were. Going down to Georgia on the Seaboard Express, I at first noticed no difference to what I had experienced in Philadelphia because these trains are desegregated. But returning to the North on local trains, I realized what segregation means. Actually, the South accepts it as a way of life which both colored and white people seem to accept without thinking that it could be different. They go as a matter of course into segregated waiting rooms, passenger cars, rest rooms, etc., without giving the impression of doing so under psychological pressure or tension. Most clearly segregated are residential areas and schools. In these areas integration appears to be the most difficult.

Negro housing in the South is still extremely poor and shabby. They live in broken-down shacks and shanties. Much labor on the plantations is still done by hand. There are many whites who refuse to accept the Negro as an equal human being. A letter in an Atlanta newspaper stated that white people would move away if what happened to Washington should happen to Atlanta. The "Freedom Riders" experiment on interstate bus lines shows the depth of anti-Negro sentiment in the Deep South. In cases of such deliberate provocation from the North, mob violence can hardly be controlled. I was in Atlanta when the "Freedom Riders" came through. Nothing happened in Georgia, but they ran into serious trouble in Alabama. In view of this situation, what has already been accomplished in Northern cities is quite remarkable. In desegregated cities like New York, Philadelphia, and in recent years Washington, whites and colored people mingle without much trouble. It is to be expected and hoped that eventually such a natural attitude in race relations will also spread throughout the South. But another generation will have to pass, before the South is desegregated in this sense.

The scenery of the South is of great beauty. Green pastures and cattle farms alternate with tobacco and cotton fields. Much land is still untilled. I saw many new clearings cut into primeval forests. The people I met were extremely courteous. The houses I visited showed exquisite taste. The Southerner thinks in agrarian terms, he loves his soil, lush forests and abundant game.

Since the South is to a great extent cut off from the outside world—there is no international harbor along the seaboard, and foreign visitors are rare—, it is rather provincial. I think nobody will ever be able to understand this region of America without having first traveled through it and come in contact with the people who have grown up there.

The Southern Drawl

The so-called "Southern Drawl" (slow, drawn-out manner of speech) may best be explained by the different intonation. The southern intonation prefers a high pitch on the main accent. The quality of tone is generally very soft and melodious, slow moving. The "Southern Drawl" is best recognized in vowels before—r—, as in "Ford" or "Georgia."

Comment on the South

[At the beginning of the 1960s the Civil Rights Movement was going into action in order to make the American public aware of the injustice of segregation. Student groups from the North—whites together with fellow black students—were traveling in buses as "Freedom Riders" into the South and organized "sit-ins" at segregated bus stops, railroad depots and public squares. Thereby, they put the legality of segregation to the test.]

Philadelphia, May 21, 1961

Besides her beauty, America has aspects of sickening ugliness.

Philadelphia, May 22, 1961

I am becoming more and more aware how much the European educational system has neglected the world outside of Europe and how much it has to catch up in this regard.

Philadelphia, May 30, 1961

Juvenile delinquency is a cancer doing damage to every big city. But here it comes to the fore in a horrifying extent. One reason for this may be seen in the insufficient vocational training.

Entire sections of this city are decaying. Its slums offer only bare shelter and refuge to an ungraspable mass of people. On the other hand, the initiatives taken by the city government for city renewal are astonishing.

Comment on City Renewal

[That was the beginning of a widespread city renewal, which in the 1960s had been advanced in most American big cities. That way, over the following three decades the American inner cities got a new face. However, mostly high rises were built that provided office space. As a result of the progressing motorization and the flight to the suburbs, the inner cities could not be saved as residential areas.]

Philadelphia, May 31, 1961

The Mobile Home—a prefabricated movable house—seems to be a belated off-spring of the covered wagon of pioneer times.

Philadelphia, June 3, 1961

The present plight of the American inner city is due primarily to the cheap construction in the second half of the last century.

[The stroll through the slums of Philadelphia was my first shock experience of the American reality. It made me aware of the special problems of the American inner cities.]

Philadelphia, June 11, 1961

The Catholic Church now has a big chance as well as a great task for the future.

Philadelphia, June 12, 1961

Building Activities on American Colleges and University Campuses

The amount of building currently in progress on virtually every college and university campus is one of the outstanding developments I have noticed so far. There is no doubt; America is assuming a leadership role in research and university life in the world today.

Faculty-Student Ratio

Where one professor teaches only ten students, individual attention can be given to each one in class, but where the professor lectures to five hundred students or more, as is the case in many European universities, the student body unfortunately degenerates into a collective, whereby their best qualities are wasted.

Philadelphia, June 13, 1961

Segregation and race relations will still put the civilized world to a severe test.

[Together with a group of fellow Fulbright-scholars I was invited in June to a meeting in Washington. There was a reception in the Library of Congress at which also members of the government and the U.S. Supreme Court were present.]

Washington, June 16, 1961

At a reception in the Library of Congress today I met Senator Fulbright and Supreme Court Justice Douglas.

[J. William Fulbright, U.S. Senator from Arkansas, 1945-74, founder of the international exchange program that bears his name; William 0. Douglas, Supreme Court Justice, 1939-75.]

Philadelphia, June 23, 1961

As long as the European nations do not find themselves together in a union, Europe will more and more be at a disadvantage compared with the rest of the world.

Philadelphia, June 25, 1961

Impressions of Washington

Washington, more than any other city I know, gives the impression of being the pulsing heart of the world today. It is an active, beautiful and alert city which is assuming ever more the qualities of the nerve center of an empire.

National Gallery of Art

The collections of the National Gallery of Art are less impressive on a second visit than on the first. They are still uneven, assembled haphazardly, filling large halls with little content. The architecture of the building, however, is of imposing beauty; the entrance hall is particularly memorable.

[The large neo-classical building of the National Gallery of Art was completed in 1941. The main entrance leads into the Rotunda, in whose center stands, surrounded by marble columns, the statue of Mercury by Giovanni Bologna. The hall impresses by its well-balanced design.]

The Rembrandt Collection

The Rembrandt Collection in the National Gallery of Art struck me as the most beautiful group of paintings assembled in any one place. It was there that I developed a predilection for Rembrandt. What a climax in the portrayal of the human soul—it is the deep humaneness that emanates from the characters which renders his paintings unsurpassed among the long gallery of works in the art of portraiture.

[Two rooms of the National Gallery of Art are devoted exclusively to the paintings of Rembrandt—one of the most significant collections of his works in the world.]

Philadelphia, June 26, 1961

What is the idea of the educated person today?

He/she is not only the connoisseur of art and literature, versed in Latin, Greek, and several European languages, but is also someone who has achieved a fuller understanding of the world in which he/she lives. This may give Western education a new sense of direction.

The essential issue of higher education today is still humanism, a cultivation of the human mind which instills a broader outlook of the present world. Humanism in this sense is not merely introspective but essentially an act to "bring man into communion with man again."

Philadelphia, June 27, 1967

This is a country of contrasts: While a super jetliner cuts majestically through the air above the statue of William Penn on the top of City Hall, a group of Highway Tabernacle Mission singers preach the Gospel to the tired homeless below.

Philadelphia, June 30, 1961

For better or for worse, English has become the *lingua franca* of the world today.

[Over the Fourth of July Weekend, I had planned a short visit to Cambridge, Massachusetts. It was my first contact with Harvard University: A stroll over the Harvard Yard, a first orientation in the large Widener Library, and finally a first introduction to the Houghton Library. As the literary archive of Harvard University, the Houghton Library holds extensive manuscript collections, particularly of American literature. It was above all the Houghton Library which brought me back to Harvard time and again. Harvard College, the oldest college of America, was founded in 1636 and named after John Harvard. In the course of the 19th century, it developed into the leading university of the country.]

Cambridge, Massachusetts, July 5, 1961

A Common World Civilization

Each generation should become aware of the most pressing problems it has to solve. For our generation, it seems to me, there is no other problem as important as creating a common world civilization that comprises mankind as a whole.

Harvard Impressions

The American university has become a crossroad of young people from the Occident and the Orient.

Hardly anything is so reminiscent of the Old World as the chimes of a carillon on a college campus.

Philadelphia, July 9, 1961

The way north or south from Washington leads into two worlds that are still very different from each other.

The American big city has at night a unique glamour and splendour all its own. This is especially true of the New York skyline and of Time Square.

[For the summer I had been accepted as Reader by the Huntington Library in Pasadena, California. That gave me on the one hand the opportunity to use the source materials for the California author Frank Norris (1870-1902), and on the other hand it fulfilled a long intended wish of mine to once cross the continent from coast to coast, from the Atlantic to the Pacific, by railroad.]

Altoona, Pennsylvania, July 15, 1961

Left North Philadelphia Station at 9 a.m. today on a westbound trip from coast to coast.

Indianapolis, July 16, 1961

Indiana gives for the first time the impression of continental space. Here one is accustomed to orient oneself following the cardinal points. Here, it is also possible that someone gets off the train and starts a conversation about the Church of Nazareth.

St. Louis, Missouri, July 17, 1961

St. Louis the Gateway to the West

Here, the traces of the French settlement of the Mississippi region are still visible: An excellent cuisine and decorative wrought ironwork. Also, the missionary work of the Jesuits has left its mark. With the Louisiana Purchase of 1803 the West was opened to the throng of new settlers.

The ride through the Midwest gives the impression of the enormous agricultural abundance of this country. But because of the short time of settlement, no village culture has developed. Instead of "village" the word "township" is used. It is more of a small town environment that has developed on the countryside with single homesteads in-between.

Grainfield, Kansas, July 18, 1961

From horizon to horizon, as far as the eye can see, nothing but grainfields, that's Kansas.

Denver, Colorado, July 19, 1961

Denver is a modern booming city with a steadily growing skyline. The romance of the former Wild West continues, however, to lurk in the background, best visible in the frontier shop on the corner and the rodeo show for tourists.

The diorama exhibitions in the State Museum depict beautifully how this area developed from a frontier settlement of a hundred years ago to the jet age metropolis of today.

The river namers, audacious trail blazers, fur traders and prospectors opened the path for settlement. The gold rush of 1859 at Pikes Peak near Colorado Springs unleashed a great migration from the East to this primarily mining area.

The pioneers set out in covered wagons on a six week journey across the Great Plains. They usually moved in teams with a government of their own, rules written down, and elected officers. For their collective protection against Indian raids, the nightly wagon camps were arranged in elephant corrals. In the beginning, the contact with the Indians in this area was carefree. Fur traders, mountain men, beaver trappers adopted the Indian way of life; they were dressed in deerskin, or buckskin leggings, traded with the Indians and married squaws.

From here to the South and Southwest, the impact of the early Spanish settlements becomes visible. One becomes aware of the effects of Coronado's expedition into the Northern parts of Mexico, the hacienda culture and large Spanish land grants. The influence of the Indian culture of the pueblos and Navajos of the Mesa Verde region also becomes very obvious. The Indian folklore attraction and handicrafts stand out from the otherwise drab souvenir displays.

Denver is the gateway to a mountainous area of great natural beauty. The nearby Rocky Mountains rise to altitudes of 12 to 14 thousand feet. Mount Evans, Andrews Peak and Snowdrift Peak in the Arapaho National Forest form a panorama of impressive magnitude. The scenic view is different from that of the Central Alps. For the most part, it is still untouched wilderness.

Salt Lake City, Utah, July 21, 1961

Seen from the Train

From Denver over Cheyenne, Laramie to Ogden in Utah, a grassland of about 1,000 km (625 miles) stretches across the plains. The high plains along the foothills of the Rocky Mountains are a unique pasture which gradually turns into a semiarid steppe. The entire area is very sparsely settled. Except for widespread ranges, some coal strip mining and oil drilling stations, nothing else was to be seen that showed signs of human habitation. The ride through Wyoming from Laramie over Rawlins to Rock Spring made a deserted impression. It led over the high plains of the Continental Divide, the watershed between the Atlantic and the Pacific, an arid plateau covered by sagebrush, through which occasionally a few antelopes were jumping.

Comment

[The exceptionally beautiful natural sites of Wyoming are located in the northwest corner of the state—in the Grand Teton National Park and the Yellowstone National Park. Each year these world-famous National Parks attract hundreds of thousands of visitors from all over the world.]

Salt Lake City, July 21, 1961

Notes on Utah and Salt Lake City

Father Escalante discovered Utah Lake in 1776.

Comment

[In his effort to find a connecting passage from Santa Fe in New Mexico to the missions in California, the Franciscan missionary Father Silvestre Valez de Escalante undertook an expedition in 1776 through the unknown territory of the Ute Indians. He thereby reached the Great Salt Lake.]

The name Utah is of Indian origin and means "high in the mountains."

Trappers and Fur Traders

Peter Skene Ogden, a trapper in the service of the Hudson Bay Company, came to the Salt Lake area in the 1820s. He explored the territory between the Great Salt Lake Basin and the Sierras along the river route. The river named after him was later changed to Humboldt River, but Ogden, the second largest city of Utah, retained his name. John C. Frémont from the U.S. Army Topographical Engineers surveyed the Great Lake Basin in 1843-44.

The Mormons

The history of the present state of Utah and the development of Salt Lake City are invariably linked to the Mormons and their historic migration.

The Mormons or The Church of Jesus Christ of Latter-Day Saints have their own Bible, The Book of Mormon, which is the word of the Prophet Mormon. Although the members of this sectarian group provoked controversy wherever they settled and were thus persecuted for their beliefs, the Mormons attracted many followers throughout the nineteenth century. In their search for religious freedom and the Kingdom of God, these people demonstrated unbelievable endurance in the face of sheer insurmountable hardships.

Brigham Young (1801-1877)

In 1847 Brigham Young, the resourceful Head of the Church, led the great Mormon exodus of 20,000 people from Nauvoo, Illinois [situated in the western part of the state near the Mississippi River], across Iowa, the Nebraska Territory and along the North Platte River to the Great Salt Lake valley where he founded Salt Lake City.

The Mormon migration to Utah continued during the second half of the nineteenth century. Altogether about 80,000 people crossed the plains to settle there. A few of the pioneers of the late nineteenth century are still alive. In 1947 they were able to participate in the "Centennial Celebration of the Days of '47."

By Handcarts across the Plains

Mormon families who had no oxen or horses banded together in groups and pulled their few possessions and children on handcarts across the plains. On the way, hundreds of them died of exhaustion and starvation.

The covered wagon on which Brigham Young came to Salt Lake City can still be seen in the Pioneer Museum.

It should be remembered that in their covered wagons the pioneers carried into the wilderness the full load of the civilization of their times: Furniture, books, utensils of all kinds, anvils, and surveyor's instruments.

They also brought with them the contemporary expertise in agriculture and craftsmanship.

The early pioneer period ended with the arrival of the transcontinental railroad. The driving of the golden spike at Promontory, Utah, on May 10, 1869, connected the Union Pacific from the East with the Central Pacific from the West.

Salt Lake City, July 21, 1961

The Capitol of Utah in Salt Lake City is one of the most attractive sights in the country; the view from its hilltop site across the valley is especially impressive.

I had been looking for California and in my search discovered Utah.

Utah is a peculiar cultural achievement of the American West. This is an example how the desert can be turned into a blooming garden.

[With the Winter Olympics of 2002 Utah and Salt Lake City attracted the world's attention as never before.]

[Over the night of July 21/22 a ride on a Greyhound Bus brought me from Salt Lake City through the Mojave Desert to Los Angeles.]

San Bernardino, California, July 22, 1961

The states in the Rocky Mountains are still a very thinly populated region. Irrigation is the question of survival in the desert areas. Coming from Salt Lake City, San Bernardino offers the first contact with the Spanish missionary culture in California.

Los Angeles, July 23, 1961

The size of Los Angeles is no tall tale: The diagonal distance of the city is almost 70 miles, the circumferal distance 265 miles.

The first impression of Los Angeles is that of a hustle and bustle, of aimless motion and exuberance, as well as of a jumble of different architectural styles.

Santa Monica Beach, California, July 23, 1961

The First Time on the Pacific

Reached the Pacific today at Santa Monica. It is a curious feeling to think now of home through the back door. [Looking to the West and not to the East.]

Precious moments

There are a few moments in life which one will never forget, like seeing the Pacific for the first time.

Note

Cabrillo discovered Santa Monica Bay in 1542. There was a quadricentennial celebration of this historic event. This part of America is not young anymore.

Pasadena, California, July 25, 1961

The Henry E. Huntington Library and Art Gallery

[Upon my arrival I was completely surprised by the Huntington Library. Located in San Marino, a small township south of Pasadena, it offered all the benefits which one could only have hoped for in a research stay. The neo-classical building with the Library and the Art Gallery stands in the midst of a botanical garden. Room and board were provided in the nearby Atheneum, the guest house for visiting scholars. The Huntington Library and Art Gallery was founded by Henry Edwards Huntington (1850-1927) in 1919. The Library, one of the leading research institutions for the humanities in North America, excels by its rich holdings of manuscripts in the areas of English and American literatures as well as documents of California history. Among the special treasures of the Huntington Library are the Ellesmere Ms. of Chaucer's *Canterbury Tales*, the manuscript of Benjamin Franklin's *Autobiography*, and in the Art Gallery "The Blue Boy" by Thomas Gainsborough.]

The Berlin Crisis

The current unanimous opinion from coast to coast, to stay firm in the Berlin crisis, is indeed remarkable.

Pasadena, July 30, 1961

The European University Crisis

The crisis of the Humboldtian university ideal is not just a phenomenon of the present time or the result of the post-war era, but has been long in coming. Humboldt's ideal suited the central European university of the 19th century, but has become woefully inadequate in fulfilling the needs of higher education in the 20th century. The European university today finds itself in a profound crisis, which can only be overcome by modernization and a structural reform.

[Transl: Wilhelm von Humboldt (1767-1835), the brother of the world-famous explorer Alexander von Humboldt, reorganized the educational system in Prussia. In 1810 he founded the Humboldt University in Berlin. He advocated a research university that served a small group of scholars, but which did not take into account the needs for higher education of the growing population of an industrial state.]

Pasadena, July 30, 1961

The Mission San Gabriel Archangel

The Mission San Gabriel Archangel was founded September 8, 1771. The original main entrance of the Mission opened out on the Camino Real, the King's Highway, the artery connecting the twenty-one Missions of California.

In the Camposanto, the graveyard of San Gabriel, a commemorative tablet records that between 1778-1865 about 6,000 Indians were buried there. The largest number of them had been carried away by the smallpox and cholera epidemics of 1820.

[The Mission is located in the town of San Gabriel near Pasadena.]

Junipero Serra (1713-1784)

Friar Junipero Serra, the founder of the twenty-one missions in California, succeeded in creating a unique missionary work.

[The Franciscan missionary Father Junipero Serra is also called "Apostle of California." In 1988 he was beatified by Pope John Paul II.]

Pasadena, August 2, 1961

Covered Wagons on the Overland Trail

It is quite possible to converse here with people who not only remember the San Francisco earthquake of 1906, but who can also relate the experience of their parents' birth on a covered wagon on the overland trail. California has both: on the one hand an older civilization represented by her Missions, and on the other, a still vividly new frontier.

Because of the lower cost of freight and transportation of household goods and livestock, covered wagons crossed the plains even after the first railroads had been built.

The axles of the Conestoga wagon [named after Conestoga, Pennsylvania, where it was built] were extremely stout so that they could withstand rough roads. The Conestoga could haul virtually everything a household needed: the kitchen with its iron stove, beds and furniture, food supply, and useful tools. It made a long migratory existence possible. The largest display of Conestoga wagons and prairie schooners can be seen at Knott's Berry Farm Ghost Town, south of Los Angeles.

Pasadena, August 5, 1961

Fundamentalism and a Marriage Chapel

Within an hour's drive from Hollywood one can find a fundamentalist religious community that forbids the sale of alcoholic beverages and cigarettes.

The Marriage Chapel is an institution that takes care of everything: the ceremony of any religious affiliation, the meal and the entertainment.

Pasadena, August 10, 1961

The World Convention for the Space Age

The World Convention for the Space Age, Astrophysics and Astronomy, which is taking place here at this time, clearly illustrates the current actuality of questions about outer space. One has the feeling as if a trip to the moon was just around the corner.

[The World Convention for the Space Age took place at that time at the California Institute of Technology which lies across from the Huntington Library in Pasadena. The Convention was organized and carried out by the Jet Propulsion Laboratory (JPL). The JPL, founded in 1936, and since 1958 has been administered by the National Aeronautics and Space Administration (NASA). From here, probes launched into space that may be on their way for years are controlled, course corrections carried out, and pictures sent back to earth from other planets processed. These pictures are then telecast on TV around the world.]

Pasadena, August 10, 1961

Striking Contrasts

It is still possible in this area for someone to "squat" on a tract of land for a period of time and then obtain a legal title to that land.

[The contrast between the highly developed space technology of the JPL and the customs of the frontier that one finds next to it is indeed striking.]

Explanation

[To "squat" means in colloquial speech to crouch or settle down. A squatter is someone who settles down on a piece of free government land and later buys the lot. This widespread custom of the frontier goes mainly back to the Pre-emption Act of 1841 whereby settlers could stake out 160 acres of government land and later legally acquire it at a minimum price.]

Pasadena, August 11, 1961

[At the Huntington Library I got acquainted with Professor John A. Hawgood of the University of Birmingham. Hawgood was the leading British historian on the American West. He was working at that time on the book, *The American West* (London, 1967). As he was just examining the German correspondence of John August Sutter with his family in Switzerland, I was able to help out in explaining various expressions. On my part, I gained a great deal from Hawgood's profound knowledge of California history. The acquaintance resulted in a fruitful collaboration that lasted until John Hawgood passed away in 1971.]

John August Sutter (1803-1880)

In 1841 the Mexican Governor of California Juan Bautista Alvarado granted Sutter over 48,000 acres of land in the Sacramento Valley. Sutter's Fort provided a form of protected civilized life on the frontier. It was for the most part an adobe construction, i.e. mud and straw bricks dried in the sun, which were much used as building material in California. Sutter was very prudent in his treatment of the Indians. He dreamed of New Helvetia, a new empire he hoped to develop in Northern California.

[Sutter's dream of New Helvetia was shattered when in 1848 gold was found on the American River. His land was simply overrun by thousands of gold diggers and squatters.]

Pasadena, August 14, 1961

The Berlin Wall

[As the Berlin Wall went up on August 13, 1961, the Berlin crisis dramatically came to a head. The fear which had always been present that the Third World War could break out suddenly surfaced again.]

I seriously considered flying home because of the Berlin crisis.

[With a railroad and a ship line ticket in my pocket, Innsbruck appeared to be intolerably far away.]

Pasadena, August 15, 1961

The Helplessness of Europe

The past week has again shown how helpless Europe is in confronting its own problems. Europe urgently needs a reorganization overcoming the nation states. There are no national solutions for Europe—German, French or British—, which would be meaningful and effective. Only if these strongest national forces work together instead against each other, the unity of Europe will make itself noticeably felt.

Pasadena, August 21, 1961

A Hot-bed of Sects and Cults

Southern California or the Southland, the area of Los Angeles with its host of surrounding townships, is a hot-bed of sects and cults, culturally immature and insecure of itself, a garden land and playground, turbulent with excessive extravagances. It is a place groping for a future that is still not clearly visible.

Pasadena, August 27, 1961

The Journey Home

On my journey home, I am crossing once again the full length of the so-called Free West, from its most-western to its most-eastern point.

[The journey home by railroad first led from Los Angeles to San Francisco, from there to Chicago and back to Philadelphia where part of my luggage was in storage.]

San Francisco, August 29, 1961

San Francisco is not large but it has the tempo and glamour of a world metropolis. When one sees San Francisco, one should be reminded that 120 years ago there were only four houses standing in the entire Bay.

Union Square in San Francisco is one of the most elegant metropolitan centers I have seen so far.

Berkeley, August 29, 1961

The Golden Gate Bridge is undoubtedly one of the most beautiful sights in the world.

Sacramento, August 29, 1961

[The Union Pacific Express left in the afternoon from Oakland and made its way through Sacramento up to the Donner Pass.]

The Sacramento River is reminiscent of John Sutter and the pioneer beginnings of Upper California.

Cheyenne, Wyoming, August 31, 1961

[During the night of August 29 to 30 the Union Pacific Express had crossed Nevada. Already at daybreak the desolate flats of the Great Salt Lake came up. After 24 hours the train reached Cheyenne. That was halfway to Chicago and also the right time for a stop to get some sleep.]

The Museum in the State Office Building here contains one of the most remarkable collections of Indian artifacts, especially good specimens of colorful beadwork and ceremonial decorations.

Chicago, Illinois, September 3, 1961

Note:

In 1681 La Salle traveled from here along the Chicago River and then down the Mississippi, thus laying the foundations of a new empire for France.

[Robert Cavelier, Sieur de La Salle (1643-87) undertook an expedition in 1681-82 in order to find the waterway from the Great Lakes to the Gulf of Mexico. He thereby turned at the southwest shore of Lake Michigan into the mouth of the Chicago River and took advantage of the short portage to reach the Illinois River which flows into the Mississippi. La Salle traveled down the Mississippi and reached as first *explorateur* its mouth in the Gulf. He took possession of the entire Mississippi region for France and named it in honor of his King Louis XIV "Louisiana."]

From 1803-1812 Fort Dearborn stood at the mouth of the Chicago River as a control point for the waterways between the Great Lakes and the inland rivers.

[The name Chicago derives from the Indian word "checagou" what could mean as much as "wild onion" or "onion field." In 1803 Fort Dearborn was erected at the mouth of the Chicago River. The Fort was named after Henry Dearborn who served as Secretary of War in the cabinet of Thomas Jefferson. In the War of 1812 Fort Dearborn was raided and completely destroyed. Only years later the settlement Chicago developed, which finally in 1833 was incorporated as a village with about 200 inhabitants. With the opening of the Midwest as new area for settlements as well as the progressing industrialization and the arrival of the railroad, Chicago advanced quickly. At its silver jubilee in 1858, the city already had a population of 90,000.]

Philadelphia, September 12, 1961

The opening of school this fall witnessed a noticeable step forward in the struggle for integration. Schools have been integrated which even a year ago were strongly opposed to it.

[In the historic Brown vs. Board of Education decision of the U.S. Supreme Court on May 17, 1954, the principle of "separate but equal," which had allowed segregation in equal school facilities, was declared unconstitutional. It demanded the admission of colored children to public schools. From that time on schools had to adjust to integration, which finally led to "school busing." Accordingly, children from different residential districts were brought on buses across town to integrated schools.]

Philadelphia, September 12, 1961

Heard the evangelist Rev. Billy Graham speak today in the Irvin Auditorium of the University of Pennsylvania. His Philadelphia Crusade clearly illustrates the fundamentalist religious attitude in American life. Billy Graham is a great orator who is capable of convincing his audience.

[In September of 1961 Billy Graham (1918—) from Charlotte, North Carolina, was on his Philadelphia Crusade. Already at that time his great charisma was recognizable. During the following decades, he attracted in his public ministry millions of people around the world.]

New York, September 17, 1961

Saw the Leningrad Kirov Ballet at the Metropolitan Opera tonight. I have rarely heard such an enthusiastic ovation from an audience.

New York, September 17, 1961

Something very hopeful is happening in our generation which has never been experienced before to such an extent: The contact of all people, cultures and races from every continent. These newly established international ties have to be strengthened at whatever cost, whatever the circumstances. This is not just a fashion or ephemeral phase of our time, but is more akin to a tidal wave that will mold and shape mankind into a new form and way of existence.

New York, September 21, 1961

I attended the steering committee of the United Nations for the General Assembly agenda. In the discussion—with Dean Rusk, Zorin, and India's Krishna Menon speaking—on the ban of nuclear tests, it became clearly visible how the Cold War is being fought on the East River and how the United Nations are misused as a forum for Cold War propaganda.

[Dean Rusk (1909-1994), U.S. Secretary of State, 1961-69; Valerian Zorin (1904-1986), permanent representative of the USSR in the Security Council, 1960-62; Krishna Menon (1897-1974), chairman of the Indian Delegation to the United Nations, 1953-62.]

Mid-Atlantic, September 25, 1961

Back to the cauldron and yet so much loved Europe.

[The passenger ship *United States* landed three days later in Le Havre where my wife had waited for my arrival.]

Historic Events 1962-64

The Second Vatican Council

The Second Vatican Council opened on October 11, 1962, and closed on December 8, 1965.

October 1962

The Cuban Missile Crisis

After it had been established beyond a doubt that the USSR was installing a medium-range missile base with nuclear warheads in Cuba, U.S. President John F. Kennedy demanded in the form of an ultimatum that the launch pads be dismantled and the missiles taken back. In those days, the world was brought to the brink of a nuclear war. On October 28, Nikita Khrushchev yielded to Kennedy's demand whereby the Cuban missile crisis was defused and war averted.

August 28, 1963

The March on Washington

The historic March on Washington took place on August 28, 1963. The nearly 200,000 participants in this peaceful civil rights demonstration gathered in front of the Lincoln Memorial and heard toward the end of this event the compelling speech by Martin Luther King, Jr. The speech concluded with the words: "I have a dream . . ."—a moving appeal for racial equality which has been indelibly imprinted in the consciousness of the American nation.

November 22, 1963

The Assassination of John F. Kennedy

In the noon hours of November 22, 1963, U.S. President John F. Kennedy was assassinated by a bullet fired from an ambush in Dallas. The news ran like a shockwave around the world. First there was confusion and uncertainty about what would happen in the United States. U.S. Vice President Lyndon B. Johnson, who had accompanied Kennedy on the campaign trail to Texas, was sworn in as 34th president of the U.S.A., while Air Force One was still standing on the Dallas airport.

[The news of the assassination of John F. Kennedy reached me in the evening hours in my home in Innsbruck, while my family and I were packing the trunks for the voyage to New York which had been booked for January. Under the impression of the first shock, we considered to possibly cancel our journey to America.]

SECTION 2

January 18–September 5, 1964

[At the beginning of January, 1964, my family and I set out on our journey to the United States. That was the beginning of our American adventure. Helping the family with the still small children, eight and four years old, my wife's sister joined us on the journey. We sailed on the Italian passenger ship *Leonardo da Vinci* from Genoa to New York. While the voyage through the Mediterranean was like a cruise, after Gibraltar a heavy storm awaited us on the open Atlantic that did not subside until we landed in New York. The volcanic peaks on the Azores were snow-covered. And during the passage, our four year old daughter got chicken pox.]

New York, January 18, 1964

To enter New York Harbor and to pass the examination by the Health Authorities with a child who got chicken pox aboard ship is a nerve-racking experience never to be forgotten. We barely missed the quarantine station on Staten Island.

[The Health Authorities feared smallpox at the time. It was required to have been vaccinated against smallpox before entering the U.S. But the Certificate of Vaccination against smallpox notwithstanding, it took awhile until it was definitely determined that those were chicken pox and not smallpox.]

New York, January 19, 1964

The Lincoln Center for the Performing Arts

The new Lincoln Center for the Performing Arts opened with a play by Arthur Miller, while Menotti's opera *The Last Savage* premiered at the Metropolitan Opera House.

[The new Lincoln Center between West 62nd and 66th Streets in Manhattan was in part still under construction. The Metropolitan Opera, which was still performing in its old house on 39th Street and Broadway, moved to the Lincoln Center in September of 1966. The large complex of the Lincoln Center comprises the Metropolitan Opera House, the Avery Fisher Hall (Concert Hall of the New York Philharmonic), the New York State Theatre (Stage for the New York City Ballet), and the Vivian Beaumont Theatre (Repertory Theatre). The famous Juilliard School of Music is also connected with the Lincoln Center. As a whole, the Lincoln Center is the most significant center for the performing arts in the United States. Gian Carlo Menotti (1911—) had his musical education in Milan as well as in Philadelphia and in Boston. As a composer he gave modern opera new impulses. Menotti directed the "Festival of the Two Worlds," which he had founded, from 1958-93. These festivals take place in Spoleto, Italy, and also in Charleston, South Carolina. Menotti connected America and Europe like nobody else.]

Arrival in South Bend and Notre Dame

[We arrived by the end of January by the overnight-express from New York in South Bend, Indiana, at 6 a.m. in the morning. It was one of the last trains that approached South Bend. Shortly thereafter passenger train service was discontinued. In front of the Union Station was a "For Sale" sign, what to some extent astonished us. The ride by taxi cab first passed along streets with abandoned factory buildings, for the Studebaker Automobile Plant had just closed its doors forever. When we reached the Golf Course and saw the Golden Dome of Notre Dame from a distance, the somewhat dreary atmosphere on that cold January day brightened up.]

Notre Dame, Indiana, End of January, 1964

The Catholic university in America has adopted many of the forms of the prevailing American way of life.

[When we arrived at Notre Dame, we could immediately move into the apartment that had been reserved in advance in the newly-opened University Village for Married Student Housing. After the household had been established, I began my teaching as Visiting Assistant Professor in the Department of Modern and Classical Languages. The following more extensive entries refer to general observations on the way of life in the Midwest.]

Notre Dame, February 22, 1964

By its well-balanced, solid way of life, the Midwest has an agreeable effect. This region of the United States is very healthy at its core. It is a rising, up-and-coming area that is little known outside the United States. What has been created here in hardly a century and a half is surprising. The wide stretches of territories from the Appalachians in the East to the Great Plains in the West, which at the turn of the century were still thinly settled, have now numerous advancing young communities.

The cultural life concentrates on the universities and colleges, which gain more and more in influence. Next to the traditional institutions of higher learning in the East, new universities and colleges have originated here that need not shy away from comparison with the East coast. Above all one can notice that a generous building policy is being planned for the future. The new, just completed 14-story high and state of the art university library building of Notre Dame is a visible testimony to that. In general one can say that a surprisingly high number of schools and churches are being built. Here in St. Joseph County the many houses of worship built in a modern architectural style come to one's attention. On Sundays churches of all denominations are surprisingly well attended.

Notre Dame, February 22, 1964

The Division according to Ethnic Origin and the Melting Pot

The division according to ethnic origin is here still clearly visible. The City of South Bend has a strong Polish and Hungarian population who form their own section of town. Separated from that is the German settlement, which is more limited to small farms towards the northwest. On the other hand, the manufacturing zone is concentrated on the westside of the city. According to an unwritten law, these various ethnic groups live separate from each other and at the same time together without much tension, whereby their ethnic characteristics remain for the most part preserved. In order to define a salient feature of American civilization, it would be important to determine to what extent these various immigrant groups have maintained their ethnic character and how fast they have adapted to the mainstream of American life.

The fastest adaptation has ensued in acquiring the English language. The native tongue has to a large extent already been lost in the second generation. Education, the judicial system, and social manners are next to language and literature primarily of English origin. However, religious affiliations, the way of living in the home, how food is prepared, and customs from the country of origin have been preserved over generations.

Preservation vs. Assimilation

a) Preserving elements

Religion: The population of Irish, Polish, Hungarian, Italian, and French, as well as Spanish-Latino descent belongs overwhelmingly to the Catholic Church. Americans of Norwegian and Swedish descent are for the most part Lutherans, while Americans of Greek descent adhere to the Orthodox Church. Generally speaking, one can say that belonging to a religious faith is determined by the country of origin and remains preserved over generations.

Ways of life and preferences of taste in the home are also determined by the country of origin. This applies to ethnic food, preferences for certain colors, styles of furniture and clothing. Skills from the old countries have especially been preserved in restaurants, cabinet-making, tailoring, the butcher's and the baker's trade, as well as in crafts. In its sum total, this has produced an immense variety of consumer goods in America.

b) Assimilation or adaptation

By quickly acquiring the English language, the native tongue is given up in the second generation. New immigrant groups have always been eager to learn English as quickly as possible in order to advance in mainstream America. Mixing of languages is for the most part avoided. This also explains the desire to adapt to the American system of education as well as the high value that is attributed to a college education in American life. Immigrant groups have also quickly adapted to the American political system and have shown strong loyalty to the American government. The allegiance to the country of origin diminishes at the moment of emigration.

Adaptation to the American legal system and to the political structure of the country as well as emphasizing personal freedom—there are hardly any national separatist movements.

There is linguistic tolerance towards the foreigner who is learning the language and speaks English with a heavy accent.

The foreigner is not coming as a tourist into this country but is immediately accepted as a full member of society; essentially without prejudice.

Despite the commercial conformity, there is enough room for individual peculiarities.

Notre Dame, February 22, 1964

Life has here a delightful unspoiled vitality and an unshakable optimism. Here, the young generation still has great opportunities open for the future.

Chinese New Year

Americans of Chinese descent celebrate the New Year on February 13. Schools, television and businesses celebrate with them. Announcements like "Celebrate Happy New Year with Americans of Chinese Descent" invite to participate.

Notre Dame, February 24, 1964

The Question of Race Relations is Coming to a Head

The question of race relations and signs of an economic regression are at the moment obvious difficulties the United States has to deal with. One can notice that the question of race relations is becoming increasingly radicalized.

The closing of the Studebaker Automobile Factory evoked, especially in this area, the specter of unemployment. It brought with it economic hardships for a large part of the population of South Bend and Mishawaka. But the reason for closing the Studebaker Plant seems more to be mismanagement than the result of the general economic regression.

Notre Dame, February 24, 1964

The Astronaut John Glenn was presented the "Patriot of the Year Award" by the Senior Class of the University of Notre Dame. In his address, John Glenn made the impression of a strong-willed, deeply religious personality. Space travel has become here a matter of course.

Notre Dame, March 1, 1964

The First Time by Car to Chicago

One can best experience the modern, industrialized America between Gary, Hammond, East Chicago and the center of the City of Chicago. The Indiana Toll Road streaks through the steel mills of Gary and the refineries of Hammond to the Chicago Skyway which spans over the Harbor of Chicago. The Skyway runs into the 14-lane Dan Ryan Expressway that leads directly to the Loop in the center of town. To drive for the first time on these freeways is an impressive, although also a stressful experience. One gains the impression that America has solved the technological problems of population density and the sprawl of the industrial areas as well as the traffic jams in the big cities in a most rational way. The population is overall moving into the suburbs. The suburbs or residential areas surround the city in a 60 mile radius, while they are more and more extending.

Comment

[In a circumference of about 100 miles Chicago has, after New York and Los Angeles, the third largest population concentration in America. Despite continuous improvements and new road constructions, it is difficult to meet the needs of the increasing traffic volume. At rush hours long traffic congestions on the Dan Ryan Expressway are not rare anymore.]

Notre Dame, March 2, 1964

A Country of Asylum for the Aristocracy

It is surprising to find out that the United States, since its foundation, has always been a country of asylum also for the European aristocracy. During the French Revolution members of the French high aristocracy sought refuge in the Etats-Unis. Also during the revolutionary upheavals in the 19th and 20th centuries, aristocrats from Europe who had been persecuted for political reasons fled to America, where they were received with openheartedness.

Notre Dame, March 5, 1964

Campus Architecture

On a tour through an American university campus, one can study the various architectural styles the United States has gone through in the course of its history. Inevitably, one will at first come across some of the raw brick and wooden structures from the colonial period or pioneer times. Then one will see the temple-like buildings with their many columns from the "Greek Revival" period. Predominantly, however, are the ivy-covered halls of the "College Gothic" style with their pointed arch windows, narrow entrances, turrets, adornments and Latin inscriptions. They give the campus a nearly medieval, scholastic ambience. But at the moment, as the new, large library building on the Notre Dame campus demonstrates, a new architectural style is emerging that is, detached from European models, more functional. It will give American colleges and universities a new look.

Notre Dame, March 10, 1964

Cut Off from the Outside World

The American Middle West remains to a large extent cut off from the outside world. For example, it is not possible to exchange a note in a foreign currency into dollars at a bank in South Bend.

Notre Dame, March 18, 1964

The Civil Rights Bill

The Civil Rights Bill is up for a vote in Congress. It is regarded as the most important legislation to overcome racial discrimination in the United States since the Fourteenth Amendment of 1866 that gave the colored population citizenship after emancipation.

The Civil Rights Bill was already adopted by the House of Representatives on February 10 by a vote of 290:130, and was then passed on to the Senate. The debate that is now unfolding in the Senate puts this important legislation again in doubt. The representatives of the South argue among other things that this law would limit the right of a private citizen to make his own decisions. The owner of a restaurant, for example, would lose his right to decide who may enter his establishment or who may not. Furthermore, the senators from the South point out that the execution of this law would give the federal government in Washington too much power. They also express their concern that mob violence could break out.

[The debate in the Senate dragged on until June. Voting was mostly delayed by filibuster, i.e., obstruction policy by marathon speaking. See entry below of June 10, 1964.]

Addendum

[The Fourteenth Amendment to the Constitution was proposed by a resolution of Congress in 1866. After it had been ratified by three fourths of the States in the Union, it became law in 1868. Section 1 of the Fourteenth Amendment reads: "All persons born or naturalized in the United States, and subject to the jurisdiction thereof, are citizens of the United States and of the State wherein they reside." Thereby, the foundation for American citizenship was laid. At the same time, about four million people of color who had been emancipated from slavery received citizenship.]

[March 23-April 1, 1964]

After eight years of construction, the Gateway Arch was completed and opened to the public in May of 1968. This masterpiece of modern architecture stands on the right hand bank of the Mississippi River in St. Louis at the center of the Jefferson National Expansion Memorial park. The stainless steel Arch, which rises 630 feet into the sky, is a symbol of the gateway to the Western expansion and settlement of the American West in the 19th century. Inside the two columns of the Arch, a narrow-track cog railroad leads to the top. The observation station at the top of the Arch affords a magnificent panoramic view: To the East, one can look across the Mississippi far into Illinois, and to the West, across St. Louis far out into the suburbs. This photo was taken the middle of October, 2000.

Round Trip during Easter Vacation

The three states tour: Indiana, Illinois, and Kentucky—eight days by car—2,000 miles (3,200 km) covered.

The Itinerary:

Indiana: From South Bend in southwesterly direction via Rochester to Lafayette/West Lafayette (location of Purdue University); further on westward to:

Illinois: Via Danville to Urbana/Champaign (location of the University of Illinois); further on to Springfield, the capital of Illinois. In Springfield a visit of the Lincoln Memorial sites, including the Pioneer Village of New Salem, which is located ten miles to the northwest. There, Abraham Lincoln started practicing law and being active in politics. From Springfield we drove south to the Mississippi River and St. Louis, Missouri. On the right hand bank of the Mississippi one could see the gigantic construction site of the "Gateway Arch" project. [The Gateway Arch, which with its altitude of 630 feet (192 m) frames the skyline of the city, has become the landmark of St. Louis.] After a short stop in St. Louis, we traveled south on the Illinois side of the Mississippi; at first to Fort Kaskaskia, and then further on to the area of "Little Egypt" via Thebes to the promontory of Cairo, where the Ohio River flows into the Mississippi. Cairo, Illinois, was on the itinerary of this journey because the surrounding area is reminiscent of a famous scene in French literature. In his novel *Atala* (1801), Francois Chateaubriand had chosen the mouth of the Ohio River as the fictitious backdrop for "Les Funérailles d'Atala."

Kentucky: After crossing the bridge over the Ohio, we visited the "Mounds," the burial grounds of various Indian tribes at Wickliffe in Kentucky. From there we moved on via Paducah to the Kentucky Dam Village State Park. Here, at the dam of the TVA (Tennessee Valley Authority) a recreational resort area has been developed. At a length of 183 miles (293 km), the Kentucky Lake is regarded as one of the longest man made lakes in the world. From the Kentucky Dam Village we drove on the newly-built Western Kentucky Parkway eastward through marvelous natural scenery to Elizabethtown and Bardstown in Central Kentucky. In Hodgenville near Elizabethtown we visited the birthplace of Abraham Lincoln. The Log Cabin in which Abraham Lincoln was born in 1809 stands in a museum like building open to visitors. As had been planned in advance, the family spent Easter in Bardstown, a bishop's see with a well-known cathedral. The renovated plantation "Old Kentucky Home" stands on Federal Hill in Bardstown. It was named after the song "My Old Kentucky Home," which Stephen Foster had composed there in 1853. In the Old Stone Inn we could enjoy a delicious Kentucky Easter meal. From Bardstown we drove directly north via Louisville to Indianapolis and then back to South Bend. Thus, this long and very informative round trip came to a happy conclusion.

The Big Surprise

The big surprise of this journey was the small town of Bardstown in Kentucky. Central Kentucky belongs to the oldest areas of settlement west of the Appalachians. Bardstown was founded in 1788. Little known is the fact that Louis Philippe of Orleans (1773-1850), the later King Louis Philippe of France, after having fled the French Revolution, spent the winter of 1796 in the Old Stone Inn in Bardstown. During the long winter, he supposedly painted al fresco on the walls of his room. The allegorical figures of these murals show the demise of the Old World in contrast to the flowering of the New. They express specifically the view of the "bon sauvage," the idea of the noble savage. As a token of his gratitude for the hospitality that had been extended to him, Louis Philippe as King of France sent as gifts to the St. Joseph's Cathedral in Bardstown a number of paintings that are attributed to the school of Van Dyck.

Observations and Travel Impressions

Indiana and Illinois have rich agricultural areas, where also large industries have developed; altogether a high living standard and progressing communities.

The racial problem shifted to a large extent to the ghettos of the big cities, where it represents a serious danger and is urgently pressing for a solution.

The Mississippi and Ohio Rivers are a distinct cultural border line between North and South. While the agricultural areas in Indiana and Illinois thrive and prosper, even a Border State like Kentucky shows long stretches of images of poverty and neglect.

What comes to the particular attention of the traveler from Europe is the historical continuity of American institutions. This applies at first to the enduring political order since the foundation of the Union in 1789. Upheavals, changes of public institutions as well as changing borders, as they happened in Europe as the result of revolutions and wars, are practically non existent. One gains the strong impression of an extraordinary stability of the legal and political system in this country.

Notre Dame, April 3, 1964

The Polka Party

The Polka Party of the local Slavic population has preserved a good part of the Polish and Czech folklore heritage. For the most part, they still converse in their native tongues, but mainly in Polish.

Notre Dame, April 4, 1964

Jean Madeira

In today's matinee of the South Bend Symphony Orchestra Jean Madeira gave a concert. In 1955 the world-famous alto celebrated triumphs as Carmen in the Vienna State Opera, which have become part of operatic history. As a sign of her affection for Vienna, she sang at the end of the concert "Wien, Wien, nur du allein."

[Jean (Browning) Madeira was of native Indian-Irish descent. Born 1924 in Centralia, Illinois, she grew up in St. Louis where she had her first music education. From 1948-71 she was a member of the Metropolitan Opera. Jean Madeira died in 1972.]

Notre Dame, April 10, 1964

Amish Country

The area that stretches from here about 50 miles to the east is known as Amish country of Indiana. In the midst of well cared for farm land a number of attractive villages and small towns have developed, among them especially Bremen, Nappanee, Goshen, Bristol, Middlebury and Shipshewana stand out. The Amish are a separate sectarian group of Mennonites, who in the 18th century had emigrated from Southern Germany and Switzerland to the New World. The name derives from the founder of this sect, Jacob Amann, from Bern in Switzerland. Searching for more fertile land, the Amish, starting in the 19th century from Pennsylvania, moved farther west and settled in Ohio, Indiana, and Illinois. The Amish are Anabaptists who live strictly according to the Bible and who are very mindful of their independence as a group. In modern America the Amish are a conspicuous curiosity. They cling unbendingly to their old traditional simple lifestyle foregoing electricity, television and the telephone. They also reject the use of motor vehicles, driving instead across the countryside in a "buggy," a small black carriage drawn by a single horse. They are mostly dressed in black. The men grow beards and wear broad-brimmed black hats. Besides agriculture, small active industries have developed primarily good homespun eateries as well as furniture and cabinet-making. The Amish are known for being good farmers. Their natural produce is liked in the food departments of super markets.

Notre Dame, April 15, 1964

The Michigan Fruit Belt

South Bend and Notre Dame are situated close to the Michigan state line. The area north from here along the eastern shore of Lake Michigan surprises by its natural beauty and large wooded dunes. Favored by the steady climate on the lakeside, an extensive fruit belt has developed. Here, apples, pears, cherries, peaches, and grapes are grown. Immigrants from Holland, Germany, and Eastern European countries have contributed to the development of this area. The southwest corner of Michigan is like one vast orchard. Especially at this time of the year, the landscape resembles a sea of blossoms.

Notre Dame, April 22, 1964

The Civil Rights Bill and the Wallace Campaign

[As Governor of Alabama George C. Wallace had made his decision known that he would be a candidate in the 1964 primaries of the Democratic Party in the North. He eventually ran his campaign in the Wisconsin and Indiana primaries. Wallace's sharp polemics against the Civil Rights Bill was a direct challenge of President Johnson.]

The civil rights question is taking center stage as the decisive issue in this year's presidential election. The votes Governor Wallace gained in the

Wisconsin primary (Wallace gained nearly 35% of the Democratic votes) worries Democrats as well as the liberal wing of the Republican Party. The Wallace campaign north of the Mason-Dixon Line raised awareness that political forces are at work also in the Northern States opposed to the Civil Rights Bill.

Notre Dame, April 24, 1964

President Johnson Visits South Bend

President Lyndon B. Johnson paid a surprise visit to South Bend today. He visited the vocational retraining centers for the former Studebaker Automobile Plant workers who had lost their jobs. This visit by the President called national attention to the retraining programs supported by the government. At the same time L.B. Johnson started his campaign. The clever domestic policy tactics of Johnson goes in the direction of personally visiting the so-called "poverty pockets" in order to make his anti-poverty program explicit to voters. Johnson's visit passed by remarkably quiet, whites and blacks alike showed a great deal of sympathy towards him.

Notre Dame, April 30, 1964

The Indiana Primary

[After Wisconsin, the Wallace Campaign concentrated on Indiana.]

Wallace's entry into the Indiana primary had an alarming effect. Governor Matthew Welsh of Indiana, who stood in as proxy candidate for President Johnson in the primary of his state, led a crusade against Wallace. Welsh warned voters not to repeat the example of Wisconsin.

The Welsh vs. Wallace controversy in the Middle West moved the civil rights question to the foreground of the national interest. Under the pretext of "States' Rights," to protect the rights of the individual states, Wallace presented himself shamelessly as advocate of race discrimination. This evoked the unanimous resistance of church communities and university campuses. At yesterday's campaign speech on the Notre Dame campus, Wallace saw himself confronted with vociferous demonstrations. He was able to escape only with the greatest difficulty from the incensed crowd.

Notre Dame, May 5, 1964

The Results of the Indiana Primary

Governor Matthew Welsh won the Indiana primary for Lyndon B. Johnson, but nevertheless 30% of the Democratic votes went to George Wallace. The following reasons may explain Wallace's high share of the votes: (1) The widespread uncertainty about the consequences of the Civil Rights Bill; (2) the latent fear among the white population that jobs could be lost by racial integration; (3) the apprehension that by desegregation in the area of education children could be forced to attend integrated schools.

On the Republican side Barry Goldwater won the majority of votes, followed by Harold E. Stassen. Nelson A. Rockefeller and Cabot Lodge did not run as candidates in the Indiana primary.

Notre Dame, May 7, 1964

The Theodore M. Hesburgh Library of the University of Notre Dame. (Courtesy of the University of Notre Dame Photography)

The dedication ceremony of the Library took place on May 7, 1964

Dedication of the Memorial Library

On today's Solemnity of the Ascension of the Lord the Memorial Library, the new main library of the University of Notre Dame, was dedicated. The dedication ceremony turned out to be an academic event of the first order. Cardinal Eugene Tisserant, the Dean of the College of Cardinals, celebrated the Pontifical Mass on the open Mall in front of the Library. He conveyed the blessing of the Holy Father. Present were also Albert Cardinal Meyer of Chicago and Joseph Cardinal Ritter of St. Louis besides many representatives of American colleges and universities. The President of Columbia University, Grayson Kirk, remarked in his address that the traditional university structure is in a fast process of change, and that the great days of the American universities still lie ahead. The construction of the 14-story high building has been completed in three years: Only a few days ago, the lawn of the Mall was laid out, and in addition the trees along either side were planted. The large mosaic with the figure of Christ the teacher in the center, which covers the entire wall of the building towards the south, has become the defining symbol of the Memorial Library.

[In 1987 the Memorial Library was renamed Theodore M. Hesburgh Library. The Reverend Theodore M. Hesburgh, C.S.C. (1917—) was president of the University of Notre Dame from 1952-1987. Father Hesburgh was the driving force behind the construction of this great university library.]

Notre Dame, June 6, 1964

Barry Goldwater in California

Barry Goldwater from Arizona won a decisive victory in the California primary. All 86 votes of the Republican delegates from California go to Goldwater. It is therefore highly probable that Goldwater will receive the nomination of the Republican Party at its national convention in San Francisco. As far as can be anticipated, it will be Goldwater who will confront Johnson in the campaign for the presidential election this fall. Goldwater's ultraconservative attitude gives even fellow Republicans discomfort, who have started a "stop Goldwater campaign." The thought that Goldwater could possibly move into the White House triggered, especially in the European press, severe alarm.

Notre Dame, June 10, 1964

Vote on Cloture in the Senate

Today the Senate voted 71:29 for cloture, closing the unlimited filibuster. The adoption of the Civil Rights Bill has been delayed for months by the tactics of marathon speeches. Last night, a senator from West Virginia held such a marathon speech which lasted from 6 p.m. until 8:50 a.m. in the morning.* From now on, each senator will have only one hour to speak on the Civil Rights resolution. The chances for adopting the Civil Rights Bill have increased considerably.

[Cloture, that is putting an end to the tactics of obstruction by marathon speeches, was introduced in the Senate only in 1917. A two-thirds majority is needed to achieve cloture. That happened by the vote taken on the Senate floor on June 10, 1964, in connection with the debate over the Civil Rights Bill. Before, Senators had unlimited time to speak, cloture usually limits the time to speak to one hour.]

*[Senator Robert C. Byrd, Democrat from West Virginia, had joined the filibuster tactics of the Democrats from the South. During the night of June 9 to 10, 1964, he gave his longest speech that lasted more than 14 hours.]

[The academic year at the University of Notre Dame finished with the commencement exercises on June 6 and 7. My family and I left Notre Dame by the middle of June and embarked on the journey by car along the Great Lakes to Boston that had been planned long in advance. It first led us in a northwesterly direction across Illinois to Galena and then on to Waverly, Iowa, where we met with friends, the family of a Lutheran pastor and professor at Wartburg College. From Waverly we drove directly north via Minneapolis to Duluth, the western end of Lake Superior. From there the journey continued on Interstate 2 across the sheer endless woods of the Ottawa National Forest to Escanaba and then along the northern shore of Lake Michigan to St. Ignace and a visit to Mackinac Island. From St. Ignace we drove over the Mackinac Bridge and then through Michigan to Port Huron. After a short distance through Canada, we reached the Niagra Falls. From there the journey went on via Buffalo to Cooperstown, New York, and finally over Pittsfield, Massachusetts, to Boston. Wherever on this 3,000 mile stretch we came to a place of literary interest, we stopped.]

June 15-17, 1964

Galena, Illinois

Galena, situated in the northwest corner of Illinois, was one of the most peculiar small towns which we encountered in the Midwest. Its history and old culture go back to the Mississippi steamboat era. Until 1850 Galena was regarded as the great "metropolis" of the West, a role which was later taken over by San Francisco. It was the hometown of Ulysses Grant. The wealth of the town was based on its copper mines. In the summer of 1840 Herman Melville had come to Galena to visit his uncle. The journey over the Great Lakes to Galena, and then down the Mississippi and up the Ohio back to Albany, New York, left a lasting influence on his writing.

[Escanaba, Michigan], June 20, 1964

The Center of the Lutheran Church

Wisconsin, Iowa and Minnesota form the center of the Lutheran Church in America. This goes back to the strong immigration in the 19th century from Scandinavian countries, mainly from Norway and Sweden. The Church was for the settlement of these vast and lonesome territories an indispensable help to get started. It was also the spiritual center for schools and the cultural development. A good number of well-known private colleges in these states have been founded by the Lutheran Church.

St. Ignace, Michigan, June 21, 1964

On the Upper Peninsula of Michigan French place names and topographical designations like Sault [su:] Ste. Marie, St. Ignace, Pt. aux Chenes, Epoulette, Manistique, Marquette and many more prevail. That was in the 17th and 18th centuries the entry area for French *explorateurs* and *missionnaires*. The missionary area of the Jesuit Order stretched, starting from Quebec, all over the Great Lakes. The French influence today is still visible everywhere.

Mackinac Island

Mackinac Island was a surprise. It is during summer without a doubt one of the most beautiful vacation resorts in the Midwest. The small island, which is reached by ferry from St. Ignace, lies in the Straits of Mackinac that connects Lake Huron with Lake Michigan. This important connecting passage was discovered in 1634 by the *explorateur* Jean Nicolet (1598-1642). Due to its location, Mackinac Island was of special strategic significance during the colonial period. It was an essential starting point for the exploration of the North American Continent as well as an emporium for the fur trade. The Jesuit missionary Père Jacques Marquette (1637-75) founded the town of St. Ignace on the shore across from the island. In 1673, starting from this place, Marquette advanced as far west as the Mississippi River and thereby prepared for La Salle the way for the exploration of the Mississippi to its mouth in the Gulf. Fort Mackinac still played a decisive role during the War of 1812. Today, Mackinac Island is a major tourist hub. As no motor vehicles are permitted on the island, visitors move around on horse-drawn carriages. The well-preserved Fort, its terrace and restaurant with the magnificent view of the Straits, rank foremost among the many attractions.

St. Ignace, June 21, 1964

Senate Adopts Civil Rights Bill

On Friday, June 19, the U.S. Senate adopted by a vote of historic significance 73:27 the Civil Rights Bill. Only the signature of President Johnson is still needed for this fiercely debated Bill to be enacted as federal law.

[The *Congressional Record* (Bill H.R. 7152) shows that the Senate vote on June 19 on the Civil Rights Bill of 1964 was taken in tribute to John F. Kennedy. As Senator George McGovern elaborated: The Civil Rights Law "was passed in tribute to John F. Kennedy, who on June 19, 1963 had sent a message to Congress calling for the passage of a comprehensive civil rights law." (*Congressional Record*, 88th Congress, Second Session, vol. 110, pt. 11, p. 14,432).]

Port Huron, Michigan, June 22, 1964

From St. Ignace we first drove over the Mackinac Bridge. This bridge, which was opened as recently as 1959 to public traffic, spans the Mackinac Straits and connects the Upper with the Lower Peninsula of Michigan. Then the day's journey continued on Interstate Highway 75 south to Flint and from there east to Port Huron on the Canadian Border. The highways, parks and rest areas of Michigan are exceptionally well kept, to the advantage of the vacation areas in the northern part of the state.

Niagara Falls, Ontario, Canada, June 23, 1964

It was only a short distance across the Province of Ontario to Niagara Falls. The Canadian side of the Falls offers the best view of this unique display of Nature's wonder. On the American side, on the other hand, one can join a guided tour and, protected by long waterproof jackets, walk down close to the Falls.

Cooperstown, New York, June 26, 1964

The Gem Cooperstown

After the long drive from Buffalo to Albany, the side-trip through the Mohawk Valley to Cooperstown was a welcome change. The small town lies like a jewel on Lake Otsego. It is named after its founder Judge William Cooper, the father of the author James Fenimore Cooper (1789-1851). The settlement Cooperstown originated around 1800; some of the original buildings have been preserved. The Cooper heritage, in regard to the family as well as to the author's works, is being well looked after. Cooperstown was the original home of the author, from which he drew the narrative materials for "The Leatherstocking Tales." Lake Otsego and the source of the Susquehanna River form the authentic background for *The Pioneers* (1823), the first of the five novels in "The Leatherstocking Tales" series. Today, Cooperstown is a sought after place for excursions. It is also the place of attraction for baseball fans from around the world, for it is the home of the Baseball Hall of Fame.

Pittsfield, Massachusetts, June 28, 1964

Arrowhead

The Farm Arrowhead was tightly closed, just as generally speaking the entire estate looked rather dilapidated.

[Pittsfield lies in the Berkshire Hills in Western Massachusetts. The stay there offered me the opportunity to visit the Farm Arrowhead, where in 1850-51 Herman Melville had written *Moby-Dick*. Only years later, the Melville Society acquired Arrowhead, a place which is of significance for American literature.

The Farm House was renovated and appropriately turned into a Museum with Melville memorabilia.]

[I had already made arrangements in Innsbruck with a Fulbright-guest professor in Austria that during our six week sojourn in Boston my family and I could move into his home in West Newton. From there I drove every day to Cambridge to Harvard University in order to pursue my research at the Houghton Library. I had permission to examine the manuscripts of Thomas Wolfe. Just at that time, the extensive literary estate of Thomas Wolfe in the William P. Wisdom Collection had been made accessible to research. In the summer of 1964, Richard S. Kennedy and Paschal Reeves had begun their work of editing the pocket notebooks of Thomas Wolfe. That monumental work was published in 2 vols. as *The Notebooks of Thomas Wolfe* in 1970. Paschal Reeves called my attention to the many entries on Europe in Wolfe's notebooks. Out of this, finally the idea emerged for *Jason's Voyage: The Search for the Old World in American Literature,* which appeared as a book in 1989.]

Cambridge, Massachusetts, July 1, 1964

The Harvard Summer School looks like an artist colony of French existentialists and pseudo-cosmopolitan Midwesterners.

West Newton, Massachusetts, July 3, 1964

The Civil Rights Act Signed into Law

Yesterday evening, President Lyndon B. Johnson signed the Civil Rights Act of 1964, which now has become the law of the land. This was the decisive step taken by the U.S. government to normalize race relations and to give the colored minority equality within the American society.

The essential provisions of this law are:

1. To enforce the constitutional right to vote.
2. Injunctive relief against discrimination in public accommodations.
3. Equality in public facilities and public education.

(This means the desegregation of public parks, playgrounds, pools, libraries and public schools.)

The execution of these provisions will basically change American society in the decades ahead. There is a special symbolic significance to the circumstance that the Civil Rights Act was signed on the evening before the Fourth of July Weekend.

West Newton, July 11, 1964

The Boston Pops Orchestra

In summer time, Boston and the surrounding New England villages have a festival atmosphere, which by comparison is not much different from that of the tourist resorts in Europe. Above all a great deal of music and theater is offered. Especially liked are the concerts of the Boston Pops Orchestra on the Esplanade. The 36th season of the Pops with their remarkable program has just ended. The open air concert conducted by Arthur Fiedler took place free of charge in the Hatch Shell on Memorial Drive in the Back Bay of the Charles River. We heard an excellent rendition of Gershwin's "Rhapsody in Blue."

[Arthur Fiedler (1894-1979) was born in Boston, but had descended from a family of musicians in Vienna. In 1930 he took over the direction of the Boston Pops Orchestra, a position he maintained until his death in 1979. As conductor Fiedler was master of a wide-range repertoire that reached from classical to popular music. The Pops had on their program familiar tunes from operettas and musicals, and Fiedler conducted with equal verve the march music of John Philip Sousa. The concerts on the Esplanade in Boston attracted hundreds of thousands of people. Fiedler was one of the most liked and successful figures, indeed an institution of the musical scene in America.]

West Newton, July 12, 1964

Salem, Massachusetts

Salem is situated on the Northern coast of Massachusetts Bay at a distance of about 20 miles from Boston. The township, which was first settled in 1626, belongs to the oldest settlements in New England. Salem has become known by the witchcraft trials of 1692 and as the birthplace of Nathaniel Hawthorne (1804-64). The unhappy victims of those notorious trials were sent to the gallows. Hawthorne, the author of *The Scarlet Letter* (1850), was born here and spent most of his life in the Puritanical environment of this small town. In total seclusion, Hawthorne wrote here his psychologically profound tales.

In Salem, the houses from the early colonial period are kept preserved with great care. On the grounds of "The House of the Seven Gables," which served as the backdrop for Hawthorne's romance of the same title, a Hawthorne Memorial has been established. Thus, the simple house where the author was born was transferred there and opened for visitors.

West Newton, July 13, 1964

The Plight of the Inner City

The inner districts of the cities on the East Coast are for the most part neglected; they virtually suffocate by their own debris. The flight to the residential areas in the suburbs is constantly increasing, what again contributes to the growing plight of the inner cities.

[Plymouth and New Bedford, Massachusetts], July 18-19, 1964

After the *Mayflower* had landed on Cape Cod on November 11, 1620, the Pilgrim Fathers were looking for a suitable place where they could establish a permanent settlement. They found such a place on the shore across the Bay and named the settlement Plymouth after the harbor in England from which they had ventured into the unknown. On December 16, the *Mayflower* dropped anchor at Plymouth Rock. The Pioneer Village of Plymouth gives a vivid impression of how the pilgrims lived during the first years following their arrival in the New World. During the severe first winter close to half of the 102 settlers died of disease and hunger. But in October of the following year 1621 the pilgrims together with the Indians, who had helped them to survive, could celebrate their first Thanksgiving. Out of that, the very own American celebration of Giving Thanks and of families coming together has emerged.

[George Washington declared the Thanksgiving of November 26, 1789 a national holiday. But only in 1941 was it determined by an act of Congress that Thanksgiving Day should be observed on the fourth Thursday in November.]

New Bedford

New Bedford, which at its peak had a fleet of 329 whaling vessels, was by the middle of the 19th century the most important whaling harbor in America. When mineral oil was discovered in Pennsylvania in 1857, the whaling industry lost its economic significance. In addition to that, the New Bedford whaling fleet lost about half of its ships during the Civil War 1861-65. The historic New Bedford has a special relationship to American literature. Herman Melville (1819-91) had come to New Bedford by the end of December 1840 with the intention to sign on to a whaler. On January 3, 1841 he began from Fairhaven aboard the whaler *Acushnet* the long voyage that led him around Cape Horn into the South Pacific. This adventurous whale hunt and the odyssey through the South Pacific archipelagos, which altogether lasted for four years, was the decisive experience in Melville's life. Ten years later, it offered him the narrative material for *Moby-Dick*. The New Bedford Whaling Museum holds a number of documents and objects that are instructive for the understanding of *Moby-Dick*. Especially impressive was the visit to the Seamen's Bethel of New Bedford. Most likely, that church served as a model for the Whaleman's Chapel in *Moby-Dick* (Chap. VII) from whose pulpit Father Mapple delivers his sermon to the sailors.

[Transl: In January, 2003, the Melville Society Archive was inaugurated at the New Bedford Whaling Museum and the Kendall Institute.]

West Newton, July 20, 1964

Goldwater Nominated

As expected, last Wednesday, July 15, Senator Barry Goldwater was nominated by the National Republican Convention in San Francisco as the Republican Party candidate for the presidency. The nomination of Goldwater demonstrates that the ideology of the Republican Party has changed from a liberal to an extreme conservative political attitude. The center of gravity of the Party has shifted from the East to the West concentrating its power in the Southwest, California, and the Northwest. The new, extremely radical tone became apparent by the acceptance speech of the nominee. Goldwater verbatim: "Extremism in the defense of liberty is no vice, moderation in the pursuit of justice is no virtue."

West Newton, July 25-27, 1964

Racial Incidents

Recently, there occurred a racial incident which prompted the New York Police to cordon off the residential area north of 125th Street. A similar incident happened over this weekend in Rochester, New York, after a police patrol helicopter had crashed into the colored section of town. Due to the emergency situation in the ghettos of the northern cities, more and more of the black population are venting their anger by violence. The American dilemma of racial conflicts is still far removed from a solution. But nevertheless, the America of the future can only be imagined as an integrated society in which whites and blacks have equal rights and live together in peace.

Boston, August 20, 1964

In Memoriam of John F. Kennedy

How much the name of John F. Kennedy is rooted in the hearts of the American people, is demonstrated by the exhibition to establish the Kennedy Library that takes place this week in the Boston Museum of Fine Arts. An incessant throng of thousands of people from all walks of life are making a pilgrimage to this exposition. They stand deeply moved before the memorabilia of the late president who so tragically had lost his life. The Kennedy Memorial Library is an idea that meets with overwhelming approval.

New York, August 25, 1964

The Pietà on the World's Fair

The Pavilion of the Vatican is a special attraction at this year's World's Fair in New York. Michelangelo's Pietà is on display for visitors passing by. In making this possible, the Catholic Church has shown courage as well as a world open spirit. Critics had warned of the dangers to take the Pietà out of St. Peter's Basilica, from where it has never been removed since 1499, to ship it across the Atlantic and expose it to the turmoil of a world's fair. They should see the rush of people from all around the world, who deeply touched, pass in silence in front of this sublime work of art. The exhibit of the Vatican promotes without a doubt the ecumenical idea.

[The voyage home had been booked for August 26 on the *United States*. On the evening before, we could see from our hotel in Manhattan the large ocean liner docked on the Hudson Pier. A trace of nostalgia lay over that scene, knowing that the time of the large passenger ships crossing the Atlantic was coming to an end. In the early morning hours before departure, we could still follow on television how Lyndon B. Johnson was nominated by acclamation at the National Convention of the Democratic Party in Atlantic City. By the end of August the Atlantic remained smooth as glass. By contrast to our westbound voyage in January, the five day eastbound crossing was quiet. After landing in Le Havre, we traveled via Paris directly home to Innsbruck.]

Innsbruck, September 5, 1964

A Citizen of Two Worlds

Whoever returns to Europe after a longer sojourn in the United States, will undeniably discover a change in view of his old homeland. Anyway, this is my own experience. Already on the journey from Le Havre to Innsbruck I saw things with a different eye: The railroad, highways, cities and villages looked like a dreamy toyland. The European landscape as a whole appeared to me like a park, whereby the natural beauty of the Alps surprised me again. Upon my return, I stood amazed by the unique sight of the Altstadt, the medieval old town of Innsbruck, with the Nordkette rising precipitously in the background. On the other hand, one has to get used again to the narrow streets and to the traffic with its variegated jumble of pedestrians, bicycles, streetcars, buses, motorcycles and cars of all sizes. A certain feeling of uneasiness and estrangement in one's own home country cannot be denied. But one enjoys much more so the simple pleasures of life: A friendly waiter who serves a menu in the garden; a cup of coffee in a pastry shop; a stroll through the Hofgarten; as well as a visit to a performance in the Landestheater. After a while, one will certainly get adjusted to the daily way of living at home. Yet nevertheless, the longing will remain for once again experiencing that entirely different country with its spaciousness and generosity. One has become a citizen of two worlds, which are very different from each other, but their advantages and disadvantages complement each other.

Historical Events 1964-67

1) U.S. presidential election November 1964

> In the U.S. presidential election on November 3, 1964, Lyndon B. Johnson won a landslide victory. With 61.3% of the votes cast, Johnson gained the largest share of the votes, which up to that time had ever been achieved by a candidate in a presidential election.

On January 20, 1965 he was sworn in as President of the United States. His running mate Senator Hubert H. Humphrey assumed the office of Vice President.

2) On September 9, 1965 Charles de Gaulle declared the withdrawal of France from the North Atlantic Treaty Organization (NATO).

On December 19, 1965 Charles de Gaulle was reelected president of France.

3) The escalation of the war in Vietnam 1965-67

After American installations had been attacked by units of the Vietcong, President Johnson ordered in February, 1965 air strikes against military targets in North Vietnam. With the increasing deployment of ground troops, the war in Vietnam escalated more and more.

4) Racial unrests in American cities 1965-67

From 1965-67 severe racial unrests occurred in the ghettos of American cities, which took on the character of a civil war. It began with the riots in the Watts district of Los Angeles in August, 1965. During the summer of 1967 the unrests spread like wild fire through the cities in the North and the Midwest, among them especially severe in Newark, New Jersey, Detroit, Michigan, and in Kansas City, Missouri. Added to that were the wild demonstrations against the war in Vietnam on American university campuses.

SECTION 3

April 9, 1967-December 27, 1968

Innsbruck, April 9, 1967

The Tarnished Transatlantic Relationship

The recent whirlwind tour of the American Vice President Hubert Humphrey through the European capitals brought to a glaring light the uneasiness between America and Europe which has been smoldering for some time. At first the Europeans were annoyed that the Vice President was sent on this Goodwill Tour, and that the President did not come in person, although President Johnson had not spared the trouble of traveling to the much more distant Asia twice. The Europeans saw new proof that the United States pays more attention to Asian than Atlantic affairs. Indeed, during the past several years hardly anything has been more obvious than the changed relationship between America and Europe. While John F. Kennedy was cheered enthusiastically in Berlin, Hubert Humphrey's reception remained cool. Furthermore, the Vice President was confronted by anti-American demonstrations in many European cities.

What has really happened that tarnished the friendly relationship between America and Europe?

In a leading article in the *Weltwoche* on April 7, Francois Bundy points out:

1) Most European countries feel offended, as they were not consulted during the American-Russian negotiations on the Non-Proliferation Treaty.*
2) The priority of the war in Vietnam over Atlantic problems.

3) France's break-up with NATO as well as the new European nationalism stirred up by Gaullism.
4) The difficulties of a trade agreement between the United States and the Common Market.

In the past years, Europe has more or less fallen behind. Economically the Common Market could become an equal partner of the United States, but politically and militarily Europe is lagging. There is a lack of constructive cooperation, above all also in the areas of science and research. Europe is in danger of falling into backwardness.

*[The Non-Proliferation Treaty, which had been agreed upon in bilateral negotiations between the United States and the Soviet Union, was signed in 1968 and came into effect in 1970. While Great Britain signed on to the Treaty, France did not join the agreement.]

Innsbruck, April 25, 1967

At the Graveside of Konrad Adenauer

[Konrad Adenauer (1876-1967) died on April 19. He was the first Chancellor of the German Federal Republic (GFR) from 1949-63. Adenauer strongly supported the policy of the GFR joining NATO in 1955. He was also a strong advocate of the European Economic Community (EC) or Common Market.]

Lyndon B. Johnson and Charles de Gaulle stood at the graveside of Konrad Adenauer to demonstrate the unity of the West in whose formation Adenauer had played a decisive role. But the encounter of Johnson and de Gaulle during the funeral ceremony in Köln showed how much the West was divided in two camps. Between the United Sates and the Gaullists a rift of misunderstanding has opened. Gaullism has gained ground in Europe and, with the opening toward the East, is getting stronger and stronger.

Innsbruck, April 28, 1967

The Resolutions of Karlsbad of 1967

The conference of the Communist parties in Karlsbad, which at the same time is a summit meeting of the heads of the Communist parties of East and

West, has again illustrated which hopes the East is nourishing. There was a clear expression of the opinion that the Atlantic Alliance should be dissolved when the NATO treaty expires in 1969. In return, they pledged also to dissolve the Warsaw Pact. After dissolving NATO, the East obviously hopes to have an easy hand in bringing the remaining Western part of Europe by peaceful infiltration on its side. The Communists would thereby achieve superiority in Europe.

Innsbruck, June 5, 1967

A Presumptuousness

De Gaulle's demand that Great Britain, before it could join the Common Market, would have to break up its relations with the United States, is presumptuous to a high degree. It ignores completely the deep-rooted historical bonds within the English speaking world.

Innsbruck, June 5, 1967

The Powder Keg in the Middle East Explodes

In the early morning hours of today, the powder keg in the Middle East exploded, full-scale war between Israel and the Arab League has broken out. In a quick air strike, Israel destroyed with one blow the air forces of Egypt, Jordan, and Syria, before their aircrafts could even take off. And within a few hours, a heavy tank battle was underway. It is hardly imaginable that this small country will be able to withstand the Arab superiority.

Innsbruck, June 11, 1967

The Six-Day War

What Israel has accomplished in the past six days is unbelievable. Israel succeeded in destroying the entire Arab armed forces and to compel them to surrender within 48 hours. The Israeli tanks stormed through the Sinai Peninsula to the Suez Canal. The Israelis were also capable of taking the Old City of Jerusalem and to occupy the Gaza Strip, the West Bank of the Jordan River as well as the Golan Heights. On the urgent request by the Security Council of the United Nations, a cease-fire is being kept on all fronts.

Several lessons can be learned from the Six-Day War. A small country that is well armed and has the necessary will to defend itself can stand up against superior enemy forces. The Pan-Arabic superpower was practically only on paper. The massive Russian weapons supplies are of little help if the highly technical materials are not properly operated and serviced. A regional conflict carried out with conventional weapons does not trigger, as was feared, a nuclear war. But in the end, the war leaves behind untold misery: destroyed cities, casualties in great numbers, mutilated people, destitution, and a new flood of refugees.

Pentecost 1967

Twenty Years Catholic Student Union of Austria in Innsbruck

The twentieth anniversary of founding the Catholic Student Union of Austria in Innsbruck brings back memories of the hardships under which the generation after 1945 had to study. A warm room was already a relief. With a cup of tea and a sandwich, debates were carried on late into the night. The seriousness and maturity of that generation, who under great difficulties were building an existence for themselves, and who were searching for a new outlook on life as well as striving for a new sense of community, were unique. But despite all the difficulties, a certain optimism for the future prevailed.

Remembering Father Heinrich Suso Braun

One of the decisive and at the same time happiest encounters in my student years was Father Heinrich Suso Braun. As Director of the Campus Ministry at the University of Innsbruck, Father Braun was in charge of the Catholic Student Union. He not only impressed by his high intellect and upright personality, but even more so by his warm humanity that he extended to every single member in the community. By his sermons, which are broadcast every Sunday and heard by millions, he has arguably become the best known preacher in Austria and Southern Germany. And in addition to that, in his old age this man is also administering a home of the Seraphic Charity for handicapped children. He may serve as an example of complete Christian devotion. By his dedication and unpretentious demeanor he has become a model for me that I have deemed desirable to emulate.

[Father Dr. Heinrich Suso Braun, OFMcap. (1904-1977) came from Riedlingen in Southern Swabia on the Danube. He entered the Capuchin

Order in 1923 and was ordained a priest in 1927. He studied at the Gregorian University in Rome 1928-31 and earned a doctorate in philosophy. Thereafter, he taught in Salzburg until 1938. He served as Director of the Campus Ministry at the University of Innsbruck 1943-53. His weekly sermons "Wort am Sonntag" (Word on Sunday) were broadcast by Radio Tirol from 1945 until his death in 1977.]

Innsbruck, June 20, 1967

The detonation of the first Chinese hydrogen bomb shows again the extreme danger that threatens humanity by the nuclear armament.

Innsbruck, July 30, 1967

Racial Unrests in the U.S.

The recent racial disorders in Detroit and in a number of other American cities have demonstrated a degree of violence, which appears to be irreconcilable and seems to plunge the United States into a civil war. A national tragedy of immense proportions is happening before our eyes just at the moment when a solution to this dilemma seemed to be in sight. Left-oriented circles, not without some glee and false speculation, believe to have discovered the Achilles' heel of the protecting power of the West that could impair America's capacity to act.

With uneasiness and worries, one observes these racial unrests especially at a time when one is preparing a journey to America. It will need the cooperation of all positive forces as well as effective measures to clear up the slums in the cities in order to get these unrests under control, as they become more dangerous with every passing summer. The United States has no other choice but to solve its racial problems. But here in Europe one can hardly imagine how complex this undertaking really is.

Innsbruck, July 31, 1967

Remarks on the European Scene

Absolutism of the 17th and 18th centuries as well as the empires of the 19th century left behind sumptuous palaces where the succeeding republican citizens have established their ministries and dry offices. Humble townswomen now can take a walk with their baby carriages in the artistically designed ornamental gardens. How drab and profane would Europe be without the inherited splendor of the former ruling aristocracy?

[During the first three years (1964-67), the Foreign Study Program of the University of Notre Dame in cooperation with the University of Innsbruck established itself very well. Each year 50 students from Notre Dame came to Innsbruck for a year of studies. The group was accompanied by a professor from Notre Dame who directed the Program. As Assistant at the Amerika-Institut of the University of Innsbruck I served as academic adviser to the Program. I had the task of adjusting the curriculum requirements of an American private Catholic university to the available study possibilities in Innsbruck. In the course of this work, my relationship with Notre Dame deepened. When I was offered a position as visiting associate professor for the academic year 1967-68, I gladly accepted. Thus, in August 1967 my wife and I with our two children traveled for a second time to South Bend, Indiana. The fall semester at Notre Dame began the end of August.]

South Bend, Indiana, Labor Day, September 4, 1967

The First Flight over the Atlantic

The flight on a DC-8 from Zurich to New York (at an altitude of 10,000 m / 30,000 feet and at a speed of 800 km/h /500 mph) passes so fast that there is hardly time to eat a relaxed lunch and to fill out the customs declaration forms. And besides, these new jets fly so smoothly that one does not feel the speed. The unpleasant after-effects of a transatlantic flight are felt only after landing. With the time difference of gaining six hours, the physiological body system is mixed up. When at midnight you finally stretch out dead tired in your hotel room in New York, it is only 6 o'clock in the evening local time and still clear daylight. Unavoidably, you wake up again at 3 a.m. The effects of the jet lag cannot be denied. Only after three days does the body find its normal balance again. But the advantages of flying over traveling by boat are obvious. Flying the distance between Europe and America shrinks to such an extent that it creates the illusion of local traffic. This gives the peace of mind that in case of an emergency one would be able to return home in a few hours. It is evident that the seagoing vessels cannot compete with the airlines. Passenger ships between Europe and America will soon be a thing of the past.

First Impressions on American Soil

The impressions, which one gets in the first days and weeks after arriving in America from Europe, or vice versa, are the most fruitful and astonishing, for at this time of transition and adjustment one is most receptive to the contrasts between the two continents.

1) The first astonishing impression is the airport in New York. By comparison, the John F. Kennedy International Airport in New York makes the airports of Zurich-Kloten, Munich-Riem, or Tempelhof in Berlin look small, modest and improvised. Yet O'Hare in Chicago is even larger and its operations more impressive than the JFK. On the other hand, the decline of the railroad system in America has progressed to a degree that many of the large railroad stations are up for sale. By degrading shipping and railroads only to freight service, the mode of traveling has fundamentally changed.

2) Although the general living standard in Europe has substantially increased in recent years, one still does not trust one's eyes on arriving in the United States. As we went to the super market and filled up the shopping cart to the brim, we were surprised at the cash register how much cheaper groceries are here. Compared to Europe, income and the cost of living have further shifted in favor of the American consumer. At a higher income one spends less for the daily living expenses. A middle-class home in America has a living standard that would be thought of as being luxurious in Europe.

3) While on the contrary, the spiritual uncertainty in America has increased in past years. The Vietnam War, the racial unrests of recent summers as well as the various changes in religion and in the general outlook on life have contributed to that.

[The changes in attitude have been brought about by the "counterculture" of the 1960s. It was essentially a protest movement of the younger generation against conventional values, while they followed instead an uninhibited liberal lifestyle.]

4) The racial unrests have by no means brought about chaos or a civil war atmosphere in the country at large, yet the deep division between whites and blacks has intensified. The colored section of town, where broken shop windows, boarded up businesses and burned down houses give evidence of the recent racial violence, is more avoided now than before. Also, far-reaching changes appear to be happening within the black community.

5) The normal pace of life in America has not been thrown off balance either by the Vietnam War or the racial unrests. The white residential areas in the suburbs enjoy the peace and order they are accustomed to, while the inner cities are deteriorating even more.

South Bend, September 17, 1967

The New Sense of Security

Truly, one just lives more carefree in America than in Europe. Whoever comes here from Europe must at first free himself of his inhibitions. First, one has to get used to the informality or ease of social contacts. The freedoms to which every person is entitled here open up hesitatingly at first and not without disbelief. Gradually the anxieties and the fear of not saying the right word are overcome. Once rid of the fears and worries brought along from Europe, one feels more liberated. One would never like to miss again this newly gained sense of security.

October 1967

A Series of Strikes and Their Consequences

In order to grasp America correctly, one has to keep in mind its vast continental space. This fall is marked by a series of strikes. At the beginning of the school year, the teachers in the states of New York and Michigan went on strike. Simultaneously the teamsters, the steel truckers joined the walk-out of the Ford Motor Company work force. What are the consequences of these large strikes? Apparently the overall American economy is hardly affected by them. America is big enough to cope with strikes of this magnitude. By the loss of production at Ford, the other automobile companies hope for a larger profit.

October 1967

Foreboding Signs of the Coming Presidential Election

The Vietnam War and the racial unrests in the big cities are already the foreseeable dominant issues of the presidential election 1968. The criticism of the government is becoming so scathing that it will be difficult for President Johnson to hold out through the campaign. The governors of New York and California, Rockefeller and Reagan, have already appeared on the scene as salient candidates of the opposite party. Not without good reason, the G.O.P. is sensing a chance to win, although the electorate usually entrusts the sitting president with a second term in office.

[Nelson A. Rockefeller (1908-79), Governor of New York, 1959-73; Ronald Reagan (1911—), Governor of California, 1967-75. G.O.P. (Grand Old Party) is an epithet of the Republican Party.]

South Bend, October 18, 1967

Landing on Venus

The soft landing of a soviet space probe on Venus caused great admiration in the United States. It is generally praised as an historic accomplishment that proves again the lead of the Soviet Union in space technology. This will without a doubt spur the United States to further efforts in space exploration. In view of the expected budget cuts, this development is not inopportune for NASA. But aside from the race for the dominant role in space technology, which is only a matter between the United States and the Soviet Union anyway, this achievement of the soviet space program deserves undivided respect. Our knowledge about Venus has increased tremendously so that this mythically shrouded planet is now seen in a much more realistic light.

South Bend, October 21, 1967

Anti-War Demonstrations

Over this weekend about 50,000 young people, for the most part students from colleges and universities, gathered in Washington, D.C., in order to participate in the demonstration against the Vietnam War. They marched united on the Pentagon. The government had to mobilize the military to protect the capital from violence. This protest movement certainly attracted attention, but it hardly upset the interior of the country. Here in the Midwest people are much more interested in which team is winning in college football. Still, the pent-up anger at the way the war is being carried out in Vietnam, where at this time nearly 500,000 American troops are deployed, cannot be ignored any longer. President Johnson will have to take decisive steps to end the war before next year's election if he wants to continue staying in office.

South Bend, October 21, 1967

Little Interest in Europe

The situation in Central Europe is of little concern for the average American. It is particularly noticeable that there is little interest in the German reunification. Also, the endeavors for European integration are hardly taken seriously. One has gotten accustomed to the status quo and has adjusted to it. While the cultural heritage of Europe or the Old World is highly appreciated, the political events in Europe are hardly noticed.

South Bend, November 1967

The Devaluation of the Pound Sterling

The devaluation of the pound sterling of approximately 14% last Sunday, November 18, hit the world like a bolt from the blue, although it could not have come as a surprise for insiders. The economic crisis in Great Britain will undoubtedly have its effect on the EFTA countries. It also puts the division of the European economy into the Common Market and the EFTA in question. Furthermore, the devaluation of the pound sterling raises the specter of a worldwide economic crisis.

[The EFTA (European Free Trade Association) was founded in 1959 following a British proposal. Besides Great Britain, Denmark, Norway and Portugal also the three neutral countries Austria, Sweden, and Switzerland belonged to the European Free Trade Association.]

South Bend, November 1967

Municipal Elections

The municipal elections of November 7 have given the colored population, through the democratic process, more say in city governments. For the first time, two colored candidates have won the elections for mayor in Cleveland, Ohio, and Gary, Indiana. Although the National Guard stood ready for action in Gary, the election was carried out in an orderly fashion. Likewise, the election results were accepted without disturbances. Thereby, another step was taken, which will finally lead to racial equality.

[In the following decades a large number of Afro-American candidates won mayoral races, among others in big cities like Chicago and St. Louis. Not until the late 1970s has the expression "African-American" or "Afro-American" been accepted in everyday American speech.]

South Bend, November 24, 1967

The Escalation of the Vietnam War

Over the Thanksgiving Weekend the fiercest fighting up to now took place in Vietnam. Although little is said about it, the uncertainty as well as the progressing escalation of the war are felt as a heavy burden that dampens the spirit of the country. It becomes more evident with every day that the next presidential election will be decided by the War in Vietnam.

South Bend, November 25, 1967

200 Million Americans

Last week the demographic clock at the U.S. Department of Commerce registered the birth of the 200th million American. By the end of the century the U.S. population may well reach 300 million.

[It would be wrong to assume that counting the U.S. population is correct up to the latest born American citizen. The Bureau of Census in the U.S. Department of Commerce carries out a comprehensive census every ten years with a margin of error between 3-5%. Accordingly, the

U.S. population has grown from 151 million (1950), 203 million (1970) to 248 million (1990). See *Encyclopedia Americana,* "United States, Population, Table 1".]

South Bend, [End] November 1967

The European Dilemma

Only after coming here, one becomes fully aware of the extent of the European dilemma—here, where there are no border or customs problems, no divided cities, no demarcation lines and barbed wires, in a country that can decide its own destiny. Here one has the impression that there is permanence and that people's minds are future oriented. In contrast to America, everything in Europe got stuck in the provisional, while nobody dares to say with certainty what the future will hold.

South Bend, December 2, 1967

The Development of the Atomic Bomb

No scientific discovery has changed the power structure of the world so suddenly as the one made by Enrico Fermi 25 years ago at the University of Chicago, unleashing the nuclear chain reaction that led directly to the development of the atomic bomb.

[On December 2, 1942 the Italian physicist and Nobel laureate Enrico Fermi (1901-54) succeeded at the University of Chicago in producing the first self-sustaining nuclear reaction. Based on that discovery, the atomic bomb was developed at the Los Alamos Scientific Laboratory in New Mexico, 1942-45. In 1967 the Fermi National Accelerator Laboratory was established near Batavia west of Chicago. The Fermi Laboratory is one of the most significant centers for nuclear research in the world.]

South Bend, December 2, 1967

Cardinal Spellman Dies

With today's death of Cardinal Spellman the Catholic Church in America has lost one of its most prominent personalities.

[Francis Joseph Cardinal Spellman (1889-1967) was from 1939 until his death Archbishop of New York. He became known as Vicar of the Armed Forces during World War II. After 1945 he was instrumental in creating the system of peace.]

South Bend, December 23, 1967

Jet Age Diplomacy

Following the tragic death of Australian Prime Minister Harold Holt, President Johnson flew to Australia. On his return from the funeral ceremony in Canberra, the American president stopped at various places to talk personally with several heads of government in South East Asia. He also took the opportunity of visiting before Christmas U.S. military outposts in Vietnam. The several hours he stayed in Europe sufficed for an audience with Pope Paul VI. The main concern of Johnson's journey was finding a peaceful solution to the War in Vietnam. This new way of diplomacy that spans the globe in a week's time has been made possible by the jet aircraft.

[Harold E. Holt (1908-67), since 1966 Prime Minister of Australia, tragically lost his life by drowning in December 1967. Holt had supported President Johnson's Vietnam policy.]

South Bend, December 23, 1967

The Ignorance of Europe

In a recent interview on television, President Johnson took a position on problems of world politics. It revealed a startling ignorance of the situation in Europe. Europe was simply regarded as being contented so that it required no further discussion. The pretense that American-European relations had suffered because of the engagement in Vietnam and that European allies felt neglected was pushed aside on the grounds that Wilson and Kiesinger had been in Washington and that everything was going well.

[Harold Wilson, British Prime Minister, 1964-70; Kurt Georg Kiesinger, German Federal Chancellor, 1966-69.]

South Bend, [End] December, 1967

The First Christmas in America

The first Christmas in the United States brought for my family and me a number of surprises. The preparations for the Christmas holidays had started immediately after Thanksgiving by the end of November, much earlier than at home. The decorated Christmas trees were placed already a fortnight before Christmas Eve colorfully lit by small lamps—burning candles are not allowed in America because of fire hazard—near windows to be seen. Also, hallways and entire house fronts as well as trees in the front and backyards were colorfully illuminated. The Christian character of the holidays was by all means preserved, commercialism was not much stronger here than in Europe. Surprising were the many well presented Christmas songs, many of which come from the English carol tradition. Many German Christmas songs, "Silent Night, Holy Night" could be heard everywhere sung in English. TV networks brought a number of the favorite Christmas shows. We got our Christmas tree from a "Christmas Tree Farm," where one can select from an open field a Scotch pine or fir and cut it oneself. Midnight Mass in the Sacred Heart Church of Notre Dame, whose musical programming and readings came closest to what we were used to, made us really feel at home. The Christmas holidays came abruptly to an end on December 26, for the 26th is a regular working day in America.

[Transl: In many European countries, especially in Austria, Hungary, and Italy, December 26, St. Stephen's Day, is observed as a holiday.]

Anno 1968

All hopes of this year are directed toward ending the Vietnam War. It is quite possible that the war will come to end, although the North Vietnamese side is obviously intended to protract the war until after the American presidential election in the fall.

South Bend, January 1, 1968

The Rose Bowl Parade

The main entertainment of Americans on New Year's Day is to watch the Rose Bowl Parade in Pasadena, California on TV, as well as a number of Bowl Games that decide the national championship in college football.

[Bowl in this connection refers to a stadium. Since 1902 the college football game in the Rose Bowl has always taken place on January 1. The game is preceded by the Tournament of Roses, a parade lasting hours with marching bands and floats of fresh roses. The roses and other flowers are creatively arranged according to a given theme. The best floats are awarded prizes.]

South Bend, January 6, 1968

The U.S.A. is primarily a state idea to which regional, ethnic and racial characteristics are subordinated. This idea has overcome the nation state.

South Bend, January 15, 1968

The restriction of dollar assets as well as the announcement by President Johnson that travels abroad will be cut back in order to improve the American balance of payments are more disquieting to Europeans than the War in Vietnam.

South Bend, January 18, 1968

The State of the Union Address

As required by the constitution, the American president is obligated to deliver in January of each year his "State of the Union Address" to the joint session of Congress. This Address belongs to the most important political statements not only for the domestic agenda of the United States but also for the rest of the world because of America's global foreign policy commitments. Johnson's speech, which was broadcast on national television, remained predominantly concentrated on domestic affairs and the Vietnam War. He showed a tendency toward the utopian. He spoke continuously about the progress of the domestic development referring primarily to the new schools built and the improvements made in health care. Each week, he said, a new college is being opened so that every second youth of his age group will have the benefit of a college education. His announcement that the federal government will fight crime more vigorously received the most spontaneous applause. Johnson's references to foreign policy were naive. Europe was not mentioned with a single word. Altogether Johnson demonstrated in his speech of being a strong personality but with a mediocre understanding of world politics. The world outside

America seemed not to exist; his main interest remained directed toward domestic policy issues.

South Bend, February 22, 1968

Too Narrow

A group of 200 Amish, for whom Indiana had become too narrow or cramped to live in, moved to Missouri where there was still open land available, and where they could feel more undisturbed.

South Bend, March 3, 1968

The Kerner Report

The report of the National Advisory Commission on Civil Disorders, formed by President Johnson, or the so-called "Kerner Report" visibly shocked the American public. The report concluded that last year's unrests in Newark and Detroit were not caused by agitation from outside but by the catastrophic living conditions of the black population in the inner cities. If extensive measures are not taken, the report warns, the American population would break up into two parts, whereby peace could only be maintained by police force. To remedy the social evils in the ghettoes, billions of dollars would have to be made available for creating jobs and housing. In view of the War in Vietnam and the restrained budget situation, it is unlikely that the Congress would approve spending billions to redress the plight of the inner cities. Some members of Congress regard the "Kerner Report" as unrealistic and unfeasible.

[Irving H. Siegel, *The Kerner Commission Report and Economic Policy* (Kalamazoo, Michigan: The W.E. Upjohn Institute for Employment Research, 1969), comments on the *Report of the National Advisory Commission on Civil Disorders,* generally known as the "Kerner Report." In his view, American society is facing the greatest danger in an "extensive breakdown of the sense of community." Unemployment and part-time work of minorities in society are the main reasons for the unrests.]

[Judge Otto Kerner (1908-76) of Chicago was Chairman of the President's Commission on Civil Disorders in 1968.]

South Bend, March 11 and 12, 1968

A Historic Confrontation

What had already been expected for weeks, the hearing of Secretary of State Dean Rusk before the Senate Foreign Relations Committee chaired by Senator J. William Fulbright was televised live yesterday and today. A noteworthy argument unfolded between those who support and those who oppose the Vietnam War policy of the government. As a result, it brought to light a rift within the Democratic party that can no longer be overlooked. Fulbright emphasized the prerogative of the Senate in matters of war and peace and questioned the government's actions in Vietnam. On the other side, Dean Rusk endured the twelve hour hearing with patience, self-control and clarity of reasoning and held on unshakingly to the government's policy. Having this hearing openly televised for the entire world to see, showed the strength and the weakness of American democracy. The growing irritation at the way the War in Vietnam is being carried on became evident as the possibility of a new isolationism. It is possible that the United States would withdraw from its global treaty obligations because the assumed commitments could overstrain its reserves. It was a significant, historic confrontation.

[Dean Rusk (1909-94), U.S. Secretary of State under Kennedy and Johnson, 1961-69.]

South Bend, March 12, 1968

The New Hampshire Primary

The New Hampshire Primary brought some surprising results. Senator Eugene McCarthy succeeded in gaining half of the Democratic votes, which is a clear demonstration of no confidence in the policy of President Johnson. It is also proven at the ballot box how divided the Democratic camp really is. With 70% of the votes, Richard Nixon emerged as the dominant winner among the Republicans. It is unlikely that Governor Rockefeller would even come close to Nixon's lead.

[Eugene J. McCarthy (1916—), Senator of Minnesota, 1959-70, has above all become known for advocating thriftiness in government spending.]

March 15, 1968

The Pressure on the Dollar

The order by the Queen of England to close the banks of her country for today, while at the same time most of the banks on the Continent also remained closed, is a necessary measure to get the pressure on the U.S. dollar under control. The attempt by Charles de Gaulle to attack the gold backing of the dollar led to panic-like buying of gold. As a consequence, the international monetary system could fall into disarray. Since the conference at Bretton Woods, New Hampshire, in July 1944, the gold parity of the U.S. dollar has been based on $35 per ounce. The illusory confidence in the value of gold is much more prevalent in Europe, while here in America more trust is placed in industrial capacity and productivity.

South Bend, March 18, 1968

Over this weekend, the countries of the International Monetary Fund have reached an agreement that the central banks maintain the gold parity of the dollar of $35 per ounce, while the price of gold used for commercial purposes was left open to the free market. By this concerted effort the dollar has recently been maintained as reserve currency but under the condition that the United States reduces its high trade deficit and cut back on government spending.

[The double standard for the price of gold—one official price of the central banks and another on the free market—could not be sustained for very long. With the mounting dollar assets abroad, the gold backing of the dollar at $35 an ounce was no longer bearable. On August 15, 1971, the Nixon Administration suspended the gold parity of the U.S. dollar. In the following years, the dollar lost in value against the European currencies and the Japanese yen. In 1980 gold reached its highest value of $800 per ounce.]

South Bend, March 18, 1968

Robert Kennedy Enters the Campaign

The decision of Senator Robert Kennedy on March 16 to enter the campaign as a candidate for the Democratic Party's presidential nomination further split the Party. Following McCarthy's success at the New Hampshire Primary,

Kennedy's decision was to be expected. He is taking like McCarthy an anti-Johnson stand, but both of them decline to share a common ticket. And President Johnson on his part seems not to be willing to yield to either candidate. Only Richard Nixon can benefit from this dilemma at the top leadership of the Democratic Party.

[Robert Francis Kennedy (1925-68), the younger brother of John F. Kennedy, in whose cabinet he had served as U.S. Attorney General 1961-64, was U.S. Senator of New York 1965-68. As a candidate for the Democratic presidential nomination he won a number of primaries. After he had won the important California Primary, he participated in the victory celebration in a hotel in Los Angeles. Toward the end of the celebration he fell victim to an assassination attempt in which he was fatally wounded. Robert Kennedy died in the early morning hours of June 6, 1968. See entry of June 9, 1968, below]

South Bend, March 21, 1968

Rockefeller Withdraws His Candidacy

Governor Nelson Rockefeller's announcement today that he is withdrawing his candidacy has to some extent come as a surprise. Thereby, the Republicans have achieved unity within their Party. Practically, they have unofficially nominated Nixon as their presidential candidate.

South Bend, March 31, 1968
8 p.m.

The Renunciation of President Johnson

In his televised address to the American nation this evening, President Johnson unexpectedly announced that he will not seek and would not accept the nomination of the Democratic Party. Johnson apparently took this step in order not to further aggravate the split within his Party and to increase the confusion in the country. At the same time he informed the nation and the world that he has ordered to stop the air strikes against North Vietnam to defuse the war and to prepare peace negotiations. Johnson personally renounced a possible second term in office. He put his own ambitions last for the welfare of the state. It was the speech of a great but broken human being whose tragedy could be read in his face.

[Lyndon Baines Johnson (1908-73), U.S. Senator of Texas, 1949-61; U.S. Vice President, 1961—63; U.S. President, 1963-69. Johnson suffered from a heart condition. He died on January 22, 1973 on his ranch near Johnson City in Texas. The tragedy of Lyndon B Johnson consisted in a dilemma he could not overcome. He was concerned about the poverty in his own country and wanted to improve social conditions at home, but he was drawn deeper and deeper into the jungle warfare in South East Asia from which he found no way out.]

South Bend, April 7, 1968

The Assassination in Memphis

The brutal assassination of the Nobel Peace Prize laureate Dr. Martin Luther King, Jr., on April 4 in Memphis, Tennessee, set off a wave of outrage in all parts of the population. A profound sorrow and sadness has taken hold of the entire country. On this Sunday of prayer and day of national mourning faces have turned more serious—more serious because of the shock and a sense of shame at what happened as well as an uneasy feeling about the future. Nonviolence, which King preached, appears losing ground. In the blind uproar of recent days, the inner cities of Washington, D.C., Atlanta, Detroit, Chicago, and in a number of other places were set ablaze and looted. For a time it seemed as if civil war had broken out. With the intervention of the National Guard quiet and order have temporarily been restored.

The assassination of Martin Luther King, Jr., is a national tragedy that opens new wounds in the tense relationship between White and Black. With Martin Luther King the black minority in America has received its martyr.

[The Reverend Dr. Martin Luther King, Jr. (1929-68) was a Baptist minister and the President of the Southern Christian Leadership Conference. King fought for the Civil Rights Movement as an advocate of nonviolence; he received the Nobel Peace Prize in 1964. In 1983, January 15, the birthday of Martin Luther King, was declared a national holiday in America.]

April 8-18, 1968

The Easter Journey to Georgia

[For some time, a journey to Georgia had been planned to visit friends in Atlanta and to give a guest lecture at the University of Georgia in Athens.]

To travel with the family to Atlanta, immediately after the assassination of Martin Luther King, Jr., seemed to be a risky undertaking. However, the agreed upon date for a guest lecture at the University of Georgia in Athens left no other choice. Driving by car through Indiana, Kentucky, Tennessee to Georgia, we traveled over a distance of 800 miles. Although a certain tense situation could be felt, the South remained distinctly quiet. The National Guard had not been mobilized, and there were no road blocks on highways or other signs of an emergency. The South is not a region inclined to social unrest. Riots are usually of a local nature and the work of fanatics or individuals running amok. When we arrived on Good Friday in Chattanooga, Tennessee, an obviously berserk individual had run into the city hall and shot the deputy mayor. A curfew was issued for the city. But there were no disturbances during the night. In our hotel we were well taken care of and safe as passing travelers. Anyway, in those critical days the South was more composed and calmer, to a certain extent less involved than the outside world, especially the news media in Europe, had made to believe. There is one thing one should not lose sight of: The South is an agrarian region with a conservative, persevering way of life. In this regard, little will change for a long time to come. The social separation of the two races is deep-rooted in this way of life. Although considerable progress has already been made in a big city like Atlanta, where Whites and Blacks fill up their shopping carts in a super market next to each other unconcerned, where they sit side by side in a restaurant and use undisturbed the same public transportation, a deep social chasm between them still exists.

The American South should not be seen and judged on the race issue alone. The South is very hospitable, a gracious way of living with an aristocratic elegance that otherwise is rarely met with elsewhere in the United States. On the one hand, Atlanta represents the wealth and splendor of the Old South, and on the other, it has developed into a modern metropolis. At this time of the year, a blooming forest of azaleas surrounds the Governor's Mansion with palace-like estates in its midst, while in the center of the city a new skyline is rising similar to Rockefeller Center.

Memorial plaques of the Civil War are spread all over the South. Large stretches of the region show signs of decay. Unparalleled poverty can be seen on neglected farms and along the coal mining areas of the Appalachian Mountains. Here, the expression "poverty pocket" has real meaning. Future politicians will have to deal with this problem.

Addendum

[The reception at the University of Georgia in Athens, which lies about 70 miles east of Atlanta, was thanks to Professor Montgomery's arrangement, most cordial and friendly. Professor Paschal Reeves introduced me to the English Department. Since the summer of 1964, when I had met Professor Reeves for the first time at the Houghton Library, we were corresponding across the Atlantic and working closely together on Thomas Wolfe. Following the lecture, Professor and Mrs. Reeves gave a reception for me and my wife, which we shall never forget. It proved again that personal contacts among colleagues in the academic world are one of the best ways to overcome geographical distances and differences between America and Europe.]

South Bend, May 7, 1968

Robert Kennedy in the Indiana Primary

Today's Primary in Indiana has inasmuch drawn national attention as it was the first confrontation between Eugene McCarthy and Robert Kennedy in an open election. Robert Kennedy won the election with 42% of the Democratic votes, vs. 31% for Roger D. Branigin, the Governor of Indiana who stood in as proxy for Vice President Hubert Humphrey. 27% of the Democratic votes went to McCarthy. Kennedy regarded the Indiana Primary as a decisive test for his chances to win the presidential election. He used all means at his disposition, put in every effort, and spared no trouble or the strains, which crisscrossing Indiana demanded. The name Kennedy exerted a magic attraction. Wherever he stopped on the campaign trail, a crowd of people gathered around him among whom he mingled fearlessly shaking hands. In this campaign, Robert Kennedy brought his own personality to the fore. He won the strongest votes, at times up to 60%, in the industrial centers, in the big cities, and among the colored population who stood solidly behind him. Academics and college students were divided between Kennedy and McCarthy. The McCarthy campaign attracted large numbers of volunteers from among high school and college students. They saw in him the first candidate who had the courage to stand up against Johnson and the War in Vietnam.

Robert Kennedy had started his campaign in Indiana on April 4 in South Bend with a rally on the Notre Dame campus. Upon his arrival at noon at the St. Joseph County Regional Airport, a large crowd of his supporters had assembled. His convoy drove through the city to Notre Dame where a campaign rally had been scheduled for 2 p.m. As my wife and I drove through the Notre Dame campus that afternoon, we almost collided with the car of Robert Kennedy. We were driving slowly on the winding road along the small St. Joseph Lake, when in a curve suddenly the car of Robert Kennedy was coming toward us. Ethel Kennedy, who sat behind her husband in the car, flinched instantly, and we also were momentarily shocked, but Robert Kennedy did not turn a hair. Despite a light snow flurry, he stood upright in the open cabriolet and showed his typical friendly smile. Kennedy was on his way to Stepan Center, where about 5,000 students who had been waiting for him gave him a rousing welcome. That was the beginning of a brilliant campaign in Indiana from which Robert Kennedy emerged as a credible candidate for the American presidency.

[The University of Notre Dame Archives hold extensive records and news reports of this campaign rally, see UDIS Box 97, File 18, 1968-73.]

South Bend, [Beginning of May] 1968

The General Strike in France

The irony of Charles de Gaulle's political fortunes has it that at the very moment, when he was triumphantly welcomed on his state visit to Communist Romania, he was attacked from behind by the Communists at home. Set off by the student unrests at the Sorbonne, France has been thrown into the most serious strike crisis since World War II. After the unions had called a general strike, about 10 million people walked out of their jobs. Thereby, the entire public service has practically been paralyzed. In extreme cases, workers have occupied factories. This radical confrontation of the entire French work force with the government may well signal the end of Gaullism, even if the present crisis will be temporarily averted. The dilemma of Gaullist politics could not have been more drastically exposed. De Gaulle used Europe as an effective slogan. Pursuing national self-interests, he has been playing great power politics, although the prerequisites for doing so have been missing.

[Charles de Gaulle (1890-1970), general, first President of the Fifth Republic, 1959-69. After he had lost the referendum of April 27, 1969, he resigned. Charles de Gaulle died on November 9, 1970.]

South Bend, May 10, 1968

The Student Unrests in Europe

The student unrests at the Sorbonne were not just demonstrations but an outright revolution. The system of higher education in Europe has been shaken to its foundations. Regrettably, the justified demands for reforms have been misused by agitators and led into a direction not compatible with universities. The unfortunate combination of student organizations with political parties is taking its toll, for every student demonstration can be used for political purposes and provoke a state crisis. What happened this spring at the Universities of Paris, Rome, Torino, Milan, Brussels, Vienna, London, and Stockholm was outrageous. Those were the most destructive student unrests in the history of European universities. It was common practice to seize university buildings and to hold them like fortresses. It was a revolt against any kind of civil order, and for that reason difficult to control. To compare the student unrests in Europe with those in America would be an obvious thing to do. However, the unrests in Europe are based on very different assumptions.

Student Unrests in America

Starting in Berkeley, California, student unrests in America have become a daily occurrence. But in contrast to Europe, these revolts are not so much directed against overcrowded lecture halls, the form of instruction and study facilities as against the War in Vietnam and the draft. It has already become a routine that radical student groups occupy administration buildings on college and university campuses, whereby the entire institution comes to a standstill. If, under these circumstances, the president calls in the police because the security forces on campus are not capable to cope with the situation, violent confrontations erupt. The most spectacular riot happened toward the end of April at Columbia University in New York. A group of radical students seized the office of the president and destroyed everything they could get their hands on.

South Bend, June 2, 1968

The Words of the Patriarch

On today's Pentecost Sunday the head of the Eastern Orthodox Church, His Beatitude Maximus V Hakim of Beirut, Patriarch of Antioch, Alexandria, and Jerusalem delivered the sermon at the concelebrated Mass for the Commencement Exercises at the University of Notre Dame. He spoke to the graduating students, their parents and relatives. The Patriarch, who on his way from Beirut to South Bend, had stopped in Rome, Paris and Brussels, was still under the impression of the recent strikes and unrests. He compared these revolts to a civil war. The Patriarch emphasized that a great responsibility for the future of the world has been laid into the hands of the United States not only because of its position as a world power but also because of its spiritual and moral leadership. In our technological age, he said, the United States of America has become an example to follow for many nations in the future. The encounter with this venerable personality on the grounds of a Catholic university gives testimony to the ecumenical spirit of the Second Vatican Council.

South Bend, June 2, 1968

The Kennedy—McCarthy Debate

Last night, before the California Primary, Robert Kennedy and Eugene McCarthy confronted each other for the first time in Los Angeles in a nationally televised debate. Both candidates agreed on most issues, as they were seeking an alternative to the Johnson Administration's policy and a way out of the War in Vietnam. McCarthy remained restrained, dealing with the emotionally charged subject matter of factly. There was no doubt that the Democratic Party has split up into three camps in this campaign: The first is the Kennedy camp, the second follows McCarthy, and the third rallies around Vice President Hubert Humphrey. As the official candidate of the Party, Humphrey attracts more and more of the faithful. This division can only be to the advantage of the Republicans who, showing rare solidarity, are closing ranks behind Richard Nixon. The ruling Party makes an exhausted and burned out impression. A change in favor of the Republicans appears to be more and more likely.

South Bend, June [9], 1968

The Assassination of Robert Kennedy

In the early morning hours of June 5, shortly after he had celebrated his victory in the California Primary, Senator Robert F. Kennedy was shot by a Jordanian nationalist in the Ambassador Hotel in Los Angeles. He was so severely wounded that he died 25 hours after the assassination attempt. Since the assassination of President John F. Kennedy in November 1963, no other news has shocked the world so much as the awareness that his brother Robert Kennedy met the same fate. America, still suffering from the shock of the assassination of Martin Luther King, Jr., was paralyzed by this new politically motivated brutal murder. Dismay, shame and horror were spreading; people from all walks of life were shaken and showed genuine mourning. For three days the American public could follow on television the tragedy of the Kennedy family. The pictures around the immediate family were heartrending and full of anxiety. How the family coped courageously with this new tragedy was admirable, honest feelings of sympathy were expressed everywhere. Despite the scorching heat in the concrete sea of New York, hundreds of thousands of people did not shy away from standing in line for hours to pay their last respects to Robert Kennedy in St. Patrick's Cathedral. And an immeasurable crowd of people lined the funeral procession from New York to Washington. Robert Kennedy was laid to rest next to his brother John in the Arlington National Cemetery.

South Bend, June [10], 1968

Reflections on the Loss of Robert Kennedy

Like no other American politician today, Robert Kennedy was able to bridge the differences between Whites and Blacks, rich and poor. Minorities have lost their best advocate. Mixed with the mourning are feelings of guilt. There has been the self-accusation that the increasing violence has led to this brutal deed. The self-accusation also assumes that America is "a sick society." In such tragic moments America gets confused about itself, and the world gets confused about America.

Without a doubt, Robert Kennedy would have emerged from the primaries as the strongest candidate of the Democrats. He would have had a chance to win the presidential election in November. His tragic death has thrust the issue of violence to the forefront of the national debate. Spontaneously, thousands of people have voluntarily turned in their firearms to the police. The perennial discussion over a "gun control bill" will urgently be taken up again in Congress. At least the unrestricted delivery of firearms by mail should be prohibited. Violence is a serious problem that is more prevalent in American society than anywhere else in the world. Still, it cannot be said that America is a sick society.

Before the Requiem in St. Patrick's Cathedral, Edward Kennedy gave the eulogy on his brother Robert. At that moment, the grievous loss which the Kennedy family and America have suffered was especially painfully felt.

Through the deaths of John Fitzgerald and Robert Francis Kennedy the world has lost a vision, which had made it easier to imagine how the future can be mastered.

[During the fall semester 1967, my appointment as visiting associate professor at the University of Notre Dame had been extended for another year. And in the spring of 1968, I was offered the directorship of the Notre Dame Foreign Study Program in Innsbruck for a two year term 1969-71. Over the summer of 1968, my family and I stayed in South Bend. We planned to take a trip by car to Colorado in August.]

South Bend, June 26, 1968

The Inevitable Pull of the English Language

After a sojourn of a few months in the United States, one feels the inevitable pull of the English language. Even as trained linguists my wife and I have noticed a certain hesitation in expressing ourselves precisely in German. Loan translations have been creeping in, just as one forgets common words and idioms. It has become easier to name objects in English for which one is searching an adequate German expression to no avail. The children learn English fast in school and they chat in English with each other, although German is spoken at home. It is known from experience that the native tongue gets lost in the second generation after immigration. The third generation learns the language of their grandparents again through the foreign language instruction in college. Bilingualism can only be maintained by continuous practice, reading, language contacts and occasional visits to the old home country.

South Bend, July [1], 1968

The Non-Proliferation Treaty

The signing of the Non-Proliferation Treaty in Moscow, London, and Washington can be regarded as the most significant step to secure peace that has been undertaken in the last two decades. The threatening danger of a nuclear war has essentially been reduced. The Treaty also defuses to some extent the balance of horror. On the other hand, it strengthens even more so the partition of the world into two power blocs and spheres of influence.

[After many years of negotiations, the Soviet Union, Great Britain, and the United States signed the Non-Proliferation Treaty on July 1, 1968. The Treaty binds the signatory powers not to pass on nuclear arms materials to other nations. The nuclear powers France and the People's Republic of China did not join the Treaty. At the same time, America and Russia began talks on the Strategic Arms Limitation Treaty (SALT). Talks about non-proliferation and nuclear disarmament remained a continuous topic of negotiations for decades to come.]

South Bend, July [Middle], 1968

The Entente between America and Russia

For compelling reasons of common sense and sheer self-preservation, the United States and the Soviet Union are coming closer together in an effort to find pragmatic solutions to problems of world politics despite their undeniable ideological differences. Basically, there is no animosity between the American and Russian peoples. More likely, they see each other with mutual sympathy. An entente cordiale between America and Russia is in the making, which grants diplomatic concessions on both sides, revives cultural exchange, and furthers scientific cooperation.

South Bend, July [Middle], 1968

Searching for an Afro-American Identity

The black minority is presently searching for its identity within the American society. African-Americans are trying to find the lost heritage of their African origin and to draw attention to its contribution to American history. Instead of "colored," "black," or "Negro," the designations "African-American" or "Afro-American" are more and more used in everyday American speech. The black minority in America is at this time involved in the significant historical process of self-realization, from which it will emerge with a personal awareness of its uniqueness. After this difficult period of transition, Afro-Americans will take their place in American society with more self-confidence, individual consciousness, and self-assured appearance.

South Bend, July [End], 1968

How to Spend the Long Summer

Americans often don't know how to spend the long summer, which begins with Memorial Day Weekend, the end of May, and ends with Labor Day in early September. This is also the time for the long school vacation. Teenagers are usually looking for summer jobs, sign up for summer school, or go to a summer camp. Many adults take drawing or painting lessons. Then they show their mediocre productions in an endless series of amateur art exhibitions. However, the dream for many remains to go on a sightseeing tour of Europe. Americans rarely stay in one place for recreation. Contrary to Europeans, they are not going on a vacation just to relax. It is in any case a totally different way of vacationing. Most families spend their vacation with the children at home in their neighborhood. The standard of living of the middle class in the suburbs is such that there are enough green spaces, sports facilities, and a swimming pool available. As the summer in America can be unpleasantly hot, humid and sultry, one spends many hours of the day in air-conditioned rooms. When they travel, Americans want to see and experience something new. During the summer months, caravans of recreational vehicles of all shapes and sizes move in different directions across the country. Either one goes to the National Parks in the Rocky Mountains, to the beaches on the Atlantic or Pacific, or one visits relatives who usually live far away. Americans love the outdoors, where they can picnic, play any kind of ball games, or enjoy aquatic sports. When the schools begin again after Labor Day, the long summer is over.

South Bend, August 8, 1968

Richard M. Nixon Presidential Candidate of the Republicans

The National Convention of the Republican Party in Miami has been in session since Monday, August 5. Florida was deliberately chosen as venue for the Convention in order to gain votes for Republican candidates in the South, which since the Civil War has traditionally voted for the Democrats. The Convention began in the usual carnival atmosphere, but backstage the seasoned practitioners, who know masterly how to play the complicated game of American politics, were at work. It is always fascinating to observe how the political power play of a continent is set in motion. At the opening of the Convention, the Afro-American Senator Edward Brooke gave a remarkable speech. Looking toward the future of race relations in America, he said: "America will be an integrated society of magnificent plurality." The liberal wing of the Party was holding on to Nelson Rockefeller, although he had withdrawn from the primaries. But the radical conservative group rallied around Barry Goldwater whose speech had the strongest applause. At this Convention, the followers of Goldwater were still a noticeable force. When the voting started on Wednesday evening, there was a lot of guessing going on whether Richard Nixon would win on the first ballot. Nixon had the leading margin of votes from the primaries. When finally at 2 a.m. in the morning of August 8 the roll-call balloting was carried out, he reached the required 667 votes for his nomination on the first ballot. Surprising was Nixon's choice of Spiro Agnew for his running mate. The delegates from the Northeast and from the industrial areas felt to have been passed over, while the delegates from the South were quite satisfied with this choice. No doubt, Nixon made a concession to the conservative South by selecting the Governor of Maryland. This was a move to take the wind out of the sails of the Wallace forces. Nixon's acceptance speech aroused astonishment. If elected president, he said, he would make an effort to give American foreign policy a new direction that will again be more oriented toward Atlantic affairs. After the election in November he would generally overhaul the foreign policy situation and take care that the United States will not again be unintentionally and recklessly drawn into an international conflict.

[Richard Milhous Nixon (1913-94), lawyer and politician from California; U.S. Representative, 1947-51; U.S. Senator, 1951-53; U.S. Vice President in the Eisenhower Administration, 1953-61; U.S. President, 1969-74. Following the Watergate affair, he resigned as President in August, 1974. Nixon died on May 29, 1994 in New York; he was buried next to his wife Pat at the Richard M. Nixon Library in Yorba Linda, his place of birth on the southern edge of Los Angeles. Spiro T. Agnew (1918—), Governor of Maryland, 1967-69; U.S. Vice President in the Nixon Administration, 1969-73. Edward W. Brooke (1919—), Attorney General of Massachusetts, 1963-66. Brooke was the first

African-American to be elected to the Senate; U.S. Senator of Massachusetts, 1967-79.]

[After August 8, my family and I went on the trip to Colorado. Since my wife's sister had come from Innsbruck to visit us, we could make this journey to the West together. We drove on Interstate-80 through Illinois, Iowa, Nebraska to Denver, Colorado, altogether a distance of 1,200 miles.]

Denver, [August 15], 1968

Travel Impressions

The Mississippi River is much more of a cultural divide than one would usually assume. While the settlement east of the Mississippi is in many ways reminiscent of Europe, the character of the landscape changes drastically as soon as one crosses the River at Bettendorf. The area west of the Mississippi is still sparsely populated. Beginning in Iowa, the endless wheat and cornfields spread westward without interruption as far as the middle of Nebraska. Omaha, Nebraska, which is located on the Missouri River at the border to Iowa, is the last large city until Denver. In the Joslyn Art Museum of Omaha we could see the rare water color paintings of Karl Bodmer. These paintings show the original way of life of the Indian tribes on the Mississippi River.

[In 1833 the Swiss painter Karl Bodmer accompanied Prince Maximilian of Wied-Neuwied on his anthropological expedition to the Upper Missouri. The water colors painted on this expedition belong to the rare authentic representations of the Indian tribes of the Missouri River region.]

After Omaha we drove for hours along wheat fields. Occasionally, large grain silos surrounded by a few houses were looming on the horizon. The monotony of this landscape has an oppressive effect. Past Kearney wheat and corn gradually give way to grassland with scattered ranches. At an altitude of 1,200 m North Platte lies in the center of this pasture, where over the summer months cattle is raised for meat production. There we could visit the Buffalo Bill Ranch and see a real Rodeo.

[The legendary scout and buffalo hunter William F. Cody (1846-1917), better known as Buffalo Bill, lived in North Platte around 1880. Starting from there at the beginning of the 1880s, he put his "Wild West Show" together. Cody had his show, for which he brought along a buffalo herd, cowboys and Indians, performed in open air. The Show that lasted for 30 years was a huge success, and when brought to Europe it became a sensation. Cody contributed a great deal to the romanticized image of the Wild West and of cowboys in America as well as in Europe.]

Between North Platte and Denver, there is a stretch of semi-arid land, which on the way west only served as a passage. On this deserted, inaccessible terrain only a few shanties and forlorn trailer homes could be seen. Only when one reaches the 1,600 m or one mile high plateau of Denver, the Rocky Mountains suddenly rise up to majestic heights. But despite an altitude of 3,000 to 4,000 m, the peaks show no glaciers. The Rocky Mountains are situated much more to the south than the Alps. The climate here is warmer and drier so that there is no glacial formation.

In Denver one is immediately confronted with the Spanish-Mexican culture. The service personnel are almost exclusively Hispanic. On the southern section of Denver one passes through a sprawling ghetto that is not better than the slums in the inner cities on the East Coast. It is not difficult to foresee that the Hispanic minority of the Southwest from California to Texas will soon strive for recognition and be mindful of their rights.

[Before we traveled on to Colorado Springs, we stayed for two days in Golden, which is located west of Denver.]

Golden, Colorado, [August 19], 1968

Golden is a charming, small "Western Town" that has been developed into a tourist attraction. Something of the gold rush atmosphere is still in the air. It evokes memories of the gold mining era. On the banks of the creek that flows down from the Rocky Mountains, there are always a few hobby prospectors who hope that they can pan out a few nuggets.

[From 1860 to 1910 waves of the gold and silver rush passed through Colorado, bringing tens of thousands of fortune hunters to the Rocky Mountains. The yield of precious metals finally surpassed that of California. That turbulent as well as romantic period of Colorado's history left numerous traces behind. Especially west of Denver along the Clear Creek as far up as

Central City and on Interstate-70 to Georgetown, the area is dispersed with "ghost towns," abandoned silver mines with their dilapidated settlements, which have now become tourist attractions. But even today, one will still find a number of unswerving adventurers who are trying to pan gold out of the gravel or are prospecting for silver in remote valleys.]

Colorado Springs, August 21, 1968

The Czech Tragedy

In today's morning hours, the news reached us that during the night armed forces of the Warsaw Pact nations have invaded Czechoslovakia, and that Soviet tanks are rolling through the streets of Prague. We sat silently dumbfounded at breakfast, as the news reports incessantly came in. The reports sounded unreal on the distance, but nevertheless the reality of what was happening could not be doubted. Here in the American West, the event was hardly noticed, the vacation atmosphere of the resort town not disturbed. Public opinion in the country expressed the view that the American government should not interfere in this internal communist struggle. The existing American-Russian agreement of a partition of spheres of influence has not been thrown off balance by this intervention. The occupation of a country on the borderline of the Iron Curtain seemed to be within the limits of tolerance of both super powers. The small countries on this line should therefore be especially on guard and do more for their own security.

The line of separation between East and West that runs across Central Europe has again frighteningly been called back to mind. The precision and speed by which the troops of the Warsaw Pact overran Czechoslovakia during the night of August 20/21 is spine-chilling. At this moment, nobody could stop the advancing armored divisions. The helplessness of Europe has again come to mind in a tragic way.

The especially grave question is thrown on one's mind: Who, in case of an emergency, would protect the neutrality of Austria, should the Warsaw Pact nations for tactical considerations decide to either invade or march through Austria?

[From Colorado Springs we drove directly back to South Bend because the new school year was just about to begin.]

South Bend, August 29, 1968

Chaos in Chicago

Toward the end of August, the delegates of the Democratic Party assembled for their National Convention in Chicago in order to define the Democratic platform for the campaign and to nominate their candidate for the presidential election. The Convention has been ill-starred from the outset. It gave the impression of confusion and inner tension, accompanied by wild demonstrations that ended in an unprecedented chaos. At the opening, the delegation of Georgia left the Convention because they were not willing to split their votes with a second, racially mixed delegation of their state. The Party had urged representatives from the South to send racially mixed delegations to the Convention. Georgia was allowed to be represented by two delegations—one official white delegation and a racially mixed delegation. That led to the walk-out of the former. As a result of the controversy, the South was driven even more so into the Wallace camp. George Wallace campaigned as third party candidate for the American Independent Party. Aside from the racially motivated conflict, the Convention was even more divided on the issue of the War in Vietnam. McCarthy and his followers stood up for a peace policy and were under no circumstances ready to compromise. They were able to win over on their side about one third of the delegates, but lost the election to Vice President Hubert Humphrey whose nomination had already more or less been a given since the beginning of the Convention.

While the politically contrasting positions collided inside the Convention Hall, a street battle between police and demonstrators was going on outside. Radical groups of the "counter culture" and the peace movement had already made plans weeks ahead of time, how they could break up the Convention. The Chicago Police who had learned of these plans were prepared. They advanced with unusual harshness against the demonstrators and took dozens of them under arrest. In front of the Conrad Hilton Hotel on South Michigan Avenue, where the Humphrey and McCarthy campaigns were located, tumultuous scenes occurred. The demonstrators who were getting ready to camp out over night across the street from the Hotel in Grant Park were expelled by the Police and National Guard before nightfall. Because of these riots, it was considered to break off the Convention. But it was nevertheless brought to a conclusion. Hubert Humphrey was nominated presidential candidate of the Democratic Party, and his choice of Senator Edmund Muskie as running mate was confirmed today. In recent days Chicago has been the venue of the most serious confrontations and riots that ever happened at a National Convention in America.

[Hubert H. Humphrey, Jr. (1911-1978); U.S. Senator of Minnesota, 1949-65; U.S. Vice President, 1965-69; presidential candidate of the Democratic Party 1968.]

[Edmund S. Muskie (1914—), lawyer and Democratic politician from Maine; Governor of Maine, 1955-59; U.S. Senator of Maine, 1959-80; U.S. Secretary of State during the last year of the Carter Administration, 1980-81. As a politician, Muskie dealt more with domestic issues and the protection of the environment.]

South Bend, September 2, 1968

Labor Day

Labor Day in America goes back to the year 1882. It was declared a national holiday by a resolution of Congress in 1894. Labor Day is always observed on the first Monday in September, whereby a long weekend is guaranteed. Instead of May 1, the day honoring labor is observed in America at the beginning of September. In election years, campaigns traditionally start on Labor Day. Thus, Hubert Humphrey, the Democratic presidential candidate, began his campaign today with a big parade in New York. George Meany, the President of AFL-CIO (American Federation of Labor and Congress of Industrial Organization) stood by his side to demonstrate that the labor unions support the Democratic Party. The American Labor Day has for the most part remained free of Marxist slogans. It is more of a national holiday without stressing too much class differences.

This year's summer has remained relatively quiet in regard to racial violence. The majority of whites and blacks are presently assuming an attitude of moderation in race relations. Both parts desire to solve the problem within the framework of the law and strive, though hesitatingly, to make integration work. For example, at the beginning of the school year, integration in the educational sector is presently carried out peacefully and without much resistance.

South Bend, Wednesday, September 11, 1968

Edmund Muskie in the Stepan Center

This evening, Senator Edmund Muskie, the Democratic candidate for Vice President, spoke in Stepan Center on the Notre Dame Campus. Although Muskie attracted only a small number of students, he was more effective than previously assumed he would be. He spoke from personal conviction about the ideals of American democracy. Himself second generation of Polish descent, he was well received by an audience from the strong Polish community of South Bend. He pleasantly abstained from party politics. As he decisively expressed his view that the War in Vietnam has to come to an end, he got roaring applause.

South Bend, October 20, 1968

The End of the Liberal Era

The well-known TV Commentator David Brinkley gave a lecture yesterday in South Bend on the present political and intellectual situation. Brinkley, who had called himself a liberal, stated that liberalism in America is about going bankrupt. For 35 years, since the New Deal of Franklin Delano Roosevelt, the liberal conviction and philosophy have dominated the country. But liberalism has worn out; in part it also betrayed itself. Liberalism is about to be replaced by a conservative attitude, as it is represented by Richard Nixon. As a "lame duck" President Johnson is just waiting to be relieved from the burden of his office. He has fulfilled his mission. In Brinkley's view, the significance of Johnson may be seen in the following: He has tried in domestic policy to finish the social reforms that were still left to be done from the New Deal, and which in fact he has brought to a conclusion. Yet Johnson has failed in the area of foreign policy. The War in Vietnam has brought the Johnson Administration to the brink of disaster. It has been proven that an American president cannot carry on a war without being supported by a majority of the electorate.

South Bend, October 22, 1968

Space Flight—Apollo 7

The spacecraft Apollo 7 with three astronauts (Walter Schirra, Donn Eisele and Walter Cunningham) on board has completed an eleven day flight around the earth with a precision that can hardly be surpassed. The Apollo 7 flight was the decisive test for getting into orbit around the moon, which is expected to take place in December. The tragic setback of the American space program, when the first manned Apollo space flight had ended in a fireball at countdown just about two years ago, has been overcome by the successful flight of Apollo 7.

[The famous words by President John F. Kennedy in 1961, "landing a man on the moon, before this decade is out and safely returning him to earth," laid down the goal of the American space program. Out of that, the Apollo Program had emerged, which dominated the American space program in the 1960s. Kennedy's goal of landing a man on the moon before the decade was out was in fact realized on July 20, 1969.]

South Bend, October 27, 1968

10 Days Before the Election

The campaign for the presidential election has now entered its last stage. What only weeks ago may have looked like a burlesque show, has now become a deadly serious matter. The three candidates (Humphrey, Nixon, Wallace) are not exchanging favors with each other. Nevertheless, the campaign remains disciplined, there are no excesses. The rules of a democratic election are being observed. How decisive this election may be, the campaign is following the normal path of American politics.

South Bend, October 31, 1968

Cessation of the Bombardment in North Vietnam

This evening, President Johnson announced on national television a bombing halt, a cessation of air raids in North Vietnam. There is hope that the War may, even though with a compromise solution, be ended. It came as a surprise that this important announcement from the White House was made just an hour before the great rally of the Republicans with Nixon in Madison Square Garden in New York. This is just part of the maneuvering of the political power play in a presidential election year.

Lessons from the War in Vietnam

America has learned some painful lessons from the War in Vietnam, which has already lasted six years. In the future, the United States will engage in regional conflicts overseas with utmost restraint, and only if national interests are directly involved. American ground troops will only rarely be deployed in civil war like situations abroad. It will be firmly asked of those who need help that they should first try to help themselves. A certain return to isolationism will be unavoidable.

South Bend, November 4, 1968

On the Evening Before the Election

On the evening before tomorrow's election of the U.S. president, the outcome is still as uncertain as it was months ago. Hubert Humphrey has recently caught up with Nixon's lead, while the third party candidate, George Wallace, has the South behind him. It is quite possible that the Wallace votes can thrust the election into the House of Representatives, if neither candidate of the two major parties wins a plurality of the electoral votes. The election would then be decided in January. The War in Vietnam has been the decisive issue of this election to the very end.

South Bend, November 6, 1968

A Very Close Election Result

During last night, Nixon and Humphrey were leading alternately. Until the morning hours nobody could tell for sure who would win this election. The East Coast voted solidly for the Democrats. Altogether, the Democratic Party machinery proved to be very tenacious. But the mood of the country indicates that a political era is coming to an end. For the first time also viewers in Europe, Australia and Asia could follow this most important election of the free world on television via satellite. By 9 a.m. the result was still open. Only toward 10 a.m. the news came through that Nixon was leading in Illinois, and with its 26 electoral votes has won the election. The result is extremely close. Total popular votes:

Nixon 27,905,165, Humphrey 27,663,293, and Wallace about 8,000,000.*

The two party system in America has again proven its strength. George Wallace was leading in the South, but with only 8 million votes his American Independent Party was left far behind. With the election of Richard Nixon, American-European relations will be revived. The main attention of U.S. foreign policy will again turn to Atlantic affairs.

*[According to *The New York Times* of 8 November 1968, the final results of the election are as follows: Nixon 30,446,028, Humphrey 30,122,715, and Wallace 9,184,703 votes. In the Senate the Democrats have 58, the Republicans 41, and in the House of Representatives the Democrats have 243, the Republicans 192 seats.]

South Bend, November 28, 1968

Thanksgiving Day

America enjoyed a very peaceful Thanksgiving Day with the traditional turkey, the Macy Department Store monster parade on 5th Avenue in New York, and watching a number of football games on television. Thanksgiving is the festive occasion of the family, when relatives from across the continent visit each other. A feeling of quiet and confidence has been spreading, as peace negotiations to end the War in Vietnam are forthcoming. After having gone smoothly through the presidential election, the general mood of the country is calming down. The period of transition from the election until the new president takes office is always a political breather in Washington. The change of administration, especially when the ruling party is leaving, brings about a large move of officials and politicians. Moving companies and realtors benefit the most from this transfer.

South Bend, December 16, 1968

To Confirm the Election

Today the members of the Electoral College convened to cast their votes and to confirm the results of the presidential election of November 5. The 538 electoral votes were divided among the three candidates as follows:

Nixon 302, Humphrey 191, and Wallace 45.

This is a sheer formality hardly taken notice of by the public. Nixon has by far surpassed the required 270 electoral votes for the plurality, which has to be more than the votes of Humphrey and Wallace put together. It was therefore out of the question to have the election decided in the House of Representatives.

[The election of the U.S. president in the House of Representatives, if this ever should be necessary, provides that each state of the Union, regardless of its size or number of population, casts only one vote. In the course of American history, only one president was elected in the House. That was the election of Thomas Jefferson in the year 1800. The Union had at that time only 16 states with a population of five and a half million.]

South Bend, December 21, 1968

TLI—The Flight to the Moon

With a precision that can hardly be surpassed, the spacecraft Apollo 8 had, as scheduled, a lift-off at 7:51 EST from Cape Kennedy* on its historic flight to the moon. This is the first manned space flight to the moon with the astronauts Frank Borman, James A. Lovell, Jr., and William A. Anders on board. After orbiting the earth twice, the instruction was given to "Go for TLI" (Translunar Insertion), whereby Apollo 8 was set on course to the moon. This way, the utopian vision of a Jules Verne is translated into the plain technical language of our time. But imagining that the earth satellite, which through the millennia has been looked upon as being surrounded by myth, will now be drawn into man's sphere of influence and should become part of our world is for the moment awe-inspiring and frightening. The effects of this event cannot as yet be fully grasped.

*[In memory of President John F. Kennedy, Cape Canaveral near Orlando, Florida, was named Cape Kennedy in 1963. In 1973 the name Cape Canaveral was reintroduced, while the NASA Space Center on the Cape was named John F. Kennedy Space Center.]

South Bend, December 23, 1968

LOI—Orbiting the Moon

A few hours before the instruction will be given by the ground station for LOI (Lunar Orbit Insertion), and before Apollo 8 will enter the orbit around the moon, a number of thoughts strike me that may change our present mind set. As it has been possible to escape the force of gravity and the rotation of the earth, concepts that are based thereupon are being questioned. What after all do concepts and expressions like "heavy" and "light," "above" and "below," "ascent" and "descent," "sunrise" and "sunset" etc. still mean? Our language is full of expressions that are determined by gravity and the rotation of the earth. Without a doubt, we are at the threshold of a new era, which will open new dimensions to human experience. From now on, also cosmic space—moon and planets—will assume concrete forms in our imagination. Eventually, the exploration of the moon will not be much different from that of Antarctica. To future generations it will become so familiar as if a new continent were discovered.

South Bend, December 24, 1968

The Christmas Message

To follow Apollo 8 orbiting the moon on the television screen is an exciting experience. One is waiting anxiously until the spacecraft reappears from the far side of the moon, where the radio contact with earth is interrupted. The images of the surface of the moon show an inhospitable desert that stands motionless in the scorching sun. But the sight of the rising earth on the horizon is exalting. As Christmas message to earth, the astronauts read the opening passage of *Genesis*. Rarely have the words, "In the beginning God created the heaven and the earth," sounded as powerful as at this moment.

South Bend, December 27, 1968

The Return

After having orbited the moon ten times, Apollo 8 returned to earth. Shortly before dawn, the space capsule with the three astronauts on board splashed into the Pacific about 100 miles southwest of Hawaii. Immediately after landing, the capsule was heaved from the ocean. The first manned space flight to the moon has been performed without any visible difficulties. Thereby, the technical prerequisites for the moon landing next year have been accomplished.

SECTION 4

January 14, 1969-July 23, 1971

South Bend, January 14, 1969

Johnson's Farewell

A few days before handing over his office, President Johnson delivered his last "State of the Union Address" to the joint session of Congress. It was at the same time an occasion for a cordial and nostalgic farewell. As statesman Johnson stood above party politics. He reached out to his successor, as he asked the members of Congress for their undivided support of Richard Nixon. Johnson's farewell was less giving an account of his years in office than a request from the legislative body for continuing the social reforms which he had started. He admitted to be himself a child of the New Deal whose social programs he wanted to complete. The historical significance of Johnson lies definitely in his achievements in domestic politics, in his implementation of the American social programs. In the first place, the Civil Rights Bill of 1964, his efforts to achieve racial equality as well as better schools and housing conditions for minorities have to be mentioned. And then Johnson's accomplishments in extending Social Security should be commended. In 1965 he introduced Medicare, which guarantees government sponsored health care for every citizen over 65 years of age. He had only limited relationship to foreign policy which he could not cope with. With Johnson the liberal era in America is coming to a close.

South Bend, January 20, 1969

The Inauguration of Richard Nixon

Turning over the office of the presidency from Lyndon B. Johnson to Richard M. Nixon took place with dignity and without any disturbance. It is a tribute to the stability of the American political system. The orderly transfer of the office of the American president gives the country and the world a sense of security to which the personality of Richard Nixon is definitely a contributing factor. Without a doubt, today marks the beginning of a new era in American domestic and foreign policy. Nixon can look forward with measured confidence to the future. The War in Vietnam is coming to an end; under no circumstances could one think of an escalation of the War. The American engagement will again turn more to Europe, although the Nixon administration will act cautiously and give more the impression of a new isolationism. American foreign policy will not concentrate anymore rigidly on one issue but will remain more flexible. There is less danger that a single regional conflict could cause a global catastrophe.

South Bend, February 25, 1969

President Nixon's Journey to Europe

It will be difficult for Europeans to assess how profoundly President Nixon's journey to friendly European countries is changing public opinion in America. For years public attention has been concentrated on the Far East, understandably focused almost exclusively on the War in Vietnam. American attention is again turning toward Europe. The transatlantic question is given priority in American foreign policy, striving to achieve a balance of nuclear capabilities between the United States and the Soviet Union. A sobering word was spoken during Nixon's visit at the NATO Headquarters. Nixon explained how Europe could be meaningfully defended without being completely destroyed. Nixon's journey has the effect that questions of NATO and the European Economic Community are front page news and have once more become subjects of editorials. After a long time, also pictures of every day life in Europe are seen on American television.

South Bend, February 27, 1969

Nixon's Visit to Berlin

A visit to Berlin has become not only an obligatory act but also a test of courage for every new American president. Nixon's visit to the beleaguered city not only gives the two and a half million West Berliners new confidence but also to Western Europe more self-confidence. Surprisingly, the presence of the American president can give Western Europe a sense of solidarity, which it does not find by itself. Nixon has evoked the memory of John F. Kennedy. The frozen American-European sympathies are thawing again. By his restrained appearance and effort to understand the European point of view, Nixon was able to win over the sympathies of the Europeans on his side.

South Bend, [March 2], 1969

The Success of the European Journey

Nixon's journey to the capitals of Europe exceeded even the best expectations. He succeeded in reestablishing a relationship of mutual trust between America and Europe. The meeting with Charles de Gaulle was of special significance. It revived the American-French relationship. Altogether, Nixon's visit has noticeably strengthened the Western alliance.

South Bend, March 3, 1969

Apollo 9

The launch of Apollo 9 with the lunar module on board has not attracted much attention. Flights into space have become so much of a routine that they are seen as a matter of course. Apollo 9 orbiting the earth does not stir any sensation. No moon fever has broken out in America, yet the moon landing, expected to occur this summer, has aroused the public imagination. This event is being looked forward to with great anticipation.

South Bend, March 4, 1969

Nixon's Press Conference

Two days after his return from Europe, President Nixon gave a press conference in the White House that was aired on national television. Almost exclusively, questions of foreign policy were discussed. Although it should have been a report on the journey to Europe, questions concerning Europe were immediately superseded by the War in Vietnam and the crisis in the Middle East. The real problems of Western Europe were for the most part ignored. Nixon emphasized that a new relationship of trust with the European allies has been established, and he stressed that America will keep its European allies informed about the sought after bilateral negotiations with the Soviet Union. The new attitude of the United States toward Europe is based on non-interference in questions of European disputes. As desirable this approach may be, it nevertheless shows a certain distancing from European problems. There is obviously no intention of solving vital European problems, but more the tendency of striving for a policy of appeasement. If the Europeans do not muster the farsightedness and the political will to unify their continent, nobody else will do it for them. Then nobody in Europe should hope for playing a role in present world politics.

South Bend, [Beginning of March], 1969

A Gruesome Mathematics

Without much ado, the gruesome mathematics of megatons with their sheer unimaginable force of destruction was exercised before the public in a Senate hearing of recent days. At stake was establishing an antiballistic missile system or ABM. It was demonstrated that over the North Pole, from Russia or China, intercontinental missiles could reach the American mainland. Although much of the argument was still theoretical, the realization that the North American Continent over Alaska lies unprotected open to an attack caused some uneasiness. At the same time, the absurdity, if not the impossibility of a nuclear war was shown with compelling logic.

South Bend, [End of March], 1969

The Death of Dwight D. Eisenhower

On Friday, March 28, around the hour of noon, the former U.S. President Dwight D. Eisenhower passed away at the age of 78. Eisenhower's death did not come as a surprise, for during his severe illness the public had continuously been informed about his critical state of health by medical bulletins from the Walter Reed Army Medical Center in Washington. Yet nevertheless, when after seven heart attacks the inevitable occurred, the country and the world felt deep sorrow. Although the United States is mourning over a former president, the name Eisenhower remains indelibly connected with the invasion of Normandy in World War II. As it has only now been made clear, the decision for D-Day lay in the hands of Eisenhower, the Supreme Commander of the Allied Forces. At that time there were five million Allied troops under his command. It was Eisenhower's great historic accomplishment to have militarily subdued fascism in Europe. In a retrospective summary of his life, his high qualities have been praised. Eisenhower was a man to whom defending principles meant more than the interests of an individual or a group. Even Democrats who were in the minority during his administration admitted that he was non-partisan and objective. He was a person of absolute honesty and integrity. He had to a high degree won the trust and reverence of the American people. Service to his country meant more to him than anything else.

Eisenhower spent the last years of his life on his farm in Gettysburg, Pennsylvania. The disclosure of his last wish that he wanted to be buried in his hometown Abilene, Kansas, came as a surprise. Thereby the modesty of his early youth came to light. He was born on October 14, 1890 in Denison, Texas. But as a one year old child he came with his parents to Abilene, a small town in central Kansas. There he grew up. The name Eisenhower goes back to a Hans Nicholas Eisenhauer, who in 1741 had emigrated from the Palatinate to Pennsylvania. Dwight Eisenhower went to the Military Academy at West Point because it offered him the opportunity of a higher education without charge. After West Point he pursued a military career, which finally led him to the Supreme Command of the Allied Forces in World War II.

Eisenhower's last coming home was a dignified and solemn state funeral. Dignitaries and heads of state from all over the world arrived for the obsequies. As always at such occasions, the tall figure of French President Charles de Gaulle towered over the other guests from abroad. The personal presence of Charles de Gaulle at this state funeral was much appreciated in America. It certainly contributed to the American-French reconciliation. With the death of Eisenhower an era comes to a close, which today appears to lie much further in the past than the number of years would indicate.

[Dwight David Eisenhower (1890-1969), hometown Abilene, Kansas; attended the U.S. Military Academy at West Point, 1911-15; General, Supreme Commander of the Allied Forces in Europe, 1942-45; U.S. Army Chief of Staff, 1945-48; thereafter retired from military service. He was President of Columbia University, 1948-52; U.S. President, 1953-61. The Eisenhower Presidential Library was built in Abilene, Kansas. His mortal remains were buried in the Chapel of the Library.]

[Over Easter vacation from April 3-14 my family and I took a sightseeing trip to Washington, D.C.]

Washington, Easter 1969

Washington Seen Differently

Coming to Washington, one is, compared to European capitals, surprised by the simplicity of the government buildings. There is little splendor in Washington. It is an administration city established in an unassuming republican style. Washington was taken by surprise by the leading role it had suddenly to assume. On the surface was no hint that world politics in grand style was made here. We had just arrived at Pennsylvania Avenue in time when a helicopter with King Hussein of Jordan on board landed on the White House lawn. At the same time, the foreign ministers of the 15 NATO countries had assembled in Washington for the 20th anniversary of the North Atlantic Treaty Organization. In both cases without much fanfare, far-reaching questions of world politics were dealt with. President Nixon discussed with King Hussein the conflict in the Middle East, while talks with the NATO partners were held concerning a new peace settlement for Europe.

The White House can hardly cope with all these tasks anymore. On the one side, one state visit follows after another, and on the other, thousands of tourists stand in line to be admitted to the guided tours through the historic rooms. The entire layout of the White House is rather small and modest. It is more like a mansion than the private and official residence of the U.S. president. It would not come as a surprise if one day a new residence for the American president would be made available and the White House remained only a museum.

[The White House stands on a lot of 18 acres on Pennsylvania Avenue. It was built as a manor house in the Georgian Palladian style in part by George Washington in 1792.]

Washington still makes a provincial impression. There is no renowned theater, no opera, and no symphony orchestra to speak of. It is no wonder that the large diplomatic community along Embassy Row feels ennui from time to time.

[The John F. Kennedy Center for the Performing Arts was opened in 1971. This building at the Potomac finally gave Washington a center for the performing arts that combines in one large complex stage, concert hall and opera house.]

A special problem for Washington is the sprawling black ghetto. The city presently has a Negro population of 70% who live in the worst slums on the north side of town. The slums extend immediately behind the White House and the government buildings. As employer the capital has accepted the black population from the South. In turn, it created an inner city problem that is difficult to solve. The inner city has become unsafe for visitors to go out at night. After closing hours of museums and offices, everybody is hurrying to get out of town.

[During the previous months, the University of Notre Dame reviewed my tenure application, the decision on my permanent appointment as professor. Coming back from Washington, I found to my pleasant surprise the contract in the mail. It confirmed my appointment as associate professor with tenure. As no other university was taken into consideration, from then on my affiliation with Notre Dame was sealed for a lifetime. Consequently, also my and my family's decision to immigrate to the United States was a logical follow-up.]

[Upon the recommendation of Professor Lothar L. Tresp of the University of Georgia, I was invited for a guest lecture at the Wesleyan College in Macon, Georgia. Since the guest lecture had been scheduled for April 24, I took a flight from Chicago to Atlanta the day before.]

Chicago, O'Hare, April 23, 1969

From Chicago to Atlanta: Domestic Flights in America

Coming from Europe, one may be astonished that international flights are only a fraction of the domestic air traffic in America. Proof of that is the O'Hare Airport in Chicago. Domestic air travel has made O'Hare the most frequented airport in the world. This is an intersection of North America. From here within a few hours, one can reach any destination from Miami, Florida, to Anchorage, Alaska. Atlanta, Georgia, is only one hour and a half away by plane. Flying has become the customary mode of transportation for the general public. Modern air traffic and television have joined the North American Continent into a tangible and graspable unity.

Macon, Georgia, April 25, 1969

The Old South

[A commuter plane brought me from Atlanta to Macon located 80 miles to the south. The reception at the Wesleyan College was very cordial. That small liberal arts college founded in 1836 was the first women college in America if not the first institution of higher learning for women in the world. The lecture titled "The Image of Europe in American Literature" was accepted with great enthusiasm.]

Here one still gets an impression of the culture of the Old South, as it flourished in the 18th and 19th centuries. The first important state universities and a number of well-known colleges were founded in the South. The way of living was characterized by aristocratic elegance of which only a reflection can still be sensed today. But at the same time one cannot overlook the signs of decay and provincial seclusion. Milledgeville, the old capital of Georgia before the Civil War, is only a few miles away from here. After Atlanta had become the new capital of Georgia in 1867, Milledgeville declined into a forgotten provincial town. Despite the industrialization that was strongly accelerated by the North, Georgia has remained to a high degree an agrarian state. Although its cotton production has fallen behind, the best peaches in the country are grown here.

From the Colonial History of Georgia: The Salzburgers at Ebenezer

[The stretch of land between the Carolinas and Spanish Florida was founded as a British colony in 1733 by General James E. Oglethorpe (1696-1785) and named "Georgia" after King George II. Oglethorpe, who was appointed governor of the new colony, encouraged the immigration of persecuted Protestant groups from Europe. That facilitated the settlement of the Salzburger Protestants immediately following the foundation of the colony. From 1730-40 about 19,000 Protestants were expelled from the Prince Archbishopric of Salzburg. They first moved to Augsburg where they were taken care of by the Lutheran Mission. Many of them went on to East Prussia, but several hundreds decided to immigrate to the new Colony of Georgia. Professor Lothar Tresp, who as historian had studied the subject of the Salzburger immigrants in Georgia, called the settlement of the Salzburgers at Ebenezer to my attention.

The Salzburger emigrants were under the patronage of the Franckeschen Waisenhaus-Stiftung (Orphanage Foundation) in Halle. The Foundations created by the Protestant Pietistic theologian August Hermann Francke (1663-1727) included orphanages, hospitals, schools as well as missions for the propagation of faith. They belonged to the most important philanthropic institutions of their time. The Foundation provided two pastors who accompanied the Salzburgers to the unknown New World. Pastor Johann Martin Bolzius assumed the leadership and spiritual guidance of the settlement of the Salzburgers in Georgia. The first transport with 42 persons reached Savannah on the Atlantic coast in March 1734. Three more transports with 50 persons each, mostly families, arrived in the following years. Pastor Bolzius established the Salzburger settlement at Ebenezer 20 miles inland from Savannah. He first built the orphanage, around which the settlement gradually developed. As a multi-purpose building, the orphanage offered shelter for children who had lost their parents and also took care of persons in need. Furthermore, it was equipped as hospital, served as school, and as a house of worship until the church was built. It was the central space for spiritual guidance, and in an emergency it also took care of the social needs of the community.

Pastor Bolzius who was well aware of his unique task kept a diary, in which he recorded the development of the settlement. His diary entries together with the letters he continuously wrote to Pastor Urlsperger in Augsburg gave a vivid account of the progress of the colony. Samuel Urlsperger, Senior Pastor of the Evangelical St. Ann's Church in Augsburg, had taken special care of the Salzburger emigrants. He organized and assembled in Augsburg the transports for the emigration to Georgia, paid attention to the progress of the enterprise and asked for financial donations for the orphanage. Urlsperger found the reports of Bolzius interesting enough that he had them published by the Orphanage Press of the Francke Foundation in Halle. They appeared under the title, "Der Ausführlichen Nachrichten von der Königlich-Gross-Brittannischen Colonie Salzburgischer Emigranten in America," vols. I (1735-40), II (1741-46), III (1747-52).

I was given permission to examine the 3 vols. of Urlsperger in the Library of the University of Georgia. Among other places, the settlers had come from Werfen and Radstadt. Names like Steiner, Kogler and Schweighofer originated without a doubt from the Salzburg area. Despite their pietistic emotional exuberance, these records by Bolzius of every day events and the living conditions of the colony are exact to the minutest detail. They report of the economic difficulties at the start; of illnesses and deaths; mention the good relationship which Bolzius had maintained with Governor Oglethorpe and the colonial administration in Savannah; tell how the colonists tried to cultivate new plants and of their encounter with the Indians; also mention the difficulties they had in finding an English teacher. The Salzburgers were definitely opposed to the introduction of slavery in Georgia. But economic interests finally outweighed the various voices of opposition so that slavery was introduced in the colony of Georgia by decision of Parliament in London in 1749.

Based on the diaries of Bolzius, Lothar Tresp wrote a comprehensive study of the orphanage of the Salzburger colony titled "The Salzburger Orphanage at Ebenezer in Colonial Georgia." The article appeared in *Americana-Austriaca*, vol.3 (Wien: Wilhelm Braumüller, 1974), pp. 190-234. Next to the writings of Johann Martin Bolzius, as they were published by Samuel Urlsperger (1735-52), the Orphanage Foundation in Halle holds extensive archival materials. In their sum total, these materials offer a rare and valuable insight into the way of life and development of a German speaking Lutheran community in the early colonial period of Georgia.]

South Bend, Sunday, April 27, 1969

The Resignation of Charles de Gaulle

One had to listen twice, until one grasped the brief newscast that French President Charles de Gaulle promptly resigned after having lost the referendum. The end of the Gaullist era comes so surprisingly and without further ado that at first one has to become aware of its repercussions. In America the news of de Gaulle's departure is accepted with restraint and mixed emotions. On the one side, one expects a revival of the North Atlantic Alliance as well as an improvement of the cooperation within the West in general. It should also become easier for Great Britain to join the Common Market. But on the other side, one fears that France could plunge into economic and political chaos. It is taken for granted that the French franc will be devalued. It remains to be seen how the successors of de Gaulle will be capable of managing the economic and political crisis situation.

South Bend, May 14, 1969

The Plan for the Solution of the Vietnam War

In his first fundamental political statement on national television, President Nixon presented to the American public the following solution how to end the War in Vietnam:

1) Mutual withdrawal of troops from Vietnam within 12 months.
2) Neutralization of Vietnam.
3) Self-determination for South Vietnam, free elections with the participation of the communists under international supervision.

Even if the opposite side should not agree to accept these proposals, the Nixon administration will under any circumstances try to withdraw the United States from Vietnam.

South Bend, Sunday, May 18, 1969

Apollo 10

Today at 11:49 a.m. EST, the spacecraft Apollo 10 lifted off from the launch pad on Cape Kennedy on its flight to the moon. This is the last test flight before the moon-landing. While Apollo 10 will only circle the moon, test the maneuverability of the lunar module, and will search for a suitable landing site, Apollo 11 will carry out the first landing on the moon in July. Already now, the moon-landing is stimulating philosophical reflections. As former Vice President Hubert Humphrey remarked with correct prediction: "We have to realize that the solar system is becoming man's neighborhood." The landing on the moon will certainly encourage space travel to further explore earth's neighboring planets. At the same time, space exploration will have far-reaching repercussions for life on earth.

[The flight of Apollo 10 lasted eight days, whereby the spacecraft circled the moon 31 times.]

Impressions of Apollo 10

For the first time on this flight to the moon, colored images could be seen on the television screen. It was one of the most impressive sights of our time to see together with the astronauts on board of Apollo 10 (Thomas Stafford, Eugene Cernan, and John Young) the earth as a blue, white-marbled sphere floating in space and shrinking in size with increasing distance. The sight was continually described by the astronauts as being of phantastic beauty. The earth remained for them the only vanishing point in space visible in shining colors.

For the first time, the camera of Apollo 10 sent colored pictures of the moon back to earth. The brownish craterscape of the moon casting long shadows is of a peculiar, bizarre beauty. The moonscape will soon become a familiar environment. Following the successful testing of the lunar module on this flight, nothing anymore should hinder the landing on the moon in July. One thing has already become clear by the flight of Apollo 10: The landing on the moon will not be an escape from earth, but on the contrary will bring the moon closer to earth. Never before has an exploratory expedition been so completely controlled and guided by the station it started from.

South Bend, [Beginning of June], 1969

Campus Revolts

A series of revolts is raging through American colleges and universities these days, the effects of which cannot as yet be fully measured. Above all, the state universities in California are affected by them, but the unrests in Wisconsin and Indiana, at Harvard and Cornell University are no less alarming. The violent confrontations at New York City College have shown that these protests are also connected with the racial question. These upheavals have primarily been caused by the resistance to the War in Vietnam, but they are also a rebellion of the young generation against the traditional moral standards of the middle class. A distinguishing quality of these American campus revolts is their aimlessness. There is no common goal between students, workers and farmers, as it is widespread in Europe, Asia and Latin America. The university revolts in America are shocking by their radicalism, but their effects on society at large are limited. There is no danger that the country would be paralyzed or that higher education would shut down. On the contrary, colleges and universities will emerge from this crisis more mature and better prepared for the task ahead to house and educate the roughly 12 million young people on their campuses.

South Bend, [Beginning of June], 1969

Provincialism

Human nature tends towards provincialism. It is the understandable inclination towards security as well as clinging to what is known and familiar. The familiar environment gives a feeling of safety, ease and coziness. It may also be out of indolence that one feels comfortable with a way of life one has gotten accustomed to from early childhood on. Provincialism can be seen everywhere, here in Indiana and just as well at home in Austria, in Germany, France or Italy. It excludes what is foreign and persists with stubborn obstinacy in distrust of everything that is unknown, holding on to prejudices. Provincialism is the real obstacle to international understanding. It should be overcome by an education that goes beyond regional borders. It is necessary to go beyond the local point of view and to see the world in a larger context. First and foremost, it is necessary to be willing to understand and respect the peculiarities of a different way of life. Only by doing so, will it be possible to come to grips mentally with different continents that are fast growing together. It is also a prerequisite for creating a more world-open and humane common civilization.

[I was appointed resident director of the University of Notre Dame Foreign Study Program in Innsbruck, Austria, for the two year period 1969-71.

By mid-June my family and I flew from Chicago to Zurich and back to Innsbruck.]

Chicago, O'Hare, June 18, 1969

East and West from a Similar Point of View

From here one part of the passengers flies to Asia and the other to Europe. However different they may be, seen from here, the problems of Asia and of Europe appear to be similar. Both regions are dealing with questions that have emerged from World War II. They are both under the American sphere of influence. This is especially true of Japan and West Germany. Under the protection of the American nuclear umbrella and with substantial American economic aid, both countries have achieved hitherto unknown economic prosperity. After the United States, Japan and the Federal Republic have advanced to the second strongest economies in the world. Japanese exports to the United States are so extensive that it is hardly possible anymore to pick up a consumer good not made in Japan. The Federal Republic has assumed economic leadership in Europe and Japan the same in Asia. But by comparison to their economic significance, both countries play a subordinate role in world politics. In this respect, Asia and Europe are in a similar position. America has no other choice but to warrant their security and to do justice to their demands. When a Japanese or Korean businessman flies home from here, then there is not much difference from Europeans flying home to Frankfurt, Rome or Amsterdam. The business delegation from Tokyo pursues the same interests as the one from Munich or Milan. Both are held here in high esteem and treated equally. Chicago radiates a cosmopolitan aura. Visitors from various countries in Asia and Europe meet here freely and in an unconstrained atmosphere as hardly anywhere else in the world.

Mid-Atlantic, June 19, 3 a.m., 1969

In the Twilight Zone between America and Europe

The flight on a Swissair DC-8 from Chicago to Zurich with a stop-over in Montreal takes about eight hours. Already two hours after Montreal, at 1 a.m., the aurora of an early dawn appears on the horizon. At 3 a.m. it is already bright daylight and the coast of Ireland will soon be visible through the cloud cover. In this twilight zone over the Atlantic, my thoughts are in part still going back to America, while at the same time Europe and the familiar environment of my homeland come to mind. Modern jet travel has conquered the distance that had separated the two continents for centuries with incredible speed. Thereby the customary routines of daily life are getting ever closer to each other. One goes to bed with Johnny Carson the night before and wakes up with Heinzi Conrads the next morning.* Nevertheless, mutual understanding and communications across the Atlantic are still very inadequate.

*[Johnny Carson, arguably the best known comedian in America in the '60s, '70s, and '80s, every evening hosted the "Tonight Show" on NBC. During the same period, Heinz Conrads, the most beloved emcee in Austria, on weekends hosted the entertainment series of ORF (Austrian Radio and Television).]

What do I leave behind in America, and what do I expect of Europe? I certainly leave behind a more spacious and generous way of life and will have to get used again to the narrower and more crowded living conditions in Europe. In America one can feel the pulse of our times, witness events of worldwide importance that determine the course of history. Europe on the other hand stands in the shadow of world affairs so that the judgment of their real significance gets lost. One becomes aware again that Europe lives by provisional arrangements for which no solutions are yet in sight. Still, how delighted I am returning to Old Europe. I look forward to seeing my homeland again and to enjoy the magnificent mountain scape of Switzerland and Austria. I anticipate the pleasure of standing before a real gothic cathedral as well as taking a leisurely stroll through the Altstadt, the medieval Old City of Innsbruck. My wife and I particularly look forward to attending an opera at the Salzburg Festival.

Europe's cultural heritage is a gem that should be treasured and carefully tended to. The American longing for this heritage is undiminished; it is deeply rooted in the American character. Tourist attractions alone cannot fully explain why millions of Americans come to Europe every year.

Innsbruck, [Beginning of July], 1969

Impressions of Europe

Shortly after our return, my wife and I took a round trip tour by car to Munich and Vienna. We could not help being shocked. First, we were dismayed by the paltriness we encountered at every turn. People looked careworn and neglected. Generally speaking, despite the supposed prosperity in Europe, the inadequacies can be seen everywhere. Traffic strikes one as being like Gulliver in Lilliput. The bicycle is still a much used means of transportation. As all sorts of small vehicles are mixing with cars, trucks and horse-drawn carriages, the traffic situation is very confusing. The Autobahn exits at the periphery of the big cities. Without connecting express lanes, motorists have to maneuver their way to the center. Since multistory or underground garages are rarely available, it takes some ingenuity to find a place to park. What has been standing in Europe for centuries was built solidly to endure. But by contrast, the modern technical constructions make a rickety tin like impression. They are by design too small and overstrained. A large-scale city planning is still missing.

The Emigration

There is a big difference whether one comes back from a visit to the United States or with the declared intention to emigrate. Inadvertently, a wall of separation goes up even among relatives and close friends. There is an incomprehensible shaking of heads asking how anybody could leave such a beautiful place to go to America? Here are already the roots of a growing misunderstanding between Europe and America. Anybody who contemplates to emigrate to America would be well advised to be prepared how to cope with this reality.

Innsbruck, July 21, 1969

Apollo 11—Landing on the Moon

Yesterday, Sunday, July 20, at about 21:00 hrs. MEZ (Central European Time) or 4:17 p.m. EDT, the lunar module "Eagle" touched down in a perfect soft landing on the surface of the moon. Six hours later, Neil Armstrong, as the first human being, set foot on the moon. His first steps were cautious, but soon safe and of playful lightness. Descending from the module, Edwin Aldrin, Jr., soon followed, while Michael Collins in the spacecraft Apollo 11 orbited the moon. Armstrong and Aldrin offered a spectacle without equal to the people back on earth, who watched them on the television screens.

Although the American landing on the moon had already been accepted as a fact for months, the real occurrence brought forth an unusual psychological effect. It was one of the most exciting moments of the century. When Neil Armstrong set his foot on the surface of the moon, the entire human race identified itself with him. There was a feeling of belonging together, of solidarity, as it has not up to now been experienced. It bridged over the East West conflict and spread across all continents. There was jubilation in the streets, a whirl of enthusiasm carried by the pride of achievement. A kind of optimism was spreading which saw mankind at the beginning of a new age. Obviously, the age of space flights has begun that opens unimagined possibilities.

The American space program has without a doubt won the race to the moon. It brings with it an enormous gain of prestige for the United States. Mankind as a whole feels to be part of this NASA project. But the lunar landing has also demonstrated that only a highly advanced industrial country could provide the financial means and carry out the technological-scientific organization of such an enterprise. In a gigantic organizational effort hundreds of thousands of scientists and engineers together with the support staff have cooperated in the Apollo program over the years. Thereby, the promise of John F. Kennedy—to land a man on the moon before this decade is out—could be kept.

July 24, 1969

Splashdown in the Pacific

At 17:51 hrs. MEZ [12:51 p.m. EDT] the space capsule Apollo 11 splashed down in the Pacific near Hawaii. Following their historic flight to the moon, the three astronauts—Armstrong, Aldrin and Collins—were heaved from the ocean and brought by helicopter on deck of the carrier *Hornet* where President Nixon welcomed them back. After landing, the astronauts had to remain in quarantine to make sure that they would not bring unknown bacteria from the moon to earth.

[A series of additional lunar landings were carried out by the flights of Apollo 12-17. At the beginning of December 1972 NASA completed its manned landings on the moon with Apollo 17.]

Innsbruck, [End of July], 1969

Government Crisis in Italy

The political insecurity and lacking stability in Europe has always a surprise in store. It can spoil the pleasure of a summer vacation. In the intense July heat, the government of Italy that had resigned tried desperately to form a minority cabinet. It has finally succeeded. During the government crisis waiters as well as the entire hotel personnel started a protest strike. Vacationing tourists were mostly affected by it.

Innsbruck, [Beginning of August], 1969

The Devaluation of the Franc

On Friday, August 8, the French franc was devaluated by the new French government at a moment when nobody had expected it. The devaluation was 11.1%. What effect the devaluation of the franc will have on the European Economic Community remains to be seen. French tourists abroad have again been surprised and severely hurt by this action.

As the political crisis in Europe is continuously ongoing, it is already accepted as normal. Thereby, the abnormal is seen as normal and the political activity remains oriented to the bizarre. Europe got used to a completely upside down and disproportionate understanding of the present world situation. The desire for unity and a solution of the European problems is thwarted again and again by the divided Continent.

Nixon's Visit to Romania

As the first American president, Richard Nixon visited a communist country in the East Bloc. The enthusiasm by which he was received came as a surprise and showed how much the people in the East Bloc countries are receptive to the West. For a moment the anonymity was broken, one could see the real emotions of the people behind the Iron Curtain. The question though remains unanswered whether the visit of President Nixon was a Greek gift, and whether Romania may meet the same fate as Czechoslovakia.

[In the second half of August 49 students from the University of Notre Dame and St. Mary's College arrived in Salzburg for a year of studies in Austria. On their long journey by boat and railroad from New York via Paris to Salzburg, the group was accompanied by a priest from Notre Dame. The Salzburg Summer School of the Austrian-American Society was located in the annex of the Klesheim Palace. The main purpose of the five week summer session was further German language instruction in preparation for the academic year in Innsbruck. The German language courses were taught in cooperation with the Goethe Institute. Until the end of August, there was also the opportunity to visit some of the performances of the Salzburg Festival.]

[The Reverend Leon Mertensotto, CSC, had accompanied the student group to Salzburg. He served as Chaplain of the Program during the academic year in Innsbruck 1969-70.]

Salzburg, [Mid-September], 1969

Salzburg During and After the Festival

During the time of the Festival from mid-July to the end of August, Salzburg radiates a splendor like nowhere else in the world. The picturesque baroque city, which Max Reinhardt had turned into a single stage, gives the Festival a unique ambience. Outstanding artistic achievements and an international Festival audience make Salzburg in the summer the center of the arts in Europe. But when the Festival is over, Salzburg falls back again into the sleepy provincial town it has been since the end of the reign of the prince archbishops by the end of the 18th century. After the Festival, what is still offered on the stage and in music halls is not different from the other provincial capitals in Austria.

Innsbruck, [Beginning of October], 1969

Election to the Bundestag 1969

The big surprise of the election to the Bundestag of September 28, 1969, came at the end when the front runner of the SPD (Social Democratic Party), Willy Brandt, declared shortly before midnight in a television interview that he will assume the office of Federal Chancellor and that he had already invited the FDP (Free Democrats) to enter into coalition negotiations. That was for the moment implausible because the Unionsparteien (Union of the conservative Christian Democrats) had already celebrated victory and seen their candidate Chancellor Kurt Georg Kiesinger confirmed in office. Only in the following days, the victory of Willy Brandt turned out to be irrefutable. The SPD made to the Free Democrats, although they had suffered considerable losses in the election, far-reaching concessions in forming the government.

With the new Brandt Government, a change in German foreign policy is to be expected. The German Ostpolitik should get moving, whereby vital questions of Germany will be addressed that are also significant for securing peace in Central Europe. The acceptance of the Oder-Neisse-Linie as border to Poland is at stake as well as the possible recognition of the DDR (German Democratic Republic—East Germany) as second German state.

The Results of the Election of September 28, 1969

Of the total 38,658,363 eligible votes, 32,733,431 ballots were cast in a high voter turnout. Of these—comparable results of the election of 1965 in parentheses—46.1 % (47.6%) went to the CDU/CSU with 242 (245) seats in the Bundestag; 42% (39.3%) to the SPD with 224 (202) seats in the Bundestag; and 5.8% (9.5%) with 30 (49) seats to the FDP. The increase of votes for the SPD, together with the gain of seats in the Bundestag, made it possible for Willy Brandt to enter into a Small Coalition with the FDP and to form the government.

While a socialist liberal trend is gaining more and more ground in Europe, liberalism in the United States, after 30 year predominance, is being replaced by a conservative administration.

[Willy Brandt (1913-92), journalist and politician, lived from 1933-45 in exile in Norway and Sweden. He was mayor of Berlin, 1957-66; vice chancellor and foreign minister in the cabinet of Kiesinger, 1966-69; federal chancellor, 1969-74. He received the Nobel Peace Prize in 1971. Willy Brandt died on October 8, 1992 at the age of 79.]

Innsbruck, October 25, 1969

Revaluation of the DM

Although the revaluation of the German mark (DM) by 8.5% was a necessary and understandable measure, it brought again a factor of uncertainty into the European monetary system. To what extent will the other European currencies be forced to go along? How much of a price increase will it cause in Austria, which remains dependent on imports from the Federal Republic? It is deplorable that monetary policies in Europe are still enacted unilaterally without prior mutual consultations. Efforts for the European integration are thereby restrained. Actually, a trend of declining cooperation in essential questions of economic and political unity can be observed.

Innsbruck, November 1, 1969

Efforts for a European Security Conference

All efforts of the present international talks are aiming at a European Security Conference. Willy Brandt's Ostpolitik has given these talks a hitherto unknown boost. The states of the East Bloc are highly interested in such a Conference and would also be prepared to make concessions, while it would offer the West an opportunity for a period of relaxation in Central Europe. But the price would obviously be legalizing the status quo of the borders in Central Europe as well as the recognition of the DDR (East Germany) as a separate state. As these are already an accomplished fact anyway, such a Conference could make a significant contribution to normalize the political situation in Central Europe and at the same time ease the way for the initiated détente between the United States and the Soviet Union. After 25 years since the end of World War II, it would be time to create stable political conditions in Europe.

Innsbruck, November 19, 1969

This week bilateral talks between the United States and the Soviet Union on Strategic Arms Limitation (SALT) in Helsinki have begun in order to achieve a balance of nuclear power. This is also significant for the European Security Conference. Without a doubt, a period of negotiations has begun that could well be the most important arbitrations in deciding the destiny of Central Europe since Yalta and Potsdam.

Note

[Henry Kissinger mentions in his memoirs, *White House Years* (Boston: Little, Brown and Co., 1979, pp. 143-45) that since February 1969 preliminary talks between him and the Russian Ambassador in Washington Anatoly Dobrynin on SALT had taken place. After long negotiations and working on various drafts, the SALT I agreement was signed in Moscow in May 1972. The Final Act of the Conference on Security and Cooperation in Europe (CSCE) was signed in Helsinki by the end of July, beginning of August 1975.]

Innsbruck, [Middle of November]. 1969

Hope for the Future

Students in Europe have become very much like those in America so that it would be difficult to see much of a difference. The young generation has been following a worldwide trend by adjusting to each other the way they dress, behave and think. They give the older generation everywhere an uncanny feeling. But the positive side of this development may be seen in the circumstance that the young generation is growing into a global civilization, which furthers international understanding and brings young people from different cultures closer together than ever before. In this development, there is certainly hope for the future.

Innsbruck, [End of November], 1969

The Struggle for Democracy in Europe

Most countries in Europe are presently taking desperate efforts to achieve better and more effective forms of democracy. The continuing series of strikes in Italy, the profound discontent in France, the confrontation with the dictatorships in Spain and Greece as well as the left wing underpinnings, all threaten the stability of the liberal democratic governments in power. In addition to that, there is the historic burden to bear. Democracy in Europe has to catch up on a 150 year long neglect.

Innsbruck, [End of December], 1969

Reviving the Idea of a United Europe

Despite the frosty winter and the severe flu epidemic that afflicts Europe at this time, an unexpected euphoria of reviving the idea of a United Europe has happened in Brussels. The German Chancellor Willy Brandt and the new French President Georges Pompidou spoke up strongly for European cooperation. They held out the prospect of admitting Great Britain to the Common Market and the association of the neutral countries with it. It appears that the absurd economic partition of Western Europe into the Common Market and the European Free Trade Association (EFTA) will be overcome. As it turns out again and again, British membership in the

Common Market would be a decisive step toward European unity. For small, neutral Austria association with the Common Market would be of vital importance. If this favorable outlook can be taken as a prelude for the 1970s, then the economic and fiscal unity of Western Europe would come closer to realization.

Innsbruck, January 2, 1970

The Unsolved German Question

Although the world outside Germany never had much confidence in reunification, it completely lost credibility after the invasion of Czechoslovakia.

January 15, 1970

The dilemma of the German situation has again surfaced these days: On the one side, it is generally admitted that there is no prospect for reunification, while on the other, recognition of the DDR (East Germany) as a separate state, according to international law, has been persistently refused. As a result, a mutual understanding between the two German states, or the solution of the German question remains postponed to an unforeseeable future.

Innsbruck, January 20, 1970

The Crazy America

After having been absent from the United States for only a few months, the image of America is getting distorted. This is due to a great extent to the influence of the mass media. Opening any newspaper, one is surprised again and again to come across a section about the crazy America. Captions in bold print read, for example: "America's ghettoes are hotbeds for revolutionary ideas," "American billionaire wants to buy the whole Liechtenstein Castle," "Nine million American women take the pill," "American nun is riding on a motor scooter through the hallways of a high school in Chicago," etc. Considering that reports of this kind appear every day in the European press, radio and television, it is small wonder that Europeans have developed an image of America, which can hardly be outdone by its grotesqueness, craziness and abnormality. The awareness is being lost that there is also a normal way of life in America.

Innsbruck, January 24, 1970

Anti-Americanism

Anti-Americanism is a worldwide phenomenon that even applies to the best friends of America. In part, this phenomenon of our time has detached itself from America and has become an entity of its own. Basically, it is the revolt against the modern technological world, against consumerism and conformity, for which America has become the dominant symbol. Everywhere in the world where a four-lane highway is constructed, a new airport built, or a new super market opened, inevitably ways of life are created that were first developed in America and then in part adopted from there. Anti-Americanism has manyfold historical, political and cultural roots, but it is essentially caused by fears of an unstoppable progressing technicalization of modem life.

Innsbruck, [End of January], 1970

Nixon's Message to the World

President Nixon's State of the Union Address, a 19 page report submitted to Congress, is without a doubt for years the most important foreign policy message, which the White House has given to the world. It formulates the so-called Nixon Doctrine:

1. Shifting the emphasis of American foreign policy from Asia to Europe.
2. Introducing a more matter-of-fact, pragmatic foreign policy that serves the national self-interest.
3. Détente with the Soviet Union in regard to the limitation of strategic arms.
4. Renouncing American predominance, instead calling for partnership with the allies in Europe.

However, Europe is not ready as yet for a partnership because its defense is overwhelmingly dependent on the United States.

Innsbruck, [February], 1970

Political Attitude in Europe

European society is still very much determined by traditional class consciousness so that it is difficult for people to change political parties out of their own free democratic decision. The firmly entrenched social structures are hard to set in motion, even if economic reasoning and a modern way of thinking call for a change. Although most political parties in Europe have recently adopted the well tested American campaign tactics—rallies are like in America frequently organized as shows—, the effects are quite different. Political life in Europe is for the most part anonymous. It is burdened by anxiety and ideological differences so that a more loosened and unrestrained free expression of opinion can only slowly get through.

Innsbruck, [March 3], 1970

The Political Change in Austria

At the Austrian parliamentary elections of March 1, the SPÖ (Socialist Party of Austria) won the relative majority. The Socialists succeeded in penetrating the pool of regular voters of the conservative ÖVP (Austrian People's Party) on the countryside of the Western provinces. They also attracted swing voters and the young generation. A major political change has happened in Austria, a fundamental reorientation of the political landscape has occurred. The elections were carried out quietly and without disturbances, what proved again the democratic maturity of the country. Worn-out and stagnant after 25 years in power, the People's Party had to turn over the reins of government to the Socialists. Dr. Bruno Kreisky who dominated these elections has now the opportunity as Federal Chancellor to realize the Socialist concept of a modern Austria. The new distribution of seats in the Parliament is as follows: 81 SPÖ; 79 ÖVP; and 5 FPÖ (Liberal Party of Austria).

For many conservative circles in Austria, the Socialist victory in these national elections came like a harbinger of the end of the world, although nothing catastrophic has really happened. Voters trusted the new image of the Socialist Party, which to a high degree has abandoned its Austro-Marxist heritage. Above all, the country relied on the personality of Bruno Kreisky who stood up credibly for the basic principles of Western democracy.

[Bruno Kreisky, lawyer, diplomat, politician, was born 1911 in Vienna; since 1927 active in the Socialist workers youth movement, 1935-36 placed under detention; 1938-45 lived in exile in Sweden. From 1945-51 Kreisky served as Austrian ambassador in Stockholm; as state secretary in the Chancellor's Office, 1953-59, he was considerably engaged in bringing the negotiations on the Austrian State Treaty to a conclusion. From 1959-66 he was Austrian foreign minister; since 1967 chairman of the SPÖ. Kreisky was Federal Chancellor from 1970-83; supported by the absolute Socialist majority in Parliament, 1971-81—the Kreisky era—, he could carry out the essential domestic reforms in Austria. Kreisky died on July 29, 1990, in Vienna.]

Innsbruck, March 5, 1970

Today, when the 43 states that signed on to the Non-Proliferation Treaty deposit their ratified documents in Washington, London, and Moscow, the Treaty will come into effect.

The voluntary renunciation of developing and spreading nuclear weapons is an essential step forward for the self-preservation of mankind.

Innsbruck, March 19, 1970

The Meeting in Erfurt

For the first time in twenty years, the representatives of East and West Germany sat down at the conference table in Erfurt. Chancellor Willy Brandt went to Erfurt in East Germany to meet with his East German counterpart Premier Willi Stoph. At this meeting, subconscious emotions were set free of which nobody had thought that they existed. Demonstrations of sympathy for Willy Brandt erupted spontaneously. It remains to be seen whether the East German regime can afford to let things take their course.

There can be no doubt anymore that these negotiations will ultimately lead to the recognition of the DDR (German Democratic Republic) or East Germany as a separate state. In return one may expect an improvement of human relations between the two German states. The world has already got used to speaking of two German states so that denying their existence would be anachronistic.

The entire political development in Europe is going in the direction of maintaining the status quo. This means that the borders, as they have been established by World War II, remain in place as they are and that they will be secured by treaty. Any other solution would become more and more wishful thinking.

Innsbruck, April 16, 1970

SALT Negotiations in Vienna

The Strategic Arms Limitation Talks (SALT) were opened in the Hall of Mirrors of the Belvedere Palace in Vienna in a relaxed and friendly atmosphere. Both delegations have obviously come to Vienna, hoping to achieve positive results at the negotiations. As a good omen, not only the Austrian side but also the heads of the delegations, Ambassador Smith (USA) and Deputy Foreign Minister Semenov (USSR) were reminded of the conciliatory spirit of the Austrian State Treaty that was signed fifteen years ago at the same place. It had introduced the first phase of lessening tensions in the East-West conflict.

Addendum

[The designation "Strategic Arms" refers to intercontinental long-range missiles with nuclear warheads. The following SALT conferences alternated between Helsinki and Vienna. This way, they became the urgently needed standing institution for nuclear arms control.]

[My wife and I participated in the Annual Convention of the German Association for American Studies in West Berlin from May 21-23, 1970.]

West Berlin, May 23, 1970

The Schizophrenia of the Divided City

What remains hidden to the outside world, cannot delude the visitor to Berlin as to the absurd living situation of the city. Since there have been no changes in the status of Berlin, the absurdities have only increased and outdone each other. Next to the steel and glass constructions of modem architecture, the ruins of burned-out houses still loom ghostlike from bomb craters that are rampantly overgrown with weeds. Until the entire rubble left over from World War II will be removed, decades still may pass. West Berlin, which in fact can only be reached by air, lies as an enclave deep in East German territory.

West Berlin is being used for window dressing of the West. It is also being rebuilt as capital of a united Germany, although no signs of a possible unification are in sight. As show case for the West, it is not convincing. The imposed modernism, wherever it may come from, gives a wrong impression of the West. Next to the display of affluence, one can see at every turn poverty, human misery, and apathetic hopelessness. Although West Berlin should be a model of the free West, it has become the worst breeding ground for left-wing radical anarchy. No wonder that the absurd theater is thriving here.

The national schizophrenia also expresses itself in the idea of rebuilding West Berlin as capital. Either side of the divided city has set acts of defiance, what only deepens the division instead of overcoming it. Connections over the Wall are virtually non-existent. It would be easier from here to call San Francisco on the phone than East Berlin. Cultural institutions are doubled step by step. Humboldt University in the East is the opposite of the Free University Berlin in the West. Next to the Deutsche Staatsoper unter den Linden in the East, the Deutsche Oper was built in the West. The Reichstagsgebäude in West Berlin is being renovated as future German Parliament. The high-rise office building of the Springer Publishing House stands provocatively close to the Wall. The observation platform on the top floor offers the best panoramic view of East Berlin. The Communist regime on its part erected the high Television and Observation Tower on Alexanderplatz, which allows catching a glimpse of West Berlin.

Despite all the hardships and political conflict, Berlin remains a fascinating city. Who would like to miss a stroll along the Kurfürstendamm and to enjoy a cup of coffee with Streuselkuchen at the Kranzler's, the famous coffee shop? In the Deutsche Oper, my wife and I saw a brilliant performance of *Salome* by Richard Strauss.

If the political situation would not be so deadly serious, one could regard the Wall, which is already growing rusty, as a relict of the past. But one will only get rid of a certain tension and fearful shudder when one will land again on the other part of the world. One must have seen Berlin to understand the abysmal partition that divides one Germany from the other. One has to admire the patience and courage by which the people of this encircled city are holding out despite all the adversities.

[In July 1970 my family and I drove by car through Switzerland to the Lake of Geneva or Lac Léman, and from there over the Great St. Bernard Pass to

Aosta, and on via Torino and Bologna to the Adriatic sea-shore near Cervia where we spent our summer vacation.]

Kilchberg near Zurich, [Middle of July], 1970

At the Graveside of Thomas Mann

The unassuming grave of Thomas Mann (1875-1955) stands on the cemetery of the Church of Kilchberg, surrounded by the rural tranquility of this small town overlooking the Lake of Zurich. Nothing would indicate that this is the last resting-place of the most significant novelist of the German language.

The widow of the author, Katja Mann, still lives, advanced in years, in the Villa Thomas Mann in Kilchberg. She also takes care of the literary estate of her husband. A Thomas Mann Research Library has been established in the Conrad Ferdinand Meyer Haus on the grounds of the Zurich Technical Institute.

Vevey on the Lake of Geneva, [Middle of July], 1970

Switzerland: General Travel Impressions

It is always a pleasure to travel through Switzerland: The magnificent landscape, the refined atmosphere, and the world-renowned hotels give a feeling of comfort. But much is also outdated. Here, the lifestyle of the 19th century is still being cultivated with meticulous care as hardly anywhere else in Europe. The hotel palaces, which once were a status symbol for the haute bourgeoisie, often stand empty. Only the facade has been left. Such a world-famous resort as Vevey has lost much of its former attraction. The landscape around the Lake of Geneva is of an overwhelming beauty, but the Lake suffers from environmental pollution. The famous Hotel Des Trois Couronnes, which once was a meeting place for the international high society, lives more now on its past glamour. Henry James had used it as a setting for the first part of *Daisy Miller* (1870).

In Switzerland, too, domestic tensions can no longer be denied. They are caused by the need to join in on modern life and to be part of the ongoing process of European integration. It is questionable if on the long run Switzerland will be able to maintain her distance from what is happening in the world.

Ravenna, [End of July], 1970

Two Times 800 Years: Dante and T.S. Eliot

When in 1320 Dante Alighieri, shortly before his death, sought refuge in the Franciscan Monastery of Ravenna, the Basilica of the Monastery, built in the 6th century, was already 800 years old. There also stands Dante's Tomb erected in 1780.

St. Thomas à Becket, archbishop of Canterbury, was murdered in the Cathedral of Canterbury in 1170. This summer, on the 800th anniversary of his death, T.S. Eliot's *Murder in the Cathedral* (1935) is being performed in Italian translation as "Assassino nella Cattedrale" on the square of the Basilica. The performance of Eliot's liturgical drama in verse against the venerable historical background of the Basilica gives such an impression of a unified whole that the tragic event, which had happened in the distant past of the medieval Canterbury, can be convincingly relived in the old cathedral town of Ravenna. The translation of the English verses into Italian makes no difference. In this context, the language has only an indirect effect. What counts is the spiritual experience that unites Dante and T.S. Eliot at this special place. So deep and one unified whole are the history and cultural sphere of Europe.

Cervia, [Beginning of August], 1970

The Americans in Europe

The widespread assumption that the Americans can be met everywhere in Europe and that they virtually inundate the Old Continent is totally wrong. Here at the beaches of the Adriatic where millions of Europeans spend their vacation, Americans are rarely seen. Americans come in the summer to Europe for sight-seeing tours. They are on their way throughout Europe by motor coach, stimulating city tourism. While Europeans relax and enjoy themselves at the beaches or in the mountains, the Americans sweat through the old inner cities and endure the sticky air of palaces and museums that usually are not air-conditioned.

Cervia, [Beginning of August], 1970

Italy: Summer 1970

Although one has gotten used to government crises in Italy and is inclined to assume that Italy rules itself also without a government, the reality looks quite different. After the Cabinet of Mariano Rumor had resigned, the continuing political crisis that has caused strikes throughout the country is worrisome. The heavy unrests, which first started in Reggio Calabria in the South, are now also spreading in the Province of Veneto in the North. The demands for higher wages by the metalworkers in Mestre set off a general strike.

Italy still suffers from severe social tensions. The danger that the country may succumb to a swing to the left cannot be denied in view of the fact that the Communists are in control of the municipalities throughout Central Italy. Why does Italy compared to the rest of Europe lag behind? Modern industry is still sparse and unevenly distributed. It is for the most part limited to the Plain of the Po River in the North, stretching from Torino to Milan and Mestre near Venice. Other regions of the country are very backward. Much is still done manually, where machinery should have been used long ago. Europe's widespread economic handicap of burgeoning small trades has been thriving in Italy. As prices are rising, wages hardly cover the bare subsistence. The specter of a "sciopero generale," of a general strike is always hovering over the country. Italy clearly shows that the Common Market is not the panacea for curing the economic weaknesses of a country. Recovery must come from within. Anyway, here the Common Market has not as yet become transparent.

What further worries Italy is the increasing presence of Russia in the Mediterranean. It is indirectly connected with the reckless actions of the Lybian Revolutionary Regime, which arbitrarily confiscated the personal property of Italians living in Lybia. These destitute refugees had to seek shelter in Naples. It remains to be seen if the new Cabinet of Emilio Colombo will be able to cope with the accumulation of so many difficult problems.

Innsbruck, August 12, 1970

German-Soviet Treaty on Renunciation of Force and Cooperation

"Mit diesem Vertrag geht nichts verloren, was nicht längst verspielt worden war." (With this treaty nothing is going to be lost what had not been lost long ago.)

Willy Brandt

Today in the St. Catherine's Hall of the Kremlin, Chancellor Willy Brandt and Premier Alexei Kosygin signed the German-Soviet Treaty on Renunciation of

Force and Cooperation. Without much fanfare, after 25 years of uncertainty and illusory hopes, political reality in Europe was looked into the eye. The existing borders have been recognized and declared inviolable. With one sentence, the Oder-Neisse Line has been recognized as the Western border of Poland and the boundary between East and West Germany accepted as legitimate frontier. Rarely in European history has so much been given and given away with so few words.

After this treaty, the political integration of Europe has become all the more urgent if Europe does not want to be sucked into the Soviet sphere of influence. With the easing of tensions, the need for American protection is being diminished. This could lead to American disengagement, which has been pursued for some time anyway. Europe could enter a phase of neutralization between East and West, which could be an opportunity but also an impending danger.

The New Era of Treaty Euphoria

It may be regarded as an encouraging sign of the present world situation that the big and dangerous issues of conflict between East and West are being brought to mutually agreeable solutions at the conference table. The SALT negotiations in Helsinki and Vienna, the Nuclear Non-Proliferation Treaty as well as the German-Soviet Treaty on Renunciation of Force and Cooperation that was just signed, all have contributed their share. There is hope that the tension charged atmosphere between the two superpowers will be relieved and that solutions for peace will be found by negotiations.

Innsbruck, November 10, 1970

Farewell to Charles de Gaulle (1890-1970)

Charles de Gaulle died as he had lived—in lonely greatness that is awe-inspiring. He was the last prominent figure of World War II. He ruled France and held Europe in his spell. Will Gaullism as a political movement live on?

November 13, 1970

Charles de Gaulle gave the world at his death a gesture of reconciliation. At the official ceremony and the requiem in the Cathedral of Notre Dame heads of state from all continents and nations had assembled, who otherwise appeared to be separated by insurmountable differences. For a moment the world gave the impression of being one family. De Gaulle was buried in a pronounced unassuming way in his hometown of Colombey-Les-Deux-Eglises.

Innsbruck, December 31, 1970

Reflections at Year's End

The most important event of European politics in the past year was without a doubt the German-Soviet Treaty on Renunciation of Force and Cooperation. A logical follow-up was the German-Polish Treaty recognizing the Oder-Neisse Line as the Western border of Poland. After this territorial settlement on a grand scale, the preconditions are given for the European Security Conference, which has been aspired to by the Communist side for a long time. It would seal the status quo in Europe by an international treaty. It could be a chance to secure peace on the long-term, but it could also present the danger of splitting and weakening the Western Alliance. The Communist predominance could overshadow the rest of Europe, which is susceptible to left-wing influence anyhow.

The European economic and consequently also political integration is a slow process that may stretch over decades. But the integration cannot be stopped anymore. The new Europe, which will emerge from this process, will, despite similarities, be essentially different from the United States. A new political entity will come into being with a strong confederative character. There will be a common economy and currency, but for a long time no effective parliament. Europe cannot leave behind its past and suddenly relinquish its manifold national sovereignties. The transition to a European confederation will take time and can only be accomplished gradually.

Innsbruck, March 14, 1971

The Encounter with the Astronaut

[The City of Innsbruck had invited the Astronaut James A. Lovell, Jr., for a goodwill visit.]

The encounter with an astronaut is an exceptional experience that could not be replaced even by the best of telecasts. The opportunity of personally meeting with the most experienced American astronaut, James Lovell, offered itself last night, on Saturday evening, at a reception given in his honor by the Austrian-American Society in Innsbruck. After 700 hours in space, Lovell was an image of radiant health, giving no indication that the long exposure to weightlessness had left any physical damage. As a person Lovell is unpretentious, more of a sportsmanlike simplicity, but deeply religious. He told the story of the failed Apollo 13 mission. According to his own account, the most moving moment in his career as astronaut occurred when, on board of Apollo 8 at Christmas 1968, he entered the far side of the moon. For the first time in human experience, the earth vanished from man's sight. However, when Lovell narrated how on its return flight the Apollo 13 spacecraft had nearly missed the earth by a hair's breadth and could have revolved around the sun perpetually, the audience felt a cold shiver running down the spine.

Although spaceflights go to the limit of human endurance, and often it seems beyond it, the astronaut has incorporated space and spaceflights into the human experience. Space has become a part of our environment. For people of the 20th century, a new dimension of the heroic has been opened, which otherwise was lost long ago. While the complexity of space technology remains incomprehensible for most people, the undivided admiration stays focused on the astronaut. Lovell's visit clearly demonstrated that the human element in space exploration is necessary and that manned spaceflights fulfill a meaningful purpose.

Innsbruck, May 15, 1971

Ceterum Censeo

Whenever Mike Mansfield raises his voice in the U.S. Senate, demanding the reduction of American troops in Europe, it sounds like a *ceterum censeo*. And each time, one can sense the precarious defense situation of Europe, which is irrefutably based on the presence of American troops. Mansfield's recent demand to reduce the 300,000 American troops stationed in Europe by half until December 31 is hardly taken seriously. But in view of the growing foreign trade deficit and the weakening U.S. dollar, his arguments are gaining in significance. The reduction of American troops cannot be prevented on the long run. Europe should be prepared for this day in order not to create an unprotected power vacuum.

[Michael (Mike) J. Mansfield, born 1903 in New York, moved to Butte, Montana; a mining engineer, historian and politician, he was regarded as an expert on Southeast Asia. Mansfield served as Democrat from Montana in the U.S. Congress, 1942-77; first as Congressman, 1942-52, and then as Senator, 1953-77. Following Lyndon B. Johnson, he assumed the position of Majority Leader of the Senate. As he was many times dealing with foreign affairs, he spoke up for American troop reductions in Europe as well as in Asia. After 1977 Mansfield served as U.S. Ambassador to Japan.]

Innsbruck, [Beginning of July], 1971

The Admission of Great Britain to the Common Market

The essential event of European politics in the first half of this year was without a doubt the agreement reached by the European Community on the admission of Great Britain to the Union of Six. As the signals have been set on the go-ahead, Great Britain must now come to terms with the centuries-old reservations against the Continent and find its way to Europe. By Great Britain's joining the Common Market, new possibilities for Europe will be in the offing. A common market of 286 million people could emerge, which would soon attract all European states and inevitably also bring about political integration. The vote in the House of Commons in October on joining the Common Market is of historic importance. A United Europe with Great Britain could become the third force between the two superpowers.

Innsbruck, [Middle of July], 1971

The Distrust of America

There is still a deep-rooted distrust of America at all levels of European society. The physician does not trust his American colleague that he can make the right diagnosis. The dentist questions whether well fitting dentures can be put in place. In the view of teachers, American schools are not worth anything. The teller at the bank warns that money is losing its value in America. The innkeeper doubts whether a tasteful meal can be prepared. In general, people share the view that one cannot walk on the streets in Chicago without risking to be mugged. The most widespread assumption is that Americans have no culture at all. The list of distrust could be prolonged at will. Despite the increased transatlantic traffic, it is very difficult to overcome these prejudices.

Innsbruck, July 17, 1971

The two most remarkable artistic events, which my wife and I experienced during the past two years were the performances of *Salome* by Richard Strauss at the Deutsche Oper Berlin and Mozart's *Don Giovanni* conducted by Herbert von Karajan at the Salzburg Festival.

[My family and I left Innsbruck on July 18. We drove by rental car via Strasbourg, Nancy, Reims, Paris, Chartres, Rouen to Le Havre, where we embarked on the *France*. Being aware of the forthcoming emigration to America, this journey through Germany and France was an especially poignant experience.]

Le Havre, July 23, 1971

Travel Impressions

A journey through Germany and Northern France still shows the devastating destructions of both World Wars. Hundreds of kilometers around Verdun, the traces left by the fierce battles fought in the First and the Second World War are still clearly visible: Countless military cemeteries, where only a fraction of the nearly one million soldiers from all nations who lost their lives are buried; to a large extent ravaged stretches of land, where the vegetation and forests have not as yet fully recovered; bomb-destroyed cities, burned-down churches, evacuated houses hit by shell-fire line the streets. The horrifying losses of people, of cultivated land, as well as the loss of art treasures come into view. The wounds afflicted by two World Wars have not as yet completely healed.

The French province makes a bleak, depressed impression. Despite the abundant fertility of the country, the small towns and villages are impoverished. They seem to be going through a depression, which turns entire regions into emergency areas. It is surprising to see how little of the tourist trade has taken hold of the country outside of Paris. France suffers from serious structural problems concerning its agriculture, educational system and the retail trade.

Generally speaking, one can say that Europe as a whole would need a supranational area planning. So far, very little has been done in this regard. Area planning is still carried out according to national concepts and priorities. While North and South from Hamburg to Naples are connected by a superhighway system, East and West are not. It is hard to believe that there is no four-lane highway between Strasbourg and Paris, nor is there one planned.

Islands of Beauty

Despite the problems that depress agricultural regions and plague industrial zones, Europe has islands of beauty. Among these are the mountainscape of the Alps, the splendor of castles and palaces, like the Belvedere Palace in Vienna and Fontainebleau near Paris, the exalted architecture of medieval cathedrals, like the Strasbourg Cathedral and the Cathedral of Chartres, the picturesque, idyllic Barbizon, and much more. In order to see and to enjoy the beauty and cultural treasures of Europe, it will always be worthwhile making a pilgrimage across the Atlantic and to go on the Grand Tour in the sense of Henry James.

[The *France* left Le Havre late afternoon of July 23. After a calm, five day crossing, she landed at the Hudson River pier in New York. It was the last Atlantic crossing of this elegant passenger ship. Also for me and my family, it was our last Atlantic crossing by boat.]

PART II 1971-1979

The Decade of the Détente

Section 5: July 28, 1971-December 31, 1973

Section 6: January 20, 1974-August 17, 1976

Section 7: End of August, 1976-December 31, 1979

SECTION 5

July 28, 1971-December 31, 1973

New York, July 28, 1971

Arrival in New York City

Even after an absence of one year or two, one is surprised to find this city has changed faster and more dramatically than any other metropolis on earth. With the two new towers of the World Trade Center, the skyline of New York has changed completely. Also, the results of urban renewal with its new high-rises along Broadway between 42nd and 56th streets are stunning. On the other hand, the declining passenger steamship traffic has left the piers on the Hudson River deserted. New York is losing its significance as the main harbor of entry to North America. It is, however, holding its position as the business and financial center of the United States if not the world. The sheer abundance of material goods and the display of wealth are overwhelming. The cultural and ethnic diversity of the city is extremely fascinating. There is nothing like it anywhere else in the world. New York will always remain unfinished; here the process of the American melting pot is continuously in the making.

South Bend, August 20, 1971

The Financial Crisis

Nothing could have shaken Europe, parts of South America and Asia more than President Nixon's announcement over the television networks last

Sunday, August 15, that the United States will no longer convert the dollar into the gold parity of $35 an ounce. This means indeed a drastic change in the international monetary system which has been based on the gold parity of the U.S. dollar since the Bretton Woods agreement of July 1944. Coupled with a 90 day price and wage freeze at home as well as a 10% surcharge on foreign imports, it certainly is the most drastic turnabout in U.S. economic policy since World War II. While the United States concentrates on the price and wage freeze, foreign countries are struggling to find new parities to the dollar. Since the Common Market finance ministers could not agree on a binding solution, outright chaos is threatening the financial markets. Each individual country is trying to adopt a policy that will best guard its own interests. The floating dollar parity actually signifies a devaluation of the dollar, but this has been long overdue in any case.

St. Ignace, Michigan, [End of August], 1971

Northern Michigan

Coming from abroad, one is taken by surprise by how much of the original pioneer spirit is still alive in Northern Michigan. The areas by the Manistee and Huron National Forests near Houghton Lake offer enough room for those enterprising folks who like to live in trailer homes, clear a patch of land, and grow some corn. The atmosphere of the lumber camp still prevails immediately adjacent to an ultra-modern Ford automobile plant. In the Upper Peninsula, north of Mackinac Bridge, the wilderness is even more authentic. Here, the Hiawatha National Forest covers the strip of land between Lake Michigan and Lake Superior with an endless canopy of green. For a short vacation in pristine nature, no better place could be found.

South Bend, Labor Day Weekend, [Beginning of September], 1971

False Perception of the United States

The great ignorance of the domestic situation as well as the false perception of the United States has, at the present financial crisis, caused again helplessness and consternation. Countries in Western Europe and Asia, which carry on trade with the United States and are closely connected with America, are usually lacking in understanding of American history and of the social and political conditions. They are, therefore, in the dark when they are suddenly confronted with a decision from Washington.

South Bend, [End of September], 1971

The Question of China Before the United Nations

The incongruities within the United Nations have rarely come to light so bluntly as at this year's opening session of the General Assembly in New York. The small Taiwan or Nationalist China is holding in check the Security Council with its veto power. In the meantime, the People's Republic of China is refusing to join the United Nations as long as the representatives of Chiang Kai-shek keep their seats in the Organization. It remains to be seen if the Two China or dual representation policy stipulated by the United States will be successful.

South Bend, September 30, 1971

Fall on the Potomac and East River

With the beginning of fall, the emphasis of world politics is again shifting to Washington and New York. While the General Assembly of the United Nations is in session in New York, the finance ministers of the International Monetary Fund (IMF) are meeting in Washington to find a solution for the reserve currency. It has also become customary that the Russian foreign minister Andrei Gromyko uses his presence at the United Nations as an opportunity to meet with the U.S. president. A time of intensive diplomatic talks is at hand in which the adjustment of interests and a balanced deployment of troops in Europe are being discussed. Also, a debate on the relaxation of tension in Asia is taking place. President Nixon may count it as a success that the global situation has been decisively eased, and that the emotionally charged rhetoric has given way to a carefully considered *realpolitik*.

South Bend, October 1, 1971

In Memory of John A. Hawgood (1905-1971)

The last time I met with Professor John Hawgood was in April this year at the Hotel Grünwalderhof in Patsch near Innsbruck. As always, he was full of plans.

He was just preparing the edition of a German travel report in English translation for the Lakeside Press of the R.R. Donnelley and Sons Company in Chicago. This travel report describes the opening of the Northern Pacific Railroad which in 1883 connected Minneapolis with Portland, Oregon. John wanted by all means that I collaborated with him on this project. I finally agreed that I would try to find the German source material for that report. At the same time, John Hawgood was working on a history of San Francisco for which his profound knowledge of California would have been the best prerequisite. Furthermore, he had in mind to work on several articles. Among these would have been a study of the diplomatic correspondence of the American envoy to the Imperial Court in Vienna in the 19th century. We had agreed to meet at the Newberry Library in Chicago in October. Yesterday, the publisher of the Lakeside Press called me up and told me that John Hawgood had died after a heart attack on September 16 in Santa Barbara, California. He was 65 years old. John Hawgood was professor of American history at the University of Birmingham in England. He had studied history in Oxford, Heidelberg, and Vienna. From early on, he pursued his research interest in the American West. I got acquainted with John at the Huntington Library in the summer of 1961. In the following years we maintained a fruitful exchange of ideas. In his lifetime he had crossed the Atlantic about forty times. John Hawgood was for me a model of the world open scholar who was at home on both sides of the Atlantic.

Addendum

[The edition of the travel report on the opening of the Northern Pacific Railroad was continued by Ray Allen Billington, Professor of history at Northwestern University and Senior Research Associate at the Huntington Library in San Marino, California. The original text of Nicolaus Mohr (1826-1886), *Ein Streifzug durch den Nordwesten Amerikas. Festfahrt zur Northern Pacific-Bahn im Herbste 1883* (Berlin, 1884) appeared in the Lakeside Classics Series as *Excursion Through America* (Chicago: R.R. Donnelley, 1973). I wrote the Epilogue, "Nicolaus Mohr as Foreign Observer of the United States," pp. 353-68.]

South Bend, October 16, 1971

The Adaptation

Whoever immigrates to America will experience a distinct psychological change in the process of adaptation. At first everything is foreign and totally different. After a few months, the most familiar memories of the old home country fade away. What one gradually loses from memory are the sounds of old musical instruments, the relief over the portal of a gothic cathedral as well as the rich tint of colors of the Alps. Especially, the certainty in using one's native tongue is being lost. In a conversation with acquaintances already advanced in age that have lived here for decades, I have noticed a peculiar linguistic phenomenon. While their native tongue has become clumsy, they have never really learned to speak correct English. Many immigrants are moving in a mixed linguistic no-man's-land. As the second generation grows up speaking English, the language of the home country of their parents is gradually forgotten. Then the language of their parents or grandparents is mostly learned again through foreign language instruction in schools and colleges. America is extremely tolerant with foreign accents. But on the other hand, a strict purism in teaching English is observed in schools. After a short period of time living in the United States, the European way of life vanishes. Over time it appears to be unreal. What is left is the idealization of the old home country, which turns into an illusion.

A Feeling of Calmness

There is a feeling of calmness and unconcern in America that is unknown in Europe. Nothing seems to be so exceptionally important or distressing anymore. There is no fear anymore of an overthrow of the government, of the state interfering in the private sphere, or that a war could break out. The problems of world politics lose their frightening immediacy. One can talk with ease about Berlin, Prague, or East Pakistan without getting excited. Even the problem of the dollar devaluation is not of much concern to the individual American, unless he or she is presently living abroad. There are few events that would disrupt the flow of everyday life in America, or would set one off balance. Arriving here from Europe, one gradually begins to feel this general equanimity and connected with it a balanced calmness.

South Bend, October 17, 1971

The Strength of the Middle Class

Whatever the outside world may learn about the extravagances of America, it should not be overlooked that the American middle class is keeping things in balance. The large American middle class lives in the suburbs. Its members live a normal family life; they go to church on Sundays and care for the education of their children. This America is healthy and will endure despite all challenges.

Violence on the Streets

But it should also be kept in mind that the streets in the inner cities are dominated by sheer violence. Here, criminal offenses are worse, the victims of brutal violence more frequent than one would like to realize.

South Bend, October 18, 1971

The Cultural Isolation

When the United States goes through a period of political and economic isolation, as is the case at this time, it also affects its cultural life. Suddenly, highly-qualified persons and top performers from abroad are not to be seen or heard anymore on the stage and in concert halls. Also, well known names are missing on the guest lecture tours of American colleges and universities. Especially conspicuous is the decline of the cultural exchange with Europe. A certain intellectual dearth and cultural scantiness cannot be denied. The cultural life is in danger of becoming shallow and to relapse into provincialism.

South Bend, October 25, 1971

The Vote on China

Today the General Assembly of the United Nations voted on China. The Albanian resolution to admit the People's Republic of China as the only representation of the Chinese people passed with 76 in favor, 35 against, and 17 abstentions. On the contrary, the resolution by the U.S. Ambassador George Bush that the vote on China should require a two-thirds majority was rejected. Thereby, the American dual representation policy was defeated. After the vote, the representatives of the Republic of China on Taiwan or Nationalist China left the World Organization.

The jubilation in the General Assembly over the victory in the China question turned into pandemonium. Such scenes have never before been seen on the East River. In the frenetic ecstasy by the Marxist Afro-Asian and Euro-Communist nations it would have been difficult to distinguish what counted more the joy over the admission of the People's Republic of China to the United Nations or the glee over the American defeat. The most dejected and lonely figure in the General Assembly was Ambassador George Bush. This obvious demonstration against the United States in the United Nations shocked the American public. It will even more so strengthen the trend toward isolationism. But the decision by the United Nations does not come altogether inconveniently for the Nixon Administration, for it opens the way for a concrete China policy and relieves the President of a heavy burden before his upcoming journey to Peking.

[The later American President George Herbert Walker Bush was U.S. Ambassador to the United Nations, 1971-73; he was Chief of the U.S. Liaison Office to the People's Republic of China in Peking, 1974-75. For further biographical reference see the entry of January 20, 1989.]

South Bend, October 28, 1971

Great Britain in the Common Market

Almost ten years to the day since Charles de Gaulle's veto in 1961, the British Parliament voted in favor of Great Britain joining the Common Market. The Conservatives under Prime Minister Edward Heath won the debate on Europe in the House of Commons with 356 in favor and 244 against. Also a substantial part of the Labor opposition voted in favor. This is a great day for Europe, for a big step forward has been taken toward European unification.

South Bend, December 14, 1971

The Dollar Devaluation

After meeting with French President George Pompidou in the Azores, President Nixon announced that the dollar will be devaluated. This news made no stir in the United States because the dollar had been exposed to an unofficial devaluation months ago. Thus, the unthinkable believed to upset the entire international monetary system has come about in an undramatic fashion and has been officially confirmed without much ado.

December 18, 1971

At their meeting in Washington, the finance ministers of the ten wealthiest democratic industrial countries agreed to devalue the U.S. dollar by 7.89 or about 8%. In conjunction with it, the revaluation of the DM (German Mark) is expected to be about 14%. This means that the exchange rate of the dollar to the DM would be 1: 3.22.

The U.S. government expects that the devaluation of the dollar will make American products more competitive in Europe, and that it would create half a million new jobs. At the same time, the U.S. foreign trade deficit should be reduced by 10 billion dollars. While here in this country the dollar devaluation is hardly taken notice of, it has a severe effect on Americans living abroad. On the other hand, the standard of living in Europe is being brought closer to that in America.

South Bend, December 29, 1971

U.S. Presence in Europe Upheld

The summit meeting between President Nixon and German Chancellor Willy Brandt under the palm trees of Key Biscayne in Florida was marked by a cordial atmosphere. Brandt may have received Nixon's approval for his Ostpolitik as well as a firm pledge that the presence of American troops in Europe will be upheld. The strength of the 300,000 American troops stationed in Europe will not be reduced. To affirm the American will of engagement in Europe, the former Secretary of the Treasury David M. Kennedy was sent as ambassador to NATO. Although structural changes in the Western Alliance have been made, the core of the European defense under the nuclear umbrella of the United States has remained unchanged.

South Bend, [Beginning of January], 1972

A Friendly Word from Bonn

Americans could not have been more surprised when one morning at the beginning of the New Year they saw Chancellor Willy Brandt on the TV screen paying them an honest compliment. He praised the Americans on how polite and friendly they are. Willy Brandt had spent Christmas vacation in Miami with his family. He, thereby, learned to admire the normal American way of life.

South Bend, January 25, 1972

The Secret Negotiations on Vietnam

Tonight on national TV President Nixon lifted the veil of secrecy over the negotiations, which Dr. Henry Kissinger had conducted with North Vietnam to end the war. In fact, it was an admission that neither the secretly private nor the official negotiations in Paris led to any results. The American offer entails the complete withdrawal of American and Allied troops within six months if the opposite side agrees to an exchange of prisoners and a cease-fire. Until now the American proposals have fallen on deaf ears. But whatever can still be agreed upon, the Nixon Administration will end the War in Vietnam in any case and bring the American troops home before the presidential election in November.

Secret Diplomacy

It is hard to believe that in a time when even the smallest incident in the most remote corner of the world remains exposed to the media, a secret diplomacy to such an extent was possible. Five different ways, Henry Kissinger succeeded in getting in and out of Paris thirteen times without being noticed. [In-between, he flew secretly to Peking to prepare President Nixon's journey to China.]

[Henry A. Kissinger, born 1923 in Fürth, Bavaria; he came 1938 to the United States and was naturalized, 1943. He earned his Ph.D. at Harvard University, 1954. As a faculty member at Harvard he taught courses on government and international affairs, 1957-69. His book, *Nuclear Weapons and Foreign Policy,* was published in 1957. In 1969 he was called to the White House as President Nixon's National Security Adviser. He served as U.S. Secretary of State, 1973-77. Henry Kissinger led the negotiations to end the War in Vietnam, for which he was awarded the Nobel Peace Prize in 1973.]

South Bend, [End of January], 1972

A Continent Is Being Consolidated

The special achievement of today's America is to be found in the logistics, how, with the help of the computer, it has become possible to consolidate a continent of 200 million people. Space explorations, just as Social Security, the registration at a university, the income tax, or the advertising of a garden center are part of this process. So, for example, a garden center in Washington state mails rose bushes across the entire country, which have been cultivated to adapt to the various climatic zones. The real potential of America has by far not as yet been exhausted. It is a country that is still fermenting and growing. But a society that is organized and controlled by the computer can be frightening. A Social Security number issued to a person serves as identification for the work place, tax return, health insurance, and the driver's license. Each person is kept on record by the Social Security number.

The interest in America today is so great because future developments emerge here, which later on spread over other continents. This applies to the economic development, new technologies, as well as the education and behavior of the young generation.

South Bend, February 2/3, 1972

Sapporo, Japan

Today the Eleventh Winter Olympic Games were opened in Sapporo. It is the first Winter Olympics carried out in Asia. The opening ceremony, which was telecast via satellite throughout the world, was a splendid event. However, it was strange and highly unusual to see the slopes and runs of a Winter Olympics with an open view on the sea. Sapporo also proves that winter sports are no longer the exclusive domain of the Alpine countries. It is not so much the terrain that is all important, for mountains with snow and winter sports facilities can be found in many places. What counts for the Olympic competition are the exceptional talent and the team.

South Bend, [Middle of February], 1972

How to Write about America?

It almost takes courage to write positively about America, for it has become widespread fashionable to criticize America and to drag it through the mud. I have not come here to criticize or to glorify America, but to observe and try to understand it.

South Bend, February 17, 1972

The Journey to China

Today President and Mrs. Nixon embarked on their historic journey to China. The good wishes that accompany them come from the heart. A new wave of enthusiasm for China is surging in America. TV stations are continuously carrying programs on the history of China. Pearl S. Buck, who had lived on as a legend, was brought back to memory. There is also an attempt at explaining the Communist Revolution. China has remained for the West a big puzzling question. Just opening the gates to Peking and trying to introduce a way of understanding with the People's Republic of China would already be achievement enough for this journey. After years of hate campaigns, what impact will the arrival of the President of the United States have on the Chinese population?

February 22, 1972

The Arrival in Peking

Although, upon arriving at the Peking airport, the reception of the American President was more on the cool side, the ice broke on the second day. The addresses by Premier Chou En-lai and President Nixon at the state dinner in the Great Hall of the People left no doubt that both sides are seeking an understanding. But only when the pictures of President Nixon's meeting with Mao Tse-tung were released in the Chinese press, the interest of the Chinese population in this historic event was awakened. People stood in line to get a copy of the Peking "People's Daily."

These days a change in attitude between America and China is coming about. TV reports are bringing China closer to viewers by a human approach. Mao's Long March is presented as a heroic deed. The images from Peking show that Nixon's courageous visit has come at the right time. A twenty-year long anti-American propaganda has not been able to destroy a secret admiration for America. Also in America long hidden sympathies for China have been brought to light. Along with the fact that the contacts between the United States and Mainland China have been revived makes this journey an historical event of the first order.

February 28, 1972

The Shanghai Communiqué

Shortly before President Nixon and the American delegation returned home, a joint communiqué was issued today in Shanghai. Therein, the American side assents to the Chinese point of view that Taiwan or Nationalist China is a constituent part of the People's Republic of China. The solution of the Taiwan question is a matter of Chinese domestic affairs in which no interference from outside should take place. This is obviously the price the United States had to pay for the reconciliation with the People's Republic. Thereby, America is in agreement with the one China policy. However, since the resolution on China in the United Nations last October, this does not come as a surprise anymore.

[The passage referring to Taiwan in the Shanghai Communiqué of February 28, 1972 reads: "The Government of the People's Republic of China is the sole legal government of China; Taiwan is a province of China which has long returned to the motherland; the liberation of Taiwan is China's internal affair in which no other country has the right to interfere" (Henry Kissinger, *White House Years*, p. 1492).]

Returning Home

President Nixon had dared to take a courageous step. On his return he and Mrs. Nixon were given an enthusiastic reception at the airport of Andrews Air Force Base in Washington. It may well have been the first time that Nixon radiated a kind of charisma. He was the outstanding personality of the day. But there were also critical voices heard that he had made concessions without getting much in return. To what extent this is true, the future will show. In any case it is a fact that in the past week a decisive shift in power politics in the world has occurred.

South Bend, March 14, 1972

The Demand for Troop Reduction

Senator Mike Mansfield has stressed again his demand for the reduction of American troops in Europe. At the present time, he argued, the U.S. maintains 300,000 soldiers and 250,000 dependants in Europe, costing 14 billion dollars annually. America cannot afford this in the long run.

South Bend, March 14, 1972

Primaries

It is a certainty that Richard Nixon will be the candidate of the Republicans for reelection as president. Yet on the Democratic side a broad field of candidates has entered the primaries. At the top of the list are the Senators Edmund Muskie, George McGovern, Hubert Humphrey, and Henry Jackson. However, the great surprise in today's Florida primary was Governor Wallace who attracted 42% of the Democratic votes. Wallace campaigned against "school busing," whereby he hit a sensitive nerve in the South.

South Bend, March 27, 1972

Anxiously Waiting for the Green Card

[Since the 1960s America had a growing surplus of academics who could not find employment. This resulted in restricting to a high degree the immigration of scholars and scientists. I had entered the United States with my family on an H-1 visa, which could be changed into an immigration visa. I regarded that change as a mere formality. That was a big mistake. Toward the end of February, 1972, I was informed by the Immigration and Naturalization Service (INS) that my application for immigration had been denied. That was a hard blow. From that moment on, anxiously waiting for the green card had begun. Until that time I did not even know what the green card was. The so-called "green card" is the identification for having completed the immigration process. It grants permission for gainful employment and permanent residence in the United States. Notre Dame appealed on my behalf. The University had to prove that my teaching was indispensable for its foreign study program and that there were no local teachers available who could do the job. Waiting for the outcome of this appeal was the most difficult time my wife and I had to endure in America. It opened our eyes to how difficult and complicated immigration can be. We drove several times to Hammond, Indiana, to get information from the Bureau of the INS there about the status of our visa. The following short note of March 27 tells of our impressions during one of those visits.]

The hours in the small waiting room of the INS Bureau in Hammond, Indiana, are agonizing. The predicaments of the people who stand in line here can be seen on their faces. My wife and I are waiting here for information whether we are allowed to stay or have to leave the country by the end of June.

Addendum

[By the end of May I finally received word from the INS in Chicago that my application for immigration had been approved. Immediately thereafter the immigration was processed by the INS Bureau in Hammond, which now made a much more friendly impression. On August 29, see entry below, the immigration visas with the green cards for me and my family were issued.]

South Bend, [Beginning of May], 1972

Thinning Out

Since about half of the primaries have been held, the field of Democratic candidates is thinning out. Edmund Muskie withdrew after the primaries in Pennsylvania and Ohio. Yet Hubert Humphrey remains an attractive candidate. Also, after the primary in Florida, George Wallace stays at the top of the list. However, it is George McGovern who has turned out to be the front-runner of the Democrats. As populist he shapes the new image of the Democratic Party. He has great appeal and must be taken into account for the nomination. But everything remains open until the National Convention of the Democratic Party in Miami.

South Bend, May 8, 1972

The Blockade of Haiphong

As a measure against the latest North Vietnamese offensive, President Nixon announced a blockade of the harbor of Haiphong. Again, the world is anxiously waiting whether Russia will react to this American course of action. Should the War in Vietnam escalate into a worldwide conflict after all?

Addendum

After several days it has become apparent that the Soviet Union will not intervene. Vietnam remains a regional conflict that does not lead to a confrontation between the two superpowers. Also, the planned trip of President Nixon to Moscow will not be affected by it.

South Bend, Monday, May 15, 1972

The Assassination Attempt on George Wallace

At a campaign rally for tomorrow's primary in Maryland, an assassination attempt on Governor George Wallace occurred at the Shopping Center of Laurel, a suburb of Washington. Wallace was shot at close range. He was severely, but fortunately not fatally wounded. It was again the deed of a psychopathic individual who had mingled with the crowd of people.

[George C. Wallace, born 1919, was a four term Governor of Alabama, 1963-87. He was paralyzed by the assassination attempt and bound to a wheelchair for the rest of his life. Wallace died in September, 1998.]

South Bend, May 19/20, 1972

Die Ostverträge—The Treaties with the Eastern Bloc States

The acceptance of the Ostverträge or treaties with the Eastern Bloc states by the Bundestag, the German Parliament in Bonn, was for sure taken notice of in the United States but not commented on corresponding to their significance. The majority of Americans will therefore have little understanding of what the Moscow and Warsaw treaties mean for Europe. This demonstrates again that Americans are not adequately informed about issues like the Ostverträge or the Common Market. By and large, Americans show little interest in the political and economic questions in Europe.

[Transl: The so-called Ostverträge refer to the German-Soviet Treaty on Renunciation of Force and Cooperation and the German-Polish Treaty recognizing the Oder-Neisse Line as Western border of Poland. Chancellor Willy Brandt had signed these treaties in 1970. The Bundestag ratified the Ostverträge with the Soviet Union and the Socialist Republic of Poland on May 17, 1972. The treaties came into effect on June 3, 1972.]

South Bend, May 21, 1972

Stopover in Salzburg

The stopover in Salzburg, which President Nixon had chosen on his flight to Moscow, moved Austria into the limelight of the world press. President and Mrs. Nixon were received with hospitality at the Klesheim Palace, the guest house of the Austrian government outside the City of Salzburg. Yet the headlines and images that are disseminated by the media are not what the Festival City has expected or deserved. While Chancellor Bruno Kreisky as host of the Austrian government is entertaining the American guests in Klesheim, one sees images of Salzburg how security forces and demonstrators are engaging in regular street battles. Is it only the Austrian left or the international left in general that has gathered here to demonstrate against the American President?

[In *White House Years,* p. 1204, Henry Kissinger emphasizes the international experience and diplomatic skill of Bruno Kreisky, which had also impressed President Nixon. Kissinger does not mention the demonstrations.]

South Bend, May 26, 1972

The Moscow Summit

How pragmatic world politics has become was proven last week at the Summit in Moscow. Neither the blockade of Haiphong, nor the American rapprochement with Peking, or the differences in the Middle East could disturb the friendly atmosphere of President Nixon's state visit in Moscow. It has once more been demonstrated that the two superpowers would not allow themselves to be diverted by regional conflicts from negotiating about the urgent problems, concerning their own interests and in a wider sense the security of the world. Today the Strategic Arms Limitation Treaty (SALT) was signed in the Kremlin. Negotiations on this Treaty had been carried on for two and half years in Helsinki and in Vienna. The matter for negotiation was the Anti-Ballistic Missile (ABM) system as well as the size and number of nuclear warheads. An essential step has been taken to ease the tensions of East-West relations.

[In the chapter "The SALT Negotiations Conclude" *(White House Years,* pp. 1229-46), Henry Kissinger gives a survey of the difficult negotiations that led to the conclusion of SALT I. As he points out, the United States had a technological advantage in the Anti-Ballistic Missile (ABM) system, while the Soviet Union had a lead in Inter-Continental Ballistic Missiles (ICBMs). It was necessary to achieve a balance between these two systems.]

Addendum

At the Moscow Summit further agreements were reached in regard to cooperation in space and taking common measures against environmental pollution. At the same time, prospects were held out for strengthening cultural and scientific exchange. Without a doubt, the Moscow Summit has ushered in a new era of détente between the United States and the Soviet Union.

South Bend, May 27, 1972

The Drive for Business Expansion

[When a local concern for refrigeration engineering and air conditioning acquired a smaller family owned company in Munich, I was asked to assist in the language communication between the two partners. That way I got a first hand insight into how such a transaction is being carried out.]

American companies are driving for expansion. They usually expand on the American domestic market and at the same time in Europe and Southeast Asia. What does really happen when an American concern takes over a German company? Usually, businesses are acquired that are insolvent or can no longer stand the fierce competition. The American concern has the financial resources and the management experience to modernize the acquired company. The American parent company may also have the new technical equipment, which is not as yet available in Europe. By selling, the German owner gains a profit in the short-term, but gives up any say in the management of the company. The American concern proceeds from different assumptions. The name of the German company, which is usually maintained, helps to open new markets throughout the Common Market area as well as in North Africa and the Middle East. It also calculates with lower wages, which, however, do not always apply anymore. When different opinions in management clash, an attempt will be made to resolve differences in good understanding. The American worker is willing to accept working conditions, which his European counterpart would not take. Here, women are still standing at the lathe and do the welding, which can hardly be seen in Europe anymore.

[The strong trend of transatlantic mergers and business takeovers set in at the beginning of the 1990s. Above all, German concerns merged with American firms or acquired weaker American companies. That was an essential factor for the global development of the world economy.]

South Bend, Friday, July 14, 1972

The Democratic National Convention in Miami Beach

This week the delegates of the Democratic Party assembled in Miami Beach to nominate their candidate for the presidential election. After George McGovern had won the important California primary, he advanced to the position of favorite candidate who has dominated this National Convention. As it was declared an "open convention," delegates of minorities and various ethnic groups could be admitted. Rarely has a National Convention shown such a wide range of diverse interest groups. By his idealism McGovern attracted the young, students from high schools and colleges, who support his campaign as volunteers. The Convention has been completely under the directives of these youthful volunteers so that it resembled at times a Scouts jamboree. The Democratic Party has shown a new face. As Arthur Miller remarked: "This is not the Democratic Party anymore, this is a third party under the disguise of the former Democratic Party." At the conclusion of the Convention, George McGovern was nominated the presidential candidate of the Democratic Party by a large majority. He proposed Senator Thomas F. Eagleton of Missouri as his running mate. The proposal was accepted without objection. The question remains whether McGovern will be able to hold these manifold divergent interests together until the election in November.

[George S. McGovern, born 1922; professor of history and political science; U.S. Senator from South Dakota, 1963-81; presidential candidate of the Democratic Party, 1972.]

South Bend, August 1, 1972

The Eagleton Affair

For one week, America has been spellbound by the revelations about the clinical history of Senator Thomas F. Eagleton, the Democratic candidate for Vice President. As had been found out by the press and then was admitted by

Eagleton, he had to undergo clinical treatment for depression several times. The public pressure got so strong that even from the ranks of his own party doubts have been raised. McGovern finally had to advise his running mate to withdraw. Eagleton followed that advice and resigned from his candidacy.

August 8, 1972

Today the delegates of the Democratic Party met in Washington, D.C., to decide on a successor for Thomas Eagleton. It was a repetition of the National Convention in a smaller form. The delegates elected Robert Sargent Shriver, Jr., who was nominated by a nearly unanimous vote as candidate for the office of Vice President. Through his wife, Eunice Kennedy Shriver, Sargent Shriver is related to the Kennedy family. As Director of the Peace Corps, 1961-66, and as U.S. Ambassador to France, 1968-70, he has become known worldwide. The Democrats are now running on the George McGovern—Sargent Shriver ticket.

South Bend, Wednesday, August 23, 1972

The Republican National Convention in Miami Beach

In the same Hall in Miami Beach, where the Democrats had held their National Convention a month ago, the delegates of the Republican Party assembled for the same purpose. It was a short, lackluster National Convention because the nomination of President Nixon and Vice President Spiro Agnew for reelection was a given from the start. The real event of the Convention was the acceptance speech of President Nixon. The speech was emphatically bipartisan, more addressed to the national television audience than the assembly in the Convention Hall. Nixon reinforced his concept of world peace that is based on the strength of America as well as on his readiness for cooperation.

Addendum

At the beginning of this campaign for the presidency, Nixon is leading by a wide margin over McGovern. Opinion polls showed that 76% of the electorate is convinced Nixon will win this election. The Republicans succeeded in gaining swing voters to their side. Although Nixon is not very much liked, he is respected. He is trusted to execute his duties in the White House well.

South Bend, August 29, 1972

Permanent Residence

Today my family and I were issued the green cards by the Immigration and Naturalization Service in Hammond, Indiana. There was a big sigh of relief. Only if one immigrates oneself, one becomes aware of how many people under different circumstances have gone through a similar experience. Immigration remains a part of American life that cannot be dismissed or forgotten. Every other family has an immigration story to tell.

South Bend, September 24, 1972

An Increased Self-Awareness

Presently, a tendency can be observed in the United States that groups of diverse ethnic and racial origins are showing increased self-awareness. The Civil Rights Bill of 1964 has decisively contributed to this development. Ethnic and racial minorities, who are now thinking more about their cultural heritage, are asserting their rights as citizens. The following example may serve as a case in point: A legal adviser, who belongs to the local tribe of Potawatomi Indians, goes to his office during the week. But on weekends, he dons his feather headdress and participates in the ritual dances of his tribe. This increased self-awareness can especially also be seen in ethnic groups of European descent. There is a big difference in immigration policy between the industrialized countries in Europe and the United States. Contrary to the European countries, America does not take in foreign workers with a time-limited work permit, but gives immigrants permanent residence and grants them citizenship after five years. As a result, the millions of immigrants who had come as industrial workers into this country did not remain foreigners forever, but have assimilated into the mainstream of American life. Only that way was it possible for the American melting pot with its ethnic diversity to develop.

South Bend, September 27, 1972

A Museum for Immigration

Yesterday President Nixon opened the new Museum of Immigration at the foot of the Statue of Liberty. This Museum documents the large wave of immigration before World War I, which brought millions of people, especially from Southern and Eastern Europe, to America.

[In 1965 the Statue of Liberty and Ellis Island were combined into the Statue of Liberty National Monument. From 1892 to 1943 Ellis Island was the Processing Station for immigrants in New York Harbor. During that period about 17 million people passed through Ellis Island, immigrating to the United States. The descendants of that large wave of immigration now make up more than one third of the American population. It should not be overlooked that America is still a young nation of immigrants. In respect for the historical heritage of Ellis Island, its Main Building was restored and opened as Ellis Island Immigration Museum in 1990.]

South Bend, October 8, 1972

The Land of Unlimited Opportunities

The general idea of America as the land of unlimited opportunities has moved millions of people to try their good luck here. Opportunities in America are certainly not unlimited. Many have failed for whom the American Dream has not been fulfilled. But millions of people, who had come to America with only their clothes on their backs, were able to start a business and by being active achieve affluence and esteem. Although rising from rags to fabulous riches has become rarer, America has still remained a land of many opportunities, where by with enterprise and hard work, success can be achieved as nowhere else in the world.

South Bend, [Beginning of October], 1972

The Nobel Prize for Literature

The Nobel Prize for Literature 1972 has been awarded to Heinrich Böll. It thereby goes for the first time to a representative of German post-war literature. Through Böll's writings, the present-day city of Cologne and its environs have, as literary landscape, gained worldwide significance.

South Bend, [Middle of October], 1972

Grass-roots Politics

It is surprising to see how casual and without pretentiousness a well-known Congressman talks to a small election meeting in a public library, shaking hands with everybody and inquiring about the problems someone may have.

This is real grass-roots politics, when the candidate of a Party goes directly to the basis of the democratic election process. Congressman John Brademas, a Democrat, who had been reelected several times here in the 3rd District of Indiana, made no fuss about the fact that as "Mr. Education" in the House he controls the allocation of billions of dollars in the area of public education. Brademas mingled with ease among the people at the meeting, sipped his cup of coffee, and, of course, campaigned for his Party. He did not surround himself with an entourage, nor did he use any titles or symbols of political power. As a newcomer to this country, one has first to get used to this original feeling of democracy.

South Bend, October 26, 1972

The End of the Vietnam War

Today for the first time, Dr. Henry Kissinger confirmed on national television that the Vietnam peace negotiations in Paris have led to a positive result. The end of the War in Vietnam, the longest and bloodiest conflict since 1945, is thereby coming within reach.

[In the Chapter "From Stalemate to Breakthrough" *(White House Years,* pp. 1301-59), Henry Kissinger clearly explains how a breakthrough in the stalled negotiations in Paris was achieved. In the round of negotiations of October 8, 1972, the representative of North Vietnam, Le Duc Tho, accepted, after years of delays, the American proposals, which centered on the following three subjects: (1) Cease-fire; (2) release of prisoners of war; and (3) the withdrawal of American troops from Vietnam. The political problem of South Vietnam remained unresolved, which later turned out to be fatal for Saigon.]

October 29, 1972

Peace is Treading Softly

Peace in Vietnam is treading softly. The war has been going on for ten years. It escalated into endless jungle warfare, and finally ended in a military stalemate. There are no victors or vanquished, no triumph or capitulation. The end of the war is a compromise, in which both sides have given up some of their previous demands.

What are the results of this horrible war?

In this civil war, South and North Vietnam took a heavy toll of lives and suffered enormous damage. Approximately a million and a half lives were lost, and entire regions have been destroyed. Even worse is the barbaric brutalization which this war has produced. Also the United States has suffered heavy casualties. Nearly 45,000 American soldiers died, and in addition there are hundreds of thousands wounded or left behind as disabled veterans. The American public was divided by this war as seldom before in American history. The wounds of this war burden an entire generation.

South Bend, November 8, 1972

The Election Results

Yesterday's presidential election was decided in the evening at 9 p.m. Richard Nixon won a landslide victory over George McGovern. With about 61% of the vote cast for Nixon, the election results come close to those of Lyndon B. Johnson in 1964. It was more the victory of Richard Nixon than that of the Republican Party, for the Democrats were able to hold on to their majority in the Senate and the House.

The convincing reelection of Richard Nixon means that the Nixon era will take shape in world politics. Without a doubt, the policy of détente with the Soviet Union and China will be continued. Nixon's second term will also have special significance for dealing with the European questions that are on the agenda of the forthcoming European Security Conference.

South Bend, [End of November], 1972

Elections to the Bundestag 1972

On November 19 the German elections to the Bundestag, the Lower House of the German Federal Parliament, were held. More than other European parliamentary elections, this German election got a great deal of attention in the United States. The sympathies were from the start on the side of Willy Brandt, whose reelection as Federal Chancellor was beyond doubt. The SPD (Social Democratic Party) won 45.8%, the FDP (Free Democrats) 8.2% of the vote. This gives the coalition government of Willy Brandt over the opposition of the CDU-CSU (Union of the conservative Christian Democrats) a reliable majority. The SPD-FDP coalition received 272 seats in the Bundestag versus the 224 seats of the CDU-CSU.

The election victory of Willy Brandt clearly confirms his Ostpolitik by the German electorate. This opens the way to further talks with the DDR and for bringing the Grundvertag, the basic treaty recognizing the DDR or East Germany as a separate state, to a conclusion. It is also important for the success of the European Security Conference, which has just started in Helsinki.

South Bend, December 7, 1972

The Last Flight to the Moon

Today at 12:30 a.m. the rocket of Apollo 17 lifted off from Cape Kennedy in Florida. It streaked like a shining comet into the sky, turning the night into day. It was an overwhelming sight. This is the last flight to the moon of the Apollo Program.

December 19, 1972

On December 11 the lunar module "Challenger" landed safely in the Taurus-Littrow Valley. The astronauts Eugene Cernan and Harrison Schmitt moved across the terrain on the "lunar rover," collecting soil and rock samples. Although the images of this lunar expedition sent back to earth would have been fascinating enough, the Christmas shoppers in the malls did not let themselves to be distracted. Moon landings have already become too much of a routine. The big enthusiasm about the first moon landing three years ago has given way to the sober realization that there is not much to be gained on the moon. While the public interest in lunar landings has been fading away, their rich scientific yield will occupy laboratories for years to come. With today's perfect splashdown of Apollo 17 in the Pacific near Samoa, the series of lunar landings of the Apollo Program has been completed. No further lunar missions are planned by NASA for the foreseeable future.

Addendum

[The landing on the moon was the most significant exploratory enterprise of the 20th century. It flung the door to human spaceflights wide open. The possibility of establishing manned stations in space has become a tangible reality.]

South Bend, December 21, 1972

The Grundvertrag

By today's signing of the Grundvertrag or Grundlagenvertrag (Basic Treaty between the BRD and the DDR, recognizing each other as sovereign states) in East Berlin, the German question was brought to a temporary solution. The long expected recognition of the DDR or East Germany as a sovereign state, according to international law, has thereby been accomplished. While the world at large tacitly accepts the existence of two German states in Central Europe as a given fact, it remains to be seen how the Germans themselves will be able to cope with the situation. Can the BRD as a free, democratic society and the DDR as a totalitarian, Marxist-Leninist state exist side by side in the long run?

Note

[After the vote in the Bundestag on June 21, 1973, the Grundvertrag or Grundlagenvertrag came into effect. With this Treaty the BRD and the DDR were bound to recognize each other as sovereign states and to observe the inviolability of their borders. But the Grundlagenvertrag did not exclude reunification. The Treaty opened the way for both German states to join the United Nations. In September 1973, the BRD and the DDR were admitted as members to the United Nations.]

South Bend, January 2, 1973

Great Britain in the Common Market

On January 1, 1973, Great Britain joined the Common Market. Advocates of European integration have been waiting for this moment for two decades.

South Bend, January 3, 1973

Adaptation to American Life

Schools are crucial for the adaptation to American life. Children of parents who come from Europe and who go to school here adapt faster to the American way of life than their parents want to realize. And once they have gotten used to it, they should not be sent back and forth across the Atlantic too often. They would inevitably be confronted with an identity crisis. Only when their personality formation has been stabilized to the extent that they can handle the differences in the American and European ways of life should they decide on their own, when and under what circumstances they want to visit Europe.

South Bend, January 27, 1973

Peace in Vietnam

Today at 24 Hrs London-Greewich Time, it was 7 p.m. in the evening on the East Coast of the United States, and already early morning in Saigon, the Vietnam cease-fire has come into effect. Just a few hours earlier, U.S. Secretary of State William Rogers had signed the Vietnam peace agreement in the Hotel Majestic in Paris.

February 4, 1973

America took in the end of the Vietnam War with a sense of great relief. Millions of people felt the need to go to their churches and say a prayer of thankfulness. The longest war in American history has come to an end.

The Release of Prisoners of War

The following distressing events are occurring these days. Families of American prisoners of war, who had first received word that their sons, fathers, husbands will be coming home, had shortly to learn thereafter that the names of their missing loved ones were not on the list the North Vietnamese turned over. The tragedies happening here remind one of returning prisoners at the end of World War II.

South Bend, February 12, 1973

Prisoners of War Are Coming Home

The release and homecoming of the American prisoners of war from North Vietnam and from the jungle camps of the Vietcong led to shocking and heart-wrenching scenes. In many instances, families have been waiting five to seven years for this day, while it has always remained uncertain whether the missing family member would ever come home at all. It was touching to see how the first prisoner of war stepped off the Red Cross plane on Clark Air

Force Base in the Philippines, and how with a trembling but resolute voice he said into the microphone: "God Bless America!"

On the other hand, the release of the North and South Vietnamese prisoners of war showed images of hardly imaginable misery. It was a procession of human figures on crutches wrapped in rags. The atrocious brutality of this war has thereby once more become apparent.

South Bend, February 12, 1973

The Dollar Devaluation

President Nixon decided to devalue the American dollar by 10% in order to counteract last week's pressure caused by speculation. In America the devaluation is taken in strides as it barely affects the domestic market. A dollar devaluation stirs up more alarm in Europe and in Japan than here. But the nearly two million Americans living abroad are less pleased about it. By this devaluation, wage and price levels among the leading industrialized nations are being closer correlated to each other. The international monetary crises that flare up from time to time can only be remedied if the disparity in prices and wages between the United States and the Common Market on the one hand, and Japan on the other, are adjusted. The Nixon Administration seems to be determined to put its own house in order by striving to balance the payment deficit.

South Bend, February 25, 1973

The Downside of Affluence

Although multinational companies in America represent the economic power and affluence of the country, it is often overlooked by what sacrifices this affluence is being achieved. The managers and mid-level employees of these companies are ceaselessly moved around like pawns in a global field of operation. The families involved never really unpack their suitcases completely. One will not be able to fully imagine what this means for the wives who wish to settle down in a permanent home, or for the children who have to change schools continuously. The strained nerves frequently lead to a marriage crisis and divorce. This global movement also concerns the foreign service, the military, and to some extent also the universities. On average, Americans change their addresses every three years. As a result, America has developed one of the most active real estate businesses in the world. One buys a house here like somewhere else a car as a consumer good. But what has so far been an internal migration within the country is now spreading over five continents.

South Bend, March 11, 1973

The French Runoff Elections

Today's runoff elections to the French Parliament brought once more a narrow victory for the Gaullists. The conservative middle class in Western Europe as well as people in the United States were worried, for there was apprehension that the socialist-communist coalition could bring a swing to the left. This could have had unpredictable consequences for the Atlantic Alliance. But how long will it take until this writing on the wall will reappear? In the meantime, will Italy be able to resist the pressure from the left? Is Europe destined to become a neutral zone that will distance itself from America and then involuntarily come under Moscow's sphere of influence? Seen from here, all these questions, one was afraid, were at stake at these French elections.

South Bend, March 12, 1973

The Successful Congenial Affinity

How can you know that the wife of an American with the last name O'Leary came from Sicily and is of Italian descent, or that the grandfather of someone named Casablanca was Irish, or that the in-laws of a Preston had come from Vienna, Frankfurt or Warsaw? The European nations have connected here with one another in the most natural, uncomplicated and matter of fact way. Wouldn't that be comforting for Europe, too? For, why should it not be possible in Europe what has been so prolific and successful here in America?

South Bend, [Middle of March], 1973

Everybody Knows Germany

You wouldn't think it possible that so many Americans know Germany. On a Saturday afternoon I met at least five persons—from the barber, the gas filling station attendant to the shoe salesman—who had been stationed three to six years in Garmisch, Stuttgart or Heidelberg. They all dream now of returning as tourists to Germany or Austria. If for nearly thirty years half a million American soldiers and their families were stationed in Germany, it has had its impact. Still, the broad effect the stationing of American troops in Germany has had, is, nevertheless, surprising.

South Bend, March 28, 1973

The Last Prisoners of War

Today, with the exchange of the last prisoners of war and the withdrawal of the last American troops, the American engagement in Vietnam has come to a close. Mixed with the general feeling of relief is also the determination to say: "Never again!"

South Bend, March 30, 1973

The Surprises of an Academic Career

There are always surprises in an academic career, which at times are not without irony. As a family we had just moved into our new house here in South Bend, when I received an invitation from a well-known German university to apply for the newly-established chair for American Studies. What to do? The decision was not easy. However, after discussing the matter with my wife, the decision was clear: No moving, no change of residence anymore. We wanted to see the fresh seeded lawn in the yard grow green. Also, the fact that Notre Dame had done so much for us was a main reason to stay here.

South Bend, April 5, 1973

Meeting with Arthur Miller

The real Arthur Miller is certainly different from what one imagines him to be: A tall, gaunt figure without affected manners of the author, homespun, almost simplistic, but of compelling fascination. The world-renowned playwright gave an evening with readings from his works on the Notre Dame campus. He read excerpts from his latest work, *The Creation of the World and Other Business,* which is scheduled for its world premiere in New York. It is a Creation and the Fall of Man comedy, whereby the Fall is written with an American sense of pragmatism. The whole piece sounds as if Mark Twain had rewritten the "Prologue in Heaven" in Goethe's *Faust.* The audience was shaking with laughter, but nonetheless gained new insights into life's wisdom. In a question and answer session the next day, Miller explained that he is trying in his plays to give meaning to life. Remarkable was also the excerpt from the autobiography Miller is writing at this time. He tells about his origin in the New York ghetto. His father had come as a six year old child alone to America and grew up in the Jewish ghetto of New York. Miller narrates with a certain nostalgia how Harlem, despite its poverty, was worthwhile living in, where Jewish, Black, and Puerto Rican families lived together peacefully side by side and understood each other. Much of Miller's early life's experience flowed into his work.

Note

[The autobiography of Arthur Miller mentioned above was published as *Timebends: A Life* 1987 in New York. According to the autobiography, the Miller family had originally come from the Polish village of Radomizl, which by the end of the 19th century belonged to the Austro-Hungarian Monarchy. The family was deeply rooted in the Jewish faith and felt connected to the Austrian-German culture. In the 1880s Samuel Miller, the grandfather of the author, had emigrated with his family to America. As the money for the ship ticket was lacking, the youngest child was left behind with an uncle. Later, the barely seven year old boy Isidor, the father of the author, was sent alone across the Atlantic to join the family in New York. Arthur Miller was born 1915 in New York. Among his most important works are *All my Sons* (1947), *Death of a Salesman* (1949), *The Crucible* (1953), *A View from the Bridge* (1955), *After the Fall* (1964), and *The Creation of the World and Other Business* (1972).]

Chicago, April 22, 1973

The View from the John Hancock Center

On a clear day, the Observation Deck on the 94th floor of the still new John Hancock Center, opened in 1969, offers a magnificent panoramic view. To the north you can see along the elegant Lake Shore Drive to Evanston and beyond as far as the adjacent suburbs; to the west you can see as far out as the still open prairie; and to the south one looks with astonishment across the line of high rising new skyscrapers which are being built on North Michigan Avenue and the City Center. From there the eye may rove over Grant Park to the Field Museum of Natural History, the Adler Planetarium, and along the southern shore of Lake Michigan as far down as the industrial conglomerate of South Chicago and Gary in Indiana. Diagonally across from the Hancock Center toward the southwest, there stands the construction of the 110-story high Sears Tower, the highest building in the world that is about to be completed. What one can see here within a 50 mile radius is an encouraging view into the future. Here, the ending 20th century is passing naturally into the 21st. Chicago is a progressive, vibrant city that is continuously renewing itself.

"The largest, the tallest, the fastest in the world"

It is no accident that of all places in Chicago the attributes "the largest, the tallest, the fastest in the world" have become the proud advertisement slogans, which can be seen at every corner of the city. The entrepreneurial spirit is concentrated here to an unusual extent in a number of companies which are indeed the biggest of their kind in the world. Among these are not only the Sears Tower as the highest building in the world and O'Hare as the busiest airport, but also the Merchandise Mart as the largest commercial building, McCormick Palace as the most spacious exhibition hall as well as the Museum of Science and Industry as the largest technological museum in the world. This development had begun with the World's Fair, the World's Columbian Exposition in 1893, whereby Chicago caught the attention of the world. Not for nothing did the skyscraper architecture originate here. By its geographical location at the southwest end of the Great Lakes, Chicago developed into the largest railroad hub in the world. The notorious Chicago "stockyards" were the source for the largest meat processing industry. Sears, Roebuck and Co. advanced to the world's largest mail-order business, while the Board of Trade Building at the end of La Salle Street, the stock exchange of Chicago, became the center for the largest grain market in the world. Chicago is a good example to demonstrate how in America human activities and the potential for development have reached new dimensions. When one arrives in America for the first time, one is often surprised if not intimidated by the super-dimensional. It takes some time to get adjusted to. How did these super-dimensions in America come about? A possible answer could be that the size of the country and the fast industrial development of a continent were a challenge to think big and act in vast dimensions.

South Bend, April 30, 1973

The Scandal: Watergate

When on June 17 last year a group of overzealous Republicans broke into the Democratic Party Headquarters in the Watergate Apartment Complex in Washington, the whole affair looked like a farce or a belated First of April hoax. It was taken as an inroad by a small rightwing clique to which no further significance was attributed for the reelection campaign. Months later, the affair exploded into one of the greatest scandals the White House has ever been involved in. Court proceedings on the Watergate affair now have revealed that the closest inner circle of the President's staff were accomplices of this political espionage. In their overzealousness for the reelection of Richard Nixon, they did not shrink from criminal activity. And by the cover-up, they got even more entangled in guilt. As President Nixon today declared his point of view on the Watergate affair on national television, one could see that this was the most embarrassing speech he had to deliver before the American public. H.R. Haldeman, the White House Chief of Staff, and his closest associate, John D. Ehrlichman, resigned, while John Dean, the personal adviser of the President, was fired. Attorney General Richard Kleindienst resigned because the investigation of this case concerns personal friends. Whatever may come out of the Watergate affair, it casts a dark shadow upon the Nixon Administration and has shaken confidence in the government. Above all, the affair discredits the White House.

[Beginning of May], 1973

A Spate of Litigations

The Watergate scandal triggered a spate of public charges and hearings. They attract so much attention that all other matters are pushed into the background. Thus, the visit of Chancellor Willy Brandt in Washington was hardly taken notice of. What an irony! Just as the talks on the Security Conference in Europe and a number of other important issues should get going, the most important partner is being paralyzed because of a break-in burglary attempt.

May 17, 1973

Watergate Senate Hearings

Today the Senate Select Committee began its public hearings on the Watergate affair. Senator Sam Ervin from North Carolina, who chairs the Committee, has made it his task to find out the truth about Watergate and to make it unsparingly known to the American public. The questioning is proceeding without excuses. As the hearings are shown on national television, the public gets an insight into how the immediate associates of the President had planned a burglary, how enormous sums of campaign contributions were diverted, and how an obvious breach of the law should have been covered up. But in the center of this sordid affair stands the question to what extent the President was involved.

[Sam(uel) J. Ervin, Jr., was born in Morganton, North Carolina, in 1896. A jurist by profession, he served for decades as a judge on the bench; U.S. Senator, Democrat from North Carolina, 1954-75. Ervin was a "country lawyer," as he used to call himself. His folksiness made him a popular figure, and as Chairman of the Senate Select Committee on Presidential Campaign Activities to investigate the Watergate affair in 1973, he became a nationally known prominent personality.]

May 24, 1973

The Human Tragedy

The Watergate scandal has consumed innumerable human lives and careers leading to personal tragedies. People who blindly followed orders were dragged innocently guilty into a power struggle. Behind all this were the temptations of political power, lies and defamations. All stages of despair and hopelessness are being passed through with no way out of this conflict of loyalty.

South Bend, [End of May], 1973

Gasoline Shortage

When an attendant at the Standard gas filling station told me: "Sorry, ten gallons only!"—I realized that the gasoline shortage in America was serious. Then, it also came to my attention that more and more small filling stations had to shut down because they had no gasoline. The shortage was critical for the first time over the Memorial Day Weekend. The fact that America does not have enough crude oil on its own has at first to be grasped with all its consequences. It hits the country to the core, for American life is being controlled by the motor. The economy as well as private life depends on motor vehicles. The energy and gasoline shortage will also have a psychological effect. America has always been used to draw on abundant resources, for raw materials have been available to a nearly unlimited extent. With 6% of the world's population, America consumes annually 40% of the world's energy supply. It is not easy for Americans to change to conserving energy and to use material goods more sparingly.

South Bend, June 7, 1973

Watergate: A Feeling of Shame

America is presently going through the trauma of a national scandal. A general despondency, a feeling of shame, and distrust has been spreading. It even goes so far that no patriotic speeches are held at high school graduations. Americans are by nature open, straightforward and honest people. The feeling of having been deceived is deeply hurting. The ongoing Senate hearings are followed with a shaking of heads, but there is little talk about the matter. Yet a gloomy feeling hovers over the whole affair that the worst is still to come.

South Bend, July 16, 1973

The Tapes

The Watergate hearings have recently been dragging on so that one is tired of listening. However, when a surprise witness testified today that since 1971 the White House has been equipped with electronic listening devices, which recorded every telephone call and conversation with the President without the knowledge of the participants, listeners were for a moment breathless.

[In May 1973 the Department of Justice appointed Archibald Cox Independent Special Prosecutor. Cox was a respected constitutional lawyer from Harvard University. Given far-reaching legal authority, he was charged to independently investigate wrongdoings in the Watergate affair and take the matter to court. Immediately following the testimony on the tapes, Cox demanded their release for examination. Thereby, the Watergate affair came dramatically to a head.]

South Bend, September 19, 1973

BRD and DDR in the UN

Without a lengthy debate in the General Assembly, the two German states, the Federal Republic of Germany and the German Democratic Republic, were admitted as full members to the United Nations.

South Bend, September 21, 1973

Henry Kissinger U.S. Secretary of State

The appointment of Henry Kissinger as U.S. Secretary of State again demonstrates what is possible in America. Dr. Kissinger is the first naturalized American citizen who has been entrusted with the agenda of American foreign policy.

South Bend, October 6, 1973

Again War in the Middle East

While driving home I turned on the radio in the car, suddenly at 11 a.m. the news broke that war has erupted again in the Middle East. It was immediately clear that these are the fiercest engagements since the Six-Day War in June 1967. Yet for the moment, nobody assumed that this would be a full-out war. The various newscasts from the combat zones reported that Egyptian troops are advancing on the left side of the Suez Canal and Syrian units on the Golan Heights, no doubt that this means total war. The attack was shamelessly launched on Yom Kippur, the Day of Atonement, and the highest Jewish holiday. The fronts have soon stiffened; there is heavy fighting on all sides.

South Bend, October 10, 1973

Agnew's Resignation

Today U.S. Vice President Spiro T. Agnew announced his resignation. In a shortened court trial in Baltimore, Agnew admitted that as Governor of Maryland he had accepted bribes and that he was guilty of tax evasion. Rumors in recent months that Agnew was involved in a bribery affair have thereby been corroborated.

South Bend, October 12, 1973

Choosing a Successor

In a movingly solemn ceremony—a rare event these days in Washington—, President Nixon announced his choice of nominating a candidate to fill the vacant post of Vice President. There was a great deal of guessing about possible candidates to succeed Agnew. But when Nixon mentioned that he has chosen a man who has served 25 years in the House, it was obvious that it could only be Congressman Gerald Ford from Michigan. There was spontaneous applause, for Ford is higly respected by both Parties in Congress. He is seen as a person who can establish a basis of trust between the White House and Congress.

[Gerald R. Ford was born on July 14, 1913 in Omaha, Nebraska, but he grew up in Grand Rapids, Michigan. By profession a lawyer and politician, he represented the 5th District of Michigan in Congress, 1948-73. He supported Nixon's foreign policy in the House. Gerald Ford was sworn in as Vice President on December 6, 1973. After Nixon's resignation, he was U.S. President from August, 1974 to January, 1977.]

South Bend, October 18, 1973

The Sinai Peninsula

The largest battle of war materials since the Second World War is presently raging on the Sinai Peninsula. About 2,000 tanks are doggedly wedged in one another. The Middle East has once again become the drill field, where the latest weaponry of East and West is being tested. This war has to be stopped. The Security Council of the United Nations has urgently called for a cease-fire.

South Bend, October 20, 1973

The Tapes

How was it possible that such a harmless technical aid like a tape, which is generally used in language laboratories for foreign language teaching, could cause a government crisis? President Nixon made the compromise suggestion to give the court a summary of the tapes. After Archibald Cox had declined the suggested compromise as being insufficient, Nixon ordered Attorney General Elliot L. Richardson to immediately relieve Cox of his duties. As Richardson had doubts on constitutional grounds to carry out such an order, he resigned as Attorney General. Only Robert Bork as Acting Attorney General was willing to dismiss Cox. The dismissal of the Independent Special Prosecutor caused an uproar of indignation. The Office of the Presidency was thrown into a constitutional crisis the like of which the Republic had never seen before. How will Congress react? Will it come to the feared impeachment proceedings? One wonders what these tapes may contain that Nixon refuses with all the power at his disposal to release them.

South Bend, October 25, 1973

An Unmistakable Hint

Secretary of State Henry Kissinger warned in not to be misunderstood language that there was the danger of a nuclear war if the Soviet Union would carry out its intention to unilaterally deploy troops in the Middle East. By this unmistakable hint, the specter of a nuclear confrontation between the two superpowers was again evoked. The détente, which has been achieved with such great effort, is being tested to the breaking point. To underscore the seriousness of the situation, President Nixon put the American armed forces on global alert. In this most precarious situation, the United Nations not only proved to be a useful but a life saving institution. This should be kept in mind when the United Nations will again become the target of criticism. The resolution by the Security Council to send a troop contingent to keep the cease-fire was the only way out of this dilemma.

South Bend, [Beginning of November], 1973

On Both Sides of the Atlantic

It is a given today that an academic career can take place in Europe and in America—that is to say simultaneously on both sides of the Atlantic, although the national legal systems are ill prepared to cope with this situation

South Bend, November 7, 1973

The Energy Crisis

The oil embargo, which the Arab members of the Organization of Petroleum Exporting Countries (OPEC) had imposed upon the United States, hightened the energy crisis in America. President Nixon declared a national energy emergency and announced measures to combat it. As an immediate measure he asked his fellow-citizens not to set the thermostat higher than 68° F over the winter and to observe a general speed limit of 55 mph on all roads and highways. Nixon called the oil embargo a challenge to the United States, which has to be responded to appropriately. The goal is to make the United States independent from foreign energy import by the end of the decade. For the realization of this goal, more nuclear power plants should be built and the exploration of the available natural gas resources advanced. The construction of the Alaska Pipeline is a project of national priority.

Addendum

[President Nixon's request to save energy was followed with surprising discipline. At Thanksgiving and Christmas 1973, the use of outdoor lights by businesses and private homes was limited. The 55 mph speed limit was maintained on American roads and highways for decades. Americans also began to adjust to smaller cars. The construction of the Trans-Alaska Pipeline was completed in 1977. With a length of 800 miles, the Pipeline connected the oil fields in Prudhoe Bay on the Arctic Ocean with the ice free Harbor of Valdez in the Gulf of Alaska in the South. The Trans-Alaska Pipeline increased the crude oil supply for the country considerably. But by the end of the 1970s, there was by far no energy self-sufficiency. After the embargo had been lifted, the United States resumed the oil import from the Arab countries to its full extent.]

South Bend, December 31, 1973

The National Championship in College Football

On this New Year's Eve about 50 million Americans watched on television in suspense at the football game between the University of Notre Dame and the University of Alabama, which decided the national championship in college football. In the Sugar Bowl Stadium of New Orleans 80,000 fans cheered on their team, either the Fighting Irish of Notre Dame or the Tide of Alabama. The Fighting Irish won 24-23 and thereby became the national champion in college football 1973.

American college football is in its way unique. It has an enormously broad effect and goes far beyond what is generally seen, especially in Europe, as competitive sports on the college or university level. It is a complicated game with many rules, which requires physical strength as well as agility and quick responsiveness. The oval ball is more thrown and held than kicked. It is a matter of yards and inches, not of goals like in soccer, but of touchdowns in the end zone. College football has its own ritual with marching bands, cheerleaders and mascots. Each game is also a social event that brings friends and families together from all over America. It strengthens the bond of the alumni with their alma mater. Tonight's game in the Sugar Bowl will be remembered for a long time to come. It will be passed on as a legend from one generation to another.

SECTION 6

January 20, 1974-August 17, 1976

South Bend, January 20, 1974

Impeachment

The shadow of impeachment lies over the New Year. With inexorable inner necessity, events in Congress are moving in the direction of impeaching the president. When the Congress convenes tomorrow after the Christmas recess, the question of impeachment will be the foremost order of business. The Judiciary Committee of the House of Representatives will have to examine all the facts and then based on the available evidence either dismiss the petition for impeachment or initiate the proceedings. There is presently the widespread view that the complicated and constitutionally grave proceedings of impeachment may run their course, but that in the end President Nixon will have enough support in the Senate to prevail.

South Bend, January 30, 1974

The State of the Union Address

Who had assumed that in his State of the Union Address before the joint session of Congress President Nixon would announce his resignation, learned differently. After taking stock of his five years in office, he declared emphatically that he had not the slightest intention to resign. In his speech, possibly the most important of his political career, Nixon pointed out once more in clear terms that he saw the historical importance of his presidency in his efforts for world peace. The new foundation for peace rests on the balance of interests between the two superpowers, on the détente between West and East, which has already been tested. This speech left the impression that Nixon will certainly stay on in the White House to finish the remaining three years of his second term.

However, in his response to President Nixon's State of the Union Address, Mike Mansfield, the Democratic majority leader in the Senate, gave clearly to understand that the Watergate affair should not be regarded as having been concluded. The courts will still have to deal with the matter.

South Bend, [February], 1974

Sent Into Exile

What may have motivated the Soviet regime to expel Aleksandr Solzhenitzyn from the country and to send him into exile to Bonn in the free world? Was it in consideration of public opinion in the West holding it back from convicting the Nobel Prize laureate for literature and banishing him again to Siberia? Or, was it the political consideration that doing so could have strained negotiations at the European Security Conference?

The comparison with Thomas Mann is obvious. As Nobel Prize laureate for literature, Thomas Mann went into exile in 1933. He first went to Switzerland and in 1938 to the United states. In exile he became an important voice of resistance against fascism. Could not Solzhenitzyn in exile also become such a voice of resistance against communism?

Note

[Aleksandr Solzhenitzyn was born in Russia 1918. As author and dissident he was placed several times under detention; he spent the years from 1945-53 in various labor camps in Siberia; only in 1956 was his deportment lifted. Banished from the Soviet Union in 1974, he lived in exile first in Zurich, 1974-76, and then from 1976-94 in Vermont in the United States. As author Solzhenitzyn revealed the horrors of the forced labor camps in the Soviet Union. Among his important works before he was exiled are *A Day in the Life of Ivan Denisovich* (1962), *Cancer Ward* (1968), *The First Circle* (1968), and the three volume documentary on the labor camps, written between 1964-68, and published in the West as *The Gulag Archipelago* (1973-78). Solzhenitzyn was awarded the Nobel Prize for Literature 1970.]

South Bend, March 7, 1974

Rockefeller Passing-by

Suddenly I stood before Rockefeller, not Nelson Rockefeller, the governor of New York, but his brother David, the chairman of the board of the Chase Manhattan Bank. The unexpected encounter happened in the Faculty Club of the University of Notre Dame, where I had dinner with a faculty committee. David Rockefeller had come to Notre Dame to give a lecture on trade with Russia and China. Father Hesburgh, the president of the University, guided the guest without formalities through the Faculty Club. After a brief introduction and a few friendly words, I realized that I was talking to one of the most influential personalities in finance in the world. I was surprised how easy and nonchalant such a meeting was possible in America. Also, the natural and human way was astonishing, how David Rockefeller moved among the faculty without conceit, cool distance, or compelled friendliness. I became acquainted with the American legend that is connected with the name Rockefeller in a congenial, human way. American society is not classless. But the social barriers are pleasantly overcome by a relaxed, natural and human attitude.

South Bend, March 15, 1974

The End of the One-way Street

In his speech before the Executives' Club in Chicago, President Nixon declared, "the days of the one-way street are over." That warning was directed toward the nine countries of the Common Market. Europe cannot just rely on the protection by the United States against a military aggression, and on the other hand refuse economic cooperation with the U.S. America will solve its defense and economic problems alone, should the European countries not be ready for transatlantic solidarity. Such strong words of criticism from President Nixon have never been heard before. They were certainly exaggerated, but they nevertheless showed a latent tension within the North Atlantic Alliance. Nixon's words shocked, they hit Europe like a cold shower. The reaction was accordingly fierce. They were in part seen as extortion, and in part also understood as maneuver to distract from his domestic difficulties. It was not quite clear what Nixon had intended. Should it have been a declaration of a new trade war between America and Europe, or is America withdrawing to a new isolationism?

South Bend, March 17, 1974

Wild Irish Rose

On March 17 America celebrates with the Irish St. Patrick's Day. Everywhere shamrocks, the symbol of Ireland, are on display, parades are held, and green beer is served. In Chicago even the Chicago River is colored green. And when the song "Wild Irish Rose" resounds, many a tear is shed. The longing of the Irish for their old homeland is shared by the many Americans of European descent. This way, the day of the Patron Saint of Ireland has become a national American holiday.

South Bend, March 19, 1974

Desperate Attempts

For the third time this week, President Nixon confronted the press and the television cameras. They were desperate attempts to win public opinion over on his side. The questions of the reporters jumped alternately from the Middle East to Europe to Watergate. During today's telecast from Houston, Texas, the tone in regard to Europe was much softer. Nixon pointed out that the friendship with Europe had never been questioned and that he supports the North Atlantic Alliance. In regard to Watergate two camps have been formed in the American public: The one agrees with the President that enough has already been said about Watergate, while the other can hardly wait until Nixon either resigns or is removed from office.

South Bend, March 29, 1974

In Exile

It was a moving scene when Aleksandr Solzhenitzyn was reunited with his wife Natalya and his children at the airport in Zurich-Kloten. But the joy of seeing each other again was dimmed by the imposed destiny of living in exile and the awareness of never being able to return to their home country again.

To live abroad with the possibility of anytime being able to return to one's own home country is not so bad. Under certain circumstances, it can even be exciting and stimulating. But in the Free West, especially in the United States, hundreds of thousands of people who had to flee from their home countries—China, North Vietnam, North Korea, Poland, Czechoslovakia, Hungary, as well as from the other East Bloc countries—live with no hope of ever returning. And that is bad.

South Bend, April 4, 1974

A Quiet Jubilee

The silver jubilee of NATO, the twenty-fifth anniversary of its foundation, almost passed by unnoticed. Founded on April 4, 1949, the North Atlantic Treaty Organization has well fulfilled its function as a deterrent. But the cohesion, which should have brought the West together to a unity, did not happen. How long will the great alliance continue to exist?

South Bend, April 7, 1974

Summit at the Funeral

What diplomatic efforts recently could not achieve was accomplished by the death of the French President George Pompidou. Following the solemn requiem in the Cathedral of Notre Dame, the heads of state from East and West came together for a summit meeting. Richard Nixon met with Nikolai Podgorny, and then with the heads of government of the Common Market countries. The desire for a policy of reconciliation and détente has never been so strong. Nixon's conciliatory attitude before this world forum did not miss its effect. There came word from Paris that in the present world situation he would be needed and that the foreign leaders would dislike seeing him leave office. Thus, Nixon received unexpected help from abroad.

South Bend, May 2, 1974

Miscalculations

Mutual miscalculations between America and Europe led several times to historic catastrophes of large proportions. Nothing could therefore be more important for maintaining the North Atlantic Alliance than for the United States and the European countries getting to know and learning to understand each other better.

South Bend, May 7, 1974

Brandt's Resignation

The news of the sudden resignation of the German Chancellor Willy Brandt hit the American public, who usually takes little interest in European political affairs, like a bolt from the blue. The reason for Brandt's resignation is hard to understand. Is the espionage incident just a pretext, or is there more behind it? Willy Brandt has given European politics direction. The gap he leaves behind will be hard to fill.

South Bend, May 8, 1974

Free Delivery

Special supplements to daily newspapers are now delivering free the dirty laundry of the White House to households throughout the country. The transcripts of the Watergate affair, recently released by President Nixon, show appallingly the low standard of the working climate, which has been spreading in the immediate surroundings of the President. The language is so cynical and full of invectives that every second sentence contains an expletive. The impact of these transcripts on the impeachment proceedings remains to be seen. Anyway, they have destroyed an American myth. The Oval Office has up to now been regarded as sacrosanct. Nobody could have imagined that in the holiest office of the country such profane language is being used. The Office of the President has been dragged through the mud and given way to a shameful disillusionment.

Sunday, May 19, 1974

Once More Barely Slipped By

Today Valery Giscard d'Estaing won the run-off election for the French presidency with a slim margin (371,814 out of a total of 26 million votes) against Francois Mitterrand. Once again, France slipped by a socialist-communist government by a hair breadth. But the deep social division, which runs through the French population, has also become apparent in this election. It is expected that Giscard d'Estaing will seek a closer cooperation with the Common Market and that he will be more open-minded toward the United States.

[From the end of May to the middle of August my family and I spent our summer vacation in Innsbruck. We had booked tickets on a charter flight of the Modern Language Association of America from New York to Paris.]

South Bend, May 25, 1974

Departure from the Watergate Troubled America

Before leaving America this year, the question remains open whether the Judiciary Committee of the House of Representatives, the Rodino Committee, will recommend impeachment and whether it will come to impeachment proceedings in the Senate.

[Peter W. Rodino, born 1909 in Newark, New Jersey, by profession lawyer and politician. Democrat, U.S. Representative from New Jersey, 1948-80; since January 1973 Chairman of the Judiciary Committee of the U.S. House of Representatives. In February 1974 Rodino was charged by the House to investigate the legal transgressions in the Watergate affair, and, if necessary, to initiate the proceedings of impeachment against President Nixon.]

Innsbruck, [Beginning of June], 1974

A Uniform Global Civilization

Starting from John F. Kennedy International Airport in New York and after seven hours landing at the new, super modern Charles de Gaulle Airport in Paris, one cannot see much of a difference. Charles de Gaulle Airport is similar to the JFK in design and layout, only its widely branching out system of escalators and conveyers surpasses the latter. At airports around the world, a supranational global civilization is emerging, which follows the American model. It is characterized by a cosmopolitan lifestyle and comfort. This highly uniform lifestyle of the "jet set" can be found everywhere. A high standard of service is available to travelers in the same hotel chains at most international airports. Signs of a growing uniform global civilization can also be seen in the great museums, in concert halls and opera houses in the metropolitan centers around the world. The same world-famous soloists and singers can be heard in London, Milan, Vienna, Berlin, New York, Chicago, San Francisco, and Sidney. At universities more and more professors and students are participating in international exchange programs. Similar cityscapes of glass and concrete are arising everywhere. Equally tired motorists are resting at service areas on the super highways. Just as everywhere the same car models are on the road. Shopping malls and supermarkets, either in America or in Europe, offer consumers more and more the same brand name merchandise. The modern world is unstoppably moving in the direction of a global civilization, which, following the Western model, is ever more so becoming uniform. Soon, there will be little space left for individual and indigenous expression.

Innsbruck, [Middle of June], 1974

The Differences

Nonetheless, despite the many similarities on the surface in everyday life in big cities and international travel, there are still big differences between America and Europe. These come to light as soon as one gets acquainted with the way of living and thinking of the local people. Especially conspicuous is the lack of loosening up and a widespread grouchiness as well as the resignation and indifference toward the future, which people display here. But the magnificent landscape and the cultivated feeling for beauty reward for what is otherwise missing

Innsbruck, June 20, 1974

Polarization

European society always threatens to fall apart at the threadbare seam between the extreme right and the extreme left. This polarization affects nearly all spheres of life: politics, education, religion. While the official church still indulges in baroque splendor, liberal theologians entrusted with the education of the young carry out experiments with the youth in their care that parents have their hair stand on end.

Innsbruck, [June 22], 1974

The Reform Rage

The need to catch up on democracy unleashed a reform rage in Austria and in the Federal Republic of Germany. There is nothing not deemed in need of reform and where the right of say is demanded. This goes from the elementary school up to the university or from the labor union to the management of a company. It applies to the administration of the law, to health care and the medical staff, as well as to the military service, the welfare assistance to foreigners, nursing homes, the Kindergarten and social security, let alone the political parties. Everything should be reformed. But this demand for reform looks very confusing. The reform proposals go head over heels. They are so numerous that they offset each other. In the end rarely anything new is happening.

Munich, [June 25], 1974

Pedestrian Zone

The inner city of Munich has gained a great deal by the pedestrian zone. Here a way is shown how the historic center of an old city can be redeveloped, preserved and made useful for visitors. Perhaps this way, a good many historic inner cities, which have already been written off as lost, can be saved. A quick stroll through Munich's department stores gives evidence of the high living standard and industrial potential of the Federal Republic. What one sees here, hardly differs anymore from an American department store. The abundance and similarity of the merchandise is simply striking.

Innsbruck, June 26, 1974

NATO's Continued Existence Secured

After 25 years the North Atlantic Treaty Organization could have either shrunk or dissolved had it not been for the strong will to secure its continued existence. Under the leadership of President Nixon, the 15 NATO countries signed a new declaration in Brussels. Therein, it was stated that the defense of the member countries is indivisible and that America and Europe remain dependent on each other. Just as clearly, the Federal Republic of Germany,

France, and Great Britain voiced their opinion that the presence of American troops is vital for the security of Western Europe.

Note

[According to Article 13 of the NATO agreement of April 4, 1949, each member state had after 20 years the choice to give notice of its resignation. None of the 15 NATO countries resigned. France withdrew from the integrated military structure in 1966, but remained a member of NATO. But the headquarters of NATO was transferred from Paris to Brussels. In 1974 the following 15 countries belonged to NATO: Belgium, Canada, the Federal Republic of Germany, Denmark, France, Greece, Great Britain, Iceland, Italy, Luxembourg, the Netherlands, Norway, Portugal, Turkey, and the United States of America. Greece and Turkey joined NATO in1952, the Federal Republic of Germany in 1955.]

Innsbruck, June 28, 1974

The Beginning of the End

Sixty years ago today, the Austrian successor to the throne and his wife were assassinated in Sarajevo. That was not just the beginning of the end of the Austro-Hungarian Dual Monarchy, but altogether of the Old Europe, of its position of power in the world, its order of peace, and form of life, as it had existed for centuries. Looking back, one could share with Stefan Zweig the feeling, as if the "World of Yesterday" would lie removed way back in the distant past that has long vanished from our sight. But in reality, the assassination in Sarajevo occurred not so far back. There are still enough people alive who remember the events of June 28, 1914. From that day on, Europe has not come to rest anymore. And it is still today fleeing from itself.

Innsbruck, June 29, 1974

The Brera is Being Closed

The Brera in Milan, one of the foremost Art Galleries in Europe, had to close its doors because it had not been possible anymore to pay for the superintending staff and to renovate the dilapidated rooms.

Innsbruck, [June 30], 1974

Unreal

When, after the emigration, one returns to one's home country, the living conditions appear to a large extent unreal and blurred. One can just barely share the joys and worries even of people one is closely connected with. The process of alienation is inevitably and irreversibly progressing. An inner distance has developed so that one talks at cross-purposes and actually has nothing of importance to say to each other anymore.

Innsbruck, [Beginning of July], 1974

The Wish for More Freedom

At the European Security Conference in Geneva and Helsinki, there is agreement in principle that the status quo of the European borders has to be secured by treaty. This means in real terms that the distribution of power, as it has emerged from the Second World War, is taken notice of. Standing on coexistence, the East wants to have its sphere of influence safeguarded. On the other side, the West is pushing for more freedom. Accordingly, the following items should be taken into consideration until the treaty is signed:

1) More freedom to move for the people in the East.
2) Reunion of families and marriages across the East-West border.
3) Freedom to travel to and within all countries in East and West.
4) The exchange of young people.
5) But above all, a more effective exchange of information, i.e., free admission of newspapers and magazines, as well as radio and television broadcasts.

By a less restricted movement of people and improved information across borders, the de facto partition of Europe could be eased. If this agreement should be achieved, it would be a modest, but nonetheless remarkable success. It is expected that the European Security Conference can still be concluded until the end of this year, but at the latest in 1975.

Innsbruck, July 14, 1974

The European Backbone

The German-French reconciliation as well as the cooperation between Paris and Bonn form the backbone of the European Community and hence the developing new Europe.

Innsbruck, July 20, 1974

The Cyprus Crisis

The overthrow of Archbishop Makarios as President of the independent Republic of Cyprus as well as the attempt by the national guard to unite Cyprus with Greece set off not only a serious crisis on this small island in the Eastern Mediterranean but also caused a precarious situation for the North Atlantic Treaty Organization. As a result of the Turkish invasion for the protection of the Turkish Cypriot minority, which occurred today in the morning hours, war between Greece and Turkey threatens to break out. Since both countries are members of NATO, the North Atlantic Alliance is being put to a delicate test. What should NATO do if war broke out between two of its member states? Although in this case the Soviet Union tacitly supports Turkey, the consent between the superpowers will prevent that this regional conflict will escalate.

Addendum

[Cyprus remained for years involved in a bloody civil war. A cease-fire was several times mediated by the United Nations. It came to the partition of the island into a Turkish Cypriot northern part (ca. one third of the country) and a Greek Cypriot southern part with the capital Nikosia. In the '70s Cyprus had a population of about 650,000, of which a quarter belonged to the Turkish Cypriot ethnic group. Since the partition, a UNO peacekeeping contingent has been standing guard along the demarcation line to avoid incursions.]

Innsbruck, August 1, 1974

Watergate

Following the recommendation by the Judiciary Committee of the House of Representatives to institute impeachment proceedings against President Nixon, Watergate has now gained so much interest also on this side of the Atlantic that further developments are observed continuously. Speculations about the resignation of President Nixon have received a fresh impetus. Nixon has convened his closest advisers. Will he announce his resignation before the vote on his impeachment in the House of Representatives?

August 6, 1974

The Confession of Guilt

President Nixon has now publicly admitted that in the Watergate affair he did not until now tell the full truth. He knew about the break-in into the headquarters of the Democratic Party immediately after it had occurred, and he had tried to keep it secret. Rarely has there been such a breach of confidence toward the American public as Nixon's in the Watergate affair. Nixon had several times stepped before the television cameras to assert that he had no knowledge of what had happened.

August 8, [17 hrs. Central European Time], 1974

The resignation of President Nixon is now expected any time. The Nixon era appears to be rushing to a sudden end.

The Resignation

At 9 p.m. Washington local time, what could be seen via satellite telecast from 3 a.m. on in Central Europe, President Nixon announced his resignation with the words, "therefore I shall resign the office of the presidency." It was the first time in American history that a president resigned his office.

The second term of Richard Nixon was ill-fated. From the moment on, when Federal Judge John Sirica began to uncover the background of the Watergate affair, the events took their imperturbable course. From the start the question stood in the center, as Senator Howard Baker had raised it in the Ervin Committee: "How much did he know, and when did he know it?" As it turned out, President Nixon knew too much too early, and beyond that he had helped to cover it up.

Most likely, it will always remain a mystery, how Richard Nixon, who as statesman gave world politics a new face, let himself be taken in by such a trite stupidity like Watergate in the domestic political arena. Nixon became a tragic figure whose dimension can hardly be fully fathomed.

[President Nixon officially resigned on August 9, 1974. The House Judiciary Committee presented three articles of impeachment against the President. The most serious accusations were "obstruction of justice" and "abuse of power." On grounds of the factual findings, he was advised to resign within his own Party. Nixon had resigned before the House of Representatives voted on his impeachment.]

Innsbruck, [Middle of August], 1974

Escapism

The many castles and palaces in and around Salzburg lend themselves to getting lost in illusions of the past. Here people live on dilapidated estates surrounded by hunting trophies, clinging to an aristocratic lifestyle without being aware of the shabby indigence they are in. American expatriates join their company. They are American citizens living abroad who have become obsessed with castle mania. It is a highly unreal, illusory world immersed in the splendors of the past, without paying attention to the problems of our times to begin with. But what is so typical of Salzburg proves to be a general European tendency, which, in variations, one may encounter everywhere.

South Bend, September 1, 1974

The Atlantic Vanquished

The jet-plane has vanquished the Atlantic as a centuries-old barrier between Europe and North America. If one departs from the Charles de Gaulle Airport and then after several hours lands at the John F. Kennedy International Airport in New York, one does not have the feeling anymore of having crossed an ocean, but of simply having passed a flight distance. However, although the geographical distance between America and Europe has shrunk to a few hours in the air, the outer and inner differences remain nonetheless standing. On the contrary, they may clash with each other all the more.

Nothing is more striking coming to Europe than the wealth of culture and the well kept beautiful landscape. But in contrast to this, there are the lethargy and crooked poverty, which is nesting in the alleys of the old cities as well as in the widespread tenement housing districts. This reverse side of European life frequently has a shocking effect on the visitor from America. The other way round, the European visitor coming to New York is at first surprised by the bustling activity and the modern lifestyle. On the other hand, he will soon become weary of the uniformity and feel disgusted by the dirt in the streets he just steps over. He will soon miss that he cannot move around afoot anymore. And he will at first be consternated by the amount of waste he sees at every turn.

South Bend, September 4, 1974

Exchange of Ambassadors

Between the United States and the DDR (German Democratic Republic or East Germany) treaties have been signed today in the State Department to establish mutual diplomatic relations. Without much ado and in a marked matter of fact attitude, the DDR has been recognized by the United States as a sovereign state. Thereby, hopes for reunification have been removed to a distant future. Apparently, the German partition has implicitly been accepted within the framework of détente. The enormous tragedy, which remains hidden behind the German destiny, is not being fully grasped abroad. Americans of German descent are now confronted with the dilemma whether they feel affiliated with the BRD (West Germany) or the DDR (East Germany).

South Bend, September 8, 1974

The Pardon

President Ford granted a general pardon that protects Richard Nixon from prosecution in the Watergate affair. The storm of indignation, which the pardon has unleashed, shows how much Watergate is still on people's minds. The embitterment about it sits deep. It will certainly make itself felt in the upcoming congressional elections and possibly also influence the presidential election in 1976.

South Bend, [Middle of September], 1974

What the World Expects from America

More than ever before, the expectations of a major part of the world are concentrating on the United States. America should make peace in the Middle East, negotiate between Arabs and Israelis, and at the same time mediate between Greeks and Turks in the Cyprus crisis. The United States should maintain the nuclear shield to protect the entire Free World—Europe as well as Japan—against the East Bloc and China. But it should also import Volkswagen and Toyotas, although its own auto makers have a surplus of cars stockpiled. It should persuade OPEC to not further increase the price of crude oil; furthermore, to bring its trade deficit in order and fight inflation. The developing countries expect that America delivers food and at the same time stabilizes their bankrupt national budgets. Even the East Bloc countries expect from America technical assistance and long-term loans at low interest rates. How will America be able to afford all this? It sees itself more and more placed in the position of a wealthy uncle, who for some time now cannot deliver all that is expected from him.

South Bend, September 24, 1974

The Rockefeller Hearings

President Ford has recommended Nelson A. Rockefeller for the office of vice president. The hearings before the Senate Rules Committee to confirm his candidacy puts the personality of Rockefeller or "Rocky," as people like to call him, in the limelight. Nelson Rockefeller proves to be a skilled politician who is guided by his convictions. He does not falter against the pointed questioning. He is known as a liberal from the conservative camp. He demonstrates his patriotism by referring to the Founding Fathers and quoting directly from the *Federalist Papers*. As the hearings are going, nothing should stand in the way that he will be confirmed as U.S. Vice President.

South Bend, September 29, 1974

A Union of the Fatherlands

The high expectations of the 1950s for a soon to come European union have rather given way to disappointment. Increasingly, the idea that Europe is coming together as a union of the fatherlands is having its way. This would be a compromise between a federal union and the national special interests of member states. It may well be the most comfortable solution, which in the end, however, would remain ineffective.

South Bend, [Middle of October], 1974

The Obsession to Be Number One

America is driven by the obsession to always be number one. This applies to sports, the economy, and politics. In Austria one has all along gotten used to being content with any rank one may achieve. Thereby, one has gained experience and become wiser.

South Bend, November 5, 1974

The Lesson for Watergate

At today's mid-term election, American voters taught the Republicans a lesson. The Democrats won a victory that comes close to a landslide. In the Senate they won three additional seats, increasing their majority 61:39. One of the three newly elected senators is the astronaut John Glenn, who won the vacant Senate seat in Ohio by a large margin. On the other hand, it is hard to grasp that William Fulbright will not be present in the Senate anymore. In the course of his 30 year tenure and service, Fulbright has become an institution in the Senate. In the House of Representatives the Democrats won additional 43 seats so that they have now a majority of 291: 144. The election result means altogether a nearly veto proof Congress. The Republican Ford Administration will have to show great willingness to compromise if under these circumstances any legislation will pass at all.

South Bend, [End of November], 1974

The Visit to Tokyo

As the first sitting U.S. President, Gerald Ford paid an official state visit to Japan (November 18—20). Thereby, the common American-Japanese interests have been recalled, just as the American obligations in the Pacific have been renewed.

The Summit Meeting in Vladivostok

Following his state visit to Tokyo, President Ford met with Soviet Party General Secretary Leonid Brezhnev in Vladivostok. The balance of interests between the United States and the Soviet Union was reaffirmed as well as negotiations for a SALT II agreement has been promised.

South Bend, December 2, 1974

Just Like in the 1930s

As the Chrysler Corporation has stopped its entire automobile production from Thanksgiving to January 6, the number of unemployed in the auto industry has increased to about 200,000. Detroit is especially hard hit by it. The lines before job centers and at soup kitchens are getting longer. These images bring back memories of the 1930s during the Great Depression.

South Bend, December 8, 1974

Chancellor Schmidt before the American Press

In the NBC Sunday noon program "Meet the Press," the German Chancellor Helmut Schmidt was prepared to answer questions of the American press. The discourse concentrated on the economy and the price of oil. Schmidt proved to be a very versatile politician. He not only spoke in fluent English, but he also adapted his answers so adroitly to the American mentality that they could have come from an American politician. He tactfully advocated rescinding trade restrictions and sounded optimistic in regard to the economic development worldwide in the years ahead if the present price level of crude oil can be sustained. Questions about common defense and troop reductions were not touched.

South Bend, December 19, 1974

Nelson Rockefeller Vice President

After long and hard hearings, the Senate approved nearly unanimously, the House on the contrary with only a close majority, the nomination of Rockefeller as Vice President. Nelson A. Rockefeller was sworn in today as 41 st U.S. Vice President. It was a short but cordial ceremony. Therewith, the transition from the Nixon-Agnew to the Ford-Rockefeller Administration has finally been put into effect. It speaks for the strength of the American democracy that this transition, following the Watergate drama, was carried out without revolt or dissolving the government. For the first time in American history, a President and a Vice President are in office, who had not been directly elected by the people, but who have been confirmed by Congress.

[Nelson A. Rockefeller, grandson of John D. Rockefeller, was born in 1908; he was Governor of New York, 1958-73; and U.S. Vice President, 1974-77. Rockefeller died in January, 1979, in New York.]

South Bend, January 12, 1975

Jacques Maritain on America

In his book written in English, *Reflections* on *America* (New York: Charles Scribner's, 1958), the French philosopher Jacques Maritain gave a moving testimony on America. Maritain was born 1882 in Paris. He studied at the Sorbonne and in Heidelberg natural sciences and philosophy. Maritain, who came from a Protestant family, converted to Catholicism in 1906. Starting from Thomas Aquinas, he became a renowned representative of the new Christian humanism. Maritain taught from 1914-40 at the Institut Catholique in Paris. From the early 1930s on, he took up contacts with universities in North America. He gave lectures at the Pontifical Institute of Medieval Studies in Toronto, at the University of Chicago, and at the University of Notre Dame. In 1940 he and his wife Raissa went to New York into exile. From 1945-48 he was Ambassador of France at the Vatican. In 1948 he accepted a professorship at Princeton University. After retiring as emeritus in 1953, he stayed on in Princeton, New Jersey. From there he traveled several times to the Midwest, giving guest lectures at the University of Chicago and here at Notre Dame. On the advice of his wife and out of gratitude for the friendly reception, which he had received in this country, he wrote the "reflections" on America. In the *Reflections* he calls his first encounter with America a "coup de foudre" or "love at first sight." Looking back on history, he points out: "[The Americans] were the most humane and least materialist among modern peoples which had reached the industrial age." Then he deals with the widespread European prejudice that America is exclusively materialistic. "Few things, to my mind," he declares, "are as sickening as the stock remarks with which so many persons in Europe, who are themselves far from despising the earthly goods of this world, reproach this country with its so-called materialism. The power of this fable is so great that sometimes you yourselves [the Americans] are taken in by it." Furthermore, he expresses his admiration about the efforts America has made during the past two hundred years to create a new world: "I have come to realize more and more the immensity of the human effort which was brought into play to create a new world within the course of two centuries." At the conclusion of his reflections, he arrives at the following point of view: "What the world expects from America is that she keep alive, in human history, a fraternal recognition of the dignity of man." The recognition of the dignity of the human being is most important for Jacques Maritain.

[The University of Notre Dame founded a separate Jacques Maritain Center in 1957. Maritain returned to France in 1960. He died in 1973.]

South Bend, January 19, 1975

The Depression Then and Now

Whenever there is a recession in America and the unemployment number reaches the 6-7 million mark, fearful visions of the Great Depression of the 1930s pop up. But to keep things in perspective, it would be advisable to recall some of the figures of the Great Depression. The Great Depression was triggered by the stock market crash of October 29, 1929, when stocks, without a safety net, tumbled to the bottom. As a consequence, it brought the highest unemployment rate ever recorded in America. In 1933 unemployment reached 25% of the work force. Now by comparison, unemployment stands at 7.2%. At the peak of the Great Depression in 1933, many banks had to be closed, whereby a large section of the population lost their life's savings. Furthermore, numerous mortgages were foreclosed, forcing many farmers to leave their land. In the meantime, many lessons have been learned and protective measures taken. Now, bank deposits up to a certain amount are secured by law. Also, since the New Deal a number of social security legislation has been enforced to protect the individual in an emergency. A repetition of the Great Depression is therefore very unlikely.

South Bend, February 21, 1975

The Final Closure of Watergate

Federal Judge John J. Sirica sentenced John M. Mitchel, H.R. Haldeman and John D. Ehrlichman to several years in prison. This sentence brings the Watergate affair to a final closure. The court acted impartially without regard for the high social standing of the defendants. What a tragic turn in the personal lives of these individuals, who not long ago held positions of power in the White House! That of all people, John Mitchel as former Attorney General [U.S. Attorney General from January, 1969 to February, 1972] has to serve a prison term, underscores the grotesque spectacle, which has played out on the American political arena.

South Bend, March 4, 1975

James T. Farrell

With a heavy breath, which made it difficult for him to form words in complete sentences, the author of the *Studs Lonigan* trilogy and additional twenty novels spoke to the students of Notre Dame. At the age of 72, the ailing Farrell has remained the predominant figure of Naturalism in American literature, who reaches back to Frank Norris and Theodore Dreiser. He also exemplifies that, since the beginning of the 20th century, Chicago has become a vibrant center of American letters.

[The *Studs Lonigan* trilogy (1932-35) is an autobiographical narrative of Farrell's youth in Chicago.]

South Bend, March 7, 1975

Phnom Penh

The urgent appeal of President Ford to Congress and the American public to come to a last minute rescue of the beleaguered capital of Cambodia met with no response. Following the experience of Vietnam, no one is willing anymore to send troops to Indochina. One has already resigned to the fact that Phnom Penh will fall and that the Communist regime of the Khmer Rouge will take over Cambodia.

South Bend, March 17, 1975

The President's Visit

The University of Notre Dame has three times been the historic scene of visits by sitting Presidents: Franklin D. Roosevelt in 1935, Dwight D. Eisenhower in 1960, and today on St. Patrick's Day Gerald R. Ford. The official occasion was the conferral of an honorary degree of Doctor of Laws on Gerald Ford. But beyond that, the presence of the President on the Notre Dame campus was of a more far-reaching significance. It should have a healing effect of bringing about reconciliation between the government and the universities. For the first time in ten years, a U.S. President has set foot on the campus of a major American university. Ford was given a spontaneously cordial reception.

By a random distribution of seats for the faculty, I came to sit directly in front of the podium with the "Seal of the President of the United States." Ford made the impression of an informal, straightforward, upright personality. The humanitarian theme of his address came from the heart. His habit of speech, pronouncing the "e" in judg(e)ment, could not have been missed. In his speech, Ford clearly denounced the newly growing isolationism. America will not withdraw from its international obligations. Despite the economic recession in his own country, he was determined to continue sending aid to suffering nations in the world. For one day, the Notre Dame campus was the news center in the country. Security precautions were accordingly extensive but not obtrusive. There were no demonstrations or incidents. The visit went well to mutual satisfaction—for the President and the University.

South Bend, March 30, 1975

People on the Run

In South Vietnam the tragedy of our century with all its misery is happening again: People are on the run. These days millions are fleeing from the advancing North Vietnamese troops in the Northern provinces. With only the clothes on their back, they try to find any imaginable way to escape and to seek refuge in Saigon which is still safe. Today the important harbor city Da Nang fell. What American troops have been defending by extreme effort for a decade is now given up nearly without resistance. South Vietnam is simply being overrun by the forces from the North.

South Bend, April 6, 1975

The End Is in Sight

Since it was definite that the United States would not interfere militarily in Vietnam, it has virtually been an invitation to the North and the Viet Cong to go now all out. It came as a surprise to everyone how little preparedness for defense there was in South Vietnam, which led to a hurried collapse of the South Vietnamese army. In today's televised interview on "Face the Nation," U.S. Secretary of Defense James R. Schlesinger bluntly admitted that the situation in South Vietnam is regarded as being hopeless. The American strategy is at this time already planning on what to do after the fall of Saigon. All efforts are presently concentrated on how to evacuate the American embassy personnel and other persons. The American public follows the events in South East Asia with indifference.

South Bend, April 18, 1975

Meeting Saul Bellow

At a reception in the residence of the Austrian Consul General in Chicago, given in honor of the Austrian writers Beatrice Ferolli and Peter von Tramin, I met Saul Bellow. Bellow is one of the leading novelists of present-day American literature. He is physically of a small stature, but his delicate facial feature and vivacious eyes speak of a scintillating intellect.

By character he is more withdrawn. It was not easy to engage Saul Bellow in a conversation.

[Saul Bellow was born 1915 in Lachine near Montreal, but he grew up in Chicago, which in many ways serves as background for his novels. He studied at the University of Chicago and at Northwestern University anthropology. Among his significant works are *The Adventures of Augie March* (1953), *Henderson the Rain King* (1959), *Herzog* (1964), *Mr. Sammler's Planet* (1970), *Humboldt's Gift* (1975). Saul Bellow received the Nobel Prize for Literature 1976.]

South Bend, April 19, 1975

A Prelude to the Bicentennial

Today's reenactment of the skirmish at the Bridge of Concord in Massachusetts set in motion the beginning of the Bicentennial Celebrations of the American Declaration of Independence on the Fourth of July, 1776. At the Concord Bridge on April 19, 1775, the shots were fired which started the War of Independence. Last night, swinging lanterns from the North Church in Boston gave the signal for reenacting "Paul Revere's Ride." On the night of April 18, 1775, the silversmith Paul Revere rode on horseback the ten miles from Boston to Lexington warning with a loud voice that the British were coming. General Thomas Gage, the Governor of Massachusetts at the time, had planned a surprise maneuver during that night. He dispatched a troop contingent to capture and arrest Samuel Adams and John Hancock, the leaders of the rebellion, who were hiding in Lexington. Also, the troops had orders to dismantle weapons depots in Concord. When the British troops reached Lexington at dawn, Adams and Hancock had long before fled, and the surroundings were alarmed. A group of "minutemen" confronted the redcoats at Concord Bridge. Soon the British troops were attacked from all sides. Suffering heavy losses, they had to retreat to Boston. From then on, the War of Independence took its inexorable course. Two hundred years after the events at Concord and Lexington, America is now beginning the extensive preparations for the Bicentennial in 1976.

[The legendary "minutemen" were volunteers in the War of Independence, who at any time would be available at a minute's notice.]

South Bend, April 20, 1975

At a Loss

America is completely at a loss, facing the coming catastrophe in Saigon. Should those South Vietnamese, who were employed by the Americans—about 200,000 to half a million people—, be evacuated together with the American citizens? What should happen with about two million Catholics and Christians of other denominations who fled from the North to the South? How many refugees can America realistically take in?

April 21, 1975

Under the pressure of the ongoing events, President Nguyen Van Thieu resigned. This means the end of a free South Vietnam.

April 29, 1975

A Horrifying End

Today Saigon offered its unconditional surrender. Only a few hours later, the city was turned over to North Vietnam and the Viet Cong. What had occurred before the capitulation was a horrifying end. The last televised pictures showed how people, in a last minute attempt, tried to rescue themselves into the American Embassy. Only a fraction among them could be flown out by helicopters. Then everything collapsed, total chaos broke out. The Embassy was looted by an unrestrained mob.

April 30, 1975

Ho Chi Minh City

The victorious North Vietnam did not waste any time. The advancing armored vehicles had barely reached the seat of the government and accepted the capitulation, when Saigon was forthwith renamed Ho Chi Minh City. Also, to demonstrate their triumph, the name of the rival city should be deleted from memory.

South Bend, [Middle of May], 1975

Immigration Statistics

Since 1820 the United States has been keeping records on immigration. According to these records, nearly 45 million people have immigrated in the past 150 years. The immigration of political refugees since the end of the Second World War could run up to two million, of whom more than a million have come from the Communist East Bloc countries in Europe and about 600,000 from Cuba. The present flood of immigrants from South East Asia has already reached on estimate 130,000. Although those who asked for political asylum make up only a quarter of the total immigration during the past two decades, their number elucidates that the United States is the main place of refuge for those who are persecuted for political reasons. While other countries were only temporary stations of transit, refugees have been accepted here for good. Here they felt protected, found work, and were given citizenship. In short, they found a new homeland. In moments of most serious afflictions, America has always opened its doors for those fleeing from persecution.

The refugees from Saigon were flown across the Pacific to California, where they were temporarily housed in military camps. There the lengthy processing and examining of each individual by the INS (Immigration and Naturalization Service) has begun. Whoever has a sponsor—a relative or a church community—is immediately released. But the majority of the refugees have to cope with long waiting periods in the camps until a solution will be found. Some will adapt quickly to the American way of life. Others, however, will seek refuge in a ghetto, as it has been the case many times in the history of American immigration. Such a closed district of ethnic Vietnamese is presently being formed in Los Angeles. Despite all the human misery and trials, only a handful of the refugees have opted to be repatriated. Most of them are ready to bear all the exertion and uncertainties in order to live in freedom in America and in the hope of one day being able to participate in the American dream.

[Maldwyn Allen Jones, *American Immigration* (Chicago: The University of Chicago Press, 1960) offers a comprehensive survey of American immigration history.]

South Bend, June 1, 1975

President Ford in Europe

On his first European tour, President Gerald Ford continued the policy of strengthening the North Atlantic Alliance, which had been initiated by his predecessor. The first stop of his tour in Brussels (May 28—31) served the task of invigorating NATO and to assure the European partners that America will stand firm by its obligations to the Alliance. As the Europeans, particularly after the recent experiences in Vietnam, are also in favor of further strengthening the Alliance, both sides were in agreement as they had not been for a long time. For the security of the Mediterranean area, negotiations are being held in Madrid (May 31-June 1) on retaining American Air Force Bases in Spain. From June 1-3 a meeting is planned between Gerald Ford and Anwar Sadat, the President of Egypt, at Schloss Fuschl near Salzburg, in order to further advance peace negotiations in the Middle East. While Sadat insists that the territories on the Sinai Peninsula are returned, Israel is not inclined to agree. In an audience in the Vatican on June 3, President Ford will meet with Pope Paul VI to discuss humanitarian questions.

June 5, 1975

President Ford returned in a good mood from Europe, self-assured and in a strengthened position. He was skillfully led by Secretary of State Henry Kissinger through the labyrinth of European politics. Ford also had a good understanding with the heads of governments in Europe. Although tensions between America and Europe still linger on, both sides have come much closer together again by this tour.

[In June 1975 I spent several weeks in Cambridge, Massachusetts, to pursue my research in American literature at the Houghton Library of Harvard University.]

Cambridge, Mass., June 7, 1975

The School Dispute in Boston

In an ironic turnaround of American history, the last rearguard battle of racial segregation is being fought here in Boston, where in the last century the Abolitionist Movement for putting an end to slavery had originated. For the last year, a school dispute has been raging over desegregation. U.S. District Judge W. Arthur Garrity, Jr., pronounced last year that the schools in Boston were intentionally practicing racial segregation. After he had ordered the desegregation of the school system, about 21,000 children had to be bused across town in order to achieve a balanced quota between white and colored children in all schools. There were continuously demonstrations, riots and clashes with the police. But Garrity was not to be dissuaded from his conviction by the poisoned atmosphere. With great courage he stood by his decision: The school system has, in compliance with the law and the constitution, to dismantle the barriers of segregation. In a 90 page report, he now substantiated his ruling on historical grounds. In the question of "forced busing," concessions could be made because the argument about it would not lead anywhere. But in the end, the school dispute will be solved when there are no white or black schools anymore but just simply schools in Boston.

Boston, June 12, 1975

The Social Change

From John Winthrop, the first Governor of the Massachusetts Bay Colony in the 17th century, to Michael S. Dukakis, the present Governor of Massachusetts, a profound social change has occurred. From originally a British colony of Puritan dissidents, a Commonwealth has developed with any conceivable ethnic groups coming from Europe, Africa and Asia. The Irish and Italian immigrations in the 19th and 20th centuries brought a strong Catholic element to Massachusetts. While Winthrop's main worry was how to protect the colony against raids, Dukakis faces at the moment the difficult problem of how to provide social assistance for those in need.

Cambridge, Mass., June 12, 1975

Commencement Exercises

At this year's Commencement Exercises, Harvard University conferred 4,396 degrees. Of these, 3,015 were graduate and professional degrees (M.A., Ph.D., M.D., and D.J.), while 1,381 graduating seniors received bachelor's degrees. That was the largest number of degrees Harvard University conferred at a commencement in its 350 year history. Rain dampened the ceremony on the Harvard Yard, but it did not diminish the good mood of the graduating class and the guests.

Boston, June 15, 1975

Bankruptcy of the Big Cities

A serious problem has arisen on how to finance the big cities in America. Recently New York declared bankruptcy, and Boston seems to be next in line. City governments are losing their source of revenues, as the flight to the suburbs continues. But they still have to finance the social expenditures of the impoverished inner cities. As a result of the financial squeeze, schools, police, fire departments, waste disposal, transportation, simply all the services a municipality has to provide, are affected. To get out of this vicious circle is not easy.

Cambridge, Mass., June 17, 1975

Communism in Italy

The recent regional elections of June 15 and 16 have again evoked fears of a Communist Italy. The Communists won 33.7% of the votes, whereby they come close to the Christian Democrats. They won the majority in the city governments of Rome, Milan, Torino, and Venice. Participation in the national government, if it is not formed by the Communists from the outset, is therefore very likely.

Cambridge, Mass., June 18, 1975

Walter Scheel Warns

In his address to the U.S. Congress, Walter Scheel, the President of the Federal Republic of Germany, warned that the Communist ideologies may get hold of Europe, if the social awareness of the West is not sharpened and the problems of enough food, energy and unemployment are solved. Scheel expressed concern about the Communist victory in the Italian elections. He saw the main danger for the political development in Europe in breaking up the moderate or right-center democratic parties. He warned of an increasing radicalization and of a Communist danger in Europe, which is also taken seriously in Washington.

Cambridge, Mass., June 22, 1975

The Earthquake of Las Vegas

When these days the high-rises in Las Vegas began to sway, not only the inhabitants of the casino city were harshly awakened from sleep, but the entire world was again reminded that the atomic age has lost nothing of its horror. In the Nevada desert, about 120 miles from Las Vegas, a hydrogen bomb in the megaton category was ignited 3,000 feet under ground. The power of the detonation was fifty times stronger than the bomb dropped on Hiroshima. It set off a light earthquake, whose tremors were felt within a radius of 200 miles. The power of destruction of such a bomb exceeds comprehension. It is simply a matter of common sense that the SALT negotiations will be continued and that everything is done to avoid the danger of a nuclear war.

South Bend, July 17, 1975

The Handshake in Space

In a first attempt of cooperation in manned spaceflights between the U.S.A. and the Soviet Union, an American Apollo spacecraft was docked today on a Russian Soyuz. After the successful docking maneuver, the astronauts floated through the connecting channel into the Soyuz spaceship, where they were received with a friendly welcome by the cosmonauts. The event could be clearly followed on television. The handshake in space between the commanders Thomas Stafford and Alexej Leonov not only brings the Americans and Russians closer together, but it also demonstrates to the world that the détente has become an irrefutable reality.

South Bend, August 1, 1975

The Baskets of Helsinki

Today the final accords of the Conference on Security and Cooperation in Europe (CSCE) were signed by the 35 participating countries. The various interrelated subjects were summed up in 3 Baskets.

Basket I: Formulates the security principle of the inviolability of the frontiers and of non-intervention in internal affairs.

Basket II: Aims at scientific cooperation and the exchange of experience between East and West in regard to the protection of the environment.

Basket III: Contains the humanitarian or human rights catalogue, the only real concession of the East to the West. It asks for easing the restrictions on reuniting families across borders, and it supports the exchange of information and cultural exchange.

After 22 months of preliminary diplomatic work, the representatives of East and West have finally decided to accept the agreement of Helsinki. The presence of 35 heads of state and government, who have come to Helsinki to sign the final accords of the CSCE, is reminiscent of the Congress of Vienna, 1814-15. Some similarities cannot be denied. Henry Kissinger, the chief architect of the CSCE, had carefully studied Metternich and the Congress of Vienna. Just as the Congress of Vienna, after the Napoleonic Wars, created a new peace order for Europe, Helsinki put an end to World War II. It looked the political reality in the eye and recognized the balance of strength between the two superpowers.

South Bend, September 1, 1975

Kissinger's Triumph

After incessant and tenacious negotiations in a tireless "shuttle diplomacy" between Tel Aviv and Alexandria, Secretary of State Henry Kissinger succeeded in achieving an interim agreement between Israel and Egypt. The agreement was signed today in Jerusalem and Alexandria. The U.S. Congress still has to agree that the United States will establish an early electronic warning station in the buffer zone on the strategically important Mitla and Gidi passes as well as to staff it with American civilian observers. However, there seems to stand nothing in the way anymore for signing the agreement in Geneva.

September 4, 1975

The Sinai Agreement was signed by Israel and Egypt in Geneva. Thereby, a constant trouble spot in the world has been appeased. As Anwar Sadat pointed out, the prospects for a peaceful co-existence in the Middle East between Israel and its Arab neighbors look promising.

South Bend, September 5, 1975

The Risk

In front of the Capitol in Sacramento, California, an attempt on the life of President Ford was made. It occurred during a campaign rally for the presidential election 1976, which is already underway. Shortly after the incident and still under shock, President Ford declared that he will not let himself to be deterred from mingling among the people and shaking hands. In election years, the American president has no choice but to confront the electorate, mingle among the people, and possibly risk an attack on his life. This is the risk of an open democracy, which America is ready to take.

South Bend, September 14, 1975

An American Saint: Mother Elizabeth Seton

Today, in a Mass in St. Peter's Square in Rome, Pope Paul VI canonized Mother Elizabeth Seton (1774-1821). The foundress of the Sisters of Charity is the first saint of the Catholic Church born in America.

[Elizabeth Ann Bayley was born 1774 in New York. She married the merchant William Seton in 1794. When her husband died in 1803, she was left behind as a widow with five children. After she had converted to Catholicism in 1805, she devoted her life under great difficulties to caring for and educating children. She established several Catholic schools in Maryland and founded the Order of the Sisters of Charity, which quickly spread throughout America. Leading the Order, she became known as Mother Elizabeth Seton. She was beatified in 1963 and canonized 1975.]

South Bend, October 22, 1975

Arnold J. Toynbee (1889-1975)

The world-renowned British historian died today at the age of 86 in York, England. I remember very well the spring semester 1961, which I could spend together with Toynbee at the University of Pennsylvania in Philadelphia [see entry above of April 16, 1961]. Personally not easily accessible, as a lecturer provocative and tending toward extreme formularizations, contested among colleagues, he nonetheless has influenced historiography over decades. From 1934—1961 he completed the 12 volumes of his monumental life's work, *A Study of History*. This universal history of civilization, which was originally influenced by Oswald Spengler, deals with the rise and decline of high civilizations. In Toynbee's view, religion stands in the center of human history because it informs about the mystery of life.

South Bend, November 21, 1975

Spain a Kingdom Again

After the death of Generalissimo Francisco Franco, Prince Juan Carlos de Bourbon was enthroned today as King of Spain Juan Carlos I. His spouse Princess Sophia of Greece stands on his side as Queen. Juan Carlos is the grandson of Juan Carlos Alfonso XIII, the last king of Spain (1902-31), who had to leave the country because of internal unrests. Thus, after 44 years, a cruel civil war, and a phalanx dictatorship, Spain is becoming a kingdom again. Will the constitutional monarchy be able to unite the divergent elements in the country? Spain forms an important link in the Western defense concept. Will it find under Juan Carlos the way to the new Europe?

South Bend, [Middle of December], 1975

A Wave of Terror

Although the world is experiencing at this time a period of peace and is not immediately threatened by war, the terror of radical splinter groups has spread horror all over the world. At first hostages were held for weeks in Holland, then the conference of the OPEC ministers in Vienna was raided. And now, a delayed-action bomb placed in the luggage checking area of the La Guardia Airport in New York exploded and indiscriminately hit passengers during the main traveling season. Eleven persons were killed and 70 wounded. These acts of terror are unscrupulous crimes. What should one do in the face of the danger of terror attacks? Not to go to a railway station or a department store, not to step into an airport and fly anymore? Certainly not. There is no other choice but to get used to living with terror door to door.

South Bend, [End of December], 1975

The Holy Year Has Come to a Close

On Christmas Eve, Pope Paul VI closed the Porta Santa in the St. Peter's Basilica, whereby the Holy Year 1975 has come to a close. The Year has been a call to meditation, to spiritual renewal and to reconciliation with God and among people. How much will happen until the Porta Santa will be opened again at Christmas 1999?

[In the Bicentennial Year 1976 the attention of America was markedly concentrated on immigration and ethnic groups. And it was also a year of a presidential election with its primaries.]

South Bend, January 18, 1976

The Immigration from Europe

According to the tabulation of the local daily newspaper, 46.7 million people immigrated between 1820 and 1974 to the United States [for comparison see entry above of middle of May, 1975]. Of these, 35.8 million came from Europe. Their numbers are distributed over the following countries of origin:

Germany 6.9 m(illion); Italy 5.2 m; Great Britain 4.8 m; Ireland 4.7 m; Austria-Hungary 4.3 m; Russia 3.3 m; Sweden 1.2 m; Norway 850 th(ousand); France 740 th; Greece 620 th; Poland 500 th; Portugal 400 th; Denmark 360 th; Netherlands 360 th; Switzerland 350 th; and from the remaining parts of Europe altogether about 1 million.

[These are general guiding figures, which may differ according to the interpretation of the immigration statistics. But they provide an overview of the size of the various immigration groups.]

South Bend, [Middle of February], 1976

The Adjustment

As a result of the Helsinki agreements, East and West are beginning to adjust to each other. This year scholars and scientists from East Germany and other East Bloc countries have come inconspicuously as visitors to America. Without much difficulty, one has reconciled oneself in the United States with the reality of two German states. Thus, one meets at universities here visiting scientists and guest professors from West and East Germany without seeing it as something much out of the ordinary.

South Bend, [End of February], 1976

The XII Winter Olympic Games in Innsbruck

The XII Winter Olympic Games in Innsbruck, Austria, have been carried out with exemplary organization and no incidents. For hours every day, ABC televised dazzling pictures from the Winter Olympics. Thereby, Innsbruck and the Tyrol have become widely known in America.

South Bend, [Middle of March], 1976

The Primaries

In this presidential election year, several primaries have already been held. On the Republican side, President Gerald Ford and the former governor of California, Ronald Reagan, are competing for their Party's nomination. Reagan proved to be a serious challenger. But Ford has the Republican Party behind him. He won the primaries in Massachusetts and in Florida.

There is a broad field of candidates on the Democratic side—Jimmy Carter, Birch Bayh, Fred Harris, Henry Jackson, Morris Udall and George Wallace—all contending for the nomination. Jimmy Carter, the Governor of Georgia, 1971-75, is the frontrunner at this time, especially after winning the Florida primary. He is followed by Morris Udall and George Wallace.

Chicago, March 20, 1976

The Pit

The novel by Frank Norris, *The Pit* (1903), about the mercantile or grain trade in Chicago has not lost anything of its topicality. Just as 70 years ago, also today, the mercantile exchange in the Chicago Board of Trade Building is trading the enormous harvest of the Midwest on the world market. Despite the newest electronic technology, the trading is not much different from the way Norris describes it. As ever before, the futures are auctioned off in the tense scramble of the pit. The brokers are positioned on round wooden stands, while the callers chalk up the prices on the board. One may wonder, but surprisingly the system works year after year.

The Sears Tower

The 103 story [1,454 ft/ 443 m] high Sears Tower in Chicago claims to be the tallest building in the world. The World Trade Center and the Empire State Building in New York follow thereafter. Yet the Sears Tower is in a way disappointing. Its construction follows a dry functionalism. The basalt-black rectangular blocks towering upon each other have a depressing effect. The express elevator shoots up the nearly 1,000 feet to the top in less than a minute. The panoramic view from the observation platform fully comprises the environs of Chicago. But from its dizzying height it is not possible anymore to make out details deep below. The John Hancock Center on the Lake Front comes much closer to the esthetic sensibility. It offers a magnificent view of the city's harsh modern beauty.

Addendum

[In 1996 the 1,483 ft/ 452 m high Petronas Twin Towers in Kuala Lumpur surpassed the Sears Tower in Chicago by a few feet or meters in altitude.]

South Bend, April 3, 1976

Only No.2

In a campaign speech, Ronald Reagan blamed the Ford Administration, as it follows the détente policy of Henry Kissinger, for having allowed the United States to fall back militarily to second place compared with the Soviet Union. The USSR has gained an advantage in almost all weapons categories—strength of troops, tanks, naval build-up, and even in certain areas of the nuclear arsenal. Criticizing détente introduces a volatile foreign policy topic into the campaign. Reagan wants to revise the Helsinki agreements, however, without saying how to do it.

South Bend, April 4, 1976

Fallout Shelter

Nearly at every street corner, in every school, post office or any other public building in America, one can see the yellow, somewhat faded triangle on a black background with the sign "Fallout Shelter." These are radiation safe rooms, which, in case of a nuclear attack, provide protection for the civilian population. They were built in the '50s and early '60s when the danger of a nuclear war was taken seriously. Tons of crackers were stored in these shelters to secure the food supply in case of an emergency. Although these fallout shelters are continuously checked on their suitability, they have, as a result of détente, lost their urgency. Nobody is seriously thinking of a nuclear attack anymore. These signs on fallout shelters look like relics from an era long past. This may well be the case. But how innocent were those countries that had made no contingency plans at all to protect their civilian populations from radiation in the event of a nuclear war.

South Bend, April 6, 1976

Primaries in Wisconsin and New York

Although Morris Udall was at first declared the winner at yesterday's Wisconsin primary, it turned out only in today's morning hours that Carter had again won a close victory. The New York primary held at the same time was won by Henry Jackson before Udall, while Carter landed on fourth place. Still, it is becoming increasingly clearer that the Democratic nomination cannot be taken away from Carter.

The Candidate

The surprise in this election year in the United States is the former Governor of Georgia, Jimmy Carter. He has gained the image of the candidate per se. Immediately after the primary in Wisconsin, Jimmy Carter came down to South Bend for a few hours this morning to start his campaign for the Indiana primary. His motorcade drove under heavy security through the Notre Dame Campus where he gave a campaign speech in the Stepan Center. As he drove by, his broad smile flashed up for a moment. The applause at the Stepan Center was good but far from being as enthusiastic as it had been for Robert Kennedy. The surprising thing about

Carter is that, although he has not committed himself to a specific program, he nonetheless gets the votes. First and foremost, he stands for honesty in government, which has the strongest appeal after the Watergate scandal. It has also become clear that neither the extreme left nor the extreme right have a chance in this campaign.

[The press reports on Jimmy Carter's visit to the Notre Dame Campus on April 6, 1976, mentioned that his strongest persuasive power lay in "telling the truth." They also pointed out that the popularity of George Wallace was dwindling. Carter told the press that he considered the Pennsylvania primary on April 27 as the decisive test in the confrontation with Henry Jackson. Cf. University of Notre Dame Archives, Jimmy Carter Visits, UDIS, Box 81/13 and 14.]

South Bend, May 18, 1976

The Campaign and the Tulip Festival

Gerald Ford had to win the primary in his home state Michigan in order to remain a credible candidate of the Republicans. He fell back on an old form of campaigning, the "whistle stopping." Traveling by train, President and Mrs. Ford stood on the platform at the rear of the train and stopped at small towns and villages. They talked to campaign rallies and mingled among the people. The highlight of this campaign trail was the Tulip Festival in Holland, Michigan, which takes place every year with parades and large floats. Ford won the Michigan primary by a considerable margin before Reagan.

South Bend, May 24, 1976

France and the United States in the Bicentennial Year

On the occasion of the Bicentennial, the President of France Valery Giscard d'Estaing paid a state visit to the United States. As it was not to be expected otherwise, he flew on the Concorde to America. That he had to promote this new French-British supersonic commercial airplane, which crosses the Atlantic in 3 hours and 50 minutes, is understandable. The French President finally achieved that the disputed landing rights for the Concorde were granted in Washington, D.C., and in Dallas, Texas.

In Washington Giscard d'Estaing proved to be a far-sighted statesman of stature. Referring to the historic French-American Alliance during the War of

Independence, he stressed that since then the Franco-American friendship has never faded. Speaking of the "malaise American," he said that the Americans in their self-doubt could forget their destiny in the world. He was confident that the United States will overcome the crises of Vietnam and Watergate. In his "Message to America" he emphasized four points of America's mission in the world: 1) Uphold the commitment to defend the West; 2) make an active contribution toward safeguarding the international monetary and financial order; 3) assist in the effort of establishing Europe as political entity of its own based on friendship and cooperation; 4) engage in an increased participation in the dialogue with the Third World to create a more just and stable world order.*

The exceptional success of 200 years of American history strengthens in Giscard d'Estaing's view the confidence that America will meet the challenges of the modern world; while at the same time remain true to the ideal of freedom and humanity.

*[The English text of Giscard d'Estaing's "Message to America" is printed in *Time* Magazine of May 24, 1976, p. 21.]

South Bend, [Beginning of June], 1976

New Elections in Italy

The new elections in Italy scheduled to be held by the end of June have given rise to concern because it is feared that the Communist Party could come into power. The West has to deal with the question whether classified material of NATO can be entrusted to Italy should the Communists be in the government, or whether it would be better to transfer the headquarters of the 6th Fleet from Naples to somewhere else. How will Western Europe react to a possible victory of the Communists in Italy? And what will be the reaction of the United States?

The Danger of Euro-communism

The possible failure of social democracy in Italy is a matter of conscience for the West. Should the West trust the assertion of Enrico Berlinguer who, like a wolf in sheep's clothing, propagates that the Communism in Italy will follow democratic rules? The form of Euro-communism in Italy could spread to other countries. In that, an eminent danger can be seen.

South Bend, June 9/10, 1976

Carter the Leading Democratic Candidate

The primaries of June 8 brought for Jimmy Carter the decisive breakthrough. After he had won the primaries in Ohio and New Jersey, the opposition against him collapsed. Senator Hubert Humphrey of Minnesota as well as Governor George Wallace of Alabama announced that they will no longer seek the Democratic nomination and that they will support Carter. Mayor Richard Daley of Chicago also declared that he will support Carter. As a result, the nomination of Jimmy Carter as presidential candidate of the Democrats is practically assured.

It speaks for the strength of American democracy that such a radical political force as launched by George Wallace did not lead to disintegration but has been absorbed within the Democratic Party and now stands unified behind Carter.

South Bend, June 15, 1976

Before the Italian Elections

America is deeply concerned about the upcoming Italian elections. If it should not be possible to protect Italy from Communism, how should the rest of Europe be protected. The organization "Americans for a Democratic Italy" started a letter writing campaign. About 200,000 Americans of Italian descent have been writing their relatives in Italy not to vote for the Communists. This apparently happened out of fear that Italy could in part turn into a people's republic. At any rate, it is an indication how alarmed people are looking forward to these elections.

June 23, 1976

After the Elections

On June 20/21 a new parliament was elected in Italy. These were in many ways regarded as the most important parliamentary elections in Europe since 30 years. The result is neither encouraging nor disappointing. The Communists did not win to the extent they had hoped for. The Democrazia Christiana was able to stand its ground. Whether the Communists will be conceded a say in the new government remains to be seen. There is a general sigh of relief. But even if the Communists had won, America would have recognized the results of democratic elections.

Cincinnati, [End of June], 1976

Over the Rhine

An old district of Cincinnati with a view over the Ohio River is called "Over the Rhine." It once was the residential area of German immigrants in the 19th century, who out of nostalgia for their homeland thought they had found a piece of the Rhine in America. In a way, this riverscape meets the illusion. But the German residents left long ago, the old half-timbered houses are dilapidated, the entire district has declined into one of the worst slums. As I was myself enticed by the name, I have come here expecting to find a Rhine idyll on the Ohio. The disappointment is therefore twice as great. Cincinnati has been mercilessly overrun by the new industrial development. It once was a flourishing metropolis, which had prospered from the Mississippi shipping industry and had given a boost to the American food business. Nowadays, the city is to a large extent run down. There is a lesson to be learned: Whatever has lost its function in America, goes down more so without mercy than anywhere else in the world.

South Bend, July 4, 1976

The Bicentennial: Fourth of July, 1976

It was a gigantic birthday party. Among the highlights of the day: President Gerald Ford spoke to the national wagon train at Valley Forge*; then he addressed a special audience at Independence Hall in Philadelphia; at 2 p.m. he struck the bell on the Carrier Forrestal in New York Harbor whereby he started the bell ringing throughout the nation. The most spectacular sight was the parade of sailing vessels up the Hudson River from maritime nations all over the world. The largest fireworks ever were displayed in the evening and the giant birthday cake at Fort McHenry in Baltimore added to the festive spirit.**

It was a remarkably harmonious 4th of July. America was at peace and at ease and everyone enjoyed the celebrations from the Jazz Festival in New

Orleans to the rodeo in Flagstaff, Arizona. After two hundred years, the entire world celebrated America's birthday. There were observations in Berlin, Paris, Jerusalem, Leningrad and Warsaw, just to mention a few. It has been a great day and a magnificent spectacle altogether.

Although born by an act of rebellion, the idea of America has grown more by evolution than revolution during the past two hundred years, and it is still evolving. The foundations of American democracy have stood the test of time and will continue to do so in the future.

Now as the yearlong celebrations are over, it is time again to store away the wigs, bonnets, buckles, drums and fifes until the Tricentennial comes around. How will America look in a hundred years from now?

*[That was the horse—and oxen-drawn wagon train accompanied by settlers dressed in their old costumes, how they had conquered the American West in the first half of the 19th century. The national wagon train was set in motion months ago in California. It moved slowly eastward until it reached its destination in Valley Forge, Pennsylvania. Valley Forge, located west of Philadelphia, was the camp where George Washington and his troops had survived under difficult circumstances the winter of 1777-78.]

**[Toward the end of the War of 1812-14 Fort McHenry, which protected the entry to the Harbor of Baltimore, held out against the attack of the British fleet. When the poet Francis Scott Key saw the American flag still waving on the Fort at early dawn, he wrote the lyric of "Star-Spangled Banner," which finally in 1931 was adopted by the U.S. Congress as the National anthem of the United States.]

Addendum to the Bicentennial

The Bicentennial was the 200 year celebration of signing the Declaration of Independence by the Second Continental Congress in Philadelphia on July 4, 1776. The Declaration unleashed irrevocably the War of Independence. The introductory sentence to the second paragraph of the Declaration of Independence—"We hold these Truths to be self-evident, that all Men are created equal, that they are endowed by their Creator with certain unalienable Rights, that among these are Life, Liberty and the Pursuit of

Happiness"—has become the fundamental principle for American political and judicial thinking. In a study to the Bicentennial, I have examined the foreign response to the American Declaration of Independence. For that purpose, I have carried out an inquiry with a number of European National and University Libraries in order to ascertain how widespread the Declaration had been received. Although the news of the rebellion of the British colonies in North America had spread like wildfire throughout Europe, it took a long time for the Declaration to cross the Atlantic. Except for London and Paris, the Declaration remained mostly unknown until late in the 19th century. It seems that most libraries in Europe received a copy of the Declaration of Independence only after 1945. Had the original 13 colonies not succeeded in gaining independence, the Declaration of Independence would have without a doubt been forgotten.

[See Klaus Lanzinger, "The Foreign Response to the Declaration of Independence," in *Americana-Austriaca,* vol.4 (Vienna: Wilhelm Braumüller, 1978, pp. 40-54.]

South Bend, July 15, 1976

The Democratic National Convention

Last night the Democratic National Convention in Madison Square Garden in New York nominated Jimmy Carter by acclamation as the presidential candidate of the Democratic Party. Governor Jerry Brown of California released his 73 delegates for Carter. Following the same example, Morris Udall released his 348 delegate votes. Today Carter proposed Senator Walter Mondale from Minnesota as his running mate for the office of Vice President. The proposal was accepted without opposition to speak of.

Addendum

[At the Republican National Convention in Kansas City on August 19, Gerald Ford was nominated with a narrow majority before Ronald Reagan as the presidential candidate of the Republican Party. Ford chose Senator Robert Dole from Kansas as his running mate for the office of Vice President. Thus, Carter-Mondale and Ford-Dole confronted each other at the presidential election in November.]

South Bend, July 20, 1976

The Mars Landing

With the soft landing of the American probe Viking I on the planet Mars further progress has been made in the exploration of space. The pictures transmitted back to Earth from a 200 million miles distance are stunningly clear. One has the impression as if they were taken on any boulder somewhere on Earth. The surface of Mars is much more similar to Earth than that of the Moon. The thin carbon dioxide atmosphere creates a light-blue horizon, changing to yellow and red. It is assumed that under the icy cap on the North Pole are large quantities of water frozen in. This could be the prerequisite that signs of life will be found on Mars.

The pictures from Mars let us forget the year long journey of the Viking probe through space. Remarkable are the planning and programming of this enterprise by the Jet Propulsion Laboratory in Pasadena, California. No less surprising is the fact that all the equipment and instruments are functioning without a hitch over this distance.

New York, August 17, 1976

[As I reassumed the directorship of the Notre Dame foreign study program in Innsbruck for the two year period 1976-78, my wife and daughter Christine traveled with me to New York where I met the student group. Christine, who had just been admitted as a student to the University of Notre Dame, was given permission to participate in the foreign study program in Innsbruck. Our son Franz stayed on campus in Notre Dame to finish his senior year for the B.A.]

New York Impressions

From the rooftop swimming pool of the Holiday Inn in Upper Manhattan one has an extensive view of the New York Harbor installations along the Hudson River. The piers of Manhattan are empty. What was just a few years ago a busy port, where the big vessels of the world's major shipping lines were docked, no passenger ship is to be seen anymore. The famous Harbor of Manhattan has turned into a ghost town.

At a fruit stand on 9th Avenue, 57th Street, an older gentleman was offering his produce. He spoke no English. My wife, who is versed in the Romance languages, was able to start a conversation. We learned that he had fled from Cuba and just recently found refuge in New York. The room service maid at the Holiday Inn only spoke French. She came from Haiti to New York. The taxi driver, who brought us to the John F. Kennedy International Airport, had fled two years earlier from Russia to America. This has always been the way how millions of people who were searching for freedom and a better life started in New York. It is surprising for me to find out that this process of immigration and assimilation is happening today with the same intensity as it did under similar circumstances at the beginning of the century.

[At the JFK International Airport I met with the 37 students in my charge, who had come together from all parts of the United States for the flight across the Atlantic. We departed from the JFK in the early evening hours of August 17. The new "Jumbo Jet," a Boeing 747, brought us to the Charles de Gaulle Airport in Paris. After a short stopover, we flew on a Caravelle to Munich, landing there at 10 a.m. A motor coach brought us from Munich to Salzburg for the Summer School. The academic year in Innsbruck began on October 1.]

SECTION 7

End of August, 1976-December 31, 1979

Innsbruck, [End of August], 1976

The First Days Back in Austria Again

The beauty of the landscape that one enjoys on a train ride from Salzburg via Zell am See to Innsbruck is much more impressive than I remembered. The beauty of the Alps and the cultural wealth of the country surprise one time and again when one returns to Austria after a longer period of absence. But the drawbacks of living in Europe are felt the moment one starts driving a car. The Autobahn between Salzburg and Munich and from Munich to Stuttgart is hopelessly congested, stalled for hours in a traffic jam. At the border crossings, there are mile-long backups. The access to cities is still a nuisance, for one drives continuously over torn up road constructions. Furthermore, it is nearly impossible to find a place to park the car. On the other hand, the recently opened pedestrian lanes in the inner cities are pleasant. They are charming and preserve the old, historical character. This is rarely to be found in America.

Innsbruck, Tuesday/Wednesday, November 2/3, 1976

The Night of the Election

From 11 p.m. to 9 a.m., Europeans have followed in suspense the outcome of the American presidential election. Via satellite and by the cooperation between the American and the European broadcasting systems, people here can follow live the election in America. The neck-and-neck race between

Carter and Ford makes this election the more suspenseful. Europeans are more inclined to wish that Gerald Ford remained President and that Kissinger's foreign policy would be continued. One is accustomed to it, while Jimmy Carter is still unknown. Carter's statement that America would not intervene if Soviet troops invaded Yugoslavia shocked the Europeans. The great interest in Europe in the American presidential election may be explained by the fact that one is witnessing an event, which can have a decisive influence on Europe's destiny. Whatever the outcome, the American presidential election is a matter of worldwide political significance. It is undisputedly accepted in Europe that the President of the United States takes on the leadership role of the free West.

In the early morning hours it has become increasingly clear that Jimmy Carter has won this election. The Deep South voted solidly, the industrial North, especially the black population, with a large majority for Carter.

November 4, 1976

According to the tabulation in today's edition of the *International Herald Tribune* Carter won 51% vs. Ford 48% of the nearly 80 million ballots cast. 272 electoral votes go to Carter, 235 to Ford. The Democrats also won big in the Senate and the House. The new Senate is made up of 62 Democrats and 38 Republicans; in the House the Democrats now have 288, the Republicans 142 seats.

Newly elected to the Senate are S.I. Hayakawa, R-California; Howard M. Metzenbaum, D-Ohio; Daniel P. Moynihan, D-New York; and Richard G. Lugar, R-Indiana.

Jimmy Carter is the first politician from the South, who has been elected U.S. President since the time before the Civil War.

Innsbruck, November 7, 1976

Like an Unreal Shadow Play

Returning from America, life here appears like an unreal shadow play. One cannot separate from the life in Europe, yet neither can one be fully part of it anymore.

Innsbruck, November 28, 1976

The Entertainment Industry

The popular entertainment industry here is more and more fed by American models. This applies to jazz, rock, country music, thrillers and western films, and to an increasing extent to shows on television. Unfortunately, often third-rate American productions are shown or imitated.

Innsbruck, December 31, 1976

Reflections on the Conclusion of the Bicentennial Year

The signing of the Declaration of Independence on July 4, 1776, was an act of far-reaching historical significance. The 13 British colonies in North America, who had already at the signing of the Declaration of Independence named themselves the "thirteen united States of America," achieved independence in 1783. In the following years they united into a federal state named the United States of America. With the adoption of the U.S. Constitution in 1787, which is the foundation of American democracy, the United States was nearly 150 years ahead of Europe in establishing a democratic government. The Declaration of Independence proclaimed the unalienable rights of all human beings to "Life, Liberty, and the Pursuit of Happiness." This guiding principle is in accordance with the Bill of Rights, the first ten amendments or articles added to the American Constitution in 1791. These articles warrant the protection of the individual from infringement by the government, especially in regard to freedom of religion, freedom of speech, and freedom of the press. They have become the model for basic constitutional rights of civil liberties and have awakened the conscience for the protection of human rights, which finally led to the declaration of universal human rights by the United Nations in 1948. The surprising thing about the Bicentennial was that the whole world spontaneously participated in this American birthday celebration.

Innsbruck, January 20, 1977

Today Jimmy Carter was sworn in as 39th President of the United States. There is every indication that Carter will be a popular President. His inauguration turned out to be a huge public festival in Washington. Carter gives America again a sense of optimism and idealism.

[Jimmy (James Earl) Carter, Jr., was born in Plains, Georgia, 1924; by profession he is a farmer, an engineer, and a politician. Carter was Governor of Georgia, 1971-75, and U.S. President, 1977-81. Following his presidency, he has been actively engaged in peacemaking missions, working for many humanitarian organizations and defending human rights. Next to numerous other honors, he received the Albert Schweitzer Prize for humanitarian work in 1987, and the Felix Houghouet-Boigny UNESCO Peace Prize in 1995.]

[Transl: Jimmy Carter was awarded the Nobel Peace Prize 2002.]

Innsbruck, [January 21], 1977

Vigilance is in Order

The out-going Ford Administration cannot warn enough that the Soviet Union has gained military superiority. A sudden thrust into Western Europe cannot be excluded anymore. In fact, it is in the long-term strategic planning of the Soviet Union. How would one otherwise understand the extensive protective measures taken in Russia against a nuclear war on the one hand, and the offensive nuclear armament on the other. *Time* Magazine bluntly published operational plans of the East for an advance to the Rhine. Similar plans were also confirmed by the French media. Although these gloomy predictions may be exaggerated, a heightened vigilance is nevertheless in order.

Innsbruck, January 23, 1977

Americanism without Awareness

Without being aware of it, most areas of European life have been penetrated by American life styles. This refers to common habits of every day life, how people dress, interior furnishings, television and radio programs, merchandise, toys, clubs of any kind, discotheques, shopping malls, advertising, cars, sports, etc.

The European attitude toward America is ambivalent: On the one hand, America is vehemently rejected, but on the other hand, Europeans, in their daily lives, follow consciously or unconsciously American models. Despite all the revolt against America, there is a hidden "Amerikasehnsucht," a longing for America.

Innsbruck, [Beginning of March], 1977

Vienna as Transit Station

Hardly a day goes by without a dissident from the East Bloc countries arriving in Vienna with hopes of being able to go on to the United States. The human rights catalogue of the final accords of the Helsinki Agreement has proven to be a time fuse. The voices demanding more freedom in the East Bloc are not to be silenced anymore—first the Charta 77 in Czechoslovakia,* then the group around the physicist Sakharov in Moscow.** The hope for more freedom is being nourished by President Carter's firm stand on human rights. The follow-up Conference on Security and Cooperation in Europe (CSCE), which will convene by the end of summer in Belgrade, promises to have an intense debate on a timely issue.

*[On January 5, 1977, 257 citizens of Czechoslovakia signed the Charta 77. They demanded that the human rights catalogue of the Helsinki Agreement be fulfilled, as had been promised.]

**[The renowned Russian nuclear physicist Andrei Sakharov, who was born in Moscow in 1921, fought relentlessly for human rights. In 1970 he founded the Committee for Human Rights, and in 1975 he received the Nobel Peace Prize. Sakharov was sent into internal exile to Gorky, 1980-86. After a short period of freedom in the Gorbachev era, he died in Moscow in 1989.]

Passed on the Left

In the last decades the understanding of democracy in America and Europe has been reversed. While American democracy has always been too liberal for Europe, a conservative America now stands opposite to a radical progressive Europe. Aside from the people's republics of Eastern Europe, which have turned the democratic idea into communist dictatorships, the increasing radicalization in Western Europe is evoking a crisis in the mutual understanding with the United States. How should the United States adjust to the growing Euro-communism, and how can the radical leftist-leaning reformers in Europe be understood in Washington? In its understanding of democracy, Europe has passed America on the left.

How Far Left is Left?

At the University of Rome a downright street battle broke out when a communist union official addressing the striking students was stormed by radical leftist student groups. Sworn to anarchy, how far left are these students standing? Yet what happened in Rome was only a visible sign of the inner social unrest which is threatening large parts of Europe. Most European countries are facing an avalanche of unemployed academics. The masses of young people, who leave the universities every year with or without a degree, are quite in the air in regard to their future. A great deal of misery, hopelessness and disappointment is hiding behind this uncertainty. The futility and aimlessness for the future harbor an explosive danger that can lead to violent riots.

European Pessimism

Coming from America to Europe, one is confronted with a pessimistic attitude that is difficult to grasp. There is a widespread sullenness nourished by the assumption that whatever one does is of no use anyway. People here live in the past; they keep their eyes closed to the future. It takes a while until one gets used again to this defeatism. This pessimistic attitude is destructive. It is a heavy burden on the young generation who is striving to develop its abilities.

Marbach, Baden-Wurttemberg, [Middle of March], 1977

Naples on the Neckar

Whoever visits Marbach on the Neckar these days, the birthplace of the German playwright Friedrich Schiller, will be surprised to see that this small town has assumed a southern Italian character. Italian foreign workers have moved into the half-timbered houses where well-established burghers once lived. The inns have been turned into pizzerias, and the laundry hangs across the narrow alleys for drying. In front of the town's fountain produce stalls have been set up. All this gives the small town a certain Mediterranean charm. But Marbach only illustrates what is happening to many small towns north of the Alps. It is the sociological infiltration from the poorer European countries in the South. While the affluent middle class is moving to the suburbs, the foreign workers take over the empty, old and partly dilapidated buildings left behind. This reminds me of a similar event, which I was able to observe in Cincinnati, Ohio.* Basically, such shifts in social structure are not unusual. They will increase here to the extent the European Community will be united and will allow free movement to its population.

*[Transl: See above entry "Over the Rhine," end of June, 1976.]

Innsbruck, March 16, 1977

Austrian Studies in America

Today Chancellor Bruno Kreisky presented the University of Minnesota a donation of 1 million dollars for the purpose of establishing a Chair for Austrian Studies. At the same time also an Institute for Austrian Studies will be established. The financial means for this donation were procured by selling "Amerikasterne" (America Stars) during the Bicentennial Year. All sections of the Austrian population participated in this fund-raising campaign out of gratitude for the help Austria had received through the Marshall Plan.

March 18, 1977

Concerned about Human Rights

In his address to the United Nations, President Carter made an impassioned plea to the world community to make every effort for the protection of human rights. No state, Carter emphasized, can regard maltreating its citizens as a domestic affair.

Vienna, [End of March], 1977

Refugee Tragedies

Austria is by its geographic location an outpost of the Free World. Not a day goes by without a number of people fleeing, at the risk of their lives, across the border to Austria. Here refugees from the East arrive first, here they are accepted, taken care of, and transferred to Western missions. More than ever, refugee tragedies play out at the U.S. Consulate in Vienna. People who fled from the East are standing in line under heavy security. They all hope to be admitted to the United States and to start a new life there. This opportunity is offered only to a few, while many others have adjusted to years of waiting and endless petitions. Despite favorable signs of easing tensions, the border here to the East has lost nothing of its harsh reality.

Vienna, March 31, 1977

Easing of Travel Restrictions

The détente between East and West shows here in Vienna that travel restrictions with Hungary and Czechoslovakia have been eased. On Sunday mornings tour buses arrive here with tourists from Budapest and Prague who spend the day in Vienna. These guests from the East can now be seen in the Prater amusement park, in the Schönbrunn Palace, and in the museums. It is astonishing how devoted these visitors stand before the remnants of the Habsburg Monarchy. It may also be regarded as progress of détente that a Hungarian restaurant chain can now operate establishments in Budapest, East-Berlin, and in Vienna. Here in the Danube region, the lessening of tensions has become irreversible.

Innsbruck, April 8, 1977

Political Terror

The assassination in broad daylight of Generalbundesanwalt Siegfried Buback in Karlsruhe not only left the German population horror-stricken, but made also the public throughout Europe once more realize that there is an underground terrorism at work, which does not recoil from any act of brutality.

[Transl: Generalbundesanwalt is the Chief Prosecutor of the German Federal Republic at the Federal Constitutional Court in Karlsruhe.]

Easter Sunday, April 1 0, 1977

Urbi et Orbi

It is one of the most moving moments in the Christian world when the Holy Father proclaims, from the Loggia of the Vatican, the Easter message and gives the blessing Urbi et Orbi in 14 languages before 200,000 faithful assembled at St. Peter's Square. Pope Paul VI is keeping up his physical strength admirably, although the frailty of advanced age is being felt.

Innsbruck, May 8, 1977

President Carter in Europe

At the summit of the seven leading industrial nations (Canada, the Federal Republic of Germany, France, Great Britain, Italy, Japan, and the United States) in London, President Carter met for the first time with the heads of government in Europe. Will he succeed in passing on his unfailing optimism to his European partners? Carter used his stay in England to visit the George Washington Memorial in Sulgrave, located in the northwest of London. A branch of the Washington family had come from there in the 17th century to America. On the occasion of his visit, Carter was made an honorary citizen of that small town.

[The Washington family, who belonged to the landed gentry, had their estate and manor in the village of Sulgrave in Northamptonshire. Following the Civil Wars in England, the great-grandfather of George Washington immigrated to Virginia in 1657, where he could establish himself as plantation owner. Sulgrave erected a monument to George Washington, the first President of the United States.]

Innsbruck, May 19, 1977

South Africa

The continued apartheid policy in South Africa has become a scandal, which the world community cannot accept indifferently any longer. How widely the points of view between Pretoria and the rest of the world differ, has come to light these days at the meeting between U.S. Vice President Walter Mondale and the South African Prime Minister Johannes Vorster in Vienna. While Walter Mondale spoke up in unmistakable language for human rights, Vorster said that the situation of the Negroes in South Africa could not be compared with those in the United States. And he added that South Africa has already done everything anyway the world expects of it to do.

Innsbruck, May 20, 1977

Goal Achieved

When I was informed by the Provost Office of the University of Notre Dame that I have been promoted to full professor, I felt a great sense of happiness and relief. After twenty years of striving, many roundabout ways and overcoming many difficulties, the goal of my academic career has been achieved.

Innsbruck, May 22, 1977

President Carter at Notre Dame

Already the 10 p.m. evening news here reported on the speech, which President Jimmy Carter had given this afternoon at the commencement exercises of the University of Notre Dame in Indiana. Carter, who received the degree of Doctor of Laws honoris causa, gave the commencement address. It was a declaration of principle of the new American foreign policy, which attracted much attention in Europe. Accordingly, Carter will put American foreign policy on new moral grounds. He announced that the cooperation with developing countries will be increased and that efforts will be made to alleviate the North-South disparity between the rich and poor nations. Above all he emphasized that he will endeavor to overcome the fear of communism. Nor will America be ready to support rightwing dictators just to fight communism. The policy of casting out the devil by Beelzebub has failed. America will continue to advance détente and to cooperate with the Soviet Union and China. But the priority of his policy will remain the protection of human rights.

[Transl: For the full text of President Carter's historic commencement address at the University of Notre Dame on May 22, 1977, see Wilson D. Miscamble, ed., *Go Forth and Do Good: Memorable Notre Dame Commencement Addresses* (Notre Dame, Indiana: University of Notre Dame Press, 2003), pp. 196-203.]

Innsbruck, [Beginning of June], 1977

Escapism

The American Indians are a favorite theme of escapism in Europe. Talking about the Indians in North America stimulates the romantic imagination. One can get excited about a faraway exotic topic, which diverts from the real problems at home. In America, on the other hand, it is a favorite theme of escapism, especially on parties, to talk about trips made or about going to Europe.

Innsbruck, June 15, 1977

Elections in Spain

In the first free parliamentary elections in Spain in 41 years, the electorate has shown surprising democratic maturity. The Democratic Centrist Party under Prime Minister Suarez gained 35%, the Socialist Workers Party 26%, while the rightist Phalanx as well as the extreme Left got 8% each. The Iberian Peninsula, which had been cut off for decades, has become present in Europe. Spain now has an open road to the European Community.

Innsbruck, June 20, 1977

Warning About Euro-communism

At a conference in Washington, former U.S. Secretary of State Henry Kissinger gave a remarkable speech, in which he spoke about the development of Euro-communism. Kissinger warned that Euro-communism was a danger for the Western Alliance. Should the Communist parties, above all in Italy and France, come to power, NATO would be undermined and the presence of American troops in Europe put in question. It would also have far-reaching consequences for America's relations with its treaty partners. Europe should free itself from the feeling that Communism be unpreventable.

Innsbruck, [Beginning of July], 1977

A Common Currency

Europe would gain a great deal if it would finally succeed in introducing a common currency. Be it a Euro-Dollar, Euro-Schilling or Euro-Franc, there would be no need any more to change money at the borders between German Marks, Schillings, Francs, Liras, Guilders, Kronas or Pounds.

July 24, 1977

Hope for a Common World Civilization

This year's Salzburg Festival was opened with the notable address by the President of Senegal Léopold Sédar Senghor. The philosopher, poet and statesman spoke about Austria representing a common world civilization. Today, the music of Mozart is understood everywhere, no matter on which continent it is heard. Austria, whose music, poetry and art has originated from the manifold intellectual encounters in Central Europe, offers an example for a possible universal world civilization, which could unite all peoples in a sense of a common humanity.

[End of July], 1977

In a Festive Mood

At the time of summer festivals in Austria, a special festive mood arises, which spreads among the native population as well as the many guests from abroad. Who wouldn't like to be carried away by it and spend at least one evening in a good mood?

Innsbruck, [Beginning of September], 1977

Frustrated

"Frustriert"—this frequently used and misused word fits the present European mentality in a disquieting way. Conditions in Europe are apt to nourish frustration. The stiff social situation freezes human relations. Travels to far away continents are only an escape but no solution for the real problems. One problem is the fact that professional development is still constrained to national borders. Thereby, the young generation is being deprived of further personal growth and the chances of professional advancement. The older generation, whose life's expectations have frequently been left unfulfilled, have, for a long time, already resigned. This widespread morose atmosphere festers distrust and narrows the view how the world is seen. There is a lack of vision how the future can be mastered and new opportunities for the young generation be opened beyond national borders. By this self-centered attitude and by continuously looking backward, there is the danger of an increasing suffocating provincialism and of failing to see what matters.

Innsbruck, [Middle of September], 1977

The European Parliament

The first general elections to the European Parliament should take place in the fall of 1978. What kind of legislative power will this European Parliament be able to exercise? Will it have only an advisory function, or will it become a legislative body that can pass binding laws for the member states of the European Community (EC)?

As long as the EC is not coming together to a political union, being able to speak with one voice and to make binding decisions for all member states, the wish of becoming an equal partner of the United States will remain an illusion.

[The first general elections to the European Parliament in Strasbourg were held June 7-10, 1979. The original 410 seats were distributed among the nine EC countries according to the size of their populations. Each of the four large countries—France, the German Federal Republic, Great Britain, and Italy—were entitled to 81 seats. General elections to the European Parliament, which in the meantime has been enlarged to 518 seats, are held every five years.]

Innsbruck, October 16, 1977

The Terror Scene

Since weeks, news reports in the German Federal Republic have been dominated by the terror scene. At first, one had taken waiting for hours on end at the border crossing from Austria to Germany, especially on the Walserberg near Salzburg and in Kufstein, in good stride with the understanding that intensified border controls were necessary. One also acquiesced in the belief that this crisis will go by and solve itself. But by the hijacking of a Lufthansa airplane on its flight from Mallorca to Frankfurt, it has become clear that this terror scene is being commanded by an international conspiracy.

While the public at large fears for the life of the president of the German Federation of Industry, Hans-Martin Schleyer, who was kidnapped, the anxiety about the fate of the 87 hostages on board the hijacked Lufthansa airplane is growing. They have been holding out for five days and were flown today from Dubai to Aden. While one ultimatum follows another, the mad and brutal behavior of the hostage takers is hardening. If it has not already become clear for a long time, the present hostage crisis proves that international terror can only be reined in by concerted action of all countries who are members of the United Nations.

October 23, 1977

The hostage crisis of the hijacked Lufthansa aircraft has come to a good end in Mogadisho, the lives of the 87 passengers could be saved. But with unimaginable brutality, the pilot of the aircraft was shot before the eyes of the hostages. Just as merciless, the terrorists killed Hans-Martin Schleyer. Terrorism cries out for an international intervention. Under the pressure of airline pilots, the UN put the fight against terrorism and air piracy on the agenda of the next session of the General Assembly.

[Hans-Martin Schleyer, born 1915, an expert on industrial management, since 1955 was on the board of trustees of Daimler-Benz AG, since 1973 president of the German Employers' Association, and since 1976 president of the German Federation of Industry. Schleyer was kidnapped by the terrorist group "Red Army Fraction" on September 5, 1977. On October 18, 1977, his body was found in Mulhouse, across the German border in France.]

Innsbruck, November 18, 1977

Dr. Kurt Schuschnigg (1897-1977)

The former Federal Chancellor of Austria Dr. Kurt Schuschnigg passed away quietly in the village of Mutters near Innsbruck. He was 80 years old. Dr. Schuschnigg personified dignity and distinction. By profession a lawyer, he had entered politics early in life: 1927-33 representative of the Christian Social Party in the Nationalrat, the Lower House of the Austrian Parliament, 1932-34 Minister of Justice and Education, and from 1934 to March 12, 1938 last Federal Chancellor of the free Austria before annexation. It is still an open question whether, in March of 1938, Dr. Schuschnigg should have accepted the ultimatum for his resignation or whether he should have offered resistance instead.

At the end of the Second World War Kurt Schuschnigg was liberated by American troops from the concentration camp. In 1948 he emigrated with his family to America. He taught political science at the University of St. Louis in Missouri. In 1956 he was naturalized as U.S. citizen. Dr. Schuschnigg returned to Austria in 1967 and spent the last years of his life withdrawn in Mutters.

Innsbruck, November 19/20, 1977

Anwar Sadat before the Knesset

As the Egyptian President Anwar Sadat had accepted the invitation of Menachem Begin to come to Jerusalem, the world could watch over this weekend an event, which just a short time ago would have been inconceivable. Anwar Sadat was welcomed in Israel with jubilation. He addressed the Knesset and presented his peace proposals. Begin and Sadat held out the prospect for a lasting peace between Israel and Egypt. With this journey, Sadat has shown great courage, farsight as well as his readiness for taking risks. Will it bring the long hoped-for peace in the Middle East?

December 4, 1977

The Arab camp has been so deeply divided by Sadat's visit to Israel that an overall solution of the Middle East crisis will not come about. However, there is the possibility that a separate peace treaty between Israel and Egypt will be concluded.

Innsbruck, December 9, 1977

Worried about NATO

Voices of concern will not go away that the North Atlantic Treaty Organization is facing difficulties. At this year's winter conference of NATO in Brussels, worries have been expressed that the U.S. is making too many concessions in the SALT II negotiations, while the Warsaw Pact countries are continuing their armament undiminished.

Innsbruck, [Beginning of January], 1978

Which Attitude to Assume?

Which attitude should one assume as an American in Europe or as an emigrant when one returns to one's old home country? The best attitude will be to keep a friendly distance and to remain open-minded for local conditions and events, but under no circumstances to interfere in domestic political affairs.

Innsbruck, January 5, 1978

President Carter's Tour of the World

Over New Year's President Carter embarked on a big journey to get acquainted with various regions of the world. In a whirlwind tour of nine days, he covered 18,500 miles, visiting seven countries on three continents. The tour led him from Warsaw to Teheran, then on to New Delhi, Riyadh, from there to the Aswan Dam in Egypt, and finally to Paris and Brussels. Carter was able to get an idea of the present international situation, before meeting with Giscard d'Estaing. Nothing could have made it clearer that Europe is only one of several regions in the world which American foreign policy has to deal with.

January 6, 1978

While President Carter had talks with representatives of NATO and the European Community in Brussels, U.S. Secretary of State Cyrus Vance handed the St. Stephen's Crown over to the Parliament in Budapest. It was a goodwill gesture. Since 1945 the St. Stephen's Crown has been in American safekeeping in Fort Knox. Without a doubt, the Carter Administration wanted to show Poland and Hungary that the East Bloc countries can count on America's confidence.

Innsbruck, January 15, 1978

Ante Portas

What has been feared for a long time, cannot, it seems, be prevented any longer: Italy's Communists are pushing to get into the government. The DC (Christian Democratic Party) at first refused to let the KPI (Communist Party of Italy) be part of the government, but the cabinet of Andreotti is about to resign. There is only the historic compromise left: Either share power with the Communists or call new elections.

This situation also challenged the Carter Administration to take a clear stand. Washington's position is now following more the view of Henry Kissinger that the participation of the Communists in a democratic West European government would strain the Atlantic Alliance.

January 16, 1978

The minority cabinet Giulio Andreotti has resigned. That was the 39th government since the end of the Second World War. Once again, Italy is without a government, until Andreotti will succeed in forming a new government under different conditions. The pressure from the street is getting noticeably louder.

Addendum

Andreotti finally succeeded in forming a new government with the exclusion of the Communists. But the Communists were conceded a stronger role in the legislative process in Parliament.

[During the semester break in February 1978, my wife and I took a tour by car through Italy, which led us from Innsbruck to Florence, Perugia, Rome, Naples, and on to Taormina in Sicily.]

Assisi, [Middle of February], 1978

Impressions of the Journey through Italy

One can share the feelings of Hermann Hesse. Tuscany and Umbria—the region around Florence, Perugia, and Assisi—belong to one of the most beautiful cultural scenes in Europe. The eye cannot see enough of it. Be it the multi-colored marble facade of the Cathedral of Santa Maria del Fiore, Brunelleschi's dome, Michelangelo's late work, the Pieta in the Duomo, the incomparable masterworks of the Tuscan school of painting in the Uffizi Gallery, or the frescoes of Cimabue and Giotto in the Basilica of St. Francis of Assisi, the eternal Italy has not lost anything of its attraction.

However, one step through the center of Perugia shows the problems of today's Italy. How can anyone still live in these centuries-old buildings? Wherever you look, the aggravating problems of the old inner cities are visible. Poverty lives in the narrow alleys, the houses are dilapidated, and the streets suffocate with the automotive traffic. The political consequences of these wretched conditions are understandable.

Rome, February 20, 1978

The plight of the inner city can especially be seen in Rome. In a graffiti scheme to an extent never seen before, any available wall has been scrawled with hammer and sickle. Without a doubt, one part of the Italian population is waiting for Communism as a salvation that will solve all problems, while the other part just as strongly abhors and fears Communism. This polarization of Italian society has created a threatening tension in the country, led to distrust and fear, if not to a civil war like situation. High schools and universities have been thrown into chaos by the continuing agitation and violent riots.

February 22, 1978

The Audience with the Pope

Pope Paul VI has scheduled for each Wednesday morning at 11 a general audience in the new Aula del Nervi with a capacity of 6,000 persons. Visitors to Rome, but especially invited schools have admission to these audiences. To see and hear the Pope speak in person is a moving experience. Paul VI spoke with a memorable, clearly articulated though fragile voice. He gave to the faithful present in the Hall as well as to Christians everywhere a Lenten sermon, which was distinguished by its depth of thought and convincing faith. The meaning of the "Quaresima," he emphasized, was to change one's ways and the renewal of the Christian conscience. Pope Paul VI radiates a deep humanity, while at the same time one can recognize a sharp intellect and an inward-withdrawn personality. The relaxed human atmosphere of this papal audience was also expressed by the participation of a troupe of acrobats from the Circus Medrano, who performed parts of their art at the beginning and toward the conclusion of the audience. Not only the visitors, also Paul VI followed their presentation with great delight.

Naples, [End of February], 1978

Who comes to Naples with the romantic image of "O sole mio," will experience a bitter disappointment. Naples has become an inferno of modern industrial society. Dense fumes from the indiscriminately dispersed refineries hang over the much praised Bay with its view of Vesuvius. In the city, the visitor is confronted with unparalleled poverty and neglect. Naples may well have one of the worst slums with all its negative side effects in the industrialized world. The decline of the maritime traffic has added its part to this sordid condition. The megalopolis, where several million people live crammed together, stretches far beyond Naples to Salerno and Sorrento. The problems of today's Italy are concentrated in the small and middle-sized cities, which, it appears, cannot cope with the industrialization. This is the tug-of-war between Andreotti and Berlinguer.

Innsbruck, March 18, 1978

Aldo Moro

Not only in Italy, all across Europe people are still in shock under the impression of the brutal kidnapping of Aldo Moro, the chairman of the Demo-Christiana (DC). Last Thursday, March 16, about 9 in the morning, the Red Brigades assaulted the car of Aldo Moro in broad daylight in the center of Rome. With hardly imaginable brutality and brazenness the escorts were shot down and Moro abducted. Moro was on his way to the Parliament where the newly formed government should have received a vote of confidence. Never before have the leading party and the opposition been so quickly of one mind. Alarmed by this criminal act, not only the center right parties closed ranks, but also the Left distanced itself from this crime and is now more willing to cooperate with the democratic center.

April 10, 1978

Carter and Europe

President Carter is simply not understood in Europe. There has not been an American president in a long time who has met here with such little understanding and sympathy. The mistakes may probably lie on both sides. Carter's human rights policy is regarded in Europe as daydreaming. But on the other hand, Carter has not made much of an effort to please Europe either. His Administration has so far not paid special attention to Europe's problems. Furthermore, the weak dollar aggravates the situation because it makes it more and more difficult to export to America. Finally, President Carter's decision to postpone the production of the neutron bomb has led to misunderstandings in Europe.

Innsbruck, April 12, 1978

Der Mann ohne Eigenschaften

Chancellor Dr. Bruno Kreisky mentioned yesterday in a television interview that the only book he had taken with him into emigration was Robert Musil, *Der Mann ohne Eigenschaften* (The Man Without Characteristics). This reminds me of an experience which I had myself with the book. Moving from Innsbruck to South Bend in 1971, a crate with books was shipped by surface freight. The crate had survived the transportation by boat across the Atlantic and the Great Lakes to Chicago. However, when it was delivered to the house, it fell from the truck on the driveway and broke apart. The first book I saw on top of the pile was Musil's *Der Mann ohne Eigenschaften*. I certainly had not packed the thick volume for patriotic reasons, but took it along out of interest for the contemporary novel. Only in the course of time, have I become aware of the Austrian substance of this great work. Living abroad, one reads one's own literature with greater interest and learns to appreciate its value.

Innsbruck, May 10, 1978

On the Streets of Rome

The anxious assumptions of recent weeks and days have turned into dreadful certainty. The body of Aldo Moro was found in a car riddled with bullets on a side street in the center of Rome. The abduction and hostage taking of the 61 year old chairman of the DC, who had also served several times as prime minister, has come to a tragic end. The civilized world is facing a frightening puzzle: How unscrupulously fanatic, how atrocious must these criminal terrorists, who took the life of Aldo Moro, be? This does not concern Italy alone but all countries where the blank terror is doing its sinister work. Rarely has the whole of Europe mourned in solidarity for a statesman as in these days for Aldo Moro.

[Toward the end of our two year stay in Innsbruck, my wife and I took a tour through the Federal Republic of Germany. Our daughter Christine, who had returned to Innsbruck after the academic year in Notre Dame, joined us on this trip.]

[End of June], 1978

German Travel Impressions

On a tour through the Federal Republic of Germany, one becomes clearly aware how strong the medieval heritage still is. The impression of the Romanesque and Gothic monuments are just as overwhelming as they have always been. There are the powerful Romanesque Cathedrals of Worms, Speyer and Trier, the great Gothic Cathedral of Cologne, and Charlemagne's Chapel at Aachen. There is the line of castles and palaces along the Neckar and Rhine from Heidelberg to Coblentz. The magnificent Rathaus of the old Hanseatic City of Bremen stands proudly on the market square. Further to the south, Lessing's Wolfenbüttel and the university town of Göttingen exude a special atmosphere. Germany has preserved much of its old cultural heritage, as there are many charming places which have maintained their traditional ambience. But in contrast to it, there is a highly developed industrial landscape, which can only be compared with America.

A Waiting Interim Solution

As capital of the Federal Republic, Bonn is still a waiting interim solution. The small city on the Rhine is more adapted to a contemplative life, less suitable for a capital of a large modern country. The Bundestag, the Lower House of Parliament, is provisionally still housed in the building of the former Technical Institute. Emergency accommodations have temporarily been changed into government buildings and diplomatic representations. The tragedy of the divided Germany has brought it about that one has adjusted to improvisations because the present political situation understandably cannot be accepted as a permanent solution.

Gegend von Schierke und Elend*

Reaching south of Göttingen a lookout point with a view over the Zonengrenze, the demarcation line between East and West Germany, one becomes aware of desolation much more cruel than Goethe describes it in the Walpurgisnacht. Along the Zonengrenze from Lübeck to Passau, a stretch of no-man's-land has been created. Here the roads simply stop and hill slopes have been clear-cut so that the view from the observation towers is not obstructed. The otherwise so impulsive activity of the Federal Republic comes to a complete standstill. People do not talk about the Zonengrenze. But there it stands as a monstrous and frightening reality.

*[Transl: Gegend von Schierke und Elend (Region of Schierke and Elend) refers, at the beginning of the Walpurgisnacht in Goethe's *Faust* Pt. I, to the location where Faust and Mephistopheles set out on their ascent of the Brocken. They try to find their way through a swampy, desolate area. The two small towns of Schierke and Elend are located east of Göttingen at the foothills of the Brocken, the highest peak of the Harz Mountains. According to legend, witches gather on the Brocken on April 30, the night before the feast day of St. Walpurgis. Faust is tempted by Mephisto to participate in the Witches' Sabbath. The Walpurgis Night is Goethe's vision of evil. As I looked across the Zonengrenze in June of 1978 and realized that Schierke, Elend and the Brocken were nearby, the Walpurgisnacht inevitably came to mind.]

[End of July, my wife and I together with our daughter Christine returned to South Bend, Indiana. Our son Franz was at the University of California Berkeley studying mathematics.]

South Bend, August 2, 1978

Coming Back to America

After an absence of two years, one sees many things which are typical of America and determine life here. Among these are: 1) The peace and easiness of everyday life; 2) the discipline on the roads, observing the 55 mph speed limit; 3) the general stability; 4) the abundance of consumer goods offered in department stores and supermarkets, which shows the common affluence of the country; 5) compared to previous years, the pacified social scene, the progress made on the racial issue; and 6) the public atmosphere, which has remained untouched by terrorism.

August 12, 1978

Mourning for Paul VI (1897-1978)

Pope Paul VI passed away on August 6. It is not saying too much that the entire world is mourning for this Pope. In the spirit of the Vatican Council, he deepened the understanding among Christians and with people of other faiths. He evoked social conscience and exemplified through his own life modesty and humility.

August 26, 1978

John Paul I

In surprising unanimity, the conclave in the Sistine Chapel elected today Cardinal Albino Luciani, the Patriarch of Venice, as Pope. He assumed, after his immediate predecessors John XXIII and Paul VI, the double name John Paul I. The new Pope will certainly continue the tasks of the Second Vatican Council, but he will most likely give the Catholic Church a conservative character.

South Bend, September 12, 1978

The Summit Meeting at Camp David

President Carter had invited President Anwar Sadat and Prime Minister Menachem Begin to Camp David in order to restart the stalled peace negotiations between Egypt and Israel. Now everyone is keenly looking forward to whether an agreement can be reached.

[The original military Camp David was converted by President Franklin D. Roosevelt into a second official residence where the American President with his family and guests can withdraw to a secluded area. Camp David is located 70 miles northwest of Washington, D.C. From the White House, it can be reached by helicopter in short time.]

September 17, 1978

Camp David Accords

In a special report, NBC broadcast this evening the historic ceremony from the East Room of the White House, in which President Anwar Sadat and Prime Minister Menachem Begin together with President Carter signed a preliminary peace agreement for the Middle East. In moving words, all three expressed their satisfaction about the successful conference. The peace treaties between Egypt and Israel should be concluded in three months hence. Prime Minister Begin called the accords of Camp David a kind of Congress of Vienna for the Middle East; for there is hope that they will become the carrying pillar for a comprehensive peace in the region.

The essential items of the accords are: 1) The Sinai Peninsula is returned to Egypt; 2) the borders of Israel with Egypt are guarantied; 3) in an interim phase of five years, autonomy status should be given to the Palestinians on the West Bank.

President Jimmy Carter has shown great courage with this conference. He brought all the power of the American presidency to bear. A failure would have damaged his political career, while its success now gives him the enhanced image of a statesman and the prestige of the peacemaker.

September 24, 1978

The news of the Camp David accords had hardly broken when reservations came to the fore. The other Arab countries rejected Egypt's unilateral action. Furthermore, the problem of the Palestinians seemed in no way having been solved. Nonetheless, Anwar Sadat was given an enthusiastic hero's welcome on his return to Cairo. Here in America, the success of the Camp David summit meeting is seen as the best moment of the Carter Presidency so far.

South Bend, September 29, 1978

In Disbelief

In disbelief and dismay the world received the news this morning that John Paul I, only 33 days after he had been elected Pope, died of a heart attack during the night.

September 30, 1978

A Minute of Silence

In the Notre Dame Football Stadium, full of the resounding voices of 60,000 fans, a minute of silence was observed in memory of John Paul I. The stadium was so quiet that one could have heard a needle drop. While the national anthem was sung, which is intoned before every football game, the American flag was raised to half-staff.

South Bend, October 16, 1978

Like a Wildfire

The news spread like a wildfire today that a cardinal from Poland, Karol Wojtyla, has been elected as the new Pope by the conclave in Rome. This is the first time in 400 years that a non-Italian and for the first time ever that a Polish cardinal has been elected pope. Cardinal Wojtyla assumed the name John Paul II.

Admirable is the foresight of having chosen a cardinal from a communist country. There is great jubilation in the Polish community in Chicago over the news that the Archbishop of Krakow now occupies the See of St. Peter. The new Pope is said to have good knowledge of the present situation of the Catholic Church, especially in regard to the confrontation with communism in Eastern Europe. He is open-minded in matters of social concern but seems to be reserved conservative on questions of theology.

Sunday, October 22, 1978

John Paul II

Today John Paul II celebrated his first Mass on St. Peter's Square in Rome. The nearly 300,000 faithful who had come to his inauguration gave him a spontaneous reception. This feeling of friendliness was also transmitted to the hundreds of millions of people who followed the Mass on St. Peter's Square on television. What makes the new Pope from Poland so engaging? He radiates goodness of heart and at the same time decisiveness. He is fluent in many languages. Besides Slavic languages, he is also fluent in Italian and French, and he can communicate in German and English. He is a splendid rhetorician and he begins his high office with almost youthful energy. But above all, there is a sense of confidence that this new Pope can lead the Church into the 21st century.

South Bend, October 24, 1978

Measures Against Inflation

President Carter announced measures to fight the creeping inflation in America. He proposed that: 1) wage increases be held at 7%; 2) price increases should not surpass the 6% limit annually; and 3) the federal government declare a hiring freeze, meaning that positions becoming vacant will not be filled. Thereby, the budget deficit should be reduced. But the success of these measures depends on the voluntary cooperation of all parties involved.

The measures of Carter against inflation have been received with great skepticism because voluntary restrictions on wages and prices usually don't work. And besides, more and more contradictions in the Carter Administration's program are coming to light. On the one hand, it continues the welfare system that increases the deficit; and on the other hand, saving measures are proposed which have little effect. Governments abroad reacted with complete distrust of Carter's proposals. As a consequence, the exchange rate of the dollar reached a new low.

October 25, 1978

Little Understood Abroad

Jimmy Carter is one of the American presidents who are little understood abroad. But Carter should not be underestimated. He was elected by the American people with a convincing majority. Carter corresponds more with what Americans consider themselves to be and not with what people abroad imagine the American president should be.

South Bend, November 6, 1978

Nuclear Power Station Rejected

Newspapers in America reported briefly that yesterday's national referendum in Austria rejected putting into operation the nuclear power station near the town of Zwentendorf west of Vienna. As a result, atomic energy as a source of producing electric power has been excluded in Austria for the foreseeable future.

South Bend, December 3, 1978

Desperate Odysseys

In recent months, it happened several times that refugees from Vietnam fled on hardly seaworthy ships, seeking asylum in the Philippines and Malaysia. But they were turned away from harbor to harbor until the boat capsized and hundreds of people drowned. How desperate must these people have been that they exposed themselves to such a danger and risked their lives for it?

December 15, 1978

Diplomatic Relations with China

President Carter announced today that the United States, beginning January 1, 1979, will enter into diplomatic relations with the People's Republic of China. America adheres to the One-China policy and regards the People's Republic as the only representation of the Chinese people. The Embassy in Taipei will be closed and the defense treaty with Taiwan terminated. This step does not come as a surprise, for it had been prepared by the Shanghai Communiqué of 1972. But what will become of Taiwan? Will it be peacefully integrated into Mainland China, or will there be military confrontation? What will be the future attitude of the United States toward Taiwan?

December 17, 1978

An Uproar of Indignation

President Carter's announcement caused an uproar of indignation on the conservative side of Congress. What will happen with the 17 million Chinese on Taiwan? Which guarantees are there that the island will not be taken by military force? Senator Goldwater from Arizona has even gone so far as to declare that he may test in court the President's decision of terminating the defense treaty with Taiwan without previous consultation of the Senate. In a burst of outrage, there were anti-American demonstrations in Taiwan, which threatened to storm the U.S. Embassy in Taipei, even before it was shut down.

December 26, 1978

Different Points of View on the China Question

1. The pragmatic point of view of President Carter: A billion people constitute such a large economic, military, and diplomatic power that only full diplomatic relations will do.

2. The opposition in the Senate: On December 22, Senator Barry Goldwater filed suit against President Carter in the U.S. District Court in Washington, D.C. The Court should decide whether or not the President has the constitutional authority to renounce the defense treaty with Taiwan without consulting the Senate. Goldwater also questions the proposition that Taiwan is only a province of the People's Republic and has no right to exist on its own. How can it be reconciled with human rights if 17 million people are turned over to Communism?
3. The economic potential: It is also a matter of market shares and spheres of influence.

South Bend, January 2, 1979

The Civil War in Iran

The events in Iran are moving in the direction of a dramatic solution. Just a year after President Carter had been given a reception with all the splendor of the imperial palace and Iran had been praised as an island of stability, the country plunged into a civil war. The oil refineries are standing still by a strike and bloody battles are being fought on the streets of Tehran between government troops and demonstrators. Will the Shah resign and leave the country? Will a democratic parliamentary form of government be able to succeed? Foreigners stationed in Iran are leaving the country in a hurry.

January 16, 1979

The Deserted Peacock Throne

Today, Reza Shah Pahlavi left Iran most likely forever. The situation in Iran remains uncertain: Can the civilian government succeed, will there be a coup by the military, or will the civil war escalate and the Islamic republic be realized? In any case, the West seems to lose a rock in the global game of chess.

South Bend, February 4, 1979

The Door Flung Wide Open

The state visit of Vice Premier Teng Hsiao-p'ing to Washington has flung the door to China wide open. The guest from Peking was given a great and cordial reception. Teng also left behind the best of impressions. He had come to America in an obliging, most friendly attitude so that the 30-year long hostile separation of the two countries appeared to have been overcome. Teng's desire for modernization and his suspicion of Russia brought him closer to America. But will this good relationship endure?

There could inasmuch be a danger in the present euphoria of American-Chinese relations as too much too fast of America comes to China. For, once the first curiosity is being satisfied and a certain saturation point has been reached, the enthusiasm for America could have the contrary effect. Then the damage would be greater than what is gained at the moment.

South Bend, February 5, 1979

Pope John Paul II in Mexico

The visit of the Holy Father to Mexico in the last week of January was a great success. Millions of people gave him a jubilant welcome. The visit of the Pope underscored the importance, which the more than 300 million Catholics in Latin America have for the Church throughout the world. It also highlighted the responsibility the Church has assumed for the people of Latin America.

Note

[Pope John Paul II followed an invitation by the Council of Latin American Bishops' Conferences, which assembled in Puebla, Mexico, in the last week of January, 1979. As Mexico had no diplomatic relations with the Vatican, John Paul entered the country on a visitor's visa. But the reception by the Mexican people was spontaneously overwhelming. The motorcade of the Holy Father from the airport to Mexico City and then along the 80 miles to Puebla became a triumphal procession with over a million people cheering on the roadside. John Paul II dealt with the theological and social problems of Latin America. Mexico was the first, and as George Weigel points out, also one of the most significant pastoral pilgrimages of the Pope. It was the beginning of a growing commitment to the Western Hemisphere, where about half of the Catholic Christians live. Cf. George Weigel, *Witness of Hope: The Biography of Pope John Paul II* (New York: HarperCollins, 1999), pp. 282-87.]

South Bend, February 6, 1979

Senate Hearing on Taiwan

While Teng Hsiao-p'ing was still on his state visit in Washington, the Senate Foreign Relations Committee began its hearing on Taiwan. The U.S. District Court had already ruled that President Carter, in his decision on China, acted within his constitutional authority. The hearing is concentrating on the question which is now the legitimate government of Taiwan. Is Taiwan only a province of the People's Republic without its own sovereignty? Who, in the future, can responsibly sign for Taiwan treaties with foreign governments? As much as Deputy Secretary of State Warren Christopher is trying to extenuate the Taiwanese situation, the fact remains that in foreign affairs Taipei is not in its own right anymore. The circumvention of letting private organizations handle all relations with Taiwan appears more like a dubious makeshift design.

South Bend, February 11, 1979

The Revolution in Iran

Prime Minister Shapour Bakhtian who had been appointed by the Shah resigned today, after a civil war had been raging on the streets of Tehran, and after it had become obvious that the loyalty of the military was divided. Thereby, the way is now open for Ayatollah Khomeini to put into effect the Islamic republic he has been striving for. Will there be a functioning government in place, or is this just the beginning of the Iranian Revolution?

February 12, 1979

Iran is demonstrating a regressive, backward looking revolution, which abolishes Western lifestyles by force and goes back to archaic customs. Without a doubt, the West has underestimated the impassionate zeal of Islamic fundamentalism. What is happening in Iran is a revolution carried out by religious fanaticism, national pride, and Marxist splinter groups.

[Toward the end of February, 1979, my wife and I participated in a conference on comparative literature and art forms at the University of

Indiana in Bloomington. That gave me an opportunity to get acquainted, though only cursory, with a big state university. The campus town of Bloomington is located about 50 miles southwest of Indianapolis, the capital of Indiana.]

Bloomington, Indiana, February 25, 1979

The State University

In 1820 the University of Indiana in Bloomington began its teaching with one professor and ten students. Today, 32,000 students are enrolled at the University of Indiana in Bloomington and 20,000 at its Medical School in Indianapolis. The intentions of its founders to make, in the spirit of democracy, higher education accessible to all the people of the state have been fulfilled. At present, the University is facing the problem of how to administer its huge institutional complex and how to take care of the large number of students. How to preserve the spirit of the humanities, which seems to get lost in the masses of people it has to handle? The 14-story building of the humanities, where 10,000 students are being taught, looks more like a beehive. Instruction can only be mastered with the help of electronic equipment.

But despite the automation, a European cultural atmosphere has been created by the highly motivated eagerness to learn and the desire for representation. Bloomington has one of the best known Schools of Music in America; affiliated with it is a large opera house. The representative halls of the University maintain an artificial ambience in the Tudor style. Thus, in the dining hall of the conference center, the Indiana Memorial Union, guests are greeted with the words: "We invite you to visit the Sixteenth Century where the Lord of the Manor and his family enjoyed a very special dining pleasure." These and similar inscriptions in the dark paneled rooms are evidence of a hidden longing for Old World culture. They are typical examples of the ambivalence, which one may come across in America, between a representative aristocratic trend of taste and the common democratic lifestyle. It also comes to my attention that, in contrast to a European university of similar size, there are no glaring Marxist slogans or graffiti scrawled on walls. Bloomington gives the impression of a study oriented campus. It is like numerous American colleges and universities an idyll in the midst of a plain industrial environment.

South Bend, March 24, 1979

The Town Meeting

Congressman John Brademas, who represents the Third District of Northern Indiana and who is also the Democratic majority whip in the U.S. House of Representatives, held a town meeting in the local Public Library. It was an open discussion with interested fellow citizens. Above all astonishing was the relaxed atmosphere of the meeting. The participants in the audience simply addressed the Congressman with "John." The topics discussed centered on Social Security and pensions for disabled veterans, but also on Europe sharing the costs of the peace settlement in the Middle East. Brademas also talked about his upcoming visit with a Congressional delegation to Moscow to explore questions concerning the SALT II negotiations. This town meeting was altogether a typical example of open democracy.

March 26, 1979

The Peace Treaty

This afternoon in an unpretentious ceremony on the lawn of the White House, the peace treaty between Israel and Egypt was signed. President Anwar Sadat signed for Egypt, Prime Minister Menachem Begin for Israel, and President Carter as witness for the United States. This brings to an end a 30-year long animosity and armed conflict between Egypt and Israel. It also provides the prerequisite for normal diplomatic relations between the two governments. In this peace dialogue, Anwar Sadat, Menachem Begin, and Jimmy Carter have risen above themselves. Despite sometimes seemingly hopeless negotiations and resistance until the end, peace has finally arrived. In the end, the spirit of Camp David has won.

South Bend, April 1, 1979

The Accident

An industrial accident happened on the Three Mile Island nuclear power plant, situated on the Susquehanna River near Harrisburg, the capital of Pennsylvania. The question whether it was caused by human error or a faulty structural design is still open. In any case, it is the hitherto most serious accident of the nuclear industry in America. Thousands of people had to be evacuated to protect them from radiation fall-out. If it should not be possible to cool the damaged reactor, a meltdown could occur. At this time, it is being considered to evacuate the population within a 20 mile radius. About half a million people would be affected by such a measure.

[Transl: The accident at the Three Mile Island nuclear plant happened on March 28, 1979.]

April 16, 1979

The accident on Three Mile Island has gone by better than feared. As it had been possible to slowly cool down the reactor, a catastrophe was avoided. There was a panic-like uproar in the area surrounding Three Mile Island, but the American public as a whole reacted to this nuclear crisis with surprising restraint and a realistic assessment of the situation. At the moment there would be no alternative to nuclear energy. There are presently 70 nuclear power plants in operation in America and the construction of 100 more is being planned. A big city like Chicago gets 45% of its electric power from nuclear energy.

Addendum

[The American nuclear industry suffered a considerable setback by the accident on Three Mile Island. The construction of several nuclear power plants was suspended and the planning for new plants reduced. The Nuclear Regulatory Commission issued strict security rules for the construction and operation of nuclear power plants. Fortunately, since 1979 no major incident has happened. In the area around Chicago one lives near several nuclear power plants without fear that something would go wrong.]

South Bend, May 20, 1979

An Endless Stream of Refugees

While 600 Jewish immigrants from the Ukraine arrived at the JFK International Airport in New York, 196 Vietnamese "boat people" came to

Des Moines, Iowa. The latter are refugees who had fled from Vietnam in makeshift vessels, risking their lives in the venture. One must have seen how these people were overcome by emotion in order to understand what it means to them to have been admitted to the United States. Having at times been waiting for years, what anxiety and hopes they must have gone through. This year, the United States will admit 50,000 Jewish immigrants from the Soviet Union and 35,000 refugees from Vietnam. The governor of Iowa has set up a special aid program for refugees from Vietnam. There are an estimated 10 million refugees dispersed over various regions of the world. Who will take care of these people?

South Bend, June 10, 1979

The First Visit to Poland

The first pastoral pilgrimage of John Paul II to his homeland last week was an event, which the world has followed with astonishment and apprehension. Millions of people gave the Holy Father a passionately enthusiastic welcome and celebrated Mass with him. Is there a more convincing testimony that religion in Poland, despite having been persecuted and suppressed for decades, is still alive? The Pope tried to find an understanding with the Communist government, but unequivocally rejected the materialistic philosophy of Marxism. He emphasized that the human being cannot be understood by his economic production alone. The words spoken in Poland will reverberate throughout the entire Communist East. It has become obvious by this papal visit how deeply rooted the Catholic Church has remained in Poland. To have been able to see this, even from a distance on television, has been consoling.

[George Weigel remarks on the reception of the Pope in Poland: "No hero in Polish history . . . had ever entered Warsaw as John Paul II did on June 2, 1979." About three million people had come from all over Poland to see their Pope and to pray with him. John Paul referred to the millennium celebrations of the Church in Poland (966-1966). He said he had come in defense of religion and to affirm anew the dignity and rights of the human being. That was the beginning of the historic change, which finally led to the fall of Communism in Eastern Europe. (See George Weigel, *Witness to Hope: The Biography of Pope John Paul II*, pp. 292-95.)]

South Bend, Sunday, June 17, 1979

The Summit Meeting in Vienna

The summit meeting over this weekend between U.S. President Jimmy Carter and Soviet Head of State Leonid Brezhnev in Vienna has moved the Austrian capital again to center stage of world attention. At stake is the conclusion of SALT II, the bilateral agreement on the limitation of strategic arms. After years of negotiations since 1972, agreement has finally been reached on the essential points so that the completed treaty will be ready to be signed tomorrow by Carter and Brezhnev. The SALT II agreement has revived public discussion about nuclear disarmament. As a lay person one can get an approximate idea what it is about. Strategic arms should be limited to a certain level. This applies to intercontinental ballistic missiles with nuclear warheads deployed in the United States and the Soviet Union, which could reach either country. The medium range nuclear weapons primarily deployed in Europe are not included in the treaty. SALT II should establish the nuclear balance between the two superpowers. The high upper level [2,250 missiles on either side], which should limit the nuclear arsenal, makes it clear that both superpowers have the capacity to obliterate each other within an hour in case of a nuclear war and to turn the Northern hemisphere into a radiation contaminated desert. By this deterrent, it should be guaranteed that a nuclear war will never happen.

In contrast to the gruesome topic of the conference, Vienna provided a charming ambience for the meeting. When could one have otherwise seen on American television pictures of the Hofburg, the Staatsoper, the Melk Abbey and Klosterneuburg? Neutral Austria proved to be an excellent host country for this summit meeting.

June 18, 1979

From the Redoutensaal Directly to the U.S. Congress

After the SALT II treaty had been signed today in the Redoutensaal of the Hofburg*, President Carter flew back to Washington to report to Congress on the agreement with the Soviet Union. He left Vienna at 2 p.m. local time and, gaining 6 hours on the flight back, was able to address Congress on the same day at 9 p.m. EST. Carter spoke with confidence about SALT II, expressing his hope that the Senate will ratify the agreement. He emphasized the importance of having achieved parity in nuclear arms with the Soviet Union, whereby a global nuclear confrontation has become unthinkable. By far not all differences between East and West have been solved, but the danger of a direct confrontation has been excluded. In Carter's view, mankind is about to overcome the cycle of world wars with periods of peace in between. The beginning of the debate on SALT II in the Senate has already been scheduled for July 6. Most likely, the Senate will ask for an amendment to the agreement.

*[Transl: The Redoutensaal, a small, delicately ornate hall in the Rococo style, was originally a meeting place for young aristocrats in the imperial palace. It later served as an intimate theatre for Mozart operas.]

Note

[The SALT II treaty was never ratified by the U.S. Senate. The debate on the matter was protracted over the summer of 1979. The opposition objected that the Soviet Union had an advantage on carrier rockets and that the verification, whether the provisions of the agreement were observed, was not reliable enough. Also, the testimony of former Secretary of State Henry Kissinger weighed in. Kissinger supported the SALT II agreement, but he had reservations. He warned that the stepped up production of SS-20 medium-range missiles in the Soviet Union exposed Europe to danger. After the Russian invasion of Afghanistan in December 1979, the SALT II treaty never made it to the Senate floor for ratification. However, the Soviet Union and the United States have adhered to the conditions of the treaty.]

[From the end of July to the middle of August, my wife and I took a trip by car from South Bend, Indiana to San Francisco, California. We visited our son Franz in Palo Alto, who had just started on his professional career in the computer industry. Once in a lifetime, one should cross the Continent from New York to California by car to get an idea of the distances and regional diversities of the United States.]

July 30-August 17, 1979

The Trip West

The trip first went along Interstate Highway 80 from Chicago to the western state line of Nebraska. Driving after 10 years again through Iowa and

Nebraska, it is striking to see how fast modern development has progressed. Especially striking is the metropolitan expansion of Omaha, Nebraska. While 10 years ago, the city hardly stretched beyond the western bank of the Missouri River, satellite communities and modern industries now extend far out into the countryside to Lincoln, the capitol of Nebraska. The Strategic Air Command (SAC), situated in Bellevue, has contributed a great deal to this development.

A Museum of a Special Kind

In Bellevue, at the southern edge of Omaha, the Strategic Air Command Museum was established. It is an open air museum of a special kind, whose unrestricted freedom is only possible in America. Next to used aircrafts of the Air Force, also older models of intercontinental rockets and missiles like ATLAS, CBM and Minute Man are on exhibition. Graphic charts illustrate the devastating destructive force of these weapons, which have just been the topic of discussion in the SALT II negotiations. This exhibition makes one think: While in most other countries the age of missiles has not even started, here outdated models are already on display.

The Cattle Kingdom

After North Platte, Nebraska, we left Interstate 80 and continued our journey on Interstate 76 to Denver, Colorado. While 10 years ago, the open country from Omaha to Denver was for the most part uninhabited, it now makes a settled impression. At least a gas filling station with a coffee shop shows up every 50 miles. After North Platte, the Great Plains with their wide pastures do not look as deserted anymore. Only now, the enormous size of the "Cattle Kingdom" has come to my attention. It stretches about 1, 500 miles from West Texas over New Mexico, Colorado, Wyoming as far up as Montana.

In the Vacationland of Colorado

From Denver we drove west on Interstate 70. The first stage led over the 10,000 feet high Eisenhower Memorial Tunnel to Vail, Colorado. The Eisenhower Tunnel lies on the Continental Divide. Beyond it, the wonderful vacationland of Colorado begins. About 100 miles around, there are the 12-14,000 feet high mountains in a number of National Parks and Forests, which together form one of the most beautiful vacation areas in the United States. Here, also the famous winter resorts—Keystone, Brackenridge, Vail and Aspen—have been created. Vail is situated just below the Eisenhower Tunnel in a valley basin. It was built in the style of an Alpine village, most likely comparable to a small Kitzbühel. The Gasthof "Pepi Gramshammer" stands in the center of the elegant resort town. There, we could feel at home and rest after a long day's ride,

The next morning we drove through the narrow canyon of the still young Colorado River near Glenwood Springs. The Colorado River remained our companion until we reached the desert in southeastern Utah. The difference in altitude and the quick change in temperature from 40 to 117 degrees F caused a flat tire. Fortunately, a young couple came along the empty highway. They stopped immediately in the desert heat, took us into their air-conditioned station wagon so that we could cool off and refresh ourselves. The young gentleman still helped me to mount the reserve. After Green River, Utah, we traveled north on the picturesque highway that passes through Price Canyon, arriving in Provo and Salt Lake City in the evening.

The Ride through the Desert

The 500 miles on Interstate 80 from Salt Lake City to Reno, Nevada, are a ride through the desert. One should be equipped as if going on an expedition. At first, one drives along the wide, dried-up flats of the Great Salt Lake. The concrete-hard salt flats are especially suitable for the car racing of the Bonneville Speedway. This is a testing ground where various automobile models are tested for the highest speed they can achieve. Heading west, one drives on Interstate 80 for hours on end along the Humboldt River. The shimmering horizon in the heat has the effect of a mirage. Rarely, a green spot with a ranch can be seen on the River. Crossing the desert of Utah and Nevada, one may involuntarily be overcome by fear of the immense and empty space one has to conquer. At Humboldt Sink the River finally trickles away into a swamp, as all running waters evaporate in this alkaline saturated desert. Arriving in the evening in Reno, one draws a deep breath to have made it.

Virginia City, Lake Tahoe, Donner Pass

From Reno we took a short side-trip to nearby Virginia City. A winding mountain road leads to the legendary silver mining town, situated on a mountain range adjacent to the Sierra Nevada. Here, the Comstock Lode, one of the richest silver veins of the Far West, was discovered. Additional gold finds made it an instant boom town which attracted a motley array of people. At its peak from 1860-70, the city had 20,000 inhabitants. Virginia City became the quintessential gold rush city of the American West. It also has its significance for American literature. Samuel Clemens started here from 1861-64 his career as a newspaper reporter. It is here, where he used his pen name Mark Twain for the first time. In the autobiographical story, *Roughing It* (1872), he narrates in a humorous way his experiences as a newspaperman in Virginia City. The years in Virginia City had a considerable influence on the development of Mark Twain's burlesque style. The printing press he had used and a few of his early articles are exhibited there. Virginia City has been rescued from decay by turning it in good time into a tourist attraction. It also served as scenery for a number of Western films.

From Virginia City we drove via Carson City, the capital of Nevada, to Lake Tahoe. The size of this dark-blue mountain lake came as a surprise. [Lake Tahoe is situated at an altitude of 6,225 feet in the Sierra Nevada; the shoreline of the lake has a length of 72 miles. The name is most likely of Indian origin and could mean "big water."] We drove along the North shore of Lake Tahoe from Nevada to the California border, which was only marked by a sign with the inscription "Welcome to California." From there the road led us to Squaw Valley and then on to the Donner Pass. The interesting visit to Virginia City and the scenic beauty of Lake Tahoe and Squaw Valley have made the by-pass from Interstate 80 worthwhile taking.

Having just driven through the Utah and Nevada desert by car, it is almost impossible to imagine how, before the railroad was built, the pioneers had been able to cross this stretch by oxen-driven covered wagons. But there were, indeed, enough accidents and catastrophes. Best known is the ill-fate that met the Donner Party in the winter of 1846-47. The wagon train led by George and Jacob Donner had reached the pass which now bears their name. But they were surprised by an early winter in the Sierra Nevada in late October 1846 so that they remained shut in over the long winter on the pass. Half of the Donner Party, among them families with women and children, died of starvation, freezing temperatures, and exhaustion. Only in spring, the survivors could be saved. A State Park was established on the pass as a memorial for the Donner Party. An impressive monument reminds visitors of the first pioneers who had come to California overland. The Donner Pass lies on the divide of the Sierra Nevada. From there, Interstate 80 rolls gently down the 100 miles to Sacramento. Ninety miles farther on through the fertile plain of the San Joaquin Valley, Interstate 80 reaches Oakland in the San Francisco Bay. [With a length of 2,148 miles, interstate 80 is the main connection between Chicago and San Francisco.]

Palo Alto, August 9, 1979

Palo Alto is situated on the Peninsula 50 miles south of San Francisco at the lower end of the San Francisco Bay. The Spanish name refers to an old, high sequoia, which had originally served the Indians as a reference point and later the Spaniards as a place to rest. The large redwood tree has been preserved as a landmark of the city. Today, Palo Alto is regarded as one of the most exclusive residential areas in the United States. Stanford University has contributed its share to it. The city combines the leisure of a resort with the newest electronic industry and space technology. At the edge of Stanford University on Page Mill Road, a clean industrial zone has originated that looks like an extension of the Stanford Campus. The revolutionary innovations in computer technology and data processing started here, changing information technologies worldwide. Santa Clara Valley, which stretches from San Jose north beyond Palo Alto, has been nicknamed "Silicon Valley," as it is known now all over the world. This area has the strongest concentration of the brain trust I have ever encountered. Also, an international atmosphere prevails here in the broadest sense of the word. The lifestyle is cultivated and liberal, but more devoted to the natural sciences than the humanities. The society is very mobile: who lives on the same address for a year is already considered a permanent resident.

August 14, 1979

Yellowstone National Park

On our journey back east, we turned north in Nevada and drove through Idaho as far as Twin Falls where we stayed overnight after a long day on the road. There, at the upper course of the Snake River one could notice a change in mentality, which was more oriented toward the Northwest to Portland, Oregon, and Seattle, Washington. The next morning, we continued our journey on Interstate 20 up to the plain of the Teton Range.

The snow-covered peaks of the Grand Teton's (13,766 feet high) could be seen from a distance. We entered the Yellowstone National Park at the West Gate and moved right on to Old Faithful. Yellowstone National Park offers a natural spectacle without equal. The Old Faithful geyser, which regularly shoots every hour 150 feet into the air, is a rarity. But there are hundreds of geysers and thousands of hot springs in the Park. It simmers, sizzles, and bubbles everywhere. 3,468 square miles of the Yellowstone River area were decreed a National Park by the U.S. Congress in 1872. It was the first nature reservation in the world, becoming a model for future nature conservancy parks. Yellowstone National Park lies on the Continental Divide at an altitude of 7,731 feet. The Park is also known as a wildlife sanctuary. Elk, moose, and buffalo roam near the highway undisturbed. Occasionally also a grizzly bear shows up. Especially impressive is the Lower Falls of the Yellowstone River that plunges into the yellow shimmering Canyon. We passed the terraced Mammoth Hot Springs and then left the Park at the North Gate in the direction of Bozeman, Montana. From there, we drove on Interstate 94 east through North Dakota and Minnesota, back to the Great Lakes and home to Indiana. We covered 10,000 miles on this three-week trip through the American West.

South Bend, October 1-7, 1979

The Visit of the Pope to the United States

Coming from Ireland, John Paul II arrived Monday, October 1, late in the afternoon in Boston. This was the beginning of his first pastoral pilgrimage to the United States. At his first Mass on Boston Common more than a million faithful had gathered. This Pope radiates a special charisma. Millions of people of all faiths feel attracted by him. His humanity and pastoral message have a convincing effect wherever he goes. The next day, October 2, he addressed the General Assembly of the United Nations in New York. He referred to the Universal Human Rights that are embodied in the Charta of the United Nations. He drew special attention to the "inalienable rights" of every individual to freedom of conscience and worship. He, thereby, related to the guiding principle of the American Declaration of Independence. His main concern remained the dignity of the human person which has to be respected. The second theme of his address dealt with the question of peace and the recent efforts made to limit the nuclear arms race.

The New Yorkers gave John Paul II, what is rare, a ticker-tape parade when his motorcade drove down Broadway to Battery Park in Lower Manhattan. With the Statue of Liberty as a backdrop, he spoke, despite a heavy rain, to a crowd of people who represented the ethnic diversity of American immigration. In Philadelphia, John Paul II spoke again about freedom, a theme that was historically suggested by Independence Hall. After a visit to a farm in Iowa, where he celebrated Mass under the free open skies of the prairie, John Paul II arrived in Chicago on Friday, October 5. Especially Chicagoans of Polish descent cheered their Pope. Half a million people congregated to celebrate Mass in Grant Park. From Chicago, John Paul II flew to Washington, D.C., where he was received by President Carter in the White House. On Sunday, October 7, his first pastoral visit to the United States came to an end.

It cannot be denied that America itself felt reaffirmed in its basic values by this papal visit. On the other hand, John Paul II has certainly gained strength from the refreshing optimism he encountered here.

South Bend, [Beginning of October], 1979

Preparation for American Citizenship

Once we had obtained permanent residence, we were recommended to aspire to achieve American citizenship. As a prerequisite, one has to fulfill the residence requirement, i.e., one has to stay five years in the country. Only if one works abroad for an American company or institution, the period spent abroad also counts toward the residence requirement. As a family we were absolutely certain that we would accept American citizenship as soon as the requirements have been fulfilled. Actually, the last steps toward American citizenship are simple. The applicant needs two U.S. citizens who serve as character witnesses. Our witnesses were Professor and Mrs. Louis Hasley from the English Department at the University of Notre Dame. We were good friends with the Hasleys since our first stay at Notre Dame. Professor and Mrs. Hasley had helped taking care of the Notre Dame student group in Innsbruck, 1964-65. As soon as one files the application, one will be called to appear with the witnesses before an examining magistrate who once more goes through all the documents and personal data. The magistrate ascertains whether one can converse in English, and he also asks a few questions on American history and government. A favorite question is who was the 16th president of the United States. Applicants are also tested if they can write their name in Latin script. This is not a matter of course, considering the strong immigration from Southeast Asia. As the essential questions had already been clarified beforehand, the entire official procedure was conducted in a friendly, relaxed atmosphere. A few weeks later, one will be invited to come before a federal judge who administers the oath on the U.S. constitution.

Wednesday, November 21, 1979

Sworn In as U.S. Citizen

Today, the day before Thanksgiving, I was sworn in as new American citizen by a federal judge. My labor of love of many years for America has not been lost, for since my year of studies at Bowdoin College in 1950-51 America has not let loose of me. The ceremony took place in a school here in South Bend, where the applicants for citizenship had assembled in the auditorium. After the oath on the U.S. constitution had been taken, the citizenship papers were solemnly presented to each new citizen.

Addendum

[As my wife was not in the service of the University but a private person while I directed the Notre Dame foreign study program in Innsbruck 1976-78, her two years abroad did not count for the residence requirement. She, therefore, could receive U.S. citizenship only two years later in 1982. Our son Franz received his U.S. citizenship in California. The one academic year 1976-77 our daughter Christine had spent as a student at the University of Notre Dame with us in Innsbruck was recognized for fulfilling the residence requirement. She was sworn in as U.S. citizen with me in November 1979. Thus, over a period of several years, our family has made the transition from Austrian to American citizenship.]

November 25, 1979

What has changed?

By becoming an American citizen, not much has changed for the moment, except that one is no longer dependent on the immigration authorities or has to worry whether a visa can be granted or extended by a consulate.

[The hardest part for my wife and myself was to turn in our Austrian passports at the Austrian Consulate General in Chicago. There was the awareness that our relationship to the Republic of Austria has unequivocally changed, although our love for our old home country has not been diminished.]

A Permanent Occurrence

The naturalization of new immigrants is a permanently continuing occurrence of American democracy. Every year hundreds of thousands of immigrants from all parts of the world are sworn in as new U.S. citizens. The five year residence requirement has contributed a great deal to the cohesion of the American state and society. This way, millions of people who had come to this country were not regarded as foreign workers but encouraged to become citizens. After the relatively short period of time of only five years, immigrants became citizens. As such they formed an integral part of American society and as voters could participate in the political process. This may in part explain how the ethnic diversity of America has been absorbed into a unified body politic.

South Bend, [End of November], 1979

The Hostage Crisis in Tehran

For many weeks, America has been under the spell of the hostage crisis in Tehran. Iranian revolutionaries raided the U.S. Embassy and have been holding its personnel—about 60 persons—hostage. They demand the extradition of the Shah who is being treated as a cancer patient in a clinic in New York. America appears to be rather helpless in this situation. Violent clashes between American and Iranian students have already occurred. The vexation among the American public is increasing. How long will President Carter be able to look on? The Security Council of the United Nations passed a unanimous resolution that Iran has to release the hostages immediately.

December 27, 1979

Over the Christmas holidays, three clergymen were allowed to visit the hostages in the American Embassy in Tehran and to hold prayer services with them. But for the moment, what will happen with the hostages remains an open question.

South Bend, December 28, 1979

Nuclear Armament in Western Europe

On its December meeting in Brussels, the Council of NATO Ministers decided to accept the American offer to upgrade nuclear armament in Western Europe. Until 1983 altogether 572 new Pershing II missiles with a 1,000 mile range should be installed—at first in the Federal Republic of Germany, Great Britain and Italy, later on also in the Netherlands and Belgium. This decision was urgently called for in view of the predominance of the Warsaw Pact in conventional weapons. But basically, it was a matter of creating a counterbalance to the Russian intermediate-range missiles targeted at Western Europe. By this decisive and serious step, the defense of Western Europe will be even closer interwoven with that of the United States.

[The mobile, ground-stationed Pershing I/II intermediate-range missiles with nuclear warheads were named after General John J. Pershing (1860-1948). Pershing was the commander of the American expeditionary forces in Europe during World War I.]

Addendum

[Margaret Thatcher explains in detail how the decision of the NATO ministers of December 12, 1979, had come about. In the area of Intermediate-Range Nuclear Forces (INF) a decision had to be made. The intermediate-range missiles at the disposition of Western Europe were out-dated and by far inferior to the Russian SS-20 intermediate range missiles. There was the danger that Western Europe could become exposed to blackmail by the Soviet Union. The West could no longer, Thatcher argues, just react passively to the course of action taken by the East. It was imperative to act. The deployment of the modernized Pershing II missiles as well as the new Cruise missiles could secure nuclear parity of Western Europe with the East. The new missiles and nuclear weapons deployed in Western Europe remained in American hands and under American control. In Thatcher's view, NATO's resolve and decision was the beginning of the historic turning point, which finally led to the collapse of the Soviet Union and the fall of Communism in Eastern Europe in the 1980s. See Margaret Thatcher, *The Downing Street Years* (New York: HarperCollins, 1993), pp. 239-44.]

[Margaret Thatcher was born as Margaret Roberts in Grantham, England, in 1925. She studied at Somerville College and Oxford University natural sciences and law and worked as research chemist and lawyer, 1947-53. In 1951 she married Denis Thatcher whose name she assumed. Margaret Thatcher soon entered politics; she was a Member of Parliament as a representative of the Conservatives in the House of Commons, 1959-92; she led the Conservative Party, 1975-79. Following the victory of her Party in the general elections in May, 1979, Margaret Thatcher became Prime Minister of the United Kingdom and held that important position until 1990. In 1992 she was ennobled with the title of baroness. As Lady Thatcher she is a Member of the House of Lords.]

South Bend, December 31, 1979

The Invasion at Year's End

During the past 36 hours, the Soviet Union has been massively invading Afghanistan with tanks and about 35,000 troops. The purpose of this move was apparently to protect the loyal Communist regime, carried to power by the Soviet Union, against Islamic insurgents. One must ask oneself what the broader intentions of this invasion could be: Is the Soviet Union planning to extend its belt of satellite countries from Eastern Europe to Central Asia and finally to advance to the Persian Gulf?

Note

[The Soviet invasion of Afghanistan started on December 27, 1979. The capital Kabul was instantly seized by airborne troops and Babrak Karmal, Moscow's faithful vassal, installed as head of state and government. The Soviet Union occupied the entire country but was soon pushed more and more into the defensive by the unyielding resistance of the Islamic population. The international indignation at the Soviet action was no less vehement.]

PART III
1980-1989

The Breakthrough

Section 8: January 5, 1980-August 5, 1982

Section 9: January 1, 1983-July 31, 1985

Section 10: August 15, 1985-December 27, 1987

Section 11: January 1, 1988-December 31, 1989

SECTION 8

January 5, 1980-August 5, 1982

South Bend, January 5, 1980

Old Hidden Fears Surfaced Again

The brazen action of the Soviet Union in Afghanistan—the precise preplanned move and cold-blooded execution of the invasion by airborne troops and advancing armored battalions—caused worldwide surprise and dismay. In Europe one was reminded of the events in Czechoslovakia in 1968. Old hidden fears of an invasion from the East surfaced again. The Russian danger has again been demonstrated as a harsh reality. What does the Soviet Union want in Afghanistan, on these barren highlands of the Hindu Kush Mountains? Without a doubt, her strategic position in Central Asia has been improved. Will she also be tempted to advance to the Persian Gulf to get a stranglehold on the oil supply of the West?

January 6, 1980

SALT II Put On Ice

In reaction to the Russian invasion of Afghanistan, President Carter recommended to the Senate that the deliberations on the SALT II agreement should be cancelled. At the same time, Carter laid an embargo on the grain shipments to the Soviet Union and ordered that the sale of computers and other desirable high-tech products be stopped. Détente, the policy of disengagement between East and West, has been, if not directly discontinued, so at least noticeably cooled off. What will become of the East West dialogue in the 1980s?

January 7, 1980

Thrown Back by 20 Years

The French ambassador to the United Nations who this month chairs the Security Council clearly characterized the present situation, before today's vote on the resolution on the Soviet intervention in Afghanistan was taken: the endeavors toward disengagement may have been thrown back by 20 years, the world today is more insecure than ever before, a new arms race between the superpowers is imminent, and the unsettled situation in Central Asia involves a serious danger of war.

The resolution of the Security Council, which condemned the Soviet intervention in Afghanistan and demanded the unconditional withdrawal of foreign troops, was of course vetoed by the Soviet Union.

South Bend, January 20, 1980

The Olympic Boycott

President Carter announced today in a televised interview on "Meet the Press" that he gives the Soviet Union a month to withdraw its troops from Afghanistan, otherwise he would recommend that American athletes not participate in the Olympic Games in Moscow. As the Russian troops will certainly not withdraw so fast, this is tantamount to a boycott of the Summer Olympic Games.

January 21, 1980

The Anxiety about Yugoslavia

As President Tito, at the age of 87, is seriously ill and close to dying, the old anxiety flared up again that with his death the unity of Yugoslavia may fall apart. This could give the Soviet Union a welcome reason for occupying the country. As a precautionary measure, Yugoslav armed forces were dispatched to the Bulgarian and Hungarian borders.

[Tito died on May 4, 1980. On the consequences of his passing, see entry of May 7, 1980.]

January 23, 1980

This Far and No Further

In his State of the Union Address today, President Carter emphasized that the Persian Gulf is of vital interest to the United States and the Free World. A further advance of the Soviet Union beyond Afghanistan, to either Pakistan or Iran, would be responded by the use of military force. The firm stand of the President—this far and no further—is supported by both parties in Congress and by a majority of the American people. The United States and the Soviet Union are once more on a collision course. One does not want to accept it for real, but the danger of war is great. President Carter ordered the return to the draft registration, which comes up to a partial mobilization. The United States is hoping for the support by the NATO countries which depend even more than America on the oil supply from the Persian Gulf.

South Bend, February 10, 1980

Difference of Opinion

In regard to the disengagement policy, a difference of opinion between the United States and its European Allies has come to the fore. While there has been a quick change of mood in the United States toward the Soviet Union and without hesitation détente has been thrown overboard, Europeans are much more guarded and disturbed by the sudden change of mood. The European Allies hesitate to jeopardize détente which has taken so much effort to achieve. Since Western Europe lies at the boundary of the East West conflict, it would have much more to lose in case of a military confrontation. There is an obvious difference between the global interests of the United States and the regional concerns of its European Allies. In this regard, the Atlantic partnership is based on unequal prerequisites. Moreover, in an election year the United States prefers to speak from a position of strength.

March 18, 1980

Presidential Election 1980—the Primaries

Except for Massachusetts, President Carter so far has defeated his challenger, Senator Edward Kennedy, in every primary. That happened in New Hampshire, Vermont, in the Southern states, and today in Illinois, where voters on the Democratic side chose Carter 2:1. Even in Chicago, although Mayor Byrne had endorsed Kennedy, Carter won. On the Republican side, Ronald Reagan has definitely emerged as the winner before Anderson who represents the liberal wing of the Party. According to the present results in the primaries, most likely the presidential election 1980 will be decided between Carter and Reagan.

South Bend, March 30, 1980

The Drawback of Mobility

The proverbial mobility of the American society is corroborated by actual numbers. About half a million Americans change their residence every year. Reasons for doing so vary. Moving to a different place may be brought about by a transfer with a promotion incentive in a company, but may also be caused by the loss of a job and the need to look for new employment in another area. After retirement, people frequently move from the North to warmer regions in the South. This extraordinary social mobility boosts the economy, but it has also its drawback. As it often happens here, families have to leave the surroundings they are accustomed to. Children have to change schools and leave their friends behind. These continuous moves strain the patience of marriages and families. As most women are working and pursuing their own professional careers, it may lead to a tug of war between spouses on who will give in and follow the other. America is a family oriented country. It is not the case—and this will increasingly apply to all advanced industrialized countries—that the family ceases to exist. In the future, it will only be a different form of family from what we have been used to.

[Beginning of April], 1980

Census 1980

April is census month. Every ten years since 1790, a census has been taken in the United States. At this year's census, a remarkable shift in the ethnic composition of the American population is beginning to show. The wave of immigration to the United States from Southern and Eastern Europe at the beginning of the century is now being replaced by a similar wave of immigration from Latin America and Southeast Asia. This new immigration is especially covered by the census 1980. The Hispanic population coming from Mexico, Cuba and Central America appears to become the largest minority in the United States. In wide areas in the West and Southwest Spanish is becoming next to English the second language spoken. Also the Asian population is becoming more and more visible. The ethnic diversity of the American population has become all the richer by these new waves of immigration.

South Bend, April 7, 1980

Diplomatic Relations Broken Off

After having waited for five months in vain, being kept in the air, and promises never kept, the Carter Administration took stronger measures today in the hostage crisis. President Carter broke off diplomatic relations with Iran. All Iranian diplomats who are still in the United States have to leave the country until midnight tomorrow. At the same time, a complete trade embargo has been declared. Further measures remain open if the hostages in the American Embassy are not released. As all diplomatic attempts at mediation seem to have been exhausted, the Iran crisis is now entering a phase of open confrontation. How much this situation will intensify is hard to tell.

April 13, 1980

Trying to Take Advantage of a Vulnerable Spot

Foreign countries who wish the United States ill have found out that every four years during the American presidential election a vulnerable spot of American democracy is being exposed. The ability of the American president to make decisions is somewhat weakened, for he has to either run for reelection and campaign to get voters on his side or, if he leaves office, as lame duck does not have the full capacity to act along with Congress. Therefore, in presidential election years, time and again attempts have been made to take advantage of this vulnerable spot, trying to influence the U.S. presidential election from abroad. That was the case in the Vietnam War, Cuba tried to do so several times, and obviously a similar method is now being applied in the Iran crisis.

April 25, 1980

The Rescue Operation

Hardly awakened, the American public was surprised this morning by a report from the White House that the rescue operation to free the 50 hostages in the U.S. Embassy in Tehran had failed. Coming from Egypt, a rescue expedition flew over Saudi Arabia into the Iranian desert to establish an outpost. At the same time, helicopters from a carrier in the Persian Gulf arrived, which should have freed the hostages in Tehran. But due to a technical malfunction of a helicopter, the operation had to be called off. Eight marines lost their lives in the mission.

April 27, 1980

Cyrus Vance Resigns

In the aftermath of the failed rescue mission to free the hostages in Tehran, Secretary of State Cyrus Vance today announced his resignation. In fact, he had already offered his resignation to President Carter days earlier, as fundamental differences of opinion over the rescue mission had arisen. Cyrus Vance is a career diplomat who was regarded as a moderate voice in the cabinet of the Carter Administration. The resignation of the American Secretary of Sate will intensify the present unsafe world situation. The fear, which is being expressed on both sides of the Atlantic not without good reason, comes from the uncertainty whether the crises in Afghanistan and in Iran could escalate into a war in the East West conflict.

May 7, 1980

Much Depends Now on Yugoslavia

After the passing of Marshal Tito, apprehensions have come up again that the Soviet Union may put a tight rein on Yugoslavia if not occupy it militarily. Although there is no imminent threat of a military occupation, the Soviet Union will not pass up the opportunity of trying to influence the Yugoslav situation in her favor. Much depends now on Yugoslavia itself whether it will be able to muster the discipline for national unity. If the old rivalries between the Serbian, Croatian, Macedonian and other ethnic groups should flare up again, not only Yugoslavia but the entire region would be affected.

[Marshal Tito held the office of President of the Socialist Federal Republic of Yugoslavia for life. After his death, the authority of governing the state was transferred to a collective body of eight members with a rotating presidency among the individual republics. The Socialist Federal Republic of Yugoslavia finally disintegrated as a result of the ethnic conflict.]

South Bend, May 8, 1980

The Exodus from Cuba

After thousands of Cubans had stormed the Peruvian Embassy in Havana seeking asylum, Fidel Castro allowed all those who wanted to leave the island to exit. That set off a massive exodus from Cuba. For weeks the Straits of Florida have been crossed by any navigable ship or boat in an attempt to reach Key West or Miami. The stream of people is so large that immigration officers and relief organizations are working beyond capacity to take care of the refugees. Tens of thousands of refugees are now joining the 600,000 Cuban exiles that live in Miami. The scenes that are playing out every day on the coast of Florida are heart-wrenching. But not all refugees are coming out of pure desire for freedom. In a cynical way, Fidel Castro used the opportunity to empty his prisons so that criminal elements have mingled among the refugees. The Carter Administration has been indulgent and humane by having until now admitted all refugees who landed on Florida's shores.

[Middle of May], 1980

A few graspable outlines are taking shape out of the chaos first created by the Cuban exodus. The stream of refugees may swell to an estimated 60,000 people. There are various reasons for this large exodus. Many have come to Florida to meet with family members whom they had not seen in 20 years. But most of them fled to escape the dire economic conditions and political repression. The criminal element among the refugees may make up for only

1% of the total. As a consequence of the Cuban exodus, the entire Caribbean got into turmoil. Also thousands of people are leaving Haiti who want to come to America. The screening process of the refugees for immigration to the United States has just begun.

Addendum

[On the 20th anniversary of the exodus from Cuba in May of 1980, the *Chicago Tribune* carried a front page article that gave a comprehensive overview of the event. From that article a number of pertinent details can be learned. The exodus from Cuba in the spring of 1980 has become known as "Mariel" because it was launched from the port of Mariel near Havana. The exodus had started on April 20, 1980 and reached its peak in May. However, it continued over the summer until the beginning of fall. The port of Mariel was closed on September 26, 1980. Altogether about 125,000 Marielitos came to South Florida. The criminal element among them may have accounted for nearly 5,000, that is 4% of the total. That new wave of Cuban exiles has completely changed the image of "Little Havana," the southern part of Miami. The original stigma which the Mariel immigrants had to endure has long been overcome. In the course of two decades, they have proved to be adaptable and successful. They were able to establish businesses of their own and to gain political influence. See the article titled "Pride has replaced stigma for 1980 Mariel arrivals," *Chicago Tribune,* May 15, 2000, sec. 1/pp. 1, 14.]

South Bend, May 15, 1980

25 Years Austrian State Treaty

I still remember vividly how on Sunday, May 15, 1955, at noon the signing of the Austrian State Treaty in the Belvedere Palace in Vienna was broadcast on radio. I was at that time with my family in Innsbruck. At first, there was a moment of disbelief until the reality of the State Treaty sank in. When Foreign Minister Leopold Figl, who together with Chancellor Julius Raab and the representatives of the signatory powers had come out on the balcony of the Belvedere Palace, holding aloft the State Treaty, proclaimed: "Österreich ist frei!" (Austria is free!)—the Austrian people erupted in jubilation. That was the moment of destiny for modern Austria.

After 25 years one can say that the State Treaty and Austrian neutrality have proved their worth exceedingly well. In the same year Austria was admitted to the United Nations and could take on the role of mediator between East and West.

[Middle of June], 1980

The Last Primaries

As Jimmy Carter as well as Ronald Reagan had already received the required number of delegates for the nomination as presidential candidates, the last primaries lacked suspense. On the Democratic side though, Edward Kennedy achieved the best results of his campaign in the last primaries. Kennedy won the important primaries of Pennsylvania, New York, New Jersey, and at the end also the primary of California. But nonetheless, he could not catch up on Carter's lead. With 1,948 delegates vs. Kennedy's 1,211 Carter is practically assured of the Democratic nomination. On the Republican side, Reagan virtually has no opponent, after Congressman John Anderson had already left the Republican fold by the end of April, campaigning as an independent. Although George Bush had won the Pennsylvania primary, he has remained far behind Reagan in the number of delegates.

South Bend, August 3, 1980

[After her graduation from the University of Notre Dame, our daughter Christine got married at the beginning of August. Her husband had graduated from Notre Dame the year before. As a student at the Law School of the University of St. Louis, he was pursuing his professional career as lawyer.]

A Sense of Conventional Decorum

American society has in many ways a sense of conventional decorum. This holds especially true to weddings for which many British customs have been acquired. It applies to the stylized form of the invitation to a wedding, the way to dress, the rehearsal dinner on the evening before the wedding and the reception following the wedding ceremony. It is also clearly defined what the parents of the bride and the parents of the groom have to do. Young people whom one usually sees in T-shirts are formally dressed up. The bridesmaids, usually friends of the bride, wear harmoniously blended dresses. The young gentlemen who stand by the groom as groomsmen wear tuxedos. For a week a wedding follows specified rules. Through the marriage of our daughter, we have suddenly become a part of a large American family. Only when your own children marry into an American family, the adaptation to American society is complete.

[Beginning of August], 1980

[After the wedding my wife and I had to recuperate. On our way to a vacation on Myrtle Beach at the Atlantic coast in South Carolina, we stopped in Asheville, North Carolina, to visit the house where Thomas Wolfe (1900—38) was born. That gave us the opportunity to also see the castle-like Biltmore House and Estate west of Asheville.]

Also America Has Its Castles

The most perfect replica of a French chateau stands in Asheville, North Carolina. Biltmore House was built by George W. Vanderbilt from 1890—95. The Loire chateaux Chambord and Blois served as models. Situated at the foot of the Great Smoky Mountains and Mount Pisgah, Biltmore House offers a stunningly beautiful view. The interior of Biltmore House is furnished with exquisite taste in a late medieval and Renaissance style. Dutch tapestries decorate the walls and valuable Dürer engravings are hanging in the alcoves. An artist craftsman from Vienna carved the wood paneling. The baroque fresco ceiling from an Italian palace has been so skillfully mounted in the library that the transatlantic transplantation could be forgotten.

Biltmore House is more than a curiosity. It is an expression of an American art form toward the end of the 19th and the beginning of the 20th centuries, which was predominantly following European models. Biltmore House is a castle in the wilderness, which surprises by its design and splendor. Looking inward, it produces a perfect illusion of a European ambience. But looking outward, it stands in an empty space, only surrounded by nature and a day's ride on horseback away from the next Cherokee Indian Reservation.

[By the end of the 19th and beginning of the 20th centuries several dozens of such castle like estates were built in the United States. Most of them are now accessible to the general public as museums. Their eclectic-historical style was primarily developed by Richard Morris Hunt (1828-95), who had also designed Biltmore House and Estate.]

[Middle of August), 1980

The Democratic National Convention

The National Convention of the Democratic Party took place in New York, August 11-14. At first, there was a vote on whether the delegates have to comply with the results of the primaries, or whether they can vote their conscience in an open convention. That would have been the chance for Edward Kennedy to win the nomination. But that decisive ballot went in favor of Jimmy Carter. Consequently, his nomination as presidential candidate of the Democratic Party was certain.

Addendum

[Carter maintained Walter Mondale as his running mate for Vice President. A month earlier, at their Convention in Detroit, the Republicans had nominated Ronald Reagan as presidential candidate. Reagan chose George Bush as his running mate. Thus, Carter-Mondale and Reagan-Bush confronted each other in the fall campaign of 1980.]

August 19, 1980

America as a Tourist Country

For the first time in the history of tourism across the Atlantic and the Pacific, the number of visitors to the United Sates is about equal to the number of Americans going to Europe or South East Asia. From among roughly 8 million tourists who visit the United States this year, approximately 1.3 million come from Great Britain, 1.2 million from Japan, 650,000 from the Federal Republic of Germany, and 400,000 from France. The interest in America has always been great. But only in recent years, due to air travel and the low exchange rate of the dollar, vacationing in the United States from abroad has become possible for short periods of time and affordable in price. America has still a great deal to offer as a tourist country.

South Bend, October 11, 1980

[After the resignation of Cyrus Vance, Senator Edmund Muskie followed him as Secretary of State.]

Edmund Muskie in Notre Dame

This morning, U.S. Secretary of State Edmund Muskie spoke on the Notre Dame Campus. It was a casual gathering of students and parents in Washington Hall, the old theatre building of the University. Muskie emphasized the need for a "balance of power" between the United States and the Soviet Union and indicated that, following the presidential election, endeavors for signing the SALT II agreement would be resumed. Muskie expressed confidence that the security of the United States and its allies was beyond question. But in the future, he said, the United States would not interfere in internal conflicts of other countries. That was an indication that the United States would not interfere in the present war between Iran and Iraq. Muskie, who above all has become known as a senator, has, in surprisingly short time, familiarized himself with the office and duties of Secretary of State. As a person and politician, who can look back on many years of experience in the Senate, he makes a trustworthy impression.

[Transl: For biographical reference on Edmund Muskie, see entry above of August 29, 1968.]

October 18, 1980

Can Carter Win?

Two weeks before the presidential election, Carter is definitely catching up on the lead Reagan has been holding in the polls. It is conceivable that his incumbency will have an effect in the last stretch of the campaign and that Carter will be elected to a second term. However, the unresolved question of the 52 American hostages in Tehran is a heavy burden on his presidency.

South Bend, October 28, 1980

The Debate

The debate between Jimmy Carter and Ronald Reagan, which was televised this evening from Cleveland, Ohio, had been expected with great interest.

The debate was fair and on a high level. While Carter laid out the policy goals of the Democrats, Reagan held firmly on to his conservative agenda, but he countered Carter's attacks with relaxing ease. About 120 million people followed the debate on television. The personality of each of the two candidates has come out in clearer profile by this confrontation.

[Reagan's relaxing reply to Carter's attack—"there you go again"—still rings in my ears after 20 years.]

November 2, 1980

Too Close to Call

Two days before the presidential election, it is still not clear who will win. According to the polls, the situation is "too close to call" to make a prediction.

November 4, 1980

The Surprise of the Election Night

The more reports of ballots cast come in, the more certain projections are getting that Ronald Reagan and the Republicans are winning higher than one had guessed. Especially here in Indiana, a Republican landslide is in the making. By this trend, also the well known Democratic Congressman John Brademas, after having served for 22 years in the House of Representatives, may lose his seat.

November 5, 1980

The Election Result

Although it has been assumed that Ronald Reagan would win, the extent of his victory is surprising. Just at this election, which was prognosticated as a neck and neck race, Reagan's landslide victory comes unexpected. The new-conservative mood in the country runs deeper than it has been seen on the surface.

With a voting turnout of 52%, the election result is as follows: Ronald Reagan won 42.4 million votes or 51% of the total; Jimmy Carter won 34.2 million votes or 41% of the total. Reagan won in 44 states. This gives him 483 electoral votes, while Carter receives only 49.

The Republicans added 10 more seats to their number in the Senate. With 51:49 seats, they have, for the first time since 1954, again the majority in the Senate. With 245 seats—several seats are still open—the Democrats could hold on to their majority in the House of Representatives.

November 10, 1980

Facing Difficult Tasks

As newly elected President, Ronald Reagan is facing difficult tasks. America has presently an inflation of 12.5% and an unemployment rate of 6.5%. What will Reagan and the incoming Republican Administration undertake to overcome this stagnation?

November 15, 1980

Pictures of Saturn

At the beginning of this week (November 12/13), the spacecraft Voyager 1, from a distance of a billion miles, sent pictures of the planet Saturn back to Earth. With astounding clarity, one could see on the television screen the images, which the Jet Propulsion Laboratory in Pasadena, California, transmitted, and thereby follow how the spacecraft flew by the ringed planet. A strange world of about 1,000 rings and of Saturn's moons, especially of the largest moon Titan, was opened to our eyes.

[The two spacecrafts Voyager 1 and Voyager 2 were launched in August and September 1977 to explore the planets in the outer solar system. Both sent pictures and data of Jupiter and Saturn back to Earth. Voyager 2 flew by Uranus in January 1986—see entries below of January 22 and 25, 1986. After passing through our solar system, the two spacecrafts are traveling practically timeless through interstellar space. Each of them carries a gold disc with records of a broad variety of our civilization. This gold disc is said to have a life span of about one billion years. It carries with it the hope that another civilization in space may receive this message of our existence. For more detailed information on the "gold plated copper phonograph record" mounted on the Voyager spacecraft see Carl Sagan, *Cosmos* (New York: Random House, 1980), pp. 287-89.]

South Bend, December 3, 1980

Worried about Poland

[In the fall of 1980, the independent union Solidarnosc under Lech Walesa had called a general strike in Poland.]

The strike situation in Poland has come to a head to the extent that there is serious danger of an intervention by the Soviet Union. About 35 divisions are standing ready at Poland's Eastern and Western borders. Will Moscow give orders to invade Poland? This is the alarming question in the world today. If the Communist Party in Poland should lose control of the situation, then there is undoubtedly the possibility that the Soviet Union, with the assistance of other East Bloc countries, may march into Poland, such as it was done in Czechoslovakia. In this case, how would the West react?

December 15, 1980

The Warning

At their recent meeting in Brussels, NATO countries have shown rare unanimity. A strong warning was given to Moscow that an invasion of Poland would have serious consequences. One can heave a sigh of relief, in the meantime the situation in Poland has calmed down.

South Bend, December 25, 1980

The Hostages in Tehran

The 52 American hostages had to spend a second Christmas in captivity in Tehran. Although the images, which had been released by Tehran over the holidays, gave the impression that the physical condition of the hostages is satisfactory, they could not delude the evil of the situation. Attempts have been made time and again at taking advantage of the hostage crisis by blackmail and excessive demands. There is no telling how this will end.

South Bend, January 11, 1981

Examination of Conscience of the Nation

The long hearings of General Alexander Haig before the Senate Foreign Relations Committee are in many ways an examination of conscience of the nation. It is about Alexander Haig's confirmation as U.S. Secretary of State by the Senate. Asked directly whether he would consider using nuclear force, Haig replied that American military power is only credible as a deterrent if the use of nuclear weapons has to be taken seriously into account. American history, he explained, offers enough examples that liberty had to be fought for and lives had to be sacrificed. After Haig's testimony, there can be no doubt that as U.S. Secretary of State he would if necessary recommend to the new Administration the use of nuclear force.

[General Alexander M. Haig, Jr., was Supreme Commander of U.S. and Allied Forces in Europe, 1974-79.]

Sunday, January 18, 1981

Free At Last

After 442 days in captivity, it's becoming more and more certain that the 52 American hostages in Tehran will be freed. The news reports from Washington, Tehran, and Algiers follow in rapid succession. Deputy Secretary of State Warren Christopher led, from the American side, the negotiations, which have now resulted in freeing the hostages. The irony of the situation has it that President Carter has brought the hostage crisis to an end without bloodshed, just a few hours before his term in office will end.

January 20, 1981

Ronald Reagan Sworn In as President

As the Constitution provides, Ronald Reagan was sworn in today at 12 noon as 40th President of the United States by Chief Justice Warren Burger. The ceremony took place, as it is customary, on the westside balustrade of the Capitol in open air despite the winter cold. Therewith, the new Republican era has begun in Washington. In his inaugural address, Reagan announced that he will reduce the bureaucracy of the federal government, strengthen States rights, and revive the economy by private initiative and reducing taxes.

[Ronald W. Reagan was born 1911 in Tampico, Illinois; he graduated from Eureka College in 1932. Reagan's conservative world view and distinct love of freedom were formed in the American Middle West. By profession radio commentator, film actor, and politician, Reagan was Governor of California, 1967-74 and U.S. President, 1981-89.]

P.S.

Half an hour after President Reagan had been sworn in, the news was broadcast that the Algerian airplane with the 52 hostages on board had departed Tehran and left Iranian air space. The freed hostages will be flown via Athens to Algiers. There, they will be taken over by an American military aircraft and flown to Frankfurt. In the American hospital in Wiesbaden, they will receive a medical check-up and be prepared for the flight home to the United States. Overwhelming was the sight when the 52 freed hostages came out of the airplane in Algiers shortly after midnight local time, about 8 p.m. EST, and walked down the boarding ramp. Free at last!—was the thought that not only moved the families and relatives of the hostages, but also millions of people around the world. Gradually, one can feel the relief that this horrible drama has come to an end.

January 27, 1981

The Homecoming

Rarely has an event moved America so much as the homecoming of the former hostages. It was not only the heart-wrenching scenes of families who had suffered the most being united again and the abhorrence of acts of maltreatment now coming to light, but also becoming aware how much personal freedom can be disregarded and made a mockery of what shook up people to the core. It touched a sensitive nerve of America's consciousness. The flood of "yellow ribbons" is gradually receding. They were bound around trees and placed on doorways throughout the country, expressing the hope that those missing would come home again.

South Bend, February 18, 1981

A New Beginning

In his first State of the Union Address before the joint session of Congress, President Reagan promised a new beginning. He offered far-reaching proposals to reduce government spending, to reduce taxes, and for deregulation. Already in the coming fiscal year, 41 billion dollars should be saved. How effective this new beginning will be, depends largely on the psychological impact the new free market economy will have.

March 1, 1981

Margaret Thatcher in Washington

In the television interview on "Face the Nation," hosted by Barbara Walters, British Prime Minister Margaret Thatcher commented on questions of European security. Leonid Brezhnev had recently proposed a summit meeting to discuss a moratorium on nuclear weapons in Europe. Asked what she thought of this proposal, Thatcher replied that the Soviet Union presently has absolute superiority in tactical nuclear weapons in Europe. As long as this imbalance exists, a moratorium is out of the question. The security of Europe depends without a doubt on the United States.

Note

[Margaret Thatcher had come to Washington on February 27, 1981, at the invitation of President Reagan. The purpose of the visit was to establish first contacts with the new Administration. Thatcher was of the opinion that Brezhnev's proposal for a summit meeting was premature and that his offer of a moratorium on nuclear weapons in Europe was deceptive. As, on the one hand, the Soviet Union had already deployed the SS-20 intermediate-range missiles, and, on the other hand, Europe had not as yet installed the Pershing II missiles, freezing the status quo would have given the Soviet Union "overwhelming superiority," to which Europe would have remained exposed. That was neither for Thatcher nor for Ronald Reagan acceptable. (On her visit to Washington, see Margaret Thatcher, *The Downing Street Years*, pp. 158-60.)]

South Bend, March 30, 1981

Not Again!

When this afternoon about 3 p.m. the news spread like wildfire that President Reagan, after delivering a speech having left the Washington Hilton Hotel, was shot at and wounded, the first reaction was disbelief and the outcry: "Not again!" As if time had shrunk, it could not have happened again. It took several hours until it was possible to get, to some extent, a clear picture of the incident. Only when word came from the George Washington University Hospital that the surgery went well and that the President is out of danger of life, one could breathe a sigh of relief.

The Press Secretary of the White House James Brady was seriously injured in the incident. With a bullet wound in his head, he is presently fighting for his life in the George Washington University Hospital.

Addendum

[The assassination attempt on President Reagan was the deed of a psychologically disturbed young man. The injury Reagan had suffered was much more serious than it had at first appeared to be. The bullet, closely passing his heart, penetrated the lung. It was a close encounter with death. James Brady remained handicapped and partially paralyzed. For a detailed description of the events on that fateful afternoon of March 30, 1981, in Washington, see Edmund Morris, *Dutch: A Memoir of Ronald Reagan* (New York: Random House, 1999), pp. 427-32. As a child Ronald Reagan was called "Dutch" by his parents. This affectionate nickname stayed with him for a long time.]

South Bend, April 12, 1981

Lift-off!

Shrouded in a white cloud of steam and with a flash of fire, the space shuttle Columbia lifted off from the launch pad on Cape Canaveral, rising into Florida's blue morning sky. Already after two minutes, it vanished from sight like a comet on the horizon. Nearly two million people had assembled on Cape Canaveral to witness this historic moment in human spaceflight. The shuttle Columbia is the first reusable spacecraft that can fly several consecutive missions.

April 14, 1981

The astronauts John Young and Robert Crippen completed the test flight of the space shuttle Columbia with a picture book landing on the runway of Edwards Air Force Base in Southern California. Half an hour before the landing, the retro-rockets were fired over the Indian Ocean. Thereafter, the shuttle entered the atmosphere and glided down for the landing. The space shuttle Columbia can now be used for another mission.

The historic significance of this test flight for the further development of human travel in space is obvious. One can easily imagine that a regular shuttle service between the launching site on Cape Canaveral and a space station will be established. The planet Earth has shrunk to an extent that would have been unimaginable only a few years ago. By the ever growing network of telecommunication via satellite, every spot on Earth can instantly be transmitted in sound and image.

Addendum

[After landing on Edwards Air Force Base, the space shuttle Columbia was flown piggyback on a Boeing 747, especially equipped for that purpose, to Cape Canaveral. There, at the Kennedy Space Center, it was examined for damages and prepared for the next flight. NASA soon had a fleet of space shuttles at its disposition, which could be used alternately for various missions in space.]

Sunday, May 10, 1981

Mitterand Wins Presidential Election

The first reports on the by-election in France showed that Francois Mitterand was leading over Giscard d'Estaing and that he will take over the presidency. Mitterand is known as a moderate Socialist. Will he be able to keep up his moderate line, or will he have to make concessions to the Communists who helped him win the election? Politics in France and in America are presently moving in opposite directions. While Reagan advocates a free market economy, Mitterand will certainly advance a Socialist program with further nationalization of industries in France.

South Bend, Wednesday, May 13, 1981

The Assassination Attempt on the Pope

About 11 a.m. here in the Midwest, the news came through that the Pope was shot at the Vatican and that his life is in danger. Daily activities in America seemed to stop for a moment. The events in Rome were hardly comprehensible. People were crying in the streets and congregated in churches. Gradually, one learned that the Pope, during his weekly Wednesday audience in St. Peter's Square, surrounded by thousands of people, fell victim to an assassination attempt on his life in the early evening hours. As soon as it became clearer what had happened, all attention was directed to the clinic in Rome where John Paul II had been undergoing nearly five hours of surgery. Only when it was announced that the Holy Father was out of danger, did worries subside. But the disgust for this senseless crime will last forever.

Addendum

[The assassination attempt on the life of the Pope was made by a shady criminal figure who had escaped from prison in Turkey and the arrest by police. The shots were fired on May 13, 1981, at about 5 p.m., when John Paul II arrived for the weekly audience in St. Peter's Square and drove through the crowd of the assembled faithful, standing in the open Popemobil, a small, jeep-like vehicle. One bullet went through the abdomen, causing life-threatening heavy bleeding. The wounded Pope was brought immediately by an ambulance to the Policlinico Gemelli where the difficult surgery was performed. Still weeks later, complications arose with high fever. That the life of John Paul was saved was almost a miracle. George Weigel gives a clear summary of the course of events of May 13, 1981, and their consequences; see *Witness of Hope: The Biography of Pope John Paul II*, pp. 411-16.]

Sunday, May 17, 1981

President Reagan in Notre Dame

At today's Commencement Exercises of the University of Notre Dame, President Ronald Reagan gave the Commencement Address. It was his first public appearance after the assassination attempt on March 30. As expected, security was tight. More than the television cameras showed, Reagan's features were still marked by what he had gone through. His voice was slightly broken.

Nonetheless, he proved to be a brilliant speaker. But the phenomenon Ronald Reagan cannot be explained by rhetoric alone. His personality radiates charisma. He has a special appeal to an audience. The 13,000 people, who filled the Athletic and Convocation Center to capacity, gave him a roaring applause. Reagan appeals especially to the broad American middle class. In his address, he clearly expounded his government agenda: The jungle of government regulations has to be simplified; the power of the federal government should be restrained and taxes reduced. At the same time, he emphasized, the defense capacity of the United States needs to be strengthened. Surprisingly, Reagan also appeals to the majority of the young generation in colleges and universities. There were no demonstrations during the Commencement ceremony. No doubt, a conservative change of heart has occurred in America.

South Bend, May 19, 1981

The Largest Wave of Immigration since 1900

According to *Time* magazine of May 18, the largest wave of immigration to the United States since 1900 is presently ongoing. Just as in the early 1900's, nearly a million people are now coming as immigrants to this country every year. Last year, about 800,000 immigrants were admitted to the United States. In addition, about a million illegal immigrants, who primarily cross the Southern border with Mexico, are also entering the country annually. Illegal immigration poses a special problem. While immigration before the First World War was made up mainly by industrial workers from Southern and Eastern Europe, the recent immigrants come from the Far East, the Caribbean and Central America. This new wave of immigration will decisively change the ethnic composition of the American population.

South Bend, August 9, 1981

Destitution in Poland

Famine, people standing for hours in line just to get basic foods; mothers on the streets begging for what they desperately need for their children—these images have shaken up the conscience of the American people. The Polish Congress in Chicago organized a telethon today, asking for help for Poland. The response has been overwhelming. Within hours, a million dollars have been pledged, which are now available for the relief of Poland.

August 10, 1981

Chaos in Transatlantic Air Traffic

The strike of air traffic controllers that has been going on for weeks is carried out with great bitterness and obstinacy. As employees of the federal government air traffic controllers on oath are not allowed to strike. After the ultimatum by the government had not been observed, President Reagan recently fired more than 12,000 air traffic controllers without notice. That triggered chaos in the transatlantic air traffic. And, as the Canadian air traffic controllers today also called a strike in sympathy with their American colleagues, the entire civil aviation between Europe and America has come to a standstill. Closing the control tower in Gander on Newfoundland has an especially serious effect. About 50,000 passengers are presently stranded at airports in Europe.

P.S.

After three days, only when the Canadian air traffic controllers, under pressure by their government, had resumed work, did air traffic normalize again. In the meantime, tired travelers, especially at the Heathrow Airport in London and the JFK in New York, have been patiently holding out.

South Bend, October 1, 1981

Economy Measures and National Debt

At the beginning of the new fiscal year, the first economy measures of the Reagan Administration are put into force: drastic cuts in spending for social programs; closing of a number of government offices; and a 5% tax cut in the first year. But despite of these measures, the national debt had to be limited to a trillion dollars because of the increased spending on defense.

October 2, 1981

A Nuclear War Cannot Be Waged

At today's press conference in the White House, President Reagan announced that the new MX missiles will be built and installed in the available silos of the Minuteman missiles. This new generation of intercontinental ballistic missiles has a range of 8,000 miles and could carry 10 nuclear warheads. It demonstrates the next to unimaginable force of destruction of the nuclear arsenal on both sides and underscores the realization that a nuclear war cannot be waged because it would result in total mutual annihilation.

October 6, 1981

Anwar Sadat (1918-1981)

The first sporadic pieces of news indicated that, at a military parade in Cairo, an assassination attempt on the life of President Anwar Sadat was made. Without further consequences, Sadat appeared to have suffered only a grazing shot. But at 1:00 p.m. EST, the full truth of this dreadful deed was confirmed. Sadat was fatally hit by a round of machine-gun fire aimed at the grandstand. He died shortly thereafter in the hospital. With the death of Anwar Sadat, America has lost one of its most reliable allies in the Middle East. The entire region is again thrown into turmoil and uncertainty.

October 10, 1981

The Funeral of Anwar Sadat

Three former American Presidents—Richard Nixon, Gerald Ford and Jimmy Carter—flew to Cairo to attend the funeral of Anwar Sadat. During their terms in office, they were all closely connected with the Egyptian President and had put great trust in him. Their cooperation culminated in the Camp David Accord of September 1978 and the following peace treaty of March 1979, whereby Egypt and Israel overcame their enmity and entered into normal bilateral diplomatic relations. But the funeral of Sadat showed with startling clarity how isolated Egypt was in the Arab world, and how split Arabs were among themselves. One has to ask whether the spirit of Camp David can be carried on, leading to a comprehensive peace agreement in the Middle East. No doubt, the peace process has been interrupted by the death of Sadat. The greatness of Anwar Sadat was manifest in his fearlessly standing up to achieve reconciliation between Egypt and Israel.

October 11, 1981

The Demonstration

While Chancellor Helmut Schmidt attended the funeral of Anwar Sadat in Cairo, nearly 250,000 people marched on the University of Bonn to protest against the deployment of Pershing II missiles on German soil as well as the nuclear armament of NATO in general. That was the largest demonstration in the Federal Republic since the end of the Second World War. Although the protest against nuclear armament is understandable, the aim of this demonstration remains confusing. Is there not the danger for a new Anti-Americanism, which could lead to the neutralization of Europe and its dependence on Moscow? How to meet with the growing discontent in Western Europe? One can only be concerned about this development.

South Bend, October 17, 1981

Yorktown

Two hundred years ago today, on October 17, 1781, the British troops under Lord Cornwallis, who had been encircled for weeks in Yorktown, Virginia, surrendered to the Continental army under the command of George Washington. That brought the War of Independence to an end in favor of the 13 colonies. The French assistance was crucial for the American victory at Yorktown. Count de Grasse, who had arrived with a large fleet and 20,000 men from the Caribbean, sailed into Chesapeake Bay. He, thereby, cut off the possibility for retreat by sea for Cornwallis.

In memory of that historic event at Yorktown, French President Francois Mitterand had come to Virginia and received President Reagan on board of the warship *De Grasse,* which lay at anchor in the Chesapeake Bay. On his part, Reagan invited Mitterand to a reception in the historic Williamsburg. The meeting between Mitterand and Reagan was pronounced cordial. Mitterand judges with a sense of realism the precarious situation Western Europe is in. He agrees with Reagan's policy of nuclear armament. Thus, Reagan's firm attitude has received unexpected support in the Elysée Palace.

South Bend, October 25, 1981

And Now in London and Rome

Protests in Europe against nuclear armament won't go away. After Bonn, demonstrations with large gatherings of people are now taking place in London and Rome. Paris and Brussels will follow. What shocked Europe and triggered the nuclear hysteria were rash remarks in the circle of the Reagan Administration that a limited nuclear war could be possible. It was obvious what Europe meant by it. One cannot fully measure in America the extent of fear Europeans have in this regard.

November 10, 1981

A Limited Nuclear War

A number of remarks have recently been made that a limited nuclear war could be waged. When asked at today's press conference what he thought of such an idea, President Reagan replied that he could not imagine to use limited nuclear force in Europe without setting in motion an exchange of intercontinental missiles between the United States and the Soviet Union. The risk of full-scale war would be very great.

Who would not feel a shiver running down the spine at this thought? By these and similar expressions, the nightmare of a nuclear war has again been aroused on both sides of the Atlantic.

November 21/22, 1981

The Struggle for Europe

While about 300,000 people rallied for a peace demonstration in Amsterdam over the weekend, Leonid Brezhnev arrived in Bonn for a state visit. Shortly before, President Reagan, alarmed by the peace movement in Europe and the growing tendency toward neutralization, announced that the United States would not deploy the Pershing II missiles if the Soviet Union on her part would dismantle the already installed SS-20 intermediate-range missiles. Brezhnev's answer was a clear "njet." Brezhnev is obviously convinced that the ever increasing peace movement in Western Europe would prevent the deployment of the Pershing missiles anyway. A gigantic struggle for the soul of Europe has broken out. Will Europe remain faithful to the Atlantic Defense Alliance, or succumb to the propaganda from the East and turn more toward Moscow?

November 29, 1981

Zero Option

At the same time when the delegations for disarmament talks arrived in Geneva, about 200,000 people demonstrated in Florence against nuclear armament in Europe. There is concern in America about the extent of these protest rallies. For the first time, President Reagan suggested "zero option," which means that all intermediate-range missiles in Western and Eastern Europe should be eliminated. Although it is unlikely that this proposal will be put into effect, it has nonetheless given new impetus to the disarmament talks in Geneva.

Note

[In a speech at the Press Club in Washington on November 18, 1981, President Reagan proposed "zero option" for the elimination of all INF (Intermediate-range Nuclear Forces) in Western and Eastern Europe. Zero option remained for years a vehemently discussed topic at the disarmament negotiations in Geneva. The historic INF treaty was finally signed by Reagan and Gorbachev in Washington in December, 1988. See Morris, *Dutch:* A *Memoir of Ronald Reagan,* pp. 454, 630.]

South Bend, December 13, 1981

Martial Law in Poland

Today after midnight, police commandos raided the main offices of the free trade union Solidarity in Warsaw, Gdansk and other Polish cities and arrested its leader. At the same time, martial law was imposed in Poland. The military is standing by on alert, news communications were cut off as well as borders and airports closed. Any stir of freedom is being crushed with brutal force. The West is confronted this morning by a number of pressing questions: Will there be an uprising in Poland? Will Solidarity, which has 9.5 million members, be able to stand its ground? Will the troops of the East Bloc countries invade Poland if the Communist regime should lose ground? Which measures should the West take against these events in the East?

December 20, 1981

Worse than Suspected

During the past week, military dictatorship has descended upon Poland. From the few reports that reached the West, one could get a rough idea of what has happened. The military and special police units cracked down with the sort of brutality one had thought would belong to the past. Where there was a strike in a factory or resistance put up, tanks moved in. There were casualties and many wounded. Lech Walesa remains under house arrest. Thousands of people fled abroad.

A convoy from the Netherlands, which had returned from a relief mission bringing food to Poland, told of violent excesses against civilians, wherever a group of people gathered. What is happening in Poland is worse than one could have suspected. As winter is approaching, there is a shortage of coal and food. What will happen with the thousands of dissidents who have been arrested? Touching scenes have occurred in Chicago, whenever it was possible to get, still in the last minute, family members out of Poland.

December 21, 1981

The Second Poland

About 10 million people of Polish descent live in America, primarily in the Chicago area. In these days of affliction of the old home country, the second Poland is getting attention. What is happening in Poland, is here not taken indifferently? Moved by reports of atrocities, terror and famine, people are prompted to act. In a blizzard and biting frost at 10 below zero Fahrenheit, thousands of people in Chicago and the surrounding suburbs went on the streets to show their compassion for the suffering Poland.

The Polish Ambassador in Washington Romuald Spasowski, an experienced career diplomat, resigned in protest and asked for political asylum. At his resignation Spasowski gave a stirring appeal to the Press Corps in Washington, saying: "This is the most flagrant and brutal violation of human rights, which makes a mockery of the Polish signature put on the final act of the Helsinki accords."

Addendum

[President Reagan who was convinced that Moscow was jointly responsible for the events in Poland, immediately announced a number of sanctions against the Soviet Union. But they met with fierce criticism in Western Europe so that they threatened more to split the Western Alliance than to unite it for a common response. Most contentious was to boycott the Siberian natural gas pipeline, which was already under construction and would have supplied Western Europe with additional energy. British, German and Italian companies had already signed binding contracts to deliver building materials for the West Siberian Gas Pipeline. Stopping the delivery would have brought financial losses and inevitably led to layoffs. Margaret Thatcher argued that the sanctions did not make much sense because they would have been more damaging to the West than the East. The dispute over which measures should be taken against the East went on for some time. See Thatcher, *The Downing Street Years,* pp. 252-54.]

South Bend, January 10, 1982

Intermediary between East and West

German Chancellor Helmut Schmidt who is presently in Washington for talks with the Reagan Administration gave a TV interview today to the well-known commentator David Brinkley. Schmidt has recently come under crossfire by the press for his critical attitude against sanctions. He is trying, as far as it is possible in the present situation, to act as intermediary between East and West. Asked what he wants to achieve by his mediatory proposal, Schmidt replied briefly and unmistakably that by breaking off talks between the United States and the Soviet Union everyone, but especially the Europeans, would be affected. Talking to his Russian partners in Moscow, he also wants to give them to understand that they should not underestimate the resolve of President Reagan. A summit meeting between Reagan and Brezhnev could correct many misunderstandings. Chancellor Schmidt regards the United States as the undisputed leading power of the Western Alliance. He pointed out that in a recent opinion poll in the Federal Republic 80% of his fellow citizens were in favor of friendship with the United States. In Schmidt's view, NATO is not, despite differences of opinion, in a crisis situation but fulfills its task quite satisfactorily.

Sunday, January 24, 1982

Football Fever

This afternoon America is divided between two camps: One is rooting for the San Francisco 49ers and the other for the Bengals of Cincinnati. Pontiac in Michigan is the venue of the 16th Super Bowl, the championship of American football. The hero of the day is Joe Montana, the quarterback of the 49ers. As quarterback of the Fighting Irish, Montana had already led Notre Dame to a national championship in college football in 1977. As the Super Bowl is shown on television, one can forget the bitter cold winter, which has covered two thirds of the country with a solid blanket of snow. The blizzards of the past two weeks brought the Northeast and the Midwest the coldest temperatures that have so far been recorded in this century.

The San Francisco 49ers won against the Bengals 26:21. By this victory in the Super Bowl, Joe Montana has become a sports legend.

March 22, 1982

Already a Matter of Routine

The space shuttle Columbia was sent this morning on its third mission. There was a smooth start, the giant rocket lifted off from the launch pad on Cape Canaveral with such ease, one had the impression that manned space flights have already become a matter of routine.

Sunday, March 28, 1982

Elections in El Salvador

Never before have elections in Central America drawn such attention as today's elections for a constituent assembly in El Salvador. The first news and pictures, which have come out from the capital San Salvador, indicate that people, despite intimidations from the left and the right, are going to vote in large numbers and are standing in line before polling stations.

March 29, 1982

It was a desperate struggle for democracy. People in El Salvador, although they stood in the crossfire between government troops and the guerillas who wanted to prevent the election, cast their ballots without letting themselves to be deterred. The American team of election observers confirmed by common consent that the election was fair. The population of El Salvador wanted to have an end to the civil war, which over two years had claimed 30,000 victims.

South Bend, Tuesday, April 6, 1982

The Side Show

The world community was startled last Friday, April 2, to learn that at dawn Argentine naval forces had invaded and occupied the Falkland Islands. What does this side show mean, which at this time is diverting attention from the East West conflict? The new military junta in Buenos Aires must have seen it as an opportune moment for risking now an international conflict by occupying the Malvines.

The indignation in Great Britain was understandably great. Foreign Secretary Lord Peter Carrington took responsibility for having underestimated the danger of the situation and resigned today. But Margaret Thatcher remained firm and resolved. A British navy task force is already on its way to the South Atlantic. Now, one can look forward in suspense to what will happen when the task force reaches the 8,000 miles distant Falkland Islands.

Note

[The Falkland Islands are situated about 400 miles northeast of Cape Horn. This group of islands in the South Atlantic was named by English sailors in 1690 after Viscount Falkland. The Falkland Sound divides the archipelago into East Falkland with the capital Stanley and the barren, virtually unsettled West Falkland. Since 1833 the Falklands have been a British crown colony, which also includes South Georgia, a small group of islands 600 miles to the east. In the 19th century, the Falkland Islands were of strategic importance for navigation around Cape Horn. The Falklands are altogether sparsely populated. The population of about 2,500, half of whom live in Stanley, is primarily of Scottish origin. Sheep-breeding and fishery are the main source of livelihood. The inhabitants of the Falklands have always declared that they wished to live under British rule and the protection of their homeland.

The Spanish name "Malvinas" derives from the French "Malouines." Citizens from Saint-Malo had, for a short period of time in the 18th century, settled on the East Island, before it was turned over to Spain. Since 1820, Argentina has asserted territorial claims on the "Islas Malvinas," including the South Georgia island group. Diplomatic efforts for many years before 1982 to find a peaceful solution in the dispute over sovereignty of the Falkland Islands were of no avail.]

South Bend, April 18, 1982

Shuttle Diplomacy

U.S. Secretary of State Alexander Haig has set a new record in shuttle diplomacy. He has been moving nonstop back and forth between Washington, London and Buenos Aires to mediate in the Falklands conflict. Both sides, however, have assumed a very obstinate and uncompromising attitude. Neither Great Britain nor Argentina has agreed somehow to yield in the question of sovereignty. While Haig is still negotiating in Buenos Aires, the British navy already crossed the equator and is sailing toward the Falkland Islands. In the meantime, Argentina has reinforced its troops on the Malvinas.

April 25, 1982

War Appears to Be Unavoidable

Since all attempts at mediation and diplomatic efforts have led nowhere, war between Great Britain and Argentina appears to be unavoidable. Today, the British task force has reached the disputed islands in the South Atlantic. South Georgia was taken without resistance worth speaking of. But the real showdown lies ahead at the Falklands, where Argentina has concentrated its armed forces.

May 1, 1982

War in the South Atlantic

In today's early morning hours, units of the Royal Air Force attacked and destroyed the airport of Port Stanley. That laid emphasis on the imposed blockade around the Falklands by air and sea. The war in the South Atlantic has begun. Its extent cannot as yet be fully measured. The United States initially assumed a neutral stance, trying to mediate in the Falklands conflict. But as all diplomatic efforts have failed, the United States is now assisting Great Britain.

Heavy Losses on Both Sides

The Argentine warship *Belgrano* was attacked by a British submarine and sent to the bottom of the sea. Hundreds of soldiers drowned in the ice-cold waters. Then, a missile fired by an Argentine combat aircraft hit the British destroyer *Sheffield,* which burst into flames and sank. Many British soldiers lost their lives. These heavy losses on both sides cast a gloomy shadow upon the war in the South Atlantic. The war also strains the relations between North and South America.

Sunday, May 16, 1982

Pierre Trudeau: Back to Détente

The Prime Minister of Canada Pierre Trudeau gave the commencement address at today's graduation ceremony of the University of Notre Dame. Trudeau is a fascinating personality. He is witty, a splendid speaker being absolutely bilingual in French and English. Trudeau is also a politician of international stature and a farsighted statesman. He urgently appealed to the two superpowers, the United States and the Soviet Union, to return to détente and resume bilateral talks to stop the nuclear arms race. In Europe as well as in Canada, anxiety is growing as long as the two superpowers are not negotiating and talking to each other.

At the United Nations

[At the beginning of the Falklands conflict, the British Ambassador to the United Nations Sir Anthony Parsons succeeded in having a resolution passed by the Security Council, which demanded the immediate withdrawal of Argentine forces from the Falkland Islands. Just like Alexander Haig, General Secretary of the United Nations Perez de Cuellar had intervened in an attempt to find a peaceful solution. Also these efforts were of no avail. It had become ever so clear that Argentina was not willing to give up the Malvinas without a fight.]

May 21, 1982

The Quotation of the Week

General Secretary of the United Nations Perez de Cuellar declared repeatedly: "Time is not on the side of peace." Time is indeed not on the side of peace. All diplomatic efforts for a peaceful solution of the Falklands conflict have failed. Last night British military units have begun to take the Falkland Islands by storm. Battle engagements are now escalating every hour.

May 23, 1982

Encircled

After British marine units have succeeded in penetrating the Falkland Sound and establishing a bridgehead, they can advance on East Falkland to the capital Stanley. As the British fleet controls the sea and the ground troops are advancing on land, the roughly 10,000 men strong Argentine garrison in Port Stanley is de facto encircled.

South Bend, May 23, 1982

Cultural Uncertainty

Talking with American intellectuals, one will encounter over and again cultural uncertainty. One will meet with astonishment and incredibility that American authors are much in demand and read abroad. Is there in Europe really a wave of enthusiasm for Melville, Hemingway, Steinbeck, Thornton Wilder, and Thomas Wolfe? Doubts about it reveal a certain cultural inferiority complex vis-à-vis Europe, which goes back to the early 19th century. Americans are very sensitive when they feel to be exposed to European criticism as to their cultural understanding.

Lorin Maazel's Farewell to Cleveland

The fact that the music director of the Cleveland Symphony Orchestra Lorin Maazel has been appointed music director of the Vienna State Opera has attracted much attention in America. How is it possible, music lovers in America are asking, that one of their own has been entrusted with one of the most coveted and hottest conductorships in the world? Maazel responded with charm that it is not only a challenge for himself to go into the lion's den but also a recognition that classical music in America is being furthered and that there are many talents to be discovered.

June 2, 1982

The Siege Has Begun

The advancing British troops on East Falkland to Port Stanley got embroiled in fierce fighting with considerable casualties on both sides. The war for the Falkland Islands, which has never been declared but has seen heavy fighting, is now entering its decisive confrontation. The nearly 10,000 men strong Argentine garrison in Port Stanley has been encircled from all sides. The siege has begun.

The Berlin Wall—Introductory Remarks

[President Reagan participated in the G-7 (Group of seven leading industrialized countries) summit meeting in Versailles from June 4-6, 1982. On June 7, he met for the first time Pope John Paul II in the Vatican, and on June 8, he gave the speech before members of the British Parliament in which he predicted that the Communist regimes in Eastern Europe will collapse by themselves. Two days later, on June 10, Reagan arrived for a short visit in Berlin. He proceeded to "Checkpoint Charlie," where he saw the Berlin Wall for the first time. When asked by a reporter what his impression of the Wall was, he replied: "It's as ugly as the idea behind it." See Morris, *Dutch:* A *Memoir of Ronald Reagan,* p. 461.]

South Bend, June 10, 1982

A Declaration of Loyalty at the Wall

Like his predecessors in office, also President Reagan declared his loyalty at the Berlin Wall. He assured that the United States will not forsake Berlin and that it remains committed to the defense of the Federal Republic and Western Europe.

South Bend, June 15, 1982

The War is Over

In the last moment, reason has prevailed. Hopelessly encircled from all sides, the commandant of the Argentine garrison in Port Stanley decided to surrender. Thereby, a senseless bloodshed possibly of thousands of lives has been avoided, for in the end 9,000 British were confronted by approximately 14,000 Argentine troops. The Falklands or Malvinas War is over.

[Margaret Thatcher offers a detailed survey of the course of events in the Falklands conflict, above all of the many-sided but failed diplomatic efforts to achieve a peaceful solution. The Falklands War was the greatest challenge of her time in office. See Thatcher, *The Downing Street Years,* pp. 173-235.]

June 27, 1982

Swift Turnover

The swift turnover in the State Department that occurred over this weekend not only took foreign countries by surprise, but it also baffled the American public. Last Friday, June 25, President Reagan announced in a brief communiqué that Secretary of State Alexander Haig had resigned, while at the same time George Shultz was nominated as his successor. What prompted the resignation of Alexander Haig? A number of speculations are circulating: Discords within the inner circle of the White House staff have already surfaced for some time. There were controversies between Haig and Secretary of Defense Caspar Weinberger. Finally, there were also differences of opinion between Haig and Reagan on foreign policy.

[Alexander Haig did not resign on his own decision. He was actually fired by President Reagan. See Morris, *Dutch:* A *Memoir* of *Ronald Reagan,* p. 463.]

South Bend, June 29, 1982

Never So True

Today, my wife was sworn in on the American Constitution at the U.S. District Court in Hammond, Indiana. Thus, all four members of our family have become

American citizens. It has been a sheer endless red tape process that lasted for ten years. But all the applications and petitions at consulates and immigration offices have now led to a happy end. It was just a matter of not losing patience and of observing the residence requirement. The swearing in on the U.S. Constitution is always a solemn ceremony. On each face of the 62 applicants for citizenship, who had assembled in the Hall of the District Court, one could see the inner emotion. Everyone has come to this point on his or her own way in life.

America never becomes so true as at the moment of naturalization. All false images and illusions fade away, and each cheap cliché would get stuck in one's mouth. Naturalization as American citizen is for everyone a new beginning.

While the judge instructed the new citizens of their rights and duties, the screeching noise and whistle of a locomotive was heard through the window. The Court House in Hammond is situated next to a railroad station in the industrial hub of Gary and East Chicago. The hardship and at the same time also the generosity and spaciousness of this country as well as a sense of freedom and security were felt at that moment with an intensity as it had never been experienced before.

Introductory Remarks

[I had once more assumed the directorship of the University of Notre Dame Foreign Studies Program in Innsbruck for the two year period 1982-84. My wife and I flew on August 1, 1982 from Chicago to Frankfurt. There we took a rental car and drove along the "Romantische Strasse" (Romantic Road)—Würzburg, Rothenburg-ob-der-Tauber, Dinkelsbühl—to Innsbruck, where we settled down for the next two years.]

[August 5], 1982

Tilman Riemenschneider (1460-1531)

On our way from Würzburg to Rothenburg-ob-der-Tauber, we stopped at Creglingen to see the nearby "Herrgottskirche" (Chapel of Our Lord) with its famous altarpiece dedicated to the Virgin Mary carved by Tilman Riemenschneider. We met there not only pilgrims to the St. Mary's shrine and a masterpiece of late Gothic art, but even more so people, who were clinging to a long gone German past and groping for something to hold on to with such deeply-moved devotion I had never seen before.

SECTION 9

January 1, 1983-July 31, 1985

Innsbruck, January 1, 1983

A Drama Without Equal

A drama without equal is playing out in Europe before our eyes. Will Western Europe in the years ahead be able to hold its own, or will it fall right into the lap of Communism in the East? The danger is just as great from the inside as from the outside. The economic recession, which in the New Year could lead to increasing unemployment in most countries in Western Europe, may put the Western democracies to a severe test. Furthermore, there are the uncertainty of the political situation in the Federal Republic, the continuously hovering government crisis in Italy, and the increasing radicalization on the periphery—in Turkey, Greece and Portugal. Into consideration should also be taken the economic slump in France and Great Britain, as well as the growingly clamorous peace movement and the widespread political defeatism. Will NATO's decision for nuclear rearmament be carried out and the 572 Peshing II and cruise missiles be deployed? Or, will Western Europe be declared a nuclear-free zone? If the latter happens, Western Europe will remain exposed to the threat by the Soviet SS-20 intermediate-range missiles that stay bluntly aimed at targets in Western Europe. In this predicament, Moscow demands, virtually in the form of an ultimatum, that the West Europeans distance themselves from the United States and dissolve NATO. An unprecedented struggle for Western Europe has begun. Whom will the Western Europeans turn to? This seems to become the decisive question for the 1980s.

Amerikasehnsucht—Longing for America

One can at present observe an unusually widespread "Amerikasehnsuchf" or longing for America. Whether one talks with students at the university, professional academics, middle-aged business people, or with politicians from the ÖVP (Austrian People's Party) as well as the SPÖ (Socialist Party of Austria), one may hear again and again the same statement: "I would like to go to America one day!" Professional interests as well as personal curiosity strongly motivate this desire to get to know the United States.

Anti-Americanism may manifest itself on the outside, but inside, in their personal views, many people feel a secret affection toward America which should not be overlooked. Roaring jubilation surrounded last night Liza Minelli at the "Silvester-Show" or New Year's Eve Concert in Bad Gastein when she sang "New York, New York."

How to React

Confused by the outbreaks of hatred for America at protest rallies, Americans frequently don't know themselves how to react. To withdraw from Europe would not only shock millions of people but would also be a historic mistake of far-reaching consequences.

[Beginning of January], 1983

Days of Historical Remembrance

Austria, as in fact the entire German cultural area, is fondly reminiscing about events of the past. In 1982, the Haydn-Year [250th birthday] and the 150th anniversary of Goethe's death were celebrated. But already new preparations are under way for days of historical remembrance in 1983. Among these are: The 500th birthday of Martin Luther; the 100th anniversary of the death of Karl Marx; the 300th anniversary of the siege of Vienna by the Turks; 100 years PSK (Österreichische Postsparkassa—Austrian Post-Office Savings Bank]; the Brahms-Year [150th birthday]; 100th anniversary of the death of Richard Wagner; symposia are being planned for the 100th birthday of Franz Kafka; also for the 500th birthday of Raffaello Santi. The list of celebrations, symposia and conferences that are being planned could be further extended.

January 7, 1983

The Peace Initiative from Prague

The seven East Bloc countries—the Soviet Union, Poland, East Germany, Czechoslovakia, Hungary, Romania, and Bulgaria—have, at their summit meeting in Prague, drafted a comprehensive peace initiative, which they submitted to the West. Next to the frequently heard propaganda appeals to renounce the first use of nuclear force, halt the arms race and to dissolve NATO and the Warsaw Pact, also a nonaggression treaty with the West has been proposed. The proposals from Prague have made the West listen; at least they have evoked readiness to talk. Much depends now on what progress will be made in the months ahead at the disarmament talks in Geneva.

January 19, 1983

Wooing Germany

On his present visit to Bonn, Soviet Foreign Minister Andrei Gromyko is clearly wooing the Federal Republic to follow a neutral course and to support Moscow's point of view in the question of disarmament. Not without good reason, this visit is directed at German voters who will have to make an important decision on March 6.

Innsbruck, January 19, 1983

Moral Support for Nuclear Disarmament

The pastoral letter of the American Catholic bishops met with unexpected worldwide response. The courageous statement by the American bishops on the present disarmament debate cannot miss its effect.

Note

[The American Catholic bishops drafted from 1981-83 a pastoral letter which addresses the question of war and peace in the atomic age. The letter passed through three drafts. The second draft has become known worldwide. To pass judgment on it, Pope John Paul II had convened a conference for January 18 and 19, 1983 in the Vatican, where representatives of the American National

Conference of Catholic Bishops together with bishops and experts in Europe could discuss and present their views on nuclear disarmament. Then in May 1983, the revised third draft was accepted by the American National Conference of Catholic Bishops as final text. The well-founded, 103 page document was published titled, *The Challenge of Peace: God's Promise and Our Response. A Pastoral Letter on War and Peace* (Washington, D.C.: United States Catholic Conference, 1983). In this pastoral letter the American bishops expressed unequivocally that they were opposed to the first use of nuclear weapons, for even a restricted use would have catastrophic, unassessable results. The statement on page 47 reads: "We do not perceive any situation in which the deliberate initiation of nuclear warfare, on however restricted a scale, can be morally justified." The letter supports most urgently the efforts for disarmament or the elimination of nuclear weapons.]

January 20, 1983

A Warning Voice

None other than French President Francois Mitterand warned in a speech before the Bundestag in Bonn about Europe being separated from the United States. Who would like to see, Mitterand pointed out, that the European Continent will be uncoupled from America.

January 30, 1983

An Unbearable Thought

The thought that Russian SS-20 intermediate-range missiles with nuclear warheads remain targeted at the most densely populated areas in Western Europe is simply unbearable. At this time, nothing could be more urgent than to dismantle the nuclear weapons arsenal on both sides of the Iron Curtain.

Innsbruck, February 4, 1983

The Repeated Declaration of Loyalty

U.S. Vice President George Bush repeated the American declaration of loyalty at the Berlin Wall. Bush assured that the United States would defend

Europe under any circumstances. Europe and America depend on each other and are inseparable from each other. In view of the national elections in the Federal Republic, in which the defense of Europe is a key campaign issue, this recent assurance of the American preparedness for defense is of significance that cannot be overlooked. The upcoming national elections for the Bundestag are inasmuch of importance as they could set the course for the future transatlantic cooperation.

Florence, [End of February], 1983

The Terror on the Streets

Also at this time of the year, when the slopes of the Apennines are still covered with snow, the stream of tourists in Florence is nonetheless moving from the Piazza della Signoria over the Ponte Vecchio to the Palazzo Pitti. The interest of the visitors stays focused as ever on the familiar sights and art treasures of singular beauty. But in contrast to previous years, passers-by fearfully hold their handbags close to their bodies to protect themselves against raids by juvenile gangs. It happens every day that a tourist is assaulted and being plundered. Crime is festering and terror rules in these narrow alleys and ancient walls.

As an Explanation

[During the semester break in February 1983, my wife and I took a short side-trip from Innsbruck to Florence. When, on a Sunday morning, we strolled unsuspectingly across the Ponte Vecchio in the direction of the Palazzo Pitti, my wife's handbag was snatched from her arm. It contained our passports and travel money. At the police station of the Carabinieri, we were shown a heap of handbags in a corner, which had been found, emptied in the streets and parks of the city. It was vividly demonstrated that we were not the only victims of such assaults.]

Innsbruck, Sunday, March 6, 1983

Election Day

Today, the long-awaited, important general elections to the Bundestag are being held in the Federal Republic of Germany. How will the approximately

43 million voters who got caught in the tug-of-war between East and West decide?

March 7, 1983

The Election Result

The CDU/CSU won the election to the Bundestag with 48.8% of the ballots cast over the SPD with 38.2% and the 6% of the FDP. The CDU/CSU will have 244 seats in the new Bundestag vs. 193 seats of the SPD and the 34 of the FDP.

[Transl: CDU/CSU=Christlich-Demokratische Union/ Christliche-Soziale Union (Christian Democratic Union/Christian Social Union); SPD=Sozialdemokratische Partei Deutschlands (Social Democratic Party of Germany); FDP=Freie Demokratische Partei (Free Democratic Party)]

Helmut Kohl has been confirmed in his office as chancellor just as the existing coalition of CDU/CSU and the FDP has been strengthened by this election.

[Helmut Kohl was born in Ludwigshafen on the Rhine in 1930. He studied history, law and political science, earning a doctorate in 1958. Since 1959 he had been active as a politician in the CDU; he served as prime minister of Rheinland-Pfalz, 1969-76 and as chairman of the CDU, 1973-98. Following the resignation of Helmut Schmidt, Kohl assumed the office of chancellor of the Federal Republic of Germany in October, 1982. Having been reelected several times, he held the office of chancellor until 1998. During his term in office, Chancellor Helmut Kohl brought about the unification of the two German states in 1989-91.]

Innsbruck, May 4, 1983

A Rare Glimpse Inside

For the opening celebrations of the Martin Luther Year in the DDR or East Germany, a Solemn Protestant Service, held today on the Wartburg at Eisenach in Thuringia, was broadcast on television that could be seen in the West. It offered a rare glimpse inside a world which has completely vanished from our consciousness. The first pictures of the Wartburg, this towering, medieval fortress, which we only know from Wagner's *Tannhäuser* and Luther's translation of the Bible, brought back into memory an almost forgotten sense of history. Surprising was the throng of people to this Service. What do their serious, grave looking faces, we may ask, want to tell us?

Innsbruck, May 30, 1983

Firmly Resolved

At the recent G-7 summit meeting in Williamsburg, Virginia, the seven leading industrial nations have proved to be firmly resolved. No doubt was left about NATO's resolution to update its nuclear force in Europe, should the disarmament conference in Geneva not lead to any result.

Innsbruck, July 3, 1983

Franz Kafka (1883-1924)

Today, the 100th anniversary of Franz Kafka's birth is being celebrated. Symposia, recitals of his works, dramatic performances, as, for example, "Ein Bericht für eine Akademie" (A Report to an Academy), as well as announcements of new editions of his works—they all mark the day. After 1945 Kafka has become one of the most significant writers of the 20th century. His works have been widely translated and received, especially in France and the United States. *The Trial*, the English translation of *Der Prozess*, reads nearly as well as the crystal-clear Pragerdeutsch, the German spoken and written in Prague, of the original. Kafka brought to the surface major themes of our century and has given us the key to our self-understanding.

Sunday, September 11, 1983

John Paul II in Austria

Hundreds of thousands of people cheered Pope John Paul II when he arrived at the Austrian Catholic Day in Vienna. It is the first visit by a pope to Austria in 200 years. The visit is of historical significance, as it coincides with Vienna's liberation from the siege by the Turks 300 years ago.*

Talking with young people yesterday evening, the longing for peace and justice, for confidence and hope was strongly expressed. At today's Mass in the Donaupark, the Holy Father, in his homily, expounded movingly the parable of the Prodigal Son. He compared the return of the prodigal son to his father with modern man's need for turning back and returning to God.

*[Vienna was liberated from the siege by the Christian expeditionary army under the command of the Polish King Jan III Sobieski on September 12, 1683.]

Innsbruck, October 23, 1983

The Yearning for Peace

Yesterday, Saturday a genuine and profound yearning for peace drove people in Europe to the streets. Human chains were formed between the embassies of the U.S. and the USSR in Vienna and in Bonn. Peace demonstrations took place in Brussels, Rome, and London. On the Autobahn between Neu-Ulm and Stuttgart, a uniform human chain closed ranks. These demonstrations were caused by the worries about NATO's nuclear armament. The approaching deployment of the Pershing II missiles caused alarm, especially in the Federal Republic of Germany, that Central Europe could become the battleground for a nuclear exchange. While the outbreaks of hatred are directed against America, the East is shamelessly taking advantage of the peace movement for its own propaganda. Nothing could be more welcome to the Communist propaganda than being able to split the public in Western Europe on the question of nuclear armament so that a mood for neutrality would gain ground. Without a doubt, a war of nerves lies imminently ahead.

Sunday, November 20, 1983

The Beginning of NATO's Nuclear Update

Threatening, ominous, as if apocalyptic shivers would run down the spine—such was the reaction to the arrival of the first cruise missiles from America at the Greenham Common Base near London in Berkshire. No doubt, this is the beginning of NATO's nuclear update in Europe. What has just started in England will soon be also carried out in Sicily, in the Federal Republic, and in the Netherlands. Deep anxiety and fear of the future have taken hold of the European public. Rarely has an action, which should serve the purpose of security, caused so much insecurity.

November 20, 1983

Courage Shown

Former German Chancellor Helmut Schmidt showed his courage at the Party Conference of the SPD. Although his own party had clearly rejected the deployment of the Pershing II missiles, he stood by his word to carry out NATO's nuclear armament update. In December 1979 Schmidt had supported NATO's "dual track" resolution. He reminded his party that the nuclear balance in Europe could only be achieved in cooperation with the leading protecting power of the West.

[Transl: The "dual track" approach in NATO's decision of December 1979 meant that, while the disarmament negotiations were ongoing in Geneva, preparations would be made for the deployment of the Pershing II and cruise missiles.]

November 23, 1983

Nuclear Armament Update Accepted

At yesterday's vote in the Bundestag, NATO's nuclear armament update was accepted by the ruling coalition of CDU/CSU and FDP against the votes of the SPD. Chancellor Kohl made a strong effort for its passage. Within the SPD Helmut Schmidt remained isolated. In one of the vital questions of the Federal Republic, a deep chasm of difference of opinion and discord has opened up. Just a few hours after the resolution in the Bundestag, the first Pershing II missiles were flown into Southern Germany.

[End of December], 1983

A Gloomy Year's End

Relations between East and West have reached a low point. All three negotiations in progress have been broken off: After the failure of the talks in Geneva on the INF (Intermediate-Range Nuclear Forces), also START (Strategic Arms Reduction Talks) have been cancelled, and consequently the MBFR (Mutual and Balanced Force Reduction) Conference in Vienna was dissolved.

Innsbruck, December 31, 1983

The Word of the Year

At the Catholic Day in Vienna, Pope John Paul II addressed scientists, artists, and those responsible in government with the exhorting words:

"Nehmt Euch des Menschen an!" (Attend to the human person!)

Innsbruck, [End of January], 1984

Peace Efforts Revived

By the middle of the month, the Conference on Confidence—and Security-Building Measures and Disarmament in Europe convened in Stockholm. The 35 participating countries consisted of:

- 16 NATO countries: USA, Belgium, Canada, Federal Republic of Germany, Denmark, France, Great Britain, Greece, Iceland, Italy, Luxembourg, Netherlands, Norway, Portugal, Spain, Turkey.

- 7 Warsaw Pact countries: USSR, Bulgaria, Czechoslovakia, German Democratic Republic, Hungary, Poland, Romania.

- 12 Nonaligned countries: Austria, Cyprus, Finland, Ireland, Liechtenstein, Malta, Monaco, San Marino, Sweden, Switzerland, Vatican City, Yugoslavia.

[The Conference on Confidence—and Security-Building Measures and Disarmament in Europe was the enlarged follow-up of the Conference on Security and Cooperation in Europe (CSCE). It had convened in Stockholm on January 17, 1984 and remained in perpetual session until its final accords of January 1, 1987.]

[Beginning of February], 1984

East-West Talks in Vienna Resumed

Having decided that the Mutual and Balanced Force Reduction (MBFR) Conference in Vienna will be resumed in March; East-West talks have been set in motion again.

Innsbruck, February 10, 1984

Yuri Andropov (1914-1984)

With due respect, the world community has received the news that Yuri Andropov, the head of state of the USSR, passed away. Despite having been secretive for months, it could not have remained a secret that Andropov was ailing and that he was mortally ill. His demise has, therefore, not come as a surprise. As he had been in office for only 15 months, Andropov remained a transitional figure who was holding on to the status quo. The Kremlin is again facing a leadership crisis. Only in the months ahead, will it become apparent who within the Central Committee of the Communist Party will be strong enough to take over the leadership. One may also hope that the new leadership in the Kremlin will seek a new relationship to the West.

[After the death of Leonid Brezhnev in November 1982, Yuri Andropov was elected general secretary of the Communist Party of the USSR. And from June 1983 to his death on February 9, 1984, he was head of state of the USSR.]

February 11, 1984

In Exile

In a French television interview at his home in Vermont, Alexander Solzhenitzyn said that he had only one more great wish: To finish his epic work on the Russian Revolution (vol. 1, *August 1914*, has already appeared) and to see his homeland again. No doubt, Solzhenitzyn shares the destiny of the émigrés of the 1930s and '40s. He cherishes the United States as a refuge, a place of freedom and security, but he feels to be a stranger and not understood in the new environment. He is worried that as a writer he could lose the liveliness and authenticity of his native tongue. Also Adorno, Thomas Mann, Brecht and many other authors in exile had expressed similar concerns.

February 12, 1984

The Lesson from the Year 1934

Fifty years ago today, on February 12, 1934, civil war broke out in Austria, when the Schutzbund (home front defense alliance) and the Heimwehr (Austrian militia) started to shoot at each other. From that moment on, the First Republic plunged into an abrupt abyss. Endless suffering came down upon the Austrian people. From the events of 1934, a lesson can be learned: The parliamentary democracy has to be taken seriously, the dialogue between parties and political adversaries should never break off and turn into violence.

Innsbruck, [Middle of February], 1984

Impressions on Passing By

There, Karl Rahner was going along the Inn River Promenade, supported by a fellow brother of the Jesuit Order. 80 years of age, physically frail, but his face still showing a keen intellect, he is a venerable figure who inspires reverence.

Innsbruck, February 24, 1984

The Blockade of the Transit Traffic

How vulnerable the European Common Market can be, is being demonstrated these days by the blockade of trucks at the Brenner Pass. A work-to-rule campaign by the Italian customs officers has caused veritable chaos on the European transit roads—at first in France and now in Austria. About 2,000 trucks are standing on the Autobahn from Rosenheim to Kufstein to the Brenner Pass. A similiar situation can be observed on all border crossings to Italy. The blockade of the transit traffic by the delayed customs clearance not only makes the feelings of the truck drivers run high, but it also affects the transport of goods in the entire Common Market area. What a burden the borders as well as the obsolete customs regulations still are!

March 4, 1984

A State Visit Turned Out Well

As first Austrian head of state, President Rudolf Kirchschläger went to the United States for a state visit last week. The reception of the Austrian president was most cordial. Altogether the state visit turned out very well. At the reception in the White House, President Reagan reaffirmed that the United States is aware of its responsibility toward Austria and as signatory power of the Austrian State Treaty would always stand up for Austria's sovereignty. Austria belongs to the union of free democracies of the West. It is aware of its freedom and role as mediator between the power blocs.

March 16, 1984

Negotiations Resumed

Without much ado, the MBFR negotiations have been resumed at the Hofburg in Vienna. This is at least one, if not a decisive, step toward lessening of tensions between East and West. Dissolving the MBFR Conference in Vienna by the end of last year caused more of a stir than its present resumption. It is after all the 359th session of the Conference in Vienna for a balanced reduction of conventional weapons on both sides of the Iron Curtain.

Innsbruck, March 31, 1984

Karl Rahner (1904-1984)

During last night, Karl Rahner, only weeks upon completion of the 80th year of his life, died of a heart failure in Innsbruck. He was one of the most prominent theologians of the 20th century. He became known worldwide as theologian at the Second Vatican Council. The scholarly work of his lifetime comprises nearly 4,000 titles. Rahner was certainly not undisputed. He had tried to bring the Catholic Church closer to the exigencies of the present time. I remember well Rahner's sermons and lectures I had heard as a student in Innsbruck. Karl Rahner was difficult to understand, but he was persistently stimulating.

[The former Universitätsplatz (University Square) in front of the Jesuit Church and the Theologische Fakultät (School of Theology) at the Old University in Innsbruck was renamed Karl-Rahner-Platz.]

Rome, April 17, 1984

[My wife and I participated in the Biennial Conference of the European Association for American Studies (EAAS) in Rome from April 16-19, 1984.]

A Common Theme

In discussions on America, Europeans have found a common theme that unites them across the many national differences.

April 18, 1984

Pilgrims

Among the throng of pilgrims coming this year for Easter to Rome, one can also see many from Poland. At today's papal Wednesday audience, also a number of buses have arrived from Poland. Looking at these pilgrims, one could sense their profound devotion with which they have come to their pope in Rome.

April 19, 1984

The Site of the Crime

Only a hundred meters from the Palazzo Antici-Mattei, where the final meeting of the EAAS Conference took place, one passes by a commemorative plague in the Via Caetani. Here, on May 9, 1978, the body of the slain Italian Prime Minister Aldo Moro was found.

Innsbruck, May 12, 1984

The Vision of a United Europe

On its recent party congress in Stuttgart, the CDU (Christian Democratic Union) conjured up again the vision of a united Europe. According to this vision, the European Community (EC) should be transformed into a federal state. It should be a Europe without borders, while a European passport should make it possible for its citizens to travel without controls. The large European transit routes—highways and railroad systems—that connect North and South, East and West should be planned and financed together. All tariffs and customs duties should be abolished. Like the EC, the "United States of Europe" could at first consist of 8-10 members. What a grandiose vision! But it always eludes realization. For the time being, the loosely connected Europe of fatherlands seems to be much closer to home than a common federal state.

Sunday, June 3, 1984

Searching for Ancestral Roots

Like his predecessors in office, John F. Kennedy and Richard Nixon, President Reagan has come to Ireland in search of his ancestors. To follow the ancestral footsteps and searching for ancestral roots in the Old World is a deep-seated need for Americans of European descent. On today's Sunday, Ronald and Nancy Reagan visited the village of Ballyporeen in County Tipperary, a small hamlet with about 300 inhabitants. When Ronald Reagan looked up the baptismal register in the parish church, he found the baptism of his great-grandfather Michael [O'Regan] recorded on September 3, 1829. Michael [O'Regan] immigrated to Illinois during the great famine in Ireland caused by the potato blight in the middle of the 19th century.

Innsbruck, June 6, 1984

D-Day after 40 Years

In a ceremony on Utah Beach, D-Day in Normandy was remembered, where on June 6, 1944, the great invasion for the liberation of Europe had begun. It was in remembrance of the 20,000 soldiers on both sides who had lost their lives on that day in June. On this occasion, President Reagan gave a statesmanlike speech on a grand scale, calling for collaboration for world peace so that the horrifying weapons, which are now available, will never be used. At the same time, he declared his loyalty for Europe. America feels obligated to defend Europe if need be. The experience of two world wars taught America a lesson: It would be of no use to anyone if America retreated and left Europe on its own.

June 17, 1984

Dull European Elections

On today's Sunday, 197 million eligible voters in Belgium, the Federal Republic of Germany, France, Greece, Italy and Luxembourg were called to the polls to elect delegates to the European Parliament in Strasbourg. Previously, citizens in Denmark, Great Britain, Holland and Ireland had already cast their votes for the European Parliament. These elections were dull; there was no real enthusiasm for a common European cause. Local problems stood more in the foreground. Paradoxically, voters in the various countries used these second direct European elections to vent their dissatisfaction with the ruling parties. The idea of a common Europe played a more subordinate role.

June 26, 1984

In contrast to the disappointing European elections, the heads of government achieved, at their European Community (EC) summit meeting in Fontainbleau, an unexpected breakthrough. First, the troubling question of Great Britain's contribution to the EC was solved. Then, concrete proposals have been made for a European passport, a common television program (Eurovision) as well as for a common history book. The idea of a united Europe has emerged strengthened from this summit meeting.

Innsbruck, July 4, 1984

Almost Forgotten

Had I not lived for years in the United States, "The Fourth of July," the celebration of Independence Day could have almost been forgotten. Little notice is taken of this American national holiday or of the Declaration of Independence abroad.

[As I had been asked by the University of Notre Dame to stay on for another year as director of the foreign study program in Innsbruck, my wife and I used the summer vacation for a short return to the United States. It gave us the opportunity to look after our house in South Bend. Our son visited us there from California, and together we drove across the Midwest to visit with our daughter and son-in-law at Lake of the Ozarks in Missouri, where our son-in-law had begun his law practice.]

August 8, 1984

In 25 Minutes over Paris

On our flight back from Chicago to Zurich, we flew, in the early morning hours, at first over Ireland and then over London. There came an announcement over the loudspeaker on Swissair's Boeing 747: "In 25 minutes we fly over Paris and in 45 minutes [thereafter] we shall land in Zurich." At that moment I became aware of how small the West European air space really is, and how vulnerable Europe has become in the age of ballistic missiles.

August 10, 1984

Drifting Apart

The short stay in the United States left behind the following impressions: 1) Economic progress can be seen everywhere, the high living standard is genuine. The country is full with vibrant life. 2) America has become more self-assured, more concentrated on its own and more patriotic. There is little if any interest in foreign countries. A new wave of isolationism is reaching its peak. 3) Although America and Europe are getting more and more similar, one cannot help noticing that at the same time they are also drifting apart from each other.

[Beginning of September], 1984

The German Dilemma

Like a festering boil, the German dilemma has again erupted. As the Chairman of the German Democratic Republic's Council of State Erich Honecker cancelled the scheduled state visit to the Federal Republic of Germany, it has brought about an intensified debate over the legal status of both German states. In this regard, there is a fundamental contradiction in the German consciousness. Based on the Preamble of the Grundgesetz (Basic Constitutional Law for the Federal Republic of Germany), the Federal Republic can claim to be the only rightful representation for the German people, including East Germany. The German Democratic Republic or East Germany maintains to the contrary to be a sovereign state of equal legal status as the Federal Republic or West Germany. While on vacation in St. Gilgen on the Wolfgangsee near Salzburg, Chancellor Helmut Kohl said in a television interview with confidence that the Berlin Wall will fall during his lifetime and that the reunification will be achieved. On the other hand, the East German Foreign Minister Fischer declared in a terse, cynical way, as two German states do exist, the German question is solved.

[Middle of September], 1984

Maneuvers in the Fall

This year on both sides of the Iron Curtain, maneuvers are being held in the fall. But in contrast to previous years, these are the biggest military field exercises of NATO and the Warsaw Pact that have ever taken place until now. On the overloaded Autobahn from Munich to Stuttgart, these days one passes endless military convoys of armored vehicles of all categories. While NATO concentrates its actions in areas of Southern Germany, the Warsaw Pact countries deploy their troops in Hungary and Czechoslovakia. As long as these maneuvers remain sand-table games, they don't stir up much fear. But a real confrontation could not be grasped by any stretch of the imagination. Hopefully, this will never happen.

Innsbruck, September 26, 1984

For the Sake of Freedom

Almost every day, there are reports how people from the Eastern countries risk their lives fleeing to the West. Just eleven days ago, a Czech family of five from Brno tried to flee over Yugoslavia into Austria. When they attempted to cross the Mur River near Radkersburg in Styria, some among them were swept away by the current. While a 15-year old girl with her 3-year old sister reached the Austrian bank of the River, the mother and the 6-year old daughter drowned. No sign of life has been received from the father. Three Polish refugees, who were locked up in a container, could have easily suffocated before reaching

Austrian territory. Another Czech family also attempted to cross the Mur River. In doing so, the wife had to turn back. For humanitarian reasons, the Yugoslav authorities allowed her to exit. How immense must be the despair of these people who risk their lives in such a way for the sake of freedom.

September 29, 1984

Contrasts

While in the city of Memmingen the medieval city wall is being reconstructed and the old city as a whole pleasantly redeveloped with a pedestrian zone, interceptor jets of the German Federal Armed Forces streak across the sky of the Allgäu. On the one hand, a medieval idyll is being carefully preserved, and on the other hand, the pace of modern technology is interfering. Many times, the latter is set upon a frame, which it threatens to burst. This contrast can be observed all over Europe: Architectural foundations and various lifestyles that have been received from former centuries must cope with the demands of a sturdy and fast advancing technical renewal.

In Southern Germany, particularly in Bavaria, this contrast is especially striking. Here, next to the Autobahn and industrial plants, an idyllic landscape prevails. Part of it are the picture book villages with their onion-shaped church towers, the green pastures with the Alps as a backdrop, the Bavarian royal castles Neuschwanstein and Linderhof, the unique rococo Wieskirche and the baroque monasteries of Ottobeuren and Ettal as well as the Tegernsee and Garmisch-Partenkirchen. These places have become a refuge from the rush of modern life.

Innsbruck, October 31, 1984

The Murder of a Priest

Eleven days after he had been abducted, the body of the Polish priest Jerzy Popieluszko was found yesterday in a reservoir of the Vistula River near Torun. Popieluszko, who was closely connected with the Solidarity movement, was brutally murdered and thrown into the River. That his murderers were "officials" of the Ministry of the Interior, or respectively members of the Secret Police, leaves one just as dumbfounded as the fact that the body of the priest could not be found for days after his assassins had confessed. Who were the instigators and wire pullers of this crime? In what murky depths will the Polish tragedy still have to sink?

Note

[Jerzy Popieluszko was a young priest who led a small parish church in Warsaw. From January 1982 on, he advocated nonviolent resistance against the Communist regime. Over time, his sermons were heard by hundreds of thousands of people. Popieluszko became a national symbol of the resistance. See George Weigel, *Witness to Hope*, p. 460.]

November 5, 1984

On the Day before the Election

Rarely was the reelection of an American president so assured as the one of Ronald Reagan. It is not a question whether Reagan will win, just by how much. There is talk about a landslide victory that could carry 48 of the 50 states. But Reagan is not the preferred candidate of the Europeans. Here, one does not understand, actually people are puzzled, why Reagan is such a favored candidate with the American voters. Yet even his critics and those who are strangers to him have to admit that, over the past four years, the reputation of the United States abroad has increased considerably.

November 8, 1984

The Election Result

As expected, Ronald Reagan won the presidential election over his challenger Walter Mondale by a vast majority. Reagan's reelection was more convincing than even optimists had dared to hope. Reagan won 49 of the 50 states, while only his home state Minnesota remained loyal to Walter Mondale. With 59% of the votes cast, 525 of the 538 electoral college votes go to Reagan. However, in the Senate, Charles H. Percy, Republican Senator from Illinois, did not make his reelection. Percy, therefore, has to relinquish the chairmanship of the Senate Foreign Relations Committee. As a result of the election, the new distribution of seats in Congress is as follows: Senate: 53 (R) vs. 47 (D)—House of Representatives: 253 (D) vs. 182 (R). From among the newly elected governorships—8 go to the Republicans and 5 to the Democrats.

Innsbruck, November 25, 1984

The Famine

It breaks one's heart to watch these days how hundreds of thousands of people in Ethiopia starve to death. Despite all the international relief efforts, help is coming too late for these emaciated people. Altogether nearly 6 million people are threatened by famine. According to this week's edition of *Time* Magazine, more than 40% of a population of 42 million are undernourished; 2.2 million are fleeing from the drought areas, only to end up in overcrowded camps. This human misery stretches all across the Sahel, the Sub-Sahara region, while famine, dictatorships and the ravages of war coincide in aggravating this affliction.

Innsbruck, December 17, 1984

Almost a State Crisis

The construction of a hydroelectric power plant on the Danube near Hainburg in Lower Austria east of Vienna has almost provoked a state crisis. About 5,000 demonstrators occupied the Stopfenreuther Au, a well-known nature preserve and Danube wetland, to prevent workers from clearing the area. To avoid being blamed for giving in to anarchy, the minister of the interior had no choice but to use force so that the clearing could proceed. He ordered the federal police and the local constabulary to dissolve the occupation by the environmentalists. His imploring admonition to use Prudence made the country listen. Most feared is the possibility that members of the ÖGB (Österreichischer Gewerkschaftsbund-Austrian Federation of Trade Unions) would go to Hainburg for a counter-demonstration, which could lead to violent clashes between workers and students.

Wednesday, December 19, in the evening

Exercising measured restraint, the feared counter-demonstration by the ÖGB did not occur. In turn, the government decided to dissolve the occupation of the Stopfenreuther Au. Early this morning, units of the police and the constabulary closed off the area and opened the road for the clearing crew to move in. There were a few scuffles between the security forces and the environmentalists. But the police action set 10,000 demonstrators in motion to march in protest on the Ringstrasse in Vienna. The question of environmental protection has become a critical issue. The preservation of the environment stirs up emotions and divides the public to an extent one could not have thought possible. Preservation of the environment could become an issue changing the political landscape in Austria and in other industrialized countries. A consensus has to be reached between commercial interests and the protection of the environment, or between economy and ecology.

Addendum

[At the beginning of 1985, the Austrian government halted the construction of the hydroelectric power plant in Hainburg indefinitely.]

Innsbruck, January 1, 1985

The New Year's Concert

The New Year's Concert of the Vienna Philharmonic Orchestra under the direction of Lorin Maazel will, for the first time, be broadcast from the Musikvereinssaal (the main concert hall of the Vienna Philharmonic) live to the United States. The broadcast of the Johann Strauss melodies throughout the world is the opening event of the Year of Music 1985 declared by the European Council.

Note

[Since 1985, the New Year's Concert of the Vienna Philharmonic Orchestra has been broadcast each year time-deferred in the evening hours by PBS (Public Broadcasting System). The New Year's celebration from Vienna has ever since been hosted with charm by the experienced commentator Walter Cronkite.]

January 7, 1985

East-West Dialogue Resumed

Today, the armament control talks between the United States and the USSR in Geneva have been resumed. The talks between Secretary of State George Shultz and Foreign Minister Andrei Gromyko give new hope for easing the tensions between East and West. They nourish the hope for a certain revitalization of détente. But on the first day of negotiations, the deep division that separates the two superpowers has surfaced. The expectations for disarmament negotiations have somewhat been dampened.

January 9, 1985

Yesterday's final talks between Shultz and Gromyko in Geneva led inasmuch to a positive result as there has been agreement to continue negotiations on armament control. The relief that the perennial danger of a nuclear war has at least been reduced is being felt everywhere.

January 10, 1985

A Political Thaw

Despite the hardest cold wave in Europe in thirty years with temperatures of 30 degrees below zero Celsius, the negotiations in Geneva brought about a thaw in world politics. Rarely has the reaction of the press of all camps been so positive as to the one in Geneva these days. An agreement has been reached to resume negotiations on comprehensive armament controls, which, under one umbrella, would discuss in the years ahead issues of weapons in space, strategic systems, and intermediate-range missiles. The goal of these negotiations would be to completely abolish nuclear weapons as proposed by President Reagan.

January 20, 1985

The Second Term

With the swearing-in ceremony in a small circle in the White House, the second term in office of Ronald Reagan as President of the United States has begun. After a long time, America has again a two term President. It is a sign of continuity and stabilization of the political climate. During Reagan's first term in office, America's domestic needs were met. Now there is hope that his second term will have a stabilizing influence on peace in the world. The talks in Geneva have raised expectations in this regard.

Note

[The 20th Amendment to the American Constitution of October 15, 1933, provides that the swearing-in of the elected American President should take place on January 20. The oath of office is usually administered in an open-air ceremony on the West Balustrade of the Capitol with the general public gathered on the Mall below. Only in extreme inclement weather, as was the case on January 20, 1985, the solemn ceremony takes place in the White House.]

Innsbruck, February 11, 1985

Yalta after 40 Years

Forty years ago today, the Yalta Agreement was signed on the Crimean Peninsula. U.S. President Franklin Delano Roosevelt, already marked by severe illness, and Prime Minister Winston Churchill conceded to Josef Stalin, perhaps under pressure by the events at the time, that the Soviet Union may have political control in the territories in Europe which she occupied. Falling under Communist rule, the fate of Eastern Europe and large parts of Southeastern and Central Europe was sealed. Yalta created the prerequisite for the partition of the Continent into a Communist Eastern Europe and a free, democratic Western Europe. In the past four decades, this distribution of power into two spheres of influence has not changed but only hardened. Two days after the conclusion of the Yalta Conference, the Red Army captured Budapest, and two months later it stood in front of Vienna and Berlin.

Note

[The Yalta Conference, which took place from February 4-11, 1945, dealt with the last phases of combat of World War II and established the zones of occupation. This summit meeting also laid the foundations for the United Nations and set up the Security Council with its veto power. Although the liberated countries had been assured free, democratic elections, soon the Communists seized power in the territories occupied by the Red Army.]

February 13, 1985

Like a Phoenix from the Ashes

Forty years after its destruction, the Dresden Opera House has indeed risen like a phoenix from the ashes. The Opera House with its long-standing tradition has been rebuilt following the designs of its original architect, Gottfried Semper. The opera *Der Freischütz* by Carl Maria von Weber was chosen for the opening performance. In this House, opera history was made. The Richard Strauss operas *Salome* (1905), *Elektra* (1909), and *Der Rosenkavalier* (1911) had their world premiere in the Semper Opera in Dresden.

Innsbruck, March 1, 1985

The High Flight

The U.S. Dollar is presently on a high flight. The psychological threshold of 3 DM to the Dollar has been passed for a long time. Today one gets for 1 Dollar 3.32 DM, 10.18 French Francs, 2,020 Italian Lira, or 23.20 Austrian Schilling. The exchange rate is fluctuating like a temperature curve. It remains, nevertheless, on highs that have not been seen in fifteen years. The high Dollar exchange rate also has its drawback. It upsets the balance of payments and heats up inflation, while prices for trade can hardly be calculated in advance. The United States is being flooded with imports, drastically increasing the trade deficit. Nonetheless, the trust in the Dollar as reserve currency for world trade and in the political stability of The United States has not been so strong for a long time. The extraordinary high flight of the Dollar cannot be sustained for the long run. Whether the exchange rate of the Dollar will fall as fast as it has risen will be seen in a few months from now.

March 11, 1985

The Succession of Generations in the Kremlin

Today at noon, the news was broadcast that the Head of State of the Soviet Union and Chief of the Communist Party Konstantin Chernenko has died. After only 13 months, the USSR has again to deal with a change in the leadership of the State and the Party. Without wasting time and certainly not without being prepared, today Mikhail Gorbachev was appointed to succeed Chernenko in office. With Gorbachev, age 54, a succession of generations is about to begin in the Kremlin.

March 21, 1985

The Bach Year

Three hundred years ago today, Johann Sebastian Bach was born in Eisenach. The numerous musical performances and commemorative events on this tercentenary celebration vividly call to mind the monumental work of Johann Sebastian Bach.

Bach sounds old and yet also surprisingly modern. His influence on Western musical culture can hardly be fully measured. Especially by his sacred music, Bach has also become in America an integral part of the general culture.

Innsbruck, March 29, 1985

Marc Chagall (1887-1985)

Yesterday, Marc Chagall, at the age of 97, has died in Southern France. With him, one of the most headstrong and significant figures of the visual arts in our century has passed away. Chagall's form and intensive colors are unmistakable. His paintings radiate a poetic touch; his freely floating figures have a magic, mystical effect. Wherever one encounters Chagall—in Zurich, New York or Chicago—, he leaves an unforgettable impression.

Commentary

[Marc Chagall was born on July 7, 1887, in the Russian city of Vitebsk on the Daugava River. He was first trained in St. Petersburg, but came to Paris as early as 1910. Chagall spent most of his life in France. He moved to Southern France in 1939. An invitation from The Museum of Modern Art in New York in 1941 made it possible for him to come with his family to America. When he returned to Southern France in 1947, he chose Vence near Nice as his permanent residence. Based on his profound religious feelings, he used many themes and motifs from the Old Testament in his art. Chagall's works are spread throughout the world. One may come across his stained glass works, paintings, mosaics, and murals in churches, synagogues, on public squares, in theaters and opera houses in Europe as well as in America. In 1966 Chagall created the two large murals, "The Triumph of Music," for the new Metropolitan Opera in Lincoln Center in New York. The famous painting from his early creative period, "The Rabbi of Vitebsk" (1914), can be seen in the Art Institute of Chicago. Marc Chagall died on March 28, 1985, in Vence, Southern France.]

March 29, 1985

The Europe of 12

After a marathon session last night in Brussels, Spain and Portugal have been admitted to the European Community (EC). The EC has now increased to 12 members. Thus, the fragmented Europe is gradually becoming a credible unified whole. Especially the Southern expansion, including the Iberian Peninsula in the Community, may have a positive effect upon Europe. After centuries of isolation, an area with a rich cultural tradition will be revived in the general European consciousness. Spain and Portugal, on their part, will be connected to the modern economy and the advanced technological development of the European Community.

May 6, 1985

A Disappointing Summit Meeting

The economic summit meeting of the G-7 in Bonn has actually been disappointing. There were only promises to curb inflation, boost the economy and create more jobs. The danger of a reciprocal restrictive tariff policy is still looming on the horizon.

In his address to about 10,000 German youth, President Reagan guaranteed the protection of Europe and the Federal Republic and held out the prospect that Europe as a whole will be free and united again. The response to his speech was friendly but nonetheless, reserved. Differences of opinion on how Europe should be united clearly came to the fore.

Innsbruck, May 19, 1985

The Stumbling Block

President Reagan's strongly advocated proposal for the Strategic Defensive Initiative (SDI) has become a stumbling block among European allies. The project, also known as "Star Wars," envisions that incoming missiles can be intercepted and destroyed in space. Should NATO member states follow Reagan's proposal, or should they develop their own defense plan? Chancellor Kohl supports European participation in the SDI project, but President Mitterand has his reservations. This matter seems to become a new source of conflict, which not only may lead to misunderstandings between America and Europe but also to discord within the European Community. The years ahead will show if the SDI project is only played as a trump card in the strategic disarmament talks in Geneva, or whether it will really offer the possibility of reducing the danger of nuclear war.

Note

[In his television address to the American nation on March 23, 1985, President Reagan announced his new plan for defending the United States against a nuclear attack. He envisioned a defense system that would intercept and destroy incoming strategic missiles in space before they reached the territory of America or its allies. He, thereby, not only surprised the international community but also his closest staff members. Secretary of State George Shultz pointed out that the Strategic Defense Initiative was inconsistent with the Anti-Ballistic Missile (ABM) Treaty of 1972, which explicitly prohibits establishing a missile defense system in space. Members of Congress were concerned about the high costs of the project, while the majority of scientists regarded it as unworkable. But the leadership in the Kremlin was extremely irritated by Reagan's SDI project. Reagan's SDI proposal also caused confusion among the European allies. It was feared that it could again derail the disarmament talks in Geneva. Reagan, however, was convinced that his SDI project could be realized, taking into account further development of satellites and progress in computer and laser technology. Despite all objections, he remained steadfast in holding on to the Strategic Defense Initiative. See Edmund Morris, *Dutch: A Memoir of Ronald Reagan,* pp. 474-80.]

Innsbruck, June 9, 1985

Opposite Views in the Atlantic Alliance

At the conference of NATO foreign ministers in Portugal, seemingly insurmountable differences of opinion within the Atlantic Alliance have openly come to light. While the European members of the Alliance urged that the SALT II Agreement, which until now has not been ratified, should be complied with, they could not decide, especially pressured by France, to participate in President Reagan's SDI project. In this regard, America and Europe appear to go divergent ways in the years ahead.

Sunday, June 16, 1985

A Horrifying Odyssey

In the Eastern Mediterranean a hijacking drama is again taking place. On Friday, a TWA plane on its flight from Athens to Rome was hijacked by

Shiite extremists. For three days, the Boeing 727 with 150 passengers on board has been going through a horrifying odyssey, flying erratically back and forth between Algiers and Beirut. While about 100 passengers have been set free, mainly 40 American male passengers are being kept as hostages. The terrorists are using the American hostages as pawns to force the release of Shiite internees from Israeli prisons. One can only guess what these people on board are going through.

June 17, 1985

Allegedly with the help of Shiite supporters, the terrorists have taken the hostages from the plane and are keeping them in a number of hideouts in the slums of Beirut. The situation reminds one of the hostage taking in Tehran six years ago. It is not to be ruled out that this time the Reagan Administration will retaliate and intervene in Beirut. Meanwhile, the hijackers are insisting unyieldingly that 700 Shiite prisoners be released. To find a solution, backstage negotiations by various intermediaries will be needed.

June 30, 1985

The hostage drama has come to a conclusion without bloodshed. This afternoon, a convoy with the hostages under the supervision of the Red Cross was on its way from Beirut to Damascus. In a hectic, secret diplomatic activity during the last few days, the release of the American hostages in Beirut was negotiated. Israel agreed to release 730 Shiite prisoners, and the United States promised not to launch a military retaliation against Lebanon after the hostages are set free. The Syrian President Hafez al-Assad took on the role of intermediary. He agreed to receive the hostages in Damascus and guaranteed their safe flight to Frankfurt. On the late evening news, one could see pictures how the convoy with the hostages arrived in Damascus. In the course of this hijacking gruesome scenes have taken place. Only now one can heave a sigh of relief that this hostage drama is over.

Innsbruck, July 16, 1985

Heinrich Böll (1917-1985)

This afternoon Heinrich Böll, at the age of 67, passed away in his house in the Eifel. The German Nobel Prize Laureate in literature has become known as an engaged post-war author, especially by his moral voice. He narrated with unsparing realism the hardships of soldiers returning from the war, the fate of war widows, and the bungled life of half-orphans that grew up without a father. He also exposed the illusory values of the Wirtschaftswunder, the German economic miracle society. And he stood up courageously for the freedom of speech of authors in East and West. In the 1950s and '60s, Böll became the conscience of the nation. His short stories and novels have been translated into all major languages. His works may have reached a total circulation of about 20 million copies.

Innsbruck, July 30, 1985

Ten Years after the CSCE Final Accords in Helsinki

Today the foreign ministers of the 35 member states of the Conference on Security and Cooperation in Europe (CSCE) have assembled in Helsinki for the 10th anniversary of signing the final accords on August 1, 1975. [See above entry of August 1, 1975.] The results of the Helsinki Agreement have been left far behind expectations. A certain disillusionment has been growing. Nonetheless, the success that has been achieved in the area of easing restrictions for the traffic of people across the borders between East and West cannot be denied.

At the beginning of the festival season in Austria this year, the tourism from Eastern countries has obviously increased. More than in previous years, one can see cars with tourists from Hungary, Czechoslovakia, and recently also from East Germany. It seems as if living in peace side by side could be possible after all.

[After completing my three-year term as director of the University of Notre Dame foreign study program in Innsbruck, my wife and I returned on July 31, 1985, to South Bend in Indiana.]

SECTION 10

August 15, 1985-December 27, 1987

South Bend, August 15, 1985

A Vast, Uninhabited Territory

On the return flight to America, the Swissair plane flew along the 60th degree of latitude, passing the Southern tip of Greenland. It was a clear day. One could see the floating ice and green shimmering icebergs below, while glacier fields were shining in the sun on the horizon. Thereafter, the jet cruised in a wide circle over Labrador, flying over the Southern end of the Hudson Bay, down to the 50th parallel to the Great Lakes. During this three-hour flight no trace of a human settlement was to be seen. Coming from Europe, one is always surprised and peculiarly touched by this vast, uninhabited territory. Between the 50th and 60th degrees of latitude, Europe still lies in the moderate climatic zone and is densely populated from Frankfurt to Oslo. By way of contrast, the same latitudes in North America are exposed to arctic temperatures. A large part of Canada with its tundra, extensive forests and thousands of lakes is situated between the 50th and the 60th parallels, encompassing a virtually uninhabited wide stretch of land. Only when the airplane reached the Great Lakes at Sault Ste. Marie and then slowed down over Michigan for landing in Chicago, farmland, villages and cities came into view as signs of a permanent settlement.

South Bend, September 1, 1985

Coming Back

Coming back to America after a long absence, one has to get used again to the way of life here. At first one is surprised by the bewildering abundance of goods and merchandise offered in malls and supermarkets. This abundance and diversity of consumer goods brought together here in one place from throughout the country and the world is made possible by a highly efficient delivery system. On the other hand, as a customer one is continuously hard-pressed by the relentless advertising on television, radio, in newspapers and by phone calls at home. One has to get readjusted to that over time.

The friendliness of the people is overwhelming. The many "welcome back!" handshakes come from the heart. They make one feel to be at home again right away.

South Bend, September 2, 1985

The Powwow

The Potawatomi Indians in Northern Indiana and Michigan gather once a year in late summer or early fall for a powwow. This is a ceremonial festival open to the public, in which the Potawatomis come together in their tribal costumes wearing feather bonnets, colorful beadwork dresses and mocassins. At the center of the festival is the ceremonial dance, which, with its songs and heavy drum beats, can intensify to a self-forgetting trance. This is not a folkloristic performance for tourism. The powwow arises from the need to preserve the tribal heritage. As a spectator one feels to be put back to a strange, mysterious age long passed.

September 9, 1985

New Perspectives for Reunification

The Consul General of the Federal Republic in Detroit gave a lecture here at the University of Notre Dame, in which he took into consideration new perspectives for the reunification of the two German states. It would be conceivable that the Federal Republic of Germany and the German Democratic Republic remained sovereign states if the interstate relationships improved and the exchange of persons would be made easier. Also, certain democratic basic rights have to be guaranteed in the German Democratic Republic. In any case, reunification remains a German hope. Even under such a modest framework, it could possibly be realized.

October 27, 1985

Mother Teresa at the United Nations

Last week the United Nations celebrated its 40th anniversary. On this occasion, Mother Teresa of Calcutta, who had been awarded the Nobel Peace Prize 1979, was invited to address the General Assembly. Last Friday, the General Assembly deeply moved listened to her address. Mother Teresa asked the members of the Assembly to join her in prayer and called to their attention that we encounter God in every human face. Each human life, above all the unborn life has to be protected. Non-believers in the audience must have been at least convinced of the profound humanity of this extraordinary woman.

South Bend, November 14, 1985

Before the Summit

In his televised address to the nation, President Reagan expounded his hopes, plans and wishes for the forthcoming summit meeting in Geneva. The campaign to win the favor of public opinion, which, for weeks, has been running in high gear in America and in Europe, has reached its peak. Reagan explained in stirring words that the meeting in Geneva could bring a turning point in the relationship with the Soviet Union. A stronger cultural exchange program to reduce mutual distrust is being planned. America is also ready to take into consideration the Russian proposal of reducing nuclear weapons by 50% if it is verifiable. If this means that an agreement could be reached for a nuclear free zone in Central Europe, remains to be seen.

[President Reagan flew with about 300 staff members and advisers on Saturday, November 16, 1985, to Geneva. The following Tuesday, November 19, he met for the first time Mikhail Gorbachev.]

Wednesday, November 20, 1985

The Historic Handshake

The historic handshake between U.S. President Ronald Reagan and the General Secretary of the USSR Mikhail Gorbachev took place yesterday at 10 a.m. in the Villa Fleur d'Eau in Geneva. From that moment on, the attention of the world has been drawn on the Geneva summit meeting.

November 21, 1985

Few Concrete Results

While America was still sound asleep, President Reagan and General Secretary Gorbachev issued today in Geneva a joint statement on the results of the summit meeting at 10 a.m. local time (4 a.m. EST). Except for an agreement on cultural exchange, no treaties were signed, nor have any tangible results been achieved on the reduction of nuclear weapons. Reagan remained steadfast on the SDI, just as the Russian side made no concessions on the reduction of offensive strategic nuclear weapons. But, nonetheless, the Geneva summit meeting was a success. The ice seems to have been broken; both sides have come closer in talking to each other. By a breath, the world has become safer. It could also mean the beginning for improved American-Russian relations, reducing the deep-seated mutual distrust. After his departure from Geneva, Gorbachev made a stopover in Prague to inform the members of the Warsaw Pact, while Reagan went to Brussels to keep the NATO partners abreast of the Geneva meeting.

This summit meeting in Geneva demonstrated once more how closely the world has become interconnected by television as a media. One simply got the impression of having been present in Geneva. Also, for the first time an

American president was visible on Russian television in larger sections, while Gorbachev was shown on American television more from his human side. Only in a few years hence, will it be possible to judge if this summit meeting really was a turning point in world politics.

November 21, 10 p.m. EST

All in One Day

An hour ago, President Reagan was enthusiastically welcomed by a joint session of Congress. After a 20-hour day—at first finishing the summit in Geneva, then meeting with the NATO allies in Brussels, flying back across the Atlantic, and immediately after landing at Andrews Air Force Base being whisked by helicopter to the Capitol—Reagan informed Congress about his talks with Gorbachev. It was a splendid speech that commanded respect from a 74-year-old after such a tour de force. As Reagan indicated, there will be further discussions on reducing the nuclear arsenals. Despite fundamental differences of opinion, both sides have decidedly come closer together. Gorbachev will come to Washington next June, and Reagan will visit Moscow the year thereafter.

South Bend, December 1, 1985

Construction Work in Space

While America enjoyed a peaceful Thanksgiving, one could see on the television screen how the crew of the Shuttle Atlantis assembled a tower in space, which should serve as a model for a planned space station. What so far have just been fantasies of science fiction is becoming tangible reality.

Addendum

[NASA's plans for building a space station were overshadowed by the Shuttle Challenger disaster end of January 1986. After long-lasting experiments with the Salyut program, the Soviet Union succeeded on February 19, 1986 putting the space station MIR into orbit. In the following years, NASA participated in the MIR project. At the same time, America and Russia collaborated in building the International Space Station (ISS). Besides America and Russia,

14 additional nations are cooperating in this project. The ISS was put in operation at the beginning of November 2000.]

Sunday, December 15, 1985

Before the Wall

Secretary of State George P. Shultz, who is presently on a visit to West Berlin, stood yesterday in pouring rain before the Wall. He declared: "The division of this city and the division of Germany are unnatural and inhuman." From West Berlin, Shultz moved on to visit, for the first time as Secretary of State, the East Bloc countries Romania and Hungary.

December 15, in the evening

Thanks for the Memory

At the annual NBC Christmas Show, Bob Hope sang again with unvarying vigor his theme song: "Thanks for the Memory." He has become a national icon. Some show arrangements are so strongly established in America that they seem to go on forever.

[Bob Hope was born 1903 in England, but came with his parents to America as a child. He made a name for himself early on as a comedian in Vaudeville, entertainment programs on radio, and as a film actor. Above all, he has become a national icon when, from 1940 on, he brought, even under danger to his life, the best entertainment to the American forces in battle zones around the world. Bob Hope is known as the entertainment artist who has received the most honorary degrees, distinctions, and awards in the world.]

December 26, 1985

The Horror of Terrorism

The Peace of Christmas was brutally disturbed by terror attacks at the airports of Rome and Schwechat in Vienna. The victims were innocent passengers who, just at the moment of the explosions, were in the hallway before departure. In the past year, the horror of terrorism has been much in evidence.

South Bend, January 1, 1986

Unexpected Good Wishes for the New Year

What had been unimaginable just a year ago, happened today: President Ronald Reagan and General Secretary Mikhail Gorbachev exchanged messages for the New Year, which were broadcast simultaneously on American and Russian television. It was an act of reconciliation and rapprochement between the two superpowers.

January 20, 1986

Martin Luther King, Jr. Day

The birthday of Martin Luther King, Jr., is being more and more observed as a national holiday. The bust of Martin Luther King was unveiled today in the Rotunda of the Capitol. Much progress has been made in overcoming race discrimination. America as a whole has become more humane for it.

[Martin Luther King, Jr. Day is observed as a national holiday on January 20, or on a Monday closest to his birthday.]

South Bend, January 22, 1986

Reason to Be Astonished

After eight years traveling through space, the spacecraft Voyager 2 is now flying by the planet Uranus and is sending perplexing pictures back to earth. The precision by which this NASA project is being carried out gives reason to be astonished. Already new moons have been discovered, which, together with the rings, orbit the faintly lit planet.

January 25, 1986

As the Jet Propulsion Laboratory in Pasadena, California, announced, especially clear images of Oberon, the outmost and second largest moon of Uranus, are being received from the spacecraft. Our knowledge of this planet at the fringe of the solar system is increasing by leaps and bounds. Voyager 2 has traversed a distance of 1.8 billion miles (2.9 billion kilometers), which equals a distance of two hours at the speed of light. From Uranus, the spacecraft will travel on to the planet Neptune, which Voyager 2 should reach in 1989.

[Voyager 2 was launched from Cape Canaveral in Florida on August 20, 1977. The spacecraft sent back to earth a large amount of new information about Uranus. In addition to the previously known 5 large moons, 10 smaller moons were discovered so that the number of known moons of Uranus has increased to 15. The newly discovered moons were named after figures from Shakespeare's plays.]

Tuesday, January 28, 1986

The Disaster

What had been feared for some time, happened today in the most unexpected and dreadful way. At the liftoff of the Space Shuttle Challenger on Cape Canaveral, a powerful explosion occurred before the eyes of the spectators and the television cameras. Within seconds, the carrying rocket and the space shuttle were engulfed in flames. All seven astronauts on board the Challenger lost their lives. This disaster shocked America. President Reagan postponed his State of the Union Address by one week.

January 30, 1986

The American nation has been overcome with deep feelings of sorrow over the tragic death of the seven astronauts. And a stream of expressions of sympathy has been coming in from all parts of the world. This has been until now the worst disaster of the manned space program. It not only saddened America deeply, but touched the entire world.

South Bend, February 16, 1986

The Election Fraud in the Philippines

Since the presidential election in the Philippines on February 7, the international community has followed the events in the Philippines with astonishment, disbelief, and finally indignation. Senator Richard Lugar who chaired the American election observer delegation said repeatedly that the election was fraudulent. The Catholic Bishops Conference of the Philippines in Manila declared outright that the election was a fraud and called on the Filipinos to exercise passive resistance. Nonetheless, last night President Ferdinand Marcos was declared the winner and confirmed in office for six more years by the National Assembly in Manila.

February 23, 1986

At the Brink of Civil War

The situation in the Philippines has come to such a pass in the last 48 hours that the country could any moment plunge into the abyss of a civil war. Since the Chief of Police, Fidel Ramos, has, together with the revolting faction in the army, established a camp in the Defense Ministry against the presidential palace, the military, police, and the general public has been divided. In stirring scenes, unarmed civilians threw themselves in front of advancing tanks in order to protect the rebels. At first, rumors were spreading that Marcos had left the country. But then, there were reports that Marcos was determined to crush the resistance and that he had already put artillery in position.

While the U.S. government had at first assumed an attitude of nonintervention, President Reagan and the Senate have now given Marcos to understand that they no longer consider the Marcos regime legitimate and therefore urged Marcos to relinquish power so that a peaceful transfer of the presidency to Corazon Aquino can take place. Above all, it was Senator Lugar who said unmistakably that in his view Marcos had no basis anymore to support his government. Many Filipinos abroad are now facing a difficult question of conscience. Thus, the Consul General of the Philippines in Lost Angeles resigned, saying: "I would rather be a traitor to one man than a traitor to my country."

February 25, 1986

Two Presidents

For a moment, the Philippines were confronted with the peculiar situation of having two presidents in office. Ferdinand Marcos as well as Corazon Aquino were sworn in as presidents. Finally, Marcos, giving in to the pressure of the unfolding events, resigned. Thereby, a larger bloodshed was prevented. While

Marcos fled with his family and a few of his supporters to the Clark Air Force Base in Manila, the masses stormed the presidential palace.

A number of remarkable events have happened in this transition of power in the Philippines. It was a revolution, which literally took place in front of the television cameras. It was a genuine popular uprising to achieve freedom and justice. The pictures of people in the streets, placing themselves in front of the armed government troops and forcing them to withdraw, remain unforgettable.

Addendum

[Corazon Aquino was the widow of the opposition leader Benigno Aquino who was murdered in 1983. She succeeded in bringing together the divided opposition against the dictatorial Marcos regime. She won the presidential election of February 1986, although Marcos had tried everything to systematically thwart the election. Corazon Aquino held the office of the presidency from 1986 to 1992. In February 1987, the referendum for a democratic constitution for the Philippines was accepted.]

February 28, 1986

Olof Palme (1927-1986)

The news that the Swedish Prime Minister Olof Palme was assassinated in broad daylight in the streets of Stockholm came tonight like a bolt from the blue. With him one of the most distinguished personalities leaves the political stage in Europe. The news struck the world with consternation just as Sweden itself. Palme was 59 years old.

South Bend, March 20, 1986

Defeated

An important debate was taking place today in the House of Representatives on President Reagan's request for 100 million dollars military aid to the Contras in Nicaragua. On the one hand, the Communist threat in Central America was evoked, and on the other, warnings were expressed about the possibility that the United States could be dragged deeper and deeper into the civil war between the Contras and the Sandinistas, which could develop into a second Vietnam close to their own front door. The motion was defeated by a vote of 222 nays against 210 yeas. The Speaker of the House, Tip O'Neill, gave an impressive speech, calling on the representatives: "Vote your conscience."

Addendum

[Thomas P. ("Tip") O'Neill, Jr., was born in Cambridge, Massachusetts, in 1912. He was third generation of Irish descent. After graduating from Boston College, he was at first active in local politics. He served for many years as representative in the State House of Massachusetts. When John F. Kennedy, before his election to the U.S. Senate, gave up his seat in the U.S. House of Representatives in 1952, O'Neill stepped into the breach. He easily won the election as Congressman for the 11th district of Massachusetts. In his home district in Cambridge with an electorate that consisted primarily of Irish and Italian immigrants O'Neill could not be beaten. He was reelected every two years time and again until 1987. For his adroit political maneuverability, he got the nickname "Tip," which soon replaced his first name. As a Democrat he was a convinced adherent to the New Deal, but remained open-minded also to different opinions. He regarded politics as the art of what is possible. Tip O'Neill advanced to majority leader of the Democratic Party in the House of Representatives and in 1977 became Speaker of the House. He held that position for 10 years. He was a tall grown man, an imposing figure, who finally became the embodiment of "Mr. Speaker" per se. The speech of March 20, 1986 was his last great appearance in the House. Tip O'Neill retired in 1987. He died on January 5, 1994 in Boston.]

South Bend, March 24, 1986

The Fire Exchange

About 5 p.m. EST the news broke that in the afternoon and early evening hours U.S. naval forces exchanged fire with the Libyan military in the Gulf of Sidra. For months the United States has made it clear that it does not recognize the off-limit "death zone" declared by Muammar Qaddafi because the zone is in international waters. When the American 6th Fleet, carrying out maneuvers, crossed the line of the barred area in the Gulf of Sidra, it was promptly attacked by the Libyans with Soviet made missiles. Thereupon, the U.S. Navy destroyed the missile launching stations on shore and sank a

Libyan fast patrol boat. The world is now waiting in suspense and worried about what the consequences of this incident will be.

Chicago, March 25, 1986

Hardly Taken Notice

At today's excursion to Chicago, I could not see, except for the headlines in the newspapers, any agitation over the events in the Gulf of Sidra. The American public has hardly taken notice of it.

South Bend, [Good Friday], March 29, 1986

Haydn's "Mass in time of war"

Joseph Haydn's "Mass in time of war" was recorded by the Bavarian Radio Orchestra under the direction of Leonard Bernstein in Ottobeuren. On today's Good Friday, this recording was broadcast on American television. The yearning for peace was strongly felt in this performance. Also, America's deep-rooted bonds with the European cultural heritage could not have been overlooked.

[After his return to Vienna from his two year sojourn in England, Joseph Haydn composed in 1796 his Mass no.7 in C major, "Missa in tempore belli," or in the English translation, "Mass in time of war." It is popularly known as "Paukenmesse" (Kettledrum Mass).]

[Transl: The Benedictine Abbey Ottobeuren in Bavaria goes back to the 8th century. After its restoration in the early 18th century, Ottobeuren became known for its monumental expression of baroque architecture.]

South Bend, April 12, 1986

A War of Nerves

After the bomb explosion of April 5 in a discotheque in West Berlin, in which Libya obviously had a hand, rumors won't go away that the United States will carry out a retaliatory strike. A war of nerves has broken out. Is now the Western Mediterranean also becoming a war zone? What would be the consequences of such an action for Europe?

April 13, 1986

A Gesture of Reconciliation

As the first Pope to do so, John Paul II visited today the Synagogue of Rome, which is situated only a mile distant from the Vatican. Thereby, a significant gesture of reconciliation between the Catholic Church and Judaism has been set, which should diminish centuries-old mutual distrust and prejudices. At this historic moment, Jews and Christians stood side by side united as brothers and sisters of a common faith tradition.

South Bend, April 14, 1986

The Retaliation

About 8 p.m. this evening, the news media reported that an hour earlier, or about 2 a.m. local time, U.S. combat planes, which had started from bases in England, struck targets in Libya.

An hour later, i.e. 9 p.m. EST, President Reagan, in a televised address, spoke to the American people. In a somber tone, he explained why he had decided to carry out a retaliatory strike against Libya. There is irrevocable proof that the Libyan regime perpetrated the bomb explosion in the discotheque in West Berlin. One American was killed and more than 50 injured by this terror attack. Reagan emphasized that the United States acted in self-defense.

In the following press conference in the White House, Secretary of State Shultz and Secretary of Defense Weinberger further clarified the situation. They underscored the determination of the United States to respond in the future if necessary to acts of terror with military force.

April 15, 1986

The Reaction

While the American public overwhelmingly approves of President Reagan's action against Libya, although with feelings of unease, the reaction abroad is a single uproar. Unfortunately, a deep rift of misunderstanding between the United States and its European allies is again being opened by the Libyan conflict. But the European concern is understandable.

April 19, 1986

Tourism Suffers a Loss

The recent wave of terrorism in Europe, which has primarily been aimed at Americans, has understandably caused fear and insecurity among American tourists. Roughly 50% of booked flights to Europe have been cancelled. According to *Time* Magazine of April 20, which is now on the newsstands, 6.4 million Americans traveled to Europe in the peak year of 1985, spending 7 billion dollars. A decrease of 25% is being prognosticated for the current year.

April 30, 1986

The Nuclear Catastrophe

It has taken a few days, until the world community has become fully aware of the scope of the nuclear catastrophe near Kiev. About 60 miles north of Kiev at Chernobyl, from Saturday to Sunday, a reactor of a nuclear power plant burned through. It caused the feared meltdown of the uranium and the graphite block, whereby large quantities of radioactivity were released into the atmosphere. The accident was only made known, after a sudden increase of radioactivity in the atmosphere in Sweden had been noticed. The wind had at first carried a radioactive cloud over Poland to Sweden. In the meanwhile, the fire in the reactor continues burning uncontrolled at about 3,000 degrees F. The authorities are rather helpless without knowing how to get at the nuclear fire.

Officially, only two casualties were admitted, but one may guess that the number may go into the hundreds. There were supposedly hurried evacuations in the Kiev area. Today, by the changing direction of the wind, a radioactive cloud was carried over Hungary to Austria, Southern Germany and Switzerland. Panic has broken out in Europe. Families are being instructed not to let their children go on the streets. There are warnings not to consume milk or fresh produce. It is still hard to grasp that an entire continent can be affected by one accident in a nuclear power plant.

[The accident in the nuclear power plant at Chernobyl happened on April 26, 1986. While carrying out an experiment at the 4th reactor block, the nuclear fuel rods, due to insufficient safety measures, burned out of control so that the reactor exploded, releasing large quantities of radioactivity into the atmosphere. It took ten days to get the fire under control.]

South Bend, May 1, 1986

Shrouded in Secrecy

The countries in the West react disturbed and with indignation to the way the Soviet Union is keeping the lid on the nuclear accident at Chernobyl. No accurate measurements or data on the present state of the fire are made available. Nor is it possible to find out whether the nuclear fire has been brought under control, or whether radioactive rays are still penetrating the atmosphere. The West depends on the measurements in Sweden where radioactivity has increased tenfold to draw conclusions on how intensive the radioactive emissions in Chernobyl really are. The radioactive cloud has now also spread over Poland and Russia to Siberia. Here in the United States, there is apprehension that the radioactivity could in reduced form drift over Alaska as far as Washington state and Nevada.

May 24, 1986

The Repercussions

Only from letters from relatives and acquaintances as well as from newspaper clips was it possible to learn how much the repercussions of Chernobyl affected the everyday life of people in Austria and the Federal Republic. Above all, it was the radioactive contamination of the soil that led to protective measures. People were advised against eating dairy products of all kinds. Especially affected are high-alpine and glacier regions in the Eastern Alps, which otherwise are preferred recreational areas. Eating fresh-collected mushrooms is out of the question. Also, the stock of game is considered contaminated. What should agriculture do, which suffers most from the repercussions? Ways of behavior have developed of which nobody up to now has thought of. Should one mow the lawn? or, fill up the swimming pool with water? In any case, people were cautioned against letting children play outdoors in sandpits.

Addendum

[The repercussions of the accident in the nuclear power plant at Chernobyl of April 1986 were thoroughly examined in the years that followed. The International Atomic Energy Agency (IAEA) in Vienna submitted a 4-part report on the matter in 1991. As it was established later on, 31 persons were instantly killed by the explosion. Nearly 600,000 soldiers who were on duty for the clean-up operation remained exposed to higher levels of radiation. By 1990, a million people still lived in a contaminated environment, which on the long term could lead to cancerous diseases. According to estimates by the Ukrainian government, about 8,000 casualties can be attributed to the catastrophe of Chernobyl. The destroyed reactor was temporarily covered with a thick casing of concrete. However, as the power supply of the Ukraine depended on Chernobyl, the two reactors that were still running remained in operation. Urged by the international community, especially by the United States, the government of the Ukraine agreed in 1994 to close the plant. The nuclear power plant at Chernobyl was shut down for good on December 15, 2000.]

South Bend, June 18, 1986

Change on the U.S. Supreme Court

As Chief Justice Warren E. Burger, at the age of 78, is retiring, the highest judicial office of the nation has to be filled anew. President Reagan has nominated a member of the Supreme Court, Justice William H. Rehnquist, to succeed Burger as Chief Justice. To fill the vacancy on the Supreme Court created by the departure of Warren Burger, President Reagan nominated Antonin Scalia from Chicago. Both nominees are expected to be confirmed by the Senate. Thus, through the Supreme Court, Reagan's hand may still be felt in the 21st century.

[For the confirmation hearings of William H. Rehnquist before the Senate Judiciary Committee, see entry of August 10, 1986, below.]

South Bend, June 18, 1986

A New Idea for a Railroad Station

In Indianapolis as well as in St. Louis, the Union Station, the large central railroad station of the city, has been redesigned as an amusement park and bazaar in order to save the building from the wrecking ball. Passenger traffic was suspended long ago. The visitor gets the impression as if railroads were of a time long past. In museums of science and industry railroad cars are shown to children as special attractions. In this regard, there is a big difference to Europe where railroad stations still serve their intended purpose.

[Thursday], July 4, 1986

Liberty Weekend

The Statue of Liberty celebrates its 100th birthday. It has been renovated and overhauled from the bottom up. On the occasion of the centennial, this Fourth of July Weekend has been declared the "Liberty Weekend." The festivities for it were prepared long before. President Reagan and French President Mitterand opened the great festivities last night. In a show, which most likely can only be put on in America, the events are now taking place. It started with last night's big fireworks in the Harbor of New York. Today, the large sailing vessels of 18 nations passed the Statue of Liberty and moved up the Hudson River, a spectacle reminiscent of the parade of sailing vessels ten years ago during the Bicentennial celebrations of 1976. President and First Lady Nancy Reagan are at the center of this big public festival, which immediately evoked a new wave of patriotism.

[The Statue of Liberty was a present of France to the United States. In 1876, during the Centennial of the Declaration of Independence, France proposed to give America a monument in memory of the French-American cooperation during the War of Independence. F.A. Bartholdi was commissioned to create an appropriate monument. Bartholdi designed a gigantic statue, which should be cast in copper. It was an allegorical female figure that symbolizes liberty. The finished work was on display in Paris on the Fourth of July of 1884. Thereafter, the various parts were disassembled and shipped across the Atlantic. The 152 feet high Statue of Liberty was set up on Bedloe's Island, a small island at the entrance to New York Harbor. It was formally unveiled and dedicated in October of 1886. In 1924 the Statue of Liberty was declared a national monument, and in 1956 Bedloe's Island was renamed Liberty Island. In 1965 the National Park Service combined Liberty Island and Ellis Island, the small island in front of Manhattan, to the Statue of Liberty National Monument.]

In the decades after its dedication, the Statue of Liberty became for millions of immigrants the symbol of freedom, just as it has become for the world the symbol of America. Next to the renovation of the Statue of Liberty and Liberty Island, special attention has been given to the restoration of Ellis Island, the most important immigration station in American history. From its opening in 1892 to its closing in 1954, about 17 million immigrants, mostly from Central, Southern and Eastern Europe, were processed. Nearly half of the American population can trace their origin to Ellis Island.

[The newly renovated main building of the Immigration Station on Ellis Island was opened in 1990 to the public as Ellis Island Immigration Museum. There, everybody can look up the Immigration Register and search for their passage ancestry.]

Saturday, July 6, 1986

The Concert

Tonight, at the conclusion of the Liberty Weekend, the long-awaited great open-air concert was given in the Central Park of New York City. The New York Philharmonic under the direction of Zubin Mehta played a favorite classical repertoire for the nearly 600,000 people who had come to hear them. Television broadcast impressive pictures of this event. The music of Haydn, Verdi, and Beethoven resounded against the backdrop of the lit skyline of New York and the shining Statue of Liberty. The "Ode to Joy" from Beethoven's Ninth Symphony had, in front of all these people of every kind of origins and in their festive mood, a special effect. Rarely have the words, "seid umschlungen, Millionen" (multitudes, be embraced), sounded as genuine as on this evening.

South Bend, August 10, 1986

The Highest Judicial Office

Justice William H. Rehnquist has been nominated by President Reagan to become Chief Justice of the U.S. Supreme Court, the highest judicial office of the nation. His brisk confirmation hearings before the Senate Judiciary Committee demonstrate once again how deeply 200 years of constitutional history are embodied in the American way of thinking. The entire constitutional history is being reviewed. The nominee is being exhaustively questioned where he stands on important provisions of the Constitution. Prime examples are among others the "First Amendment" to the U.S. Constitution of 1791, which guarantees the freedom of speech, and the "Fifth Amendment" for the due process of law. Furthermore, significant cases, which were decided by the Supreme Court in the past, are also taken into consideration, as for instance, Marbury v. Madison (1803), the decision by Chief Justice John Marshall that federal law stands above state laws; and in recent history Brown v. Board of Education (1954), whereby racial discrimination was abolished in schools. As different the expressed opinions may be, there is a general consensus: The U.S. Supreme Court is the sacrosanct last authority to decide what is constitutional or what is unconstitutional.

Addendum

[During the hearings, Rehnquist was sharply criticized by liberals for being too conservative. However, his nomination was confirmed by the Senate. On September 26, 1986 he was sworn in as Chief Justice of the U.S. Supreme Court. At the same time, Antonin Scalia was sworn in as Associate Justice of the U.S. Supreme Court.

William H. Rehnquist was born in Milwaukee, Wisconsin, 1924. He studied law at Harvard University and at Stanford University. From 1953-69 he practiced law in Phoenix, Arizona; 1969-71 he was Assistant Attorney General in the U.S. Department of Justice; 1971-86 he was Associate Justice and since 1986—Chief Justice of the U.S. Supreme Court. Rehnquist wrote several books on the Supreme Court.

Antonin Scalia was born in Trenton, New Jersey, 1936. He studied law at the University of Georgetown and at Harvard. From 1960-82 he at first practiced law and then followed an academic career. As professor of law, he taught at the University of Virginia and later at the University of Chicago. In 1982 Scalia was appointed Judge of the U.S. Court of Appeals for the District of Columbia; and in 1986 he became Associate Justice of the U.S. Supreme Court. Arguably the most difficult and historically far reaching decision, which the Rehnquist Court had to make, was on the Presidential Election 2000. On December 14, 2000, the Supreme Court decided 5:4 that the manual recount of the votes cast in Florida was unconstitutional and had to stop. As a result, the 25 electoral votes of Florida went to George W. Bush, who thereby won the election.]

[Transl: William H. Rehnquist served as Chief Justice of the U.S. Supreme Court until his death on September 3, 2005.]

South Bend, August 13, 1986

A Sad Anniversary

25 years ago, on August 13, 1961, the Berlin Wall was put up. It is a sad silver anniversary. In the meantime, little has changed at the Wall and in the status of Berlin. What will the future hold? How long will the Wall remain standing?

September 22, 1986

Progress in East West Talks

The surprising news came from Stockholm that at the Conference on Confidence—and Security-Building Measures and Disarmament in Europe, with all 35 member states participating, an agreement has been reached on troop inspections between NATO and the Warsaw Pact. This should protect against surprise attacks from either side.

The Conference of Confidence—and Security-Building Measures and Disarmament in Europe is little known in America. Here, interest is more focused on talks about global disarmament between East and West, for which positive signs of an understanding do show up. Obviously, diplomatic efforts—both on the regional and global levels—are coordinated with each other.

South Bend, Sunday, October 12, 1986

The Cold Wind of Reykjavik

The summit meeting over the weekend between U.S. President Ronald Reagan and General Secretary of the USSR Mikhail Gorbachev, which had started with great expectations, finished in disappointment. As the two partners presented themselves in front of the Loefdi House, the tension and coolness in their demeanor could be seen. And when Secretary of State George Shultz stepped petrified before the cameras, it was clear that this summit has failed. Although an agreement on reducing strategic intercontinental as well as intermediate-range missiles in Europe was within reach, the negotiations broke down because of the Soviet insistence that the United States should give up its Strategic Defense Initiative (SDI). But on that point, as he had said time and again, Reagan would not budge. After the negotiations in Reykjavik had failed, all hopes were shattered for a conference in Washington in the months ahead, which should have concluded treaties for the reduction of the nuclear arsenal.

October 14, 1986

The cold shower of Reykjavik can still be felt throughout the world, while both sides are trying to explain why the summit went wrong. The distrust that separates East and West has flared up again. In retrospect, one cannot help thinking that an historic opportunity was lost, which could have freed the world of the dreadful fear of a nuclear war. Both sides had proposed to reduce the nuclear arsenal by half, and possibly to eliminate it completely within ten years time.

Addendum

[The summit meeting in Reykjavik took place on October 11 and 12, 1986. They were bleak October days in Iceland, rain mixed with snow. Reagan and Gorbachev met at the Loefdi House, a small villa outside of Reykjavik. Gorbachev had come to the meeting well prepared. He put a comprehensive disarmament proposition on the table. The strategic nuclear weapons of all categories should be reduced by 50%, and the intermediate-range missiles deployed in Europe be eliminated altogether. Furthermore, a test-ban of nuclear weapons should be put into effect. Both sides should adhere to the ABM (Anti-Ballistic Missile) Treaty of 1972.

The American side was taken by surprise and had to respond. It was the most comprehensive disarmament proposal ever presented by the Soviet Union. Both delegations worked through the night of October 11 in order to clarify the details. U.S. Secretary of State George Shultz and Soviet Foreign Minister Eduard Shevardnadze were facing each other on the foreign minister level. During the day of October 12, a consensus was reached to the extent that all nuclear weapons should be eliminated by 1996. Yet Gorbachev insisted on his demand that he would approve of the accord only if the United States limited its SDI-Program to research in laboratories and would not carry out any tests in space. That would have meant to give up the SDI-Program. Reagan, with the support of George Shultz, declined and regarded the summit meeting as ended. It remains a mystery why the negotiations in Reykjavik had failed on a matter like the SDI, whose effectiveness was very often in doubt. Each side persisted obstinately on its position. Reagan left Reykjavik in anger. Gorbachev, on the other hand, appeared to be more optimistic. He considered the opening of discussions on disarmament between the two superpowers to be the beginning of bringing the Cold War to an end. In *Dutch: A Memoir of Ronald Reagan* (pp. 592-602), Edmund Morris describes thoroughly the tense mood that prevailed at the Reykjavik meeting. In his book, *Turmoil and Triumph: My Years as Secretary of State* (New York: Charles Scribner's Sons, 1993, chap. 38 "What Really Happened at Reykjavik," pp. 751-80), George P. Shultz explains in detail the course of events of the summit meeting, mentioning the irritated argument between Reagan and Gorbachev, which led to breaking-off the negotiations.]

South Bend, October 25, 1986

A Bishop from Austria Visits South Bend

Bishop Stefan Laszlo from Eisenstadt, who, together with a delegation of the provincial government of Burgenland, is on a goodwill tour through Mexico and the United States, has come on a visit to South Bend. The Burgenland Province of Austria lies southeast of Vienna at the border with Hungary. Eisenstadt is the capital of Burgenland. Today, Bishop Laszlo celebrated an evening Mass in Our Lady of Hungary Church, the Hungarian church on the westside of town, where many people of Slavic and Hungarian origin live. Laszlo said Mass in Croatian, Hungarian, and German. It seemed as if the nations of the former Austro-Hungarian Monarchy have gathered in prayer under the protection of Our Lady. This Bishop from the Burgenland radiates a certain charisma—deeply human, religious, but at the same time pragmatic with a down to earth attitude. An old bond of friendship exists between the local Hungarian and Burgenlander community and Bishop Laszlo, who comes to visit here every other year.

November 4, 1986

The Democrats on the Upswing again

At this midterm election, the Democrats have been on the upswing again. They regained the majority in the Senate. The Republican majority in the

Senate of 53:47 has been reversed in favor of the Democrats to 55:45. Thereby, the important chairmanships of the Senate committees are returned into the hands of the Democrats. In the House, the Democrats could increase their majority. This election proved that the "coattail effect" of Ronald Reagan has lost its effectiveness. With only 37.5%, it had the weakest voter turnout since 1942.

[Over the Christmas holiday my wife and I visited our son Franz, our future daughter-in-law Susan and her parents in Sunnyvale, California.]

Sunnyvale, December 24, 1986

Christmas in Silicon Valley

"Jingle Bells," "We wish you a Merry Christmas," "Feliz Navidad," "0 Tannenbaum," "Stille Nacht"—this is how it sounds in several languages and variations for weeks over the loudspeaker systems of the large shopping malls, providing Yuletide background music. Thousands of people in a colorful mixture of East and West—English, German, Scandinavian, Italian, Spanish-Mexican next to Chinese, Vietnamese, Japanese, Korean just to name the larger ethnic groups, which are streaming through these shopping centers. The abundance of consumer goods offered here is dazzling. The sales personnel, already visibly exhausted, are calling attention to last-minute bargains. The cashiers routinely type the serial number or scan each purchased item with the barcode scanner of the UPC (United Product Code). This enables the big retail companies throughout the United States and Canada to keep current records of even the smallest piece of merchandise of their stockholding. It has radically changed stockkeeping according to market demand.

These and similar revolutionary innovations in the market place have become possible during the last two decades by the ingenuity of Silicon Valley. The original Santa Clara Valley has become known worldwide by its nickname "Silicon Valley." The name Silicon Valley originated because since 1957 the silicon chips have been developed here, which are, as is generally known, the building blocks of the computer industry. But what really is it, the frequently mentioned and also misunderstood Silicon Valley? In short, it is the 30 mile long stretch of land at the southern end of the San Francisco Bay, which extends from Palo Alto over Mountain View, Sunnyvale, and Santa Clara to San Jose. Here, in a Mediterranean-like landscape, about 500 of the best known electronic companies have established their headquarters. It has become the world center of computer technology and data-processing. From here, the new data-processing and telecommunication age was initiated, whose development is just in its beginning stage. There is a continuous flow of traffic along the El Camino Real. One drives along Palm tree lined thoroughfares, roses are blooming in the gardens, and the ripe fruits hang on the lemon and orange trees. The air is spring-like and mild. The climate, protected at the eastern slope of the Santa Cruz Mountains against the Pacific, remains evenly moderate throughout the year.

On the surface, life in Silicon Valley does not show signs of tense competition or of continuous surveillance, suspecting industrial espionage. On the contrary, life appears to be free and easy, almost idyllic. But this should not give the wrong impression that people are not working hard here and with risks involved. Computer technology has developed a new language and lifestyle that anticipates the 21st century. There is no noise, nor does the clean industry cause air pollution. The new architecture of industrial office buildings blends into the park-like green space. It looks like a single large campus, as if the grounds of Stanford University had just been expanded. A new clicking and keyboard culture has been emerging, which organizes, stores, retrieves and forwards information at the speed of light. Attention remains completely concentrated on the screen. Books are rarely read anymore or letters written. Letter writing is being replaced by e-mail. It seems as if the humanities brought along from Europe or the East Coast belonged to an age gone by.

December 31, 1986

Steinbeck Country

After a drive by car of only a few hours south from here, one comes to the Salinas Valley in the Monterey Bay, an area that has become known as Steinbeck Country. John Steinbeck (1902-68), who was born in the city of Salinas, used the landscape and people of his immediate California homeland as background and subject matter for his short stories and novels. Among these are *The Pastures of Heaven* (1932), *Tortilla Flat* (1935), *The Long Valley* (1938), *Cannery Row* (1945), and *East of Eden* (1952). When Steinbeck won the Nobel Prize in Literature in 1962, the Salinas Valley became known worldwide. The Delta of the Salinas River is one of the most fertile plains on earth. As far as the eye can see, the artichoke and salad fields stretch out endlessly. The originally well preserved Mission San Juan Bautista stands amid eucalyptus trees in the foothills north of Salinas. From the foothills, the barren and inaccessible Diablo Range, which closes the Salinas Valley to the east, rises to the sky. Steinbeck had taken special interest in the "Paisanos," the Mexican migrant field workers whose lot he narrates with human understanding and sympathy.

The city of Monterey has become a tourist attraction. On Cannery Row sardines have not been packed for a long time. The dilapidated shacks of the former cannery have been turned into an amusement park with stores, antique shops and restaurants. But the real tourist attraction is the large Monterey Bay Aquarium that was opened in 1984.

The Monterey Peninsula has an austere beauty. Riding from Monterey along the Pacific coast on the famous "17-Mile Drive" to Carmel, one may be surprised by the rare, wild vegetation. Cyprus trees cling to the cliffs, withstanding the surf of the Pacific. And otters, seals, sea lions, and pelicans frolic on the small islands off the coast. Outside Carmel, directly on the Pacific coast, lies Pebble Beach, one of the most beautiful and also most difficult golf courses in the world.

South Bend, January 8, 1987

Notes at the Beginning of the Year

Two days ago the 100th U.S. Congress convened for its first session. The Democrats have a majority in the House and in the Senate. President Reagan presented a budget, which goes beyond the 1 trillion dollar limit. And today the Dow Jones Index exceeded 2,000 for the first time.

Note

[On February 8, 2001, President George W. Bush proposed to Congress, based on the precalculated budget surplus, a tax cut of 1.6 trillion dollars spread over a ten year period. At that time, the Dow Jones Industrial Average or Dow Jones Index (DJI) fluctuated between 10,500 and 11,000. On November 20,

1995, the DJI had reached 5,000, and on March 29, 1999, it crossed the psychologically important 10,000 bench mark.]

January 25, 1987

German Elections Went Off Smoothly

Today's elections to the German Bundestag went off smoothly. As the re-election of Chancellor Helmut Kohl had been taken for granted, there were few commentaries in the American press or on television.

March 4, 1987

150 Years City of Chicago

One hundred and fifty years ago, on March 4, 1837, Chicago was incorporated as a city. It had 4,170 inhabitants. Before that, Chicago had been founded as a village in 1833. As a railroad hub, center of commerce and industry in the Midwest, the City of Chicago advanced rapidly. Together with its suburbs, Chicago has a population of over seven million. It is presently, after New York and Los Angeles, the third largest city in the United States. In about 1893, Chicago came to be called the "Windy City." In winter and early spring, an ice-cold wind from Lake Michigan blows through the streets of Chicago.

[For information on Fort Dearborn, the original settlement, and for the meaning of the name "Chicago," see entry above of September 3, 1961.]

March 8, 1987

News from Moscow

From Moscow came the news that Gorbachev had agreed to dismantle the intermediate-range missiles in Europe without further insisting on giving up the Strategic Defense Initiative (SDI). Negotiations on the matter have already begun in Geneva. If it should be possible to free Europe of this immediate nuclear threat, while guaranteeing its security, one could draw a deep breath.

[Entry following a day trip to Chicago.]

South Bend, March 16, 1987

The Magna Charta in Chicago

The exhibition "Magna Carta in America" was opened today on the square in front of the City Hall of Chicago. A copy of the Magna Carta or Charta of 1215, together with a number of other showpieces, are shown to the public in a big, especially equipped bus. The original of the Magna Carta, the oldest document of civil rights, is in safekeeping at the Lincoln Cathedral in northeastern England. This traveling exhibition has been organized on the occasion of the 200th anniversary of signing the U.S. Constitution. Despite the winterish temperatures and the frosty wind that was blowing in from Lake Michigan, people were standing in line to see this exhibition. The great interest in this show and the efforts taken to see it demonstrated how closely connected Americans are to the democratic English tradition.

[On signing the U.S. Constitution 200 years ago in 1787, see entry below of September 17, 1987.]

South Bend, April 15, 1987

Composed and Confident

In distinct contrast to Reykjavik, U.S. Secretary of State George Shultz appeared to be composed and confident at the press conference in Moscow. Recent talks with Soviet Foreign Minister Eduard Shevardnadze and General Secretary Mikhail Gorbachev gave cause for hope that an agreement on dismantling intermediate-range missiles in Europe could be reached in the foreseeable future. This may bring about a summit meeting in Washington after all.

[From end of May to mid-August, 1987, my wife and I spent our summer vacation in Innsbruck, Austria.]

Innsbruck, May 30, 1987

The Dual Birthday Celebration

On the occasion of the 750-Year Celebration of Berlin, many dignitaries have come to the divided city, to West and East Berlin, to convey their congratulations on the city's birthday. Queen Elizabeth II opened the round of state visits in West Berlin, whereby she affirmed Great Britain's readiness to secure the freedom of West Berlin. Led by Gorbachev, the heads of state of the Warsaw Pact convened in East Berlin. Yesterday, the Warsaw Pact nations offered further negotiations to NATO over disarmament in Central Europe. President Reagan promised to visit West Berlin in early June. He indicated he would like to use this opportunity to open discussions on the reunification of Germany. But all these pledges of loyalty cannot obscure the fact that the real goal of taking down the Wall is in no way getting closer. The dual birthday celebration brings to light the grotesque situation of the divided city. Unfortunately, it has not been possible to go ahead with a common celebration for the city as a whole.

[Transl: The origin of Berlin goes back to two villages on the Spree River, which were granted a township charter in 1237.]

Innsbruck, May 31, 1987

Henry Kissinger in Aachen

Henry Kissinger was awarded the "Karlspreis" (Charlemagne Prize) by the City of Aachen. At the awarding ceremony, he gave a noteworthy speech. Speaking in fluent German, he told Europeans to be vigilant, especially at the present time. For, on the one hand, the ongoing dialogue with the Soviet Union on dismantling intermediate-range missiles should be taken advantage of; but, on the other hand, Europe should be on guard against falling into a shallow neutralism that could soften up the Atlantic Alliance. He warned against the illusion of a nuclear free future. The disarmament talks can only bring about a reasonable reduction of the nuclear arsenals. America he said is the daughter of Europe. It is imperative to uphold our common heritage, above all the freedom of the individual. A peace program can only be justified if it is compatible with our values and security.

[The "Karlspreis" (Charlemagne Prize) of the City of Aachen has been awarded every year since 1950 for outstanding service to European integration. Recipients of the "Karlspreis" before Kissinger were, among others, Jean Monnet (1953), Konrad Adenauer (1954), Winston Churchill (1955), Paul Henri Spaak (1957), Robert Schuman (1958), and George C. Marshall (1959).]

Innsbruck, June 1, 1987

The Concert Event

Last night Vladimir Horowitz gave a piano concert in the "Grossen Saal des Musikvereins," the main concert hall in Vienna. Works by Mozart, Schubert, Liszt, Schumann and Chopin were on the program. The 82-year old artist, who has become a legend, performed after 50 years for the first time again in Vienna. The concert was sold out for weeks. It has been a long time since a piano concert has been such a sensation. The technical brilliance and intuitive understanding with a restraint gesture led to a spiritual, transparent performance. A critic thought that in hearing Horowitz playing Mozart, one could experience the creative process. Wherever Horowitz performed on his European tour, the jubilation was undivided.

Innsbruck, June 5, 1987

The Historic Speech 40 Years Ago

Forty years ago today, on June 5, 1947, then U.S. Secretary of State George C. Marshall delivered an historic speech at Harvard University, which laid the foundation for the European Recovery Program (ERP), or the Marshall Plan. It was the Commencement Address to the graduating students at Harvard that year. With great foresight Marshall recognized what needed to be done in order to rescue a Europe that was ravaged by war and threatened with starvation. No other American action touched the hearts of Europeans as much as the Marshall Plan did. There is a widespread feeling of gratitude for this unique rescue operation. The Marshall Plan was a major factor that Western Europe did not succumb to Communism.

Addendum

[The 50th anniversary of the Marshall Plan in 1997 was observed on both sides of the Atlantic. On May 29, 1997, the heads of state of the countries which had participated in the Marshall Plan met in Rotterdam for a celebration. Also U.S. President Bill Clinton came to Rotterdam for that event. The Marshall Plan was praised as one of the most successful reconstruction projects in modern history.

On the occasion of the 50th anniversary of the Marshall Plan, the Harvard University Archives organized an exhibition, which showed how the Commencement Address of June 5, 1947 had come about and how the Marshall Plan was realized. U.S. Secretary of State George Marshall had accepted the invitation by Harvard University President James B. Conant to deliver the Commencement Address. However, he wrote Conant that it would not be a "formal address," but only "a few remarks." The Commencement on June 5, 1947, took place, as was customary, in open air on the Harvard Yard. In a short address that took only 15 minutes, George Marshall first called attention to the destitution of Europe at the time, which without assistance would lead to an economic and social catastrophe. Then, he briefly outlined his recovery program for the reconstruction of the war-ravaged Europe. At the conclusion, he pointed out that American policy was "directed not against any country or doctrine but against hunger."

The European Recovery Program (ERP) met at first with resistance in Congress, but was finally accepted and signed into law by President Harry S. Truman in April 1948. Truman insisted that the Program should bear the name of its founder and be called the Marshall Plan. The following 16 countries participated in the Marshall Plan: Austria, Belgium, Denmark, France, the Federal Republic of Germany, Great Britain, Greece, Iceland, Italy, Luxembourg, the Netherlands, Norway, Sweden, Switzerland, Turkey, and the United States. In the course of the Marshall Plan's operation from 1948-52, 13 billion dollars were distributed. The Marshall Plan expedited the process of European economic integration.

George C. Marshall (1880-1959) was Chairman of the Joint Chiefs of Staff during World War II. He served as Secretary of State in the Truman Administration from 1947-49. For the Marshall Plan he received the Nobel Peace Prize 1953.]

[Transl: While I was on research at the Houghton Library of Harvard University early August, 1997, I was able to visit the 50th anniversary exhibition of the Marshall Plan and by courtesy get the above information.]

Innsbruck, June 12, 1987

In Front of the Brandenburg Gate

"Mr. Gorbachev, tear down this wall!"

With these words President Reagan appealed this afternoon to Mikhail Gorbachev to get rid of the Berlin Wall. Reagan's visit to Berlin for the 750-Year Celebration was accompanied by wild demonstrations that led to violent clashes with police on the Kurfürstendamm, West Berlin's busiest thoroughfare. Oddly enough, Reagan's appeal met with greater response by youths in East Berlin, who, a few days earlier, had made similar demands, calling upon Gorbachev as their patron saint. East West politics have been set in motion these days. Should the Berlin question be solved after all?

[Notes taken following travels through West Germany, Austria, and Italy.]

Innsbruck, July 18, 1987

The Same and Yet Different

It is not only tiresome but also fruitless to continuously draw comparisons between America and Europe on what is better or worse on either side. Due to an active international trade, consumer goods on both sides of the Atlantic are much the same so that there is not much of a difference any more. Yet despite the adjustment of consumer goods, one should not overlook the differences in mentality and attitude that do exist between America and Europe. It seems as if these differences are increasing with the growing conformity of the consumer market.

Innsbruck, July 23, 1987

The Five Billion Mark Reached

Demographic observers at the United Nations recorded that the world population has reached the five billion mark. The five billionth new addition to the human race was supposedly born in Yugoslavia. To mark the occasion, United Nations General Secretary Peres de Cuellar congratulated the happy parents. The population centers are very unequally distributed: Half of the world population, i.e. 2.5 billion, lives in China, India, and in South East Asia.

Addendum

[On October 12, 1999, the demographic clock at the United Nations showed that the world population had crossed the six billion mark. While half of the world population lives in Asia, a strong increase is being expected for Latin America and Africa in the decades ahead.]

South Bend, September 8, 1987

Honecker in Bonn

After several cancellations and delays, the state visit of Erich Honecker in Bonn finally came off. This is the first time that an East German head of state was received in the Federal Republic. But the result of this encounter is rather sobering. At the state banquet, Honecker bluntly told his hosts that in his opinion a capitalist and a communist state are as incompatible as fire and water. Reunification is for him no topic of discussion.

South Bend, September 10, 1987

The Second Pastoral Pilgrimage

Arriving at the Miami International Airport, Pope John Paul II was given a warm welcome as it had rarely been bestowed unto a visitor to America from abroad. President and Mrs. Reagan came to Miami to personally welcome him. The TV networks have adjusted their programs to broadcast the papal visit. With heartfelt words John Paul II responded to the greetings by President Reagan, saying that he has come to America as a friend and a pilgrim for the cause of peace. John Paul II begins today his second pastoral pilgrimage to the United States, which, in the ten days ahead, will lead him through the South and Southwest. The following cities are on the itinerary: Columbia, South Carolina, New Orleans, San Antonio, Phoenix, Los Angeles, Monterey, and San Francisco. He will conclude his pilgrimage in Detroit, Michigan.

September 13, 1987

On his journey through the South and Southwest, John Paul II was spontaneously received with overwhelming jubilation. This was especially true today in San Antonio, Texas. This pastoral pilgrimage has been planned for the predominantly Spanish-speaking South and Southwest of the United States, where nearly half of the approximately 53 million American Catholics live. By the year 2000 the Hispanic population will presumably make up three quarters of Catholics in America. A critical shortage of priests is looming as a pressing future problem on the horizon. It has been shown time and again that this Pope radiates a special charisma. His human kindness, compassion for those who suffer and the poor as well as his convincing call for peace deeply touches people, believers and non-believers alike.

South Bend, September 17, 1987

Constitution Day

200 years ago today, on September 17, 1787, the U.S. Constitution was signed in Independence Hall in Philadelphia. Thereby, one of the great documents in history became reality. The U.S. Constitution is the oldest democratic constitution in the world, having been in effect without interruption since 1787. Eleven years after the Declaration of Independence of 1776, the historical process, which led to the foundation of the United States of America, was completed. The Founding Fathers had crafted the Constitution with legally binding clarity and also with enough flexibility so that over time it could provide legal security to a continent.

South Bend, September 18, 1987

The Long-Awaited Breakthrough

In a surprisingly called press conference at 8 a.m. in the morning, President Reagan with Secretary of State George Shultz at his side announced today that in principle an agreement has been reached between the U.S. and the Soviet Union to dismantle short-range and intermediate-range missiles with nuclear warheads worldwide. This means, concretely speaking, that a substantial reduction of nuclear weapons in Central Europe will be carried out. This is the long-awaited breakthrough in disarmament talks. But not until the treaty is signed, will it be possible to grasp the full extent of this agreement.

Monday, October 19, 1987

Black Monday

On today's Monday, which rightly can be called "Black Monday," the Dow Jones Index fell by 508 points. This is the biggest loss which has ever been quoted on Wall Street in a single day, worse than the stock market crash of October 29, 1929, the infamous "Black Friday" that led to the Great Depression in the 1930s. The news of this enormous loss of value in stocks on Wall Street spread within hours throughout the world. The stock exchanges in London, Tokyo, and Sidney have already reported heavy losses, while the stock exchange in Hong Kong remained closed for the day.

Within a few days, the Dow Jones Index plunged from 2,700 to 1,700. The stock market suddenly lost 500 billion dollars. This sizeable loss of investment value will soon trickle down through many branches of the economy. The stock market crash raises the specter of a new recession. The disquieting question is being put forward: Will the economic crisis of the 1930s repeat itself?

Addendum

[The effects of the stock market crash of October 19, 1987, cannot be compared with those of the crash of October 29, 1929. After a short recession, the American economy quickly recovered and reached its highest boost ever recorded in the 1990s.]

South Bend, November 24, 1987

Radiant with Joy

This afternoon, Secretary of State George Shultz, radiant with joy, stepped in front of the TV cameras in Geneva and, visibly moved, shook the hands of his Soviet counterpart Eduard Shevardnadze. Shultz confirmed that an agreement has been reached to dismantle medium-range missiles with mutually guaranteed verification of how it is being executed. The INF (Intermediate-range Nuclear Forces) Treaty can now be signed at the upcoming summit meeting in Washington in December. The Treaty provides that 2,000 short-range and intermediate-range missiles with a range of 300 to 3,000 miles will be dismantled in the East and West.

November 25, 1987

Today, details of the INF Treaty have been made known. Accordingly, all cruise and Pershing II missiles should be dismantled and scrapped in three years time, while the Soviet Union guaranteed to do the same with its SS-20 missiles. Furthermore, the Soviet Union agreed to eliminate 1,500 of its nuclear warheads opposite the 350 nuclear warheads that are available on the side of the West. As George Shultz stated today, following the NATO foreign ministers meeting in Brussels: "NATO foreign ministers emphatically approve of a historic superpower agreement to scrap an entire class of nuclear weapons."

Chicago, November 28, 1987

The Desire for European Culture

Hardly at any other place is the American desire for European culture as manifest as at the corner of Michigan Avenue and Adams Street in Chicago. The Chicago Art Institute stands there, and diagonally opposite to it the Orchestra Hall with its broad inscription: "Bach, Mozart, Beethoven, Wagner." The Vienna Philharmonic Orchestra conducted by Bernstein performed its guest concert in the Orchestra Hall in September. "The Marriage of Figaro" is presently on the program of the Chicago Lyric Opera. But the main attraction these days is the special exhibition of the Courtault Collection from London of "Impressionist and Post-Impressionist Masterpieces" at the Art Institute. The Chicago Art Institute's own famous collection of French Impressionists has stimulated a special receptiveness for this art form. Although tickets for the Courtault Exhibition have been sold out for weeks, people nonetheless stand in line in the cold rain on Michigan Street just to get admitted. European culture is not at all thought of here as being foreign, but is accepted as a matter of course as a common heritage one simply partakes of.

South Bend, December 8, 1987

The Historic Turning Point

The summit meeting in Washington has been scheduled for December 8 to 10. The highlight of the meeting took place right away on the first day. Today, at 2 p.m. EST, the INF Treaty was signed by President Ronald Reagan and General Secretary Mikhail Gorbachev in the East Room of the White House. It was an unpretentious ceremony, which commanded attention alone by its historic significance. According to the Treaty, short-range and intermediate-range nuclear forces, primarily in Europe on both sides of the Iron Curtain, will be dismantled. Thereby, Europe will be freed of the nightmare of being directly exposed to an immediate threat by nuclear weapons. The signing of the INF Treaty is generally seen as an historic turning point. For the first time since the end of the Second World War, an entire class of nuclear weapons will be eliminated by the two superpowers. The arms race of the Cold War may well be regarded as having been overcome, which initiates a new era of readiness for understanding between East and West. The INF Treaty still needs the two-thirds approval by the Senate. But there can be no doubt, despite several objections, that the Treaty will be ratified. The more than 200 pages of the Treaty illustrate its complexity. Affixing the signatures to the separate parts of the Treaty could be watched on TV around the world.

South Bend, December 10, 1987

Mr. Glasnost

During the three days of the summit meeting in Washington, Michael Gorbachev, who is addressed as "General Secretary," has made the catchword "Glasnost" he had coined so popular that he himself is being called "Mr. Glasnost." This new attitude toward openness is convincing. Gorbachev shaped the image of his politics by assuming the Western style of forming public opinion. He is seriously searching for conciliation with America and is striving for a new rapprochement between the two superpowers. He wants to achieve strategic stability, whereby a 50% reduction of intercontinental missiles on both sides is open for discussion. The decisive breakthrough on the thorny way of negotiating the INF Treaty came without a doubt, when both sides had agreed to let inspectors verify its execution on site.

Reagan's Judgment

After the Ilyushin airplane with Michael and Raisa Gorbachev and the Russian delegation on board had left Andrews Air Force Base, President Reagan spoke to the American nation in a televised address at 9 p.m. from the Oval Office. In Reagan's judgment the summit meeting was a great success. He called attention to the fact that years ago NATO's "dual track" decision had demonstrated the resolve of the West to squarely face the threat by the deployment of the SS-20 missiles. Thereby, the Soviet side was finally brought to the negotiating table. For the first time since 1945, the arms race has not just been halted but reduced. Beyond that, the way has been opened for START (Strategic Arms Reduction Talks), i.e. negotiations on the reduction of intercontinental missiles. Reagan emphasized that the Washington summit with the conclusion of the INF Treaty was a success for world peace. He pointed out: "I believe that this treaty represents a landmark in postwar history."

[Transl: The "dual track" decision refers to the resolution by NATO ministers on December 12, 1979, to update the nuclear capability in Europe, while at the same time to continue the arms reduction talks in Geneva. See entry of December 28, 1979 plus addendum.]

December 11, 1987

Immediately Put into Action

No time was wasted to put the INF Treaty immediately into action. At his stopover in East Berlin, Gorbachev met with the heads of government of the Warsaw Pact to report on the development of the Washington summit. It was primarily a matter of carrying out the implementations of the INF Treaty. The German Democratic Republic (East Germany) and Czechoslovakia agreed to have American inspectors on their territories. At the same time, Secretary of State George Shultz briefed the representatives of the NATO countries in Brussels on the results of the Washington summit, who on their part agreed to have Russian inspectors. The INF Treaty was unanimously welcomed by the representatives of NATO, which is also a recommendation to the U.S. Senate to ratify the Treaty.

Addendum

[Still on the same day, George Shultz, together with the foreign ministers of the five countries where intermediate-range missiles had been deployed (Belgium, the Federal Republic of Germany, Great Britain, Italy, and the Netherlands), signed an agreement that Soviet inspectors were admitted on site. See G. Shultz, *Turmoil and Triumph*, p. 1015.]

South Bend, December 24, 1987

An Austrian Christmas

This year's Christmas season in America has been dedicated to an unusual degree to Austria. It began with the special Christmas Show of Julie Andrews and Placido Domingo titled "The Sound of Christmas," which was taken live in Salzburg and broadcast on ABC TV. As every year, also the film "The Sound of Music" was shown on television. The Vienna Choir Boys participated as guests in the Christmas Concert of the Boston Pops. Their rendition of "Rudolph, the Rednose Reindeer" was particularly well received and could be heard many times on radio and on television. The Vienna Choir Boys were also part of the traditional "National Christmas Celebration" in Washington, at which President and Mrs. Reagan were present. Each time at the conclusion of these programs, the Vienna Choir Boys sang with their unmistakable voices "Stille Nacht, heilige Nacht" (Silent Night, Holy Night) in German and in English. The highlight of the Austrian Christmas presentations was tonight's "Christmas Eve Special" on CBS, which showed the Hofkirche in Innsbruck and Tyrolean Christmas customs.

South Bend, December 27, 1987

A Holiday Stroll

Although the Inner City of South Bend (population ca. 100,000), as is the case in most inner cities in America, is decaying and makes, especially on Sundays and holidays, an eerily deserted impression, the many churches are alive and thriving. The "Center City Associates" together with the "Northern Indiana Historical Society" and the "United Religious Community" have organized over the Christmas season a "Holiday Stroll" through the churches of the Inner City of South Bend. People from all walks of life have signed up for the Program. My wife and I took the Stroll yesterday. In quick succession, but with a warm reception, our group was guided through the "First United Methodist Church," "First Presbyterian Church," "Cathedral of St. James Episcopal," the synagogue "Temple Beth El," and finally the "St. Paul's Lutheran Church." These are only a few of the more than 200 churches and synagogues in South Bend and the surrounding areas. The churches in the Inner City can look back on more than a hundred years of history, which goes back to the pioneer period in Northern Indiana. They are well cared for, most of them have plans for renovations or expansions. All these churches are exclusively maintained and furthered by their faith communities. Next to their pastoral obligations, they are also devoted to social ministries, maintain kindergartens and Sunday schools. Remarkable is the friendly atmosphere that prevails among these many congregations. The need for ecumenical cooperation is as obvious here as hardly anywhere else. The "United Religious Community" has recognized this need for a long time and tried to realize it. This way, a respectful and tolerant side by side existence among the different religious communities has been created, who cooperate in solving the many family and social problems.

SECTION 11

January 1, 1988-December 31, 1989

South Bend, January 1, 1988

The Changed Atmosphere

Compared to last year, the atmosphere between East and West has noticeably improved. On this New Year's Day, the messages of greeting between President Reagan and General Secretary Gorbachev were exchanged unconstrained. Reagan spoke on Russian and Gorbachev on American television. Gorbachev has become such a familiar figure here that his greetings for the New Year are being taken as a matter of course. Moreover, his picture is on the front page of *Time* Magazine as "Man of the Year" for 1987.

January 5, 1988

The Downtrend of the Dollar

Only by the intervention of the central banks in Europe and Japan was the downtrend of the Dollar stopped. From its record low of DM 1.58 and 122 Yen the exchange rate to the Dollar was raised to DM 1.60 and 124 Yen. But how long can this cover be provided? If the high American trade and budget deficits cannot be reduced, then certainly not for long. However, in this election year every effort will be made to avoid a recession.

January 25, 1988

State of the Union Address

In his last State of the Union Address President Reagan was conciliatory and confident about the future as never before. Among other issues, he turned to school reform, the perennial topic of American domestic policy. He received undivided applause when he mentioned the INF Treaty and asked the Senate for a speedy ratification. As the Reagan era is coming to a close, it is becoming ever more clear that the initiated process of reducing the nuclear threat belongs to the great achievements of his presidency.

South Bend, February 7, 1988

Assurances for Europe

[Second thoughts arose on both sides of the Atlantic that eliminating intermediate-range nuclear forces could expose Western Europe without protection to an attack from the East, for the Warsaw Pact was far superior in conventional weapons.]

While the Senate hearings on the INF Treaty were still ongoing, a delegation of influential senators and members of the House went to Europe to inquire how the countries affected by the Treaty reacted. At the same time, they assured Europeans that America would never abandon Europe. The delegation met in Munich with politicians of the Federal Republic. It was expressed repeatedly that the security of the Federal Republic was of importance to the United States as well. Jim Wright, the Speaker of the House, emphasized the close ties of America with Europe, saying: "Europe is not only the Old Home for so many of our countrymen, Europe's security is also our security."

[The long-standing Democratic Representative from Texas, James "Jim" C. Wright, Jr., succeeded Tip O'Neill as Speaker of the House in 1986.]

Note

[The argument that by establishing a nuclear free zone, Western Europe could be overrun by the East was at first refuted by the fact that the nuclear capacity of France and Great Britain will not be diminished by the Treaty.

Moreover, George Shultz pointed out several times that when the Treaty is enacted, the American Armed Forces in Europe in the air and on the sea will retain enough nuclear striking power to fend off any attempt of an attack by the East. See G. Shultz, *Turmoil and Triumph,* p. 1082.]

South Bend, February 28, 1988

The XV Winter Olympic Games in Calgary, Alberta, Canada, ended today. It was the first Winter Olympics hosted by Canada. The Games came off splendidly. They were performed in a spirit of fair sportsmanship. National confrontations and personal rivalries remained limited to a minimum. The many guests were warmly received by the citizens of Calgary. And the Rocky Mountains provided a magnificent scenery for this great sports event.

South Bend, Tuesday, March 8, 1988

Super Tuesday

For the first time in American political history, primaries have been regionally combined. On today's "Super Tuesday," delegates for the Republican as well as for the Democratic national convention were elected in 20 Southern states. The idea was to give the South as a region noticeable significance in the upcoming presidential election. In fact, this primary, which has frequently been regarded as a "national primary," has set the course for candidates of both parties. On the Republican side, Vice President George Bush, who won 690 delegates vs. Robert Dole with only 163, has emerged as clear winner. On the side of the Democrats, Governor Michael Dukakis won 401 delegates, followed by Albert Gore with 364 and the Reverend Jesse Jackson with 344. The nomination of George Bush as presidential candidate of the Republican Party cannot be stopped anymore, while on the Democratic side the race is still open.

South Bend, March 9, 1988

How an American Legend Originated

On a nostalgic return to the Notre Dame Campus, President Reagan participated personally today in a Stamp Dedication Ceremony for the legendary football coach Knute Rockne (1888-1931). Knute Rockne led the Notre Dame football team two times to a national championship in the 1920s. On the pinnacle of his career, he died in an airplane crash in 1931. By his tragic death, Knute Rockne, who had achieved national recognition as college football coach, became a legend. Connected with Rockne was the story of George Gipp, one of his best players, who had died of a streptococcal infection in December 1920. According to tradition, Gipp, on his deathbed, supposedly expressed a wish to his coach that he should call upon the team to win for him when a game looked hopelessly lost. That moment came in 1928 when the Fighting Irish played against the superior team of the Army in the Yankee Stadium. Legend has it that during halftime Knute Rockne cheered on his team, "to win just one for the Gipper." "Win one for the Gipper" has become a familiar dictum when it matters to save a hopeless situation. This story was portrayed in the film "Knute Rockne: All American" by the end of the 1930s. As a young actor, Ronald Reagan played the role of George Gipp. The premiere of the film in South Bend in 1940 was a national event. When at today's ceremony, President Reagan cautiously repeated: "Win one for the Gipper," the audience erupted in enthusiastic applause. What happened today in the sport arena and convocation center of Notre Dame was more than a stamp dedication ceremony. One could experience how an American legend had originated and how it was brought to life again.

South Bend, March 18, 1988

U.S. Troops to Honduras

With strength of resolution, President Reagan reacted immediately to the advance of the Sandinistas on Honduran territory, where the positions of the Contras should have been taken. Within a few hours, he sent 3,200 U.S. troops to Honduras. This increases the threat of war in Central America, recently also fomented by the crisis in Panama. Apprehensions are being expressed that Central America could become a second Vietnam. Protest demonstrations in San Francisco, Los Angeles, and in Chicago have again evoked the atmosphere of the 1960s. Who will give in first? A test of wills lies ahead.

March 24, 1988

Surprisingly, Sandinistas and Contras have reached an agreement today at the negotiating table, which seems to bring an end to the civil war that has lasted for seven years and claimed nearly 40,000 lives. A 60-day truce has been agreed and the Contras were conceded the right to a say in the government of Nicaragua. New elections and democratic reforms have been considered for the future.

March 27, 1988

According to the agreed upon amnesty as part of the truce, the first 100 political prisoners were released today in Managua. As the peace negotiations in Nicaragua promise a positive result, the American troops can be withdrawn from Honduras. This intervention ended without bloodshed. No doubt, the decisiveness of the Reagan Administration contributed to bringing about the peace negotiations. Thereby, the crisis situation in Central America has been visibly eased.

South Bend, April 14, 1988

Afghanistan

The Soviet Union, the United States, Pakistan, and Afghanistan signed an agreement in Geneva, which provides the withdrawal of the Soviet troops from Afghanistan. Therewith, the conflict over Afghanistan is coming to a close. The withdrawal of the Soviet troops has been scheduled for May 15 and it should be completed in nine months. During the eight years of occupation, Afghanistan's population of 14 million lost one million lives, while five million fled over the border to Pakistan. The repatriation of the refugees poses a special problem. What will be the destiny of this war-ravaged country? Will the Communist regime fall after the withdrawal of the Soviet troops, or will it remain in power in a coalition with the *mujaheddin*? or, will there be civil war between the rivaling groups?

South Bend, May 5, 1988

Out of Time

Last night at 12 a.m., the amnesty deadline, allowing illegal immigrants to apply for residence in the United States, ran out of time. According to the new immigration regulations approved by Congress last year, illegal immigrants were granted amnesty for permanent residence in the country and applying for citizenship if they could prove that they had been in the United States since 1982. From among the estimated 6 to 8 million illegal aliens, nevertheless 1.3 million applied for amnesty. Areas of concentration were Los Angeles, Houston, and Miami. Up to the last minute, people were standing in line in front of 107 U.S. Immigration and Naturalization Service Bureaus. Above all, the new immigration regulations are supposed to stem the swelling tide of illegal border crossings from neighboring Mexico. It should also give those millions of illegal immigrants, who are hiding and living in constant fear, legal status and a humanly worthy existence. For the first time, also employers are made responsible and punishable by law if they hire foreigners without a residence and work permit. It will not be possible to fully solve the problem of illegal immigration to the United States, but by this measure at least a partial solution has been achieved.

Sunday, May 8, 1988

Reelected

With convincing majority, Francois Mitterand won today the run-off election over Chirac as president of France for seven more years. By his stoic and deliberate restraint in crisis situations, Mitterand has become a stabilizing factor in Europe and in world politics.

South Bend, May 11, 1988

Irving Berlin 100 Years Old

The popular and beloved composer Irving Berlin celebrated his 100th birthday today quietly withdrawn in his home in Manhattan. Born in 1888 in Russia, he came with his parents in 1893 to America. Among the 1,500 songs Berlin wrote are the widely known hits "Alexander's Ragtime Band," "White Christmas" ("I am Dreaming of a White Christmas" has become known the world over), "Easter Parade," and "There is No Business Like Show Business." The patriotic song "God Bless America" has virtually become a second anthem. Berlin also wrote the music for numerous Broadway musicals and films. In honor of Irving Berlin, a Gala Evening was given today in Carnegie Hall.

Note

[Israel Baline was born on May 11, 1888, in Tyumen, Western Siberia. The Baline family immigrated to the United States in 1893, passing through Ellis Island and settling down in New York. Israel Baline grew up in poverty on the Lower East Side of Manhattan. At first he started out as entertainer at the Bowery. He had a good voice and the natural talent to compose songs, which at their time had broad popular appeal. Usually, he also wrote the lyrics for his songs. As artist he assumed the anglicized name Irving Berlin in about 1909. His breakthrough as song writer came in 1911 with "Alexander's Ragtime Band." Irving Berlin died on September 22, 1989, in New York.]

South Bend, May 25, 1988

Stopover in Helsinki

On their way to the summit meeting in Moscow, President and Mrs. Reagan took a stopover in Helsinki to get adjusted to the time difference. In Helsinki they received the news that all opposition in the Senate, which could have prevented the ratification of the INF Treaty, has been overcome.

May 27, 1988

INF Treaty Ratified

The U.S. Senate ratified 93:5 the INF Treaty. At the same time, also the Supreme Soviet confirmed the agreement. Howard Baker, the chief of staff of the White House, was immediately on his way to Helsinki to bring Reagan the ratified Treaty. President Reagan can now go on to Moscow with the ratified INF Treaty in hand.

May 29, 1988

Right on time at 2 p.m. local time, Air Force One with President and Mrs. Reagan on board landed in Moscow. For the first time in 16 years, since Richard Nixon in 1972, an American president is coming again to Moscow for a summit meeting. The very fact that Ronald Reagan has taken this step, shows the fundamental change in East West relations. The reception of President and Mrs. Reagan in the Kremlin was cordial but according to protocol stiff. It seemed though as if Ronald Reagan and his host Michael Gorbachev met as old acquaintance. It is after all the fourth summit meeting—Geneva, Reykjavik, Washington, and now Moscow—that brings them together. On both sides, the willingness was visible to improve mutual relations.

May 31, 1988

A Courageous Speech

For the first time, an American president spoke to Russian academic youth. In the great Hall of Moscow University, under the mural of the Russian Revolution and in front of Lenin's bust, Ronald Reagan addressed the students, but indirectly also the Russian public about the new consent between America and the Soviet Union. He emphasized the significance of freedom, democracy and a free economy; he also pointed out the innovations of the Computer Age, which make it necessary to exchange information and to get to know each other. Reagan saw the hope for the future in the fact that he could not see any difference anymore, speaking to American, Russian, or any other students. At the conclusion of his speech, he received a standing ovation.

June 1, 1988

INF Treaty Put into Force

At the conclusion of the Moscow summit meeting, President Reagan and General Secretary Gorbachev signed the INF Treaty, putting it into force. This is a significant step toward dismantling nuclear weapons and for peace in the world. There is a general feeling as if the time of the Cold War was over.

During the summit meeting, pictures from Moscow on everyday Russian life were broadcast on television. They left impressions of a touching, simple humanity. It would be about time for Russia and the West to come closer together on a human level.

[St. Louis], June 21, 1988

The Great Drought

Since the Dust Bowl, the wide parched stretches of land in Oklahoma and the Middle West in the 1930s, America has not had such a devastating drought as this year. For two months and a half not a single drop of rain has fallen on large parts of the country. The Midwest is especially hard hit; record temperatures of 100 degrees F and above form a heat block that dries up all vegetation. From the Dakotas through Iowa, Missouri, all the way down to the Gulf of Mexico, and from Montana through Nebraska, Kansas, Illinois, Indiana to Ohio much of the harvest has been destroyed. There are emergency slaughters of cattle taking place because the forage to feed the animals is just not available anymore. Large sections of the Midwest are burned brown and river beds dried up. Crossing the mighty Mississippi here at St. Louis, one can see sandbanks sticking out. The navigation has come to a standstill. Vast areas of the United States are facing a disastrous year.

How is this drought to be explained? Is it part of a 50-year climate cycle in North America, or is it an indication of a global climate change? Is it the result of the frequently mentioned greenhouse effect caused by the constant emission of carbon dioxide by industry and the exhaust gases of motor vehicles? Climatologists agree that it is the combined effect of both elements.

South Bend, June 29, 1988

Gorbachev Put to the Test

The special Party Convention, which is presently taking place in Moscow—the first of its kind since Lenin's time—puts Mikhail Gorbachev to the test. Will he be able to succeed with his extensive reforms? Are *glasnost* and *perestroika* convincing enough to soften up the petrified Communist Party organization? Anyway, Gorbachev's attempt at renewing and democratizing the Soviet Union is a positive sign that the East Bloc is more adjusting to the West.

South Bend, July 12, 1988

Surprise at the Democrats

Michael Dukakis, who is seen as the sure presidential candidate of the Democrats, had a surprise in store today when, in the historic Faneuil Hall of Boston, he introduced Lloyd Bentsen, the senator from Texas, as his running mate. Dukakis apparently wants to repeat the example of John F. Kennedy, who in 1960 had chosen Lyndon B. Johnson, then a senator from Texas, as his running mate to achieve regional balance. Jesse Jackson, who based on his success in the primaries, asserted a claim for the second position on the Democratic ticket, was passed over, actually not even mentioned. This could again lead to a calamitous split within the Democratic Party.

July 17, 1988

In Triumphal Procession to Atlanta

Partly startled and partly amused, the American public followed the preliminary events to the Democratic National Convention in Atlanta. African-Americans felt offended and deceived by the way Governor Dukakis chose his running mate. Jesse Jackson was emotionally upset. Coming down from Chicago in a motorcade of supporters, he reached Atlanta in triumphal procession. It reminded one of the civil rights protests of the 1960s, which one thought had been overcome.

July 19, 1988

In his address at the Democratic National Convention, the Reverend Jesse Jackson surpassed himself. No doubt, he is at this time one of the best speakers in America. He can move his audience. The impressive vividness of his rhetoric comes from the tradition of the African-American Baptist preachers. Although what he said was not in line with political reality, he put his finger on the social woes of America and stirred up the conscience of the nation. Jackson mobilized sections of American society, which in apathy did not participate in the political process. He strengthened the self-confidence of those voters and encouraged them to go to the polls.

July 21, 1988

The American Dream

Michael Dukakis represents himself the realization of the American Dream. His father Panos Dukakis had arrived on Ellis Island from Greece in 1912 with 12 dollars in his pocket. He became a physician, and his son Michael, who holds the office of governor of Massachusetts, stands on the threshold of possibly becoming president of the United States. It does, therefore, not come as a surprise that Michael Dukakis chose the American Dream as theme for his acceptance speech, following his nomination as presidential candidate of the Democratic Party. Dukakis was credible in his speech. He hopes to appeal with this theme to a broad majority of the American population. He also succeeded, for the most part, in uniting the Democratic Party for the campaign ahead.

Note

[The American theme was frequently turned into its opposite in literature: From dream to nightmare and from utopia to dystopia. There are of course many instances in which the expectations of America have not have been fulfilled, especially when immigrants got stuck in the misery of slums. But it should not be overlooked that for millions of people the American Dream has been fulfilled. The success story of the Dukakis family is only one of many.

The American Dream has universal meaning, for people of any origin have the desire to be successful and to achieve affluence. It is an elemental human desire to own a piece of land and a home, to have a good job and to be able to provide for the future. Connected with it is the desire for freedom and self-realization.

In the course of American immigration history, the American Dream has been a powerful motivation for people from all parts of the world, at times under great difficulties, to come to America. The American Dream has also strongly affected social mobility. It strengthened the optimistic conviction that by making an effort and diligence everyone has a chance to take advantage of the many opportunities America offers.]

[My wife and I arrived in Sunnyvale, California, by mid-August for the wedding of our son Franz. Our daughter-in-law Susan was born in California. Her parents, who had come from Iowa to California, are third generation of Norwegian descent. Through this marriage, our American family has been enlarged by a Norwegian branch. The following entry reflects the impressions of an excursion to San Francisco and around the San Francisco Bay Area.]

Sunnyvale, August 15, 1988

California is Different

California is different from the rest of America. First of all, it is favored with its climate. While the East is sweltering under a brutal heat wave, here on the Pacific Coast one can enjoy pleasant summer days and cool nights in a steady climate of 75 degrees F. California is also more extravagant than other places; contrasts are more conspicuous here. On the one side, one is surrounded by a very high living standard, and on the other, confronted with neglect and depravity, about which nobody seems to care. San Francisco delights with the natural beauty of its environs and it radiates the splendor of its exclusive residences. But there is also another side to it: There are disgusting pictures of poverty and debasement. In the Park in front of the City Hall, figures are lying around wrapped in rags, of whom one cannot tell whether they are still alive or dead. The number of the homeless is said to have risen to 6,000. California has attracted and produced eccentrics. Next to the high-tech industry, artist colonies of every kind and shade have flourished here. Exceptual follies and craziness are openly displayed, which one would otherwise rarely encounter in America.

Of historical interest and worthwhile seeing are the Spanish missions that were built in the Bay Area toward the end of the 18th century. Among them are the Mission Dolores in San Francisco and the Mission San Jose at the lower end of the Bay Area.

California has its own character. It is a 900 mile coast line whose boundaries are defined to the West by the Pacific Ocean and to the East by the Cascade Range and the Sierra Nevada. It is complex and diverse; despite its drawbacks, it is always attractive, especially to young people. It offers professional opportunities as hardly anywhere else. Next to the highly developed industry, large areas of pristine nature of unique beauty have been preserved. California is always worthwhile visiting.

August 17, 1988

The Secret Given Away

The guessing game that has been ongoing for months, whom George Bush will choose as his running mate, has come to an end. When he arrived yesterday at the Republican National Convention in New Orleans, Bush announced, giving his secret away, that he has chosen Senator Dan Quayle from Indiana as his running mate. Even insiders of the Republican Party were surprised by the choice. Senator Quayle is only 41 years old. However, as he was reelected to the Senate two years ago, he should appeal to the younger generation of voters. Quayle is still unknown nationwide. He has to assert himself in the upcoming campaign.

August 18, 1988

Out of Reagan's Shadow

With his acceptance speech tonight at the Republican National Convention in the Super Dome of Louisiana in New Orleans, George Bush stepped out of the shadow of Ronald Reagan, at whose side he stood as Vice President for eight years. As presidential candidate, he put his own person into the center of attention. Bush clearly expressed what he stands for: The values of the individual and the family; a free market economy and a strong America in the world. He also promised that he will not raise taxes.

[In the presidential election campaign in the fall of 1988, Bush-Quayle on the Republican side and Dukakis-Bentsen on the Democratic side confronted each other.]

South Bend, August 19, 1988

The First Campaign Rally

The campaign of the Republicans could not have started simpler and closer to the people than at today's rally in Huntington, Indiana, the hometown of Dan Quayle. As the small county capital lies only 100 miles southeast of South Bend, it was easy to go there by car. Huntington, a town of about 18,000, did everything it could to give its famous son, who now has moved into the national limelight, an enthusiastic reception. About 20,000 supporters and the curious streamed into Huntington, which caused a major traffic problem. The rally took place in front of the Court House. A high school band played on the stand for the reception; and a cheerleader inspired the crowd shouting in chorus: "Bush-Quayle" "Bush-Quayle." Pepsi-Cola and pizza were handed out free. It was a public festival. George and Barbara Bush together with Dan and Marilyn Quayle arrived in their motorcade on time at 12:40 p.m. The crowd of people filled the square in front of the Court House, flowed over the railroad tracks to the abandoned depot and to the nearby half-dilapidated grain silos. A few daring teenagers climbed up the opened barriers of the railroad crossing to have a better view. Only the security guards on the roof of the Court House watched carefully what was going on. The whole scene looked like an illustration by Norman Rockwell*—real grassroots politics on the stump, as it has always been practiced in American presidential elections. Bush spoke to the people who had gathered there just how they felt. He emphasized the importance of family, community and church; he promised to create new jobs and not to raise taxes. Dan Quayle proved to be an effective speaker at the rally, but had nothing of essence to say. In Huntington, it became clear today that the Bush-Quayle campaign appeals to voters from small towns in rural areas. The campaign presented a conservative, patriotic platform which was received with enthusiasm.

*[With his subtle humor, the American painter and illustrator Norman Rockwell (1894-1978) portrayed everyday American life like no one else.]

[Chicago], September 3, 1988

Of Striking Similarity

The Art Institute of Chicago is presenting the special exhibition "Dutch and Flemish Paintings from the Hermitage." The exhibition was arranged as part of the American-Russian cultural exchange program that had been agreed upon at the summit meeting in Geneva in 1985. The paintings of Dutch and Flemish masters on exhibit, which have rarely been seen in the West, have attracted many visitors from Michigan, Illinois, and Wisconsin, who are obviously of Dutch descent. The faces of these visitors had a striking similarity with the figures shown on these paintings. They also took great pride in these magnificent works of art which they regarded as their cultural heritage. The appreciation of art treasures from Europe in America is in part based on ethnic origin.

[End] September, 1988

A Year of Natural Disasters

At first the drought, then the wildfires that consumed large areas in the National Parks, especially in Yellowstone, and now the hurricane "Gilbert," which raced with 170 mph through the Caribbean and the Gulf of Mexico, until it finally had landfall near the Mexican-American border. This up to now strongest hurricane of the century devastated nearly half of Jamaica as well as large parts of the Yucatan Peninsula. It has been a year of natural disasters. The abnormal behavior of these weather patterns points more and more to global climate change.

Sunday, October 2, 1988

In the Shadow of the Partition

Tonight the 24 Summer Olympic Games had their closing ceremony in Seoul. These Games took place in the shadow of the partition between North and South Korea. Fearful apprehensions had preceded this Summer Olympics that there could be disturbances brought on from the North and domestic violence in the South. Nothing of the kind happened. The Games were well organized and passed without an incident. After a long time, both East and West participated again in a Summer Olympics. Athletes from 160 nations competed in these Summer Olympic Games.

Government Reshuffle in Moscow

In no time over the weekend, the government in Moscow was reshuffled—the constitution was amended, the Politburo renewed, and Mikhail Gorbachev unanimously elected President of the Soviet Union by the Parliament. Gorbachev consolidated his position and moreover paved the way for his reforms.

South Bend, October 13, 1988

The Last Debate on Television before the Election

George Bush and Michael Dukakis squared off in the second and last debate before the election broadcast tonight from Los Angeles. They discussed primarily the major issues of this campaign. There were areas of agreement, but in the course of the debate, two clearly different points of view on national problems were presented to the American electorate. Altogether, George Bush emerged as the more convincing candidate from this debate.

October 26, 1988

A Brave Rescue Mission

In an effort that had lasted for three weeks, the two Californian gray whales were rescued today. The two whales were trapped in the ice by a sudden onset of cold weather at the northern tip of Alaska near Barrow. At first, the

Eskimos sawed out big holes in the ice so that the mammals could surface and breathe; then, helicopters dropped heavy concrete blocks on the ice; and finally, two Russian icebreakers plowed a path through the thick sheet of ice so that the two whales could swim out to the open sea. This brave rescue mission was followed with great interest by a worldwide audience on television. It certainly evoked a stronger international awareness of the importance of nature conservancy and the protection of animals in the wild.

South Bend, October 30, 1988

The Mountain of Debts

At the end of the fiscal year 1988 on September 30, the high American budget deficit and national debt was made public. According to the fiscal report, the federal government has a deficit of 155 billion dollars and the national debt has increased to 2.6 trillion. The government pays high interest for the bonds every year. The federal government had for the last time in 1969 a balanced budget. It will be one of the most urgent tasks of the new administration to reduce the accumulated mountain of debts.

Addendum

[The deficit of the federal government doubled in the following years, while the national debt increased threefold. Only in the second half of the 1990s was it possible to have the deficit under control. On February 2, 1998, President Clinton could, for the first time in 30 years, present a balanced budget for the following fiscal year. That goal was reached by discipline in spending and increased tax revenues during the economic boom of the 1990s. The budget for 1999 of 1.73 trillion dollars was not only balanced but also showed a substantial surplus. That was the turning point from years of deficit spending to a long-term surplus in American fiscal policy. The tax reduction policy of President George W. Bush at the beginning of his term in office in 2001 relied on the projected budget surplus for the ten years ahead.]

[Transl: Unfortunately, the budget surplus was short-lived. Following the terror attack on September 11, 2001 and the war in Afghanistan and in Iraq, the budget deficit again reached record highs.]

South Bend, November 9, 1988

The Election Result

The winner of yesterday's presidential election was already certain last night at 10:30 p.m., after Michigan had helped George Bush to pass the needed 270 electoral votes. The election result was announced today. Bush won the popular as well as the electoral vote by a wide margin. Of the 538 electoral votes 426 go to Bush and 112 to Michael Dukakis. On the other hand, the Democrats were able to increase their majority in the Senate and in the House. Election turnout was about 50%. Bush won the South and the Southwest, a large part of the Midwest and California.

[It rarely occurred in the history of American presidential elections that a sitting vice president won the election to be president. After Martin Van Buren in 1836, George Bush was only the second sitting vice president to win the presidential election. Several times though a vice president had to take over the presidency after the tragic death of the president.]

South Bend, December 7, 1988

Gorbachev Surprises the World

For weeks one has been prepared for a dramatic announcement, but what Mikhail Gorbachev had to say today in his address to the plenary assembly of the United Nations surprised and stunned the world. Gorbachev announced straightforward that the Soviet Union will unilaterally reduce its troops by 500,000 in two years. At the same time he promised to withdraw or dissolve six armored divisions from East Germany, Czechoslovakia and Hungary. This would also allow the United States to reduce its armed forces in Europe. It gives the dialogue on lessening tensions new impetus. Furthermore, Gorbachev divulged his vision of a new, interdependent world, in which the demand for democracy and social justice is getting more and more urgent. Yet the question remains open: Will Gorbachev be able to put through his far-reaching, innovative ideas also at home?

Addendum

[Immediately following his speech at the United Nations, Gorbachev met with President Reagan and Vice President Bush for a conference on Governors Island. Governors Island is located off the southern tip of Manhattan just across the Statue of Liberty and at the entrance to the East River. It was the last meeting of Ronald Reagan with Gorbachev. The meeting also gave Gorbachev the opportunity to establish contact with President-elect George Bush. It was an impressive picture that showed the President of the Soviet Union Mikhail Gorbachev together with the outgoing U.S. President Ronald Reagan and the newly elected President George Bush on Governors Island. The picture was taken against the backdrop of the Statue of Liberty, which as symbol of freedom stretched out her arm with the torch high into the sky.]

December 8, 1988

The Earthquake in the Caucasus

An earthquake in the magnitude of 6.9 on the Richter scale occurred in the Caucasian Republics of the Soviet Union—Georgia, Armenia and Azerbaijan. Entire cities were flattened, the death toll goes into the tens of thousands, those left homeless into the hundreds of thousands. President Gorbachev, cutting short his visit to America, flew back to Moscow to start emergency operations.

December 8, 1988

The New Confidence

At his last press conference in the White House this evening, President Reagan expressed his confidence in Gorbachev. When asked whether he believes that Gorbachev will turn the Soviet Union into a less dangerous country, he emphatically replied: "Yes, I do." There are changes taking place in the Soviet Union, he pointed out, which will make a closer, friendly cooperation for peace possible.

[Ronald Reagan gave a moving farewell speech to the press, which at the same time in questions and answers offered a broad overview of the foreign and domestic policy situation of the United States. The full text of the speech was printed in *The New York Times,* December 9, 1988, p. A18.]

South Bend, December 13, 1988

Already a Museum Piece

The spacecraft Apollo 8, on which the astronauts Frank Borman, James A. Lovell, Jr., and William A. Anders had for the first time orbited the moon on December 24, 1968, is presently on exhibit at the Museum of Science and Industry in Chicago. Apollo 8 sent the most impressive pictures of the surface of the moon back to earth. At the same time, the picture of earth as a blue, white-marbled sphere floating through space has from then on become the lasting image of our planet. Apollo 8 is tangible proof of how fast manned space flights have developed. Twenty years ago, the spacecraft Apollo 8 made history in human spaceflight. Now, the capsule which for the first time circled the moon has already become a museum piece.

[On the flight of Apollo 8 to the moon, see entry above of December 21, 23 and 24, 1968.]

South Bend, December 21, 1988

Lockerbie

The news just came through that a Boeing 747 of PAN AM on its flight from London to New York crashed over Southern Scotland. Parts of the airplane that went up in flames came down like a rain of fire on the village of Lockerbie.

December 29, 1988

What was presumed from the beginning has now been confirmed: The Boeing 747 of PAN AM flight 103 was the target of a terror attack. At the altitude of 33,000 feet, a bomb had exploded in the cargo space that tore the airplane to pieces. There were no survivors. Among the 258 victims were 35 students of Syracuse University who participated in a foreign study program in London and were on their way home for Christmas. About 10 people in the village of Lockerbie suddenly lost their lives by the down falling, burning parts of the airplane. The question remains to be answered: Who can be called to account for this horrible crime?

South Bend, January 1, 1989

A Good Beginning of the New Year

Not for a long time has there been such confidence in peace in the world as now. It is a hopeful, relaxed and optimistic beginning of the New Year. The New Year's greetings between President Reagan and President Gorbachev were exchanged as a matter of course as if they had always taken place. The new easing of tensions between East and West has contributed a great deal to the improved international atmosphere. It has taken away the fear of the future.

January 11, 1989

The Farewell to the Nation

President Reagan said goodbye to the nation. His farewell address, which was broadcast on television this evening, was so moving that even the otherwise very restrained anchor of NBC had tears in his eyes. Ronald Reagan leaves office with dignity as one of the most beloved American presidents of the past 50 years, actually since Franklin Delano Roosevelt. He was able to serve two full terms, which had been denied to his predecessors since Eisenhower. He gave back to his country its self-confidence, while at the same time putting peace in the world on a more trustful foundation. At the end of his time in office, he is the experienced elder statesman, who, with goodness of heart and a sense of humor, won the affection of the American people.

January 20, 1989

The Age of the Offered Hand

At 12 p.m. EST, as provided by the Constitution, George Herbert Walker Bush was sworn in today as the 41st President of the United States by Chief Justice William Rehnquist on the West Front of the Capitol. Bush took the oath of office on the Bible, on which George Washington had taken the oath of office 200 years ago in 1789. In his inaugural address, he emphasized, saying: "This is the age of the offered hand." As a conciliatory gesture, he offered his hand to Congress as well as to the world as a sign of his readiness for peace.

[George Herbert Walker Bush was born in 1924 in Milton, Massachusetts; Walker was the family name of his mother. Bush served as a young pilot in the U.S. Navy in the Second World War in the Pacific. After his plane had crashed in the area of the Bonin Islands in September 1944, he was rescued from the sea. He married Barbara Pierce in 1945; graduated from Yale with a BA degree in economics in 1948; then entrepreneur in oil companies in Texas. Bush entered politics as Congressman of the 7th District of Texas in the U.S. House of Representatives, 1967-71; U.S. Ambassador to the United Nations, 1971-73; Chief of U.S. Liaison Office in Peking, 1974-75; Director of the CIA, 1976-77. As running mate of Ronald Reagan in the presidential election of 1980, Bush won the U.S. vice presidency. He was U.S. Vice President, 1981-89, and U.S. President, 1989-93.]

South Bend, February 2, 1989

Disaster Closely Missed

Only now, at a conference in Moscow, has it come to light how closely the world had missed disaster in the Cuban missile crisis in October of 1962. Soviet missiles with nuclear warheads were indeed deployed in Cuba and targeted on American cities. After Nikita Khrushchev had given in to President Kennedy's ultimatum to dismantle and withdraw the missiles from Cuba, the crisis was overcome. But a human error or a miscalculation could have triggered the nuclear catastrophe.

South Bend, February 9, 1989

The Big Housecleaning

In his first address to a joint session of Congress, President Bush presented a long list of tough measures, which should contribute to improving the domestic situation of the nation. The measures for the big housecleaning include the fight against drugs, the improvement of teaching in schools, cleaning up and protecting the environment, but above all reducing the budget deficit.

South Bend, March 27, 1989

Free Elections in Moscow

News from Moscow on elections are such a rarity that announcing the results of yesterday's elections made headlines worldwide. Boris Yeltsin, who stood up against the orthodox party line, won 89% of the votes for the seat of Moscow in the Supreme Soviet. Those were the first free elections within the Communist regime since 1917. They are an indication that Glasnost works and that the road to more democracy, once taken, cannot be reversed.

South Bend, May 14, 1989

The Call for More Freedom

The call for more freedom in the Communist dominium is not becoming silent anymore. At first, it was heard in Poland, Lithuania, Georgia, and in the recent elections in Moscow. And now, it is heard loud and clear in the People's Republic of China. For weeks, hundreds of thousands of students have taken to the streets. There are mass demonstrations and hunger strikes in Peking. The demonstrators demand more freedom and a say in the Communist regime, which sees itself facing a dilemma.

May 17, 1989

The Tiananmen Square

The mass demonstrations on Peking's Tiananmen Square have increased today to a million people. The students were joined by workers, peasants as well as people from all walks of life. This is the largest mass demonstration for democracy that has ever taken place. The demonstrators want more basic civil liberties: Freedom of speech, freedom of the press, freedom of worship, free democratic elections, and the right to a say in the political decision making.

May 19, 1989

The News Blackout

The mass demonstrations on Tiananmen Square that have been going on for days brought the People's Republic of China on the verge of anarchy, or close to a counterrevolution, for they have spread now also to Shanghai and other cities. Broad sections of the population sympathize with the students and units of the military refused to take action. The situation has inasmuch intensified as the government has declared a state of emergency, imposed martial law on parts of the capital, and at the same time issued a news blackout for foreign reporters. Up to the last minute, until government agents pulled the plug, CNN broadcast pictures from Peking, which clearly showed that a revolution is in the making.

[On the further development of these events, see entries below of June 4 and 7, 1989.]

South Bend, May 29, 1989

40 Years NATO

NATO celebrates these days its 40th anniversary. After 40 years, one may ask: Has the North Atlantic Defense Alliance proven its worth? Yes, it has beyond all expectations. The Alliance has not only held its ground but has also consolidated internally and expanded externally. It has prevented transgressions of the East against the West and secured peace in Europe. But the time has come to reconsider the relationship of the Alliance with the East and to assume a more flexible position toward the countries of the Warsaw Pact.

On his first official visit to Europe, President Bush went to Brussels to participate in NATO's 40th anniversary celebration. Today he surprised the representatives of the Alliance gathered in Brussels when he announced that the United States intends to withdraw 20% of its troops from Europe. At the present strength of 320,000 American armed forces stationed in Europe, this would mean a reduction of 64,000. Connected with it is the request from the Soviet Union to follow suit so that the number of conventional armed forces be reduced to 270,000 on both sides of the Iron Curtain. This would provide the prerequisite for defusing the situation in Central Europe.

Addendum

[The North Atlantic Treaty Organization was founded on April 4, 1949, in Washington. The original 12 signatory countries were: Canada, Belgium, Denmark, France, Great Britain, Iceland, Italy, Luxembourg, the Netherlands, Norway, Portugal, and the United States. NATO is a collective defense alliance. Article 5 of the Treaty sets forth: "The Parties agree that an armed attack against one or more of them in Europe or in North America shall be considered an attack against them all." The Alliance was from time to time expanded. New members admitted were: 1952 Greece and Turkey; 1955 the Federal Republic of Germany and Spain; and in March 1999 Poland, the Czech Republic, and Hungary. At its 50th anniversary celebration April 23-25, 1999, the representatives of NATO's 19 member states as well as from countries applying for membership met in Washington. The Alliance has proven to be the most reliable guaranty for security in Europe and in North America.]

[Transl: In a ceremony at the White House on March 29, 2004, 7 countries that were previously under Soviet rule or part of the Warsaw Pact were admitted as new members of the North Atlantic Treaty Organization—Bulgaria, Estonia, Latvia, Lithuania, Romania, Slovakia, and Slovenia. Thereby, NATO expanded to 26 member states.]

[From the end of May until the end of July, my wife and I spent our summer vacation in Innsbruck, Austria.]

Innsbruck, June 2, 1989

The Visit to Europe Was a Success

President Bush returned to Washington today from his seven day visit to Europe with stops in Rome, Brussels, Bonn, and London. The visit to Europe was a success. Bush could strengthen the cooperation with the European allies and retake the initiative of the West by his disarmament proposal.

After the meeting of the NATO member states in Brussels, he immediately went to Bonn. Chancellor Helmut Kohl accompanied his guest on a tour boat up the Rhine River to Mainz. In the Rheingoldhalle in Mainz, Bush made a declaration of principle. He strengthened the German-American friendship and conceded to the Federal Republic a leading role within the Western Alliance. He repeated Reagan's demand to tear down the Berlin Wall and expressed his view that Glasnost should also apply to East Germany. Calling attention to the Austrian-Hungarian border, where at this time the barbed wire is being removed, he called on the countries along the Iron

Curtain to do likewise and encouraged them to continue the started process of democratization.

Innsbruck, June 4, 1989

The Massacre

Despite the news blackout, reports are currently coming through on the European and Austrian news services of the unrests in Peking. The demonstrations on Tiananmen Square have not ceased. Following the confusion in the last several days, the hard-liners within the Chinese government have obviously won the upper hand. The military was ordered to use force. The consequences of this drastic action are worse than one can imagine. Today, a massacre took place on Tiananmen Square when units of the People's Army shot indiscriminately into the crowd of demonstrators. Armored vehicles moved scurrying through the city and opened fire on defenseless civilians. News agencies tell of thousands of wounded and casualties. Similar to the "Prague Spring" of 1968, the call for more freedom was brutally crushed. Thus, the reform movement in China, which began so full of hope, and its opening to the world have come to an abrupt end.

Innsbruck, June 7, 1989

Signs of Disintegration

The world community is following the events in China with dismay and incomprehension. The reports of the reckless action by the army against defenseless civilians, of an indescribable chaos, of foreigners fleeing Peking appear in quick succession. Is China at the brink of a civil war? Assumptions are growing stronger that units of the People's Army are shooting at each other. The political leadership is in such disarray that doubts have arisen about its ability to govern. One thing is certain: This gigantic empire, where one fifth of mankind lives, will not be the same again after these events. Until now, one could not have imagined how world Communism would one day end. The events in China, the Soviet Union, and in the Communist countries in Eastern Europe show signs of internal disintegration. Suddenly, it is becoming clear that world Communism is nearing its end. Its end is coming about not by intervention from outside but by a rapidly spreading disintegration from inside. Gorbachev's reform initiative in the Soviet Union gave the impetus. In the entire Communist sphere of influence a reform movement toward democracy has been set in motion, which cannot be stopped anymore.

Innsbruck, June 12 and 13, 1989

Gorbachev in Bonn

The state visit of Mikhail Gorbachev in Bonn has brought a decisive turnabout in German-Soviet relations. Gorbachev is presently received in the Federal Republic with such ecstatic enthusiasm that one could speak of a "Gobi Mania." High hopes are placed on his reform course. Not only is an easing of tensions in the dialogue with the Soviet Union being expected of the meeting between Gorbachev and Chancellor Kohl but in the long run also a solution of the German question. Not without reason, the key to the solution of the German question is expected to be in Moscow. But how far is Gorbachev willing to go, or how far can he dare to go without pushing East Germany into the defensive and thereby destabilizing the East Bloc? Gorbachev is assuming a cautious attitude. He wishes to bring about a political reorganization of Europe—to dissolve the two power blocs (Warsaw Pact and NATO) and to bring Eastern and Western Europe closer together. At the moment though, he needs the economic cooperation of the Federal Republic in order to be able to carry out Perestroika, his economic restructuring program.

Innsbruck, June 16, 1989

Rehabilitated

A rare drama is being played out in Hungary. The former Prime Minister Imre Nagy and his followers are given a solemn state funeral. After the suppression of Hungarian uprising in November of 1956, they had been arrested, finally executed in 1958 and buried in a mass grave. The rehabilitation of Imre Nagy after 33 years means a revival of his reform course as well as resuming the goals of the Hungarian Revolution of 1956. Just as Nagy had done at the time, the new government in Budapest supports liberal economic reforms and a multi-party system. There are also talks of Hungary possibly leaving the Warsaw Pact and of neutralization. With a certain anxiety one may ask whether this time around the reforms and surprisingly fast development toward democracy will succeed. Heartwrenching are the pictures from Budapest where thousands of people are laying wreaths at the bier of Imre Nagy. This day means for Hungary a reconciliation with a national tragedy.

Innsbruck, June 26, 1989

The EC Summit

Decisive issues of European integration are being discussed at the present summit of the European Community (EC) in Madrid. It is about introducing a common European currency and the authority of a central European government. While introducing a single European currency has moved within the range of possibility, establishing a central European government remains a long-term objective hardly to be realized. Centuries-old traditions of the nation states stand in the way of establishing a central federal government. A confederate Europe of the fatherlands is more likely to be imagined.

June 26, 1989

Austria's Letter to Brussels

Today, the two major political parties, SPÖ (Sozialistische Partei Österreichs—Socialist Party of Austria) and ÖVP (Österreichische Volkspartei—Austrian People's Party), have reached an agreement that is of vital interest for the country. It addresses Austria's joining the European Community. In a letter to Brussels applying for membership, it is specified that joining the EC should not impair Austria's neutrality status. Furthermore, the limitations for foreigners to acquire land and real estate have to be upheld. The forthcoming negotiations on Austria's entry into the EC will have to decide on the most important matter the country had to deal with since the State Treaty of 1955. Yet before Austria definitely joins the EC, a referendum has to be held.

Innsbruck, July 11, 1989

The Environmental Disaster

A major environmental disaster is beginning to show in the Northern Adriatic Sea. From Venice to Ancona along the well-known beaches of the Emilia Romagna—Milano Maritima, Cervia, Rimini, Riccione and Senigallia—, the sludgy carpet of the so-called "Algae Plague" has been spreading. Authorities have discouraged going into the water, for the sludge is not only unsavory but also detrimental to health. Therewith, life on the Adriatic beaches has come to a virtual standstill, which does enormous economic damage to the entire region. The rank growth of the algae was caused by the industrial waste water in the Po River, which, across the wide Delta of the Po between Venice and Ravenna, flow directly into the Adriatic Sea. Added to it is the high quantity of fertilizers, which also flows as waste water into the sea. If no emergency actions are taken, the Adriatic is in danger of dying off.

Innsbruck, July 12, 1989

President Bush in Budapest

In his speech today at the Karl Marx Business University in Budapest, President Bush gave the Hungarians encouragement. He congratulated the country on its present reform course and offered practical help. He advocated a free market economy and promised Hungary most-favored-nation status. The United States will support Hungary as soon as the prerequisites for private investments are in place. He offered American support in mastering environmental protection. Also, a cultural exchange between the United States and Hungary was suggested. Yet altogether, the American aid Bush had promised was modest and without much commitment.

[On their way to the G-7 summit, which on the occasion of the Bicentennial of the French Revolution in 1989 took place in Paris, President Bush and his staff went first to Warsaw and Budapest to see for themselves how far the reform movements had been spreading. What they saw in Poland and Hungary was much more advanced than they had assumed. But Bush and his team of advisers proceeded cautiously in order not to provoke hard-liners in the Communist regimes to take precipitate actions. The events on Tiananmen Square were a warning. See George Bush and Brent Scowcroft, *A World Transformed* (New York: Vintage Books, 1999, pp. 112-131). Brent Scowcroft was National Security Advisor in the Bush Administration.]

Innsbruck, July 14, 1989

Le bicentenaire

In a gigantic show of superlatives, France is celebrating the "bicentenaire," the Bicentennial of the French Revolution with a big military parade from the Arc de Triomphe down the Champs-Elysées to the Place de la Concorde. The "bicentenaire" is a triumph for President Francois Mitterand. Besides the heads of state and government of the G-7 summit meeting of the seven leading industrial nations, also 20 heads of state from the francophone African countries participated in the celebrations. Paris has become richer by several more landmarks. Among them are the new Opera House on the Place de la Bastille as well as the glass pyramid, designed by I. Ming Pei, at the entrance to the Louvre. Nearly a million people lined the Champs-Elysées to watch the fantastic parade. The "grand spectacle" lasted until midnight. Unforgettable remains the impression of Jesse Norman with her powerful voice singing the Marseillaise. It was France's day which the world joined to celebrate.

The storming of the Bastille on July 14, 1789 occurred 13 years after the American Declaration of Independence. The American War of Independence from 1776 to 1783 had its influence on the events in Paris. The French Revolution was an event of great impact on world history. It was the turn of an era whose effects have been felt for the past 200 years and are still being felt today. The heads of state and government at the G-7 summit meeting (Canada, the Federal Republic of Germany, France, Great Britain, Italy, Japan, and the United States) signed today, on the 200th anniversary of the beginning of the French Revolution in Paris, a declaration. They committed themselves once more to uphold human rights. The G-7 summit meeting referred especially to the events in Eastern Europe.

Innsbruck, July 19, 1989

A Europe Whole and Free

As he had shown in last year's presidential election campaign, George Bush was never much inclined toward great visions of the future. But the recent events in the East Bloc countries also thrust on him visions of a future free Europe. In his speech at Leyden in the Netherlands, he foresaw "a Europe whole and free," a new world that is near at hand. He predicted: "The Europe behind the wall will join its neighbors to the West, prosperous and free," (See *Herald Tribune,* July 18, 1989.)

Note

[Toward the end of the 1980s, two concepts of a future Europe were facing each other: Mikhail Gorbachev stood up for a Bloc-free, largely demilitarized

Europe, in which the Communist and democratic countries would live peacefully side by side. As he had emphasized in his address to the Council of Europe in Strasbourg on July 6, 1989, both political systems should have room in a common house of Europe. Contrary to this concept, George Bush insisted on "a Europe whole and free" under the protection of NATO. The dynamic political developments at the end of 1989 and at the beginning of 1991 were unstoppably moving in the direction of the latter solution.]

Lucerne, Switzerland, July 29, 1989

The Old World and the New

A bigger contrast can hardly be imagined than staying overnight in Lucerne before flying and landing in Chicago the next day.

Lucerne, the magnificent old town in Central Switzerland, still rests comfortably in the Middle Ages. One walks in a reflective mood on covered wooden bridges from the 14th and 15th centuries across the Reuss River. The Kapellbrücke (Chapel Bridge) with its historic panel paintings and the massive Wasserturm (Water Tower) are the landmarks of the city. The old Rathaus (City Hall) with its picturesque Renaissance facade looks over the Kornmarkt (grain market), where lively small trade activities have been flourishing from time immemorial. The small excursion boats cruise leisurely on the Vierwaldstätter See (Lake Lucerne). Everything here is measured in small sizes with painstaking exactness. The ambiance is inducing to walking and quiet contemplation. City and landscape form together a magic idyll. In the evening, the illuminated circular old city wall and fortified towers leave the impression of a beautiful fairyland.

Arriving in Chicago, one enters a vibrant city of several million people with its fascinating skyline. Also Chicago has a water tower as a landmark. But the Gothic Revival structure of the Water Tower, which had been spared in the fire of 1871, stands as a unique relic on the Water Tower Place surrounded by skyscrapers. Incessant traffic moves over the drawbridge across the Chicago River. The grain market of Chicago has developed into the largest of its kind in the world. Lake Michigan has its harbor and industrial zone along the South Shore, but it extends to the North into a sheer endless nature scenery. Excursion boats have long been discontinued. Measures appear there oversized. The rhythm of life is already oriented toward the 21st century.

When one experiences Lucerne and Chicago immediately one after the other, the difference between the Old World and the New could not be more striking.

South Bend, August 10, 1989

Voyager 2 is Approaching Neptune

After a 12 year journey through space, the spacecraft Voyager 2 is approaching Neptune, the outermost of the four giant planets in the solar system. Voyager 2 had flown by Jupiter in 1979, Saturn in 1981, and Uranus in January 1986 [see entry of January 22, 1986], sending pictures back to Earth. Now, also pictures of Neptune are expected. Neptune's distance from Earth is on average 4.5 billion km, or 2.8 billion mi. Radio signals from Voyager 2 near Neptune take about 4 hours to reach Earth. While Neptune's revolution around the Sun takes 165 years, the planet rotates every 16 hours.

[Saturday], August 26, 1989

Neptune Fever

Not since the landing on the Moon 20 years ago, has a space program stirred up such enthusiasm as the pictures, which the spacecraft Voyager 2 is sending from Neptune back to Earth. A real Neptune fever has broken out. In the night of Thursday to Friday, Voyager 2 flew by close to the North Pole of Neptune and then aimed at Triton, Neptune's largest Moon. The pictures which are now televised by the Jet Propulsion Laboratory are indeed exciting. Even the scientists at the ground station reacted with outbursts of enthusiasm. Neptune appeared on television screens as a blue, cold planet (temperatures of—353 degrees F, or—214 degrees C), on which a powerful storm is raging. The planet has a thin atmosphere mostly of methane. The Moon Triton showed active volcanoes. Furthermore, 6 new moons and 5 rings that orbit Neptune were discovered. Voyager 2 is now continuing its journey beyond the solar system. The spacecraft carries with it a gold-plated disc with images of Earth and signals of our civilization. Looking into the far distant future, it carries the hope with it that, on the timeless travel of Voyager 2 through interstellar space, these images and signals will be picked up by another civilization. The fact that Voyager 2 sent images of Neptune back to Earth and has reached the outer limits of our solar system, may explain the extraordinary excitement about this successful enterprise. The precision and technical achievement of the Voyager program are indeed astonishing. It is a major scientific achievement which has tremendously increased our knowledge of the solar system.

[Transl: On the launch of the spacecrafts Voyager 1 and 2 in 1977 and the gold-plated disc they carry, see entry above of November 15, 1980.]

South Bend, Saturday, September 2, 1989

Seeking Refuge

A wave of people from the East has again been set in motion, seeking refuge in the West. At this time, thousands of people from East Germany are fleeing through Hungary to Austria. Since Hungary lifted the Iron Curtain in May, it has become easier to cross the border to Austria. From Austria, refugees are brought by train and buses to West Germany, where they can automatically claim citizenship. Over this weekend, about 15,000 to 20,000 people are expected to cross the Austrian border. They are citizens of the German Democratic Republic or East Germany, who are vacationing in Hungary and are now taking advantage of the opportunity to flee to the West.

September 10, 1989

The Way to Freedom

Today, shortly after midnight local time, the Hungarian government allowed 5,000 East German refugees, who had been retained in camps in Budapest, to leave. They did not wait until dawn, but got moving right away to the Austrian border, their faces still marked by fear and despair. With the time difference, these pictures could be seen in America on the 10 p.m. evening news. Heart-wrenching scenes have played out, which prove once more what freedom means when you don't have it.

What is happening these days, is the largest exodus from East Germany since the Berlin Wall was erected 28 years ago. By its intransigence not to allow reforms to take place, the East German regime is pushing itself into isolation within the East Bloc.

South Bend, September 30, 1989

The exodus from East Germany is widening and becoming more grotesque. Presently, about 3,000 East German refugees are waiting in cramped conditions in the Embassy of the Federal Republic of Germany in Prague for permission to depart to the West. Foreign Minister Hans-Dietrich Genscher was able, apparently through Soviet mediation at the United Nations, to obtain permission for the East German refugees to leave Prague. In the meantime, also the Embassy of the Federal Republic in Warsaw has become an asylum for East German refugees.

October 1, 1989

The news has just come through that tonight at 2:50 a.m. local time a train with 800 East German refugees on board left Warsaw in the direction of the Federal Republic. The exit was achieved by a rare agreement between NATO and the Warsaw Pact.

South Bend, October 7, 1989

A Historic Decision

This weekend, the Communist Party of Hungary made a historic decision. It dissolved itself and changed into a Western-style Socialist Party. For the first time, a Communist Party in the East Bloc ceased to exist. At the same time, the way was prepared for free democratic elections. This courageous course of action will not remain without effect on the other Warsaw Pact countries. The need to carry out domestic reforms cannot be stopped in the long run.

October 10, 1989

The reaction of the East German regime to the mass exodus of its citizens was foreseeable. The borders have again been closed and measures against demonstrators tightened up. There were protest rallies in East Berlin, Dresden and Leipzig where about 70,000 people took to the streets. Despite the tense situation, the government did not resort to drastic measures. Fortunately, there was no bloodshed.

Note

[The talk, which Honecker had with the Chinese deputy prime minister in East Berlin, shows how serious and dangerous the situation was. Honecker compared the mass rallies in East Germany to those on Tiananmen Square and hinted that the demonstrators could meet with a similar fate. See Bush/Scowcroft, *A World Transformed*, p. 147.]

Addendum

[Erich Honecker resigned on October 18, 1989. His successor Egon Krenz took charge of the affairs of the German Democratic Republic which was already in a process of disintegrating.]

South Bend, October 25, 1989

Where is It Leading to?

In a remarkable speech before the Supreme Soviet, Foreign Minister Eduard Shevardnadze announced that the Soviet Union will close its military bases on foreign soil and withdraw to her borders by the year 2,000. Furthermore, he said that the Soviet Union will not interfere in domestic affairs of neighboring countries—Poland, the German Democratic Republic, and Hungary—and will leave it up to their own free decision, which political future they wish to choose. This is a clear renunciation of the Brezhnev Doctrine, which demanded that Warsaw Pact countries take military action also against a member state if Communism should be threatened by reform movements. Once the fear of Russian tanks is taken away from the public, the reform movements leading toward democracy in the East Bloc countries cannot be stopped anymore.

October 27, 1989

Confidence in the Reunification

As farsighted statesman, President Bush expressed his view on the possibility of reuniting East and West Germany. While the German reunification gives rise to reservation and fear in West European countries, above all in France and Great Britain, Bush has no objections. On the contrary, he showed confidence in the reunification, which he sees coming as part of the present democratic movement in Eastern Europe. Bush is convinced that a reunited Germany as a democratic state will remain faithful to the principles of the Western Alliance. [Interview in *The New York Times*, weekend edition, October 25-27, 1989.]

November 4, 1989

Berlin, Alexanderplatz

Approximately, a million people moved today in East Berlin to the Alexanderplatz. They demand more democracy and freedom. It was the largest demonstration in the 40-year history of the German Democratic Republic. At the same time, about 6,000 of its citizens fled again via Prague to West Germany. In the turbulence of these events that follow one another in rapid succession, much patience is being demanded of the people in East and West. There is the undeniable danger of civil war, whose consequences can hardly be imagined.

South Bend, [Thursday], November 9, 1989

The Wall is Falling

The news spread here like wildfire this afternoon: The East German government announced that unrestricted entry and exit between the German Democratic Republic and the Federal Republic of Germany come into immediate effect. This practically means the end of the Berlin Wall. At first, it was incomprehensible, then one was moved by its historic significance, and finally, erupting in jubilation, the news took hold of both parts of Germany and the world.

November 10, 1989

Who would ever have thought that the Cold War would end with a dance on the Berlin Wall. Shortly before midnight jubilation erupted that has not ended until now. Thousands of people climbed on top of the Wall and had, like at a big New Year's party, corks of champagne bottles pop into the air. Suddenly the dam had burst, an unswerving stream of people set in motion from East to West Berlin and flowed over the Kurfürstendamm. With astonishment, they looked at the Western part of the city from which they had been shut out for 28 years. They just were looking, frequently with tears in their eyes; they met relatives, West and East Berliners just embraced each other. They returned to the Eastern section of the city with the feeling that the division is over once and for all.

With hammer, chisel, pick axe, or even with bare hands, people tried to tear down the Wall, or to take with them a memento of its dark past. Television channels in America are reporting without pause about the events in Berlin. A wave of sympathy for the German people has been spreading in America. One hopes for a fast democratization of East Germany and assumes that reunification will follow as a matter of course.

November 12, 1989

On this historic weekend, about 3 million people have crossed the border from East to West Germany. Heartbreaking scenes of encounters occurred when families, who could not see each other for almost 30 years, met again. There could not have been a better demonstration that these people from East and West belong together. But most surprising is the fact that the Communist propaganda, which had incessantly pounded the population in East Germany for forty years, suddenly dissolved like a burst bubble into nothing.

South Bend, November 16, 1989

Lech Walesa before the U.S. Congress

Lech Walesa was greeted by a joint session of Congress with roaring applause. By his courageous course of action as leader of the independent Solidarity Trade Union, Walesa had overcome Communism in Poland. He is celebrated as hero of the liberation movement in Eastern Europe. It is for the first time in 165 years that a private person has been invited to speak before a joint session of Congress. Before Walesa, this honor was granted to Marquis de Lafayette, the hero of the American War of Independence, in 1824.

November 27, 1989

Prague 1989

How deep-seated the desire for freedom and democracy is in the Czechoslovak population becomes apparent these days. Hundreds of thousands are moving again to the Wenceslas Square in Prague. They are not to be satisfied until the present Communist regime resigns and free elections are guaranteed. The call for Alexander Dubcek is getting louder as if it were needed to catch up on what was crushed by brutal force in 1968.

November 28, 1989

10 Point Program for German Unity

Chancellor Helmut Kohl presented today to the Bundestag in Bonn a 10 point program for German unity. Accordingly, free democratic elections should be held in the German Democratic Republic, economic reforms started, and finally preparations made for reunification.

[Beginning of December], 1989

The Berlin Wall Memorial on the Campus of Westminster College in Fulton, Missouri. (Photo taken by the author in August 1999)

The Relief

For those among us who have lived through the second half of the 20th century, gradually realizing that the Iron Curtain has fallen and that the Cold

War ended without military confrontation is a liberating relief, how later generations will hardly be able to imagine.

[Beginning of December], 1989

The Berlin Wall as Souvenir

In shopping malls across America, pieces of the Berlin Wall are sold as souvenirs. The price runs $10.00 a piece. They are handed out wrapped and with a warranty to make sure that these pieces of concrete and plaster are genuine. They sell well. Why are people buying them? They buy them in part out of a craving for sensation, but also because they desire to have a token in their hands of an extraordinary historical event.

A Piece of the Berlin Wall in the Middle of America

[A big junk of the Berlin Wall stands on the grounds of Westminster College in Fulton, Missouri, about 100 miles west of St Louis. How this large piece of the Berlin Wall has come to Fulton, is preceded by a long story. Westminster College established in 1937 the John Findley Green Foundation Lectures, which invite annually a prominent speaker to address a topic of international interest. Winston Churchill was invited for the year 1946. As the renowned College was located in his home state, President Harry S. Truman supported the invitation and promised Churchill that he would accompany him to Fulton and introduce him for the lecture. The speech, which Winston Churchill delivered at Westminster College on March 5, 1946, titled "The Sinews of Peace," entered post-war history as the "Iron Curtain Speech." Churchill was addressing audiences in America and in Europe. He called attention to the great danger that was threatening peace. His speech culminated in the sentence: "From Stettin in the Baltic to Trieste in the Adriatic, an iron curtain has descended across the Continent." And he pointed out that the historic capitals of Central and Eastern Europe lay behind that line. Churchill's speech was covered by the news media on both sides of the Atlantic. From then on, the expression "Iron Curtain" has become common usage, synonymous for the Cold War. In memory of that historic speech, Westminster College established at the beginning of the 1960s the Winston Churchill Memorial and Library.

The sculptress Edwina Sandys, a granddaughter of Winston Churchill who lived in New York, had decided immediately after the fall of the Berlin Wall to erect a monument in honor of her grandfather on the campus of Westminster College. She obtained permission to select from the remains of the Wall eight graffiti-sprayed sections that were near the Brandeburg Gate. Those eight concrete slabs, weighing 16 tons, were shipped to her studio in Long Island City in Queens, New York. The silhouettes of a male and female figure were cut out of the "11-foot-high by 32-foot-long" and "8-inch-thick" slabs. Edwin Sandys called her monumental sculpture "Breakthrough," symbolizing how the Wall was overcome. "Breakthrough" was installed on the campus of Westminster College next to the statue of Winston Churchill. It was dedicated and made accessible to the public in a ceremony on November 9, 1990, the first anniversary of the fall of the Berlin Wall. This large piece of the Berlin Wall now stands in the middle of America, almost ghostlike in sharp contrast to its idyllic surroundings, as a haunting testimony of a dark past.]

Note

[I am indebted to Mr. John Hensley, Curator-Archivist of the Winston Churchill Memorial and Library for the information on how the Churchill speech of March 5, 1946 at Westminster College came about, and on how "Breakthrough," the section of the Berlin Wall sculpted by Edwina Sandys was installed.]

South Bend, December 10, 1989

Prague

Today, on the Human Rights Day of the United Nations, Czechoslovakia achieved, for the first time in 40 years, a government, in which the Communists are in the minority. This strengthens the awareness that the days of repression, of flagrant disregard of human rights by a police state based on Marxist doctrine are finally over.

South Bend, December 18, 1989

Romania

The Ceausescu regime in Romania stubbornly refuses to give up its Stalinist course. Using brutal force, over the weekend demonstrators were indiscriminately shot at. The number of fatalities could go into the hundreds if not thousands. In spite of it, also in Romania the movement for democracy cannot be stopped anymore.

December 22, 1989

Nicolae Ceausescu Resigns

Following the bloody conflicts in Timisoara and Bucharest, Nicolae Ceausescu resigned. Ceausescu and his wife Elena fled in haste from the government palace. Although Ceausescu had gone his own willful way within the East Bloc, as Stalinist he has ruled Romania with a tight grip since 1965. How brutal and dictatorial his regime has been, has still to be uncovered. At this time, the supporters of Ceausescu and the liberation army in Bucharest are confronting each other in bloody street battles. The events in Romania serve as a warning example for what could have happened in the other East Bloc countries. The more surprising is the "velvet revolution," which, in recent months, has spread all over Eastern Europe and moved without bloodshed in the direction of democracy.

December 23, 1989

The world community has learned with horror that at the massacre in Timisoara about 4,500 people lost their lives. Outside the city, the bodies, among them women and children, were found in open mass graves. They were mercilessly shot down by rounds of machine gun fire. [*The New York Times,* front page, December 23, 1989.]

December 25, 1989

Christmas in Romania

Despite the civil war and the confusion throughout the country, Christmas trees were lit in Romania. Christmas was celebrated in public, which, for decades, had only been possible to do in secret.

Washington, D.C., December 30, 1989

The MLA Annual Convention

[The Modern Language Association of America (MLA), founded in 1883, is the most important professional association for the modern languages in America. The MLA Annual Convention takes place each year from December

27-30. With 8,000 to 10,000 participants, it is the largest convention for the modern languages in the world. I attended several MLA Annual Conventions and occasionally wrote reports on them in the *Neueren Sprachen* (Frankfurt, Diesterweg). The MLA Annual Convention is not an international congress. It is primarily dealing with problems of teaching modern languages and literatures in North America. The numerous lectures and short 20 minute presentations address any conceivable theme of modern language teaching and research. The MLA Annual Convention operates a Job Information Center for scheduled interviews; it also gives room to large exhibits of newly published books in the field of modern languages and literatures. In teaching foreign languages in the United States, Spanish has by far the highest enrollment, followed by French and German. Italian, Russian, Japanese and Chinese come thereafter. My wife and I participated in the MLA Annual Convention 1989, which took place in Washington, D.C., December 27-30. My book, *Jason's Voyage: The Search for the Old World in American Literature,* which had appeared in the fall of 1989 at Peter Lang in New York, was put on display by the publisher.]

Washington is giving more and more the impression of a real capital, although its character of being strictly a government administration center has been maintained. The city renewal of the past ten years has given Washington a refreshing face-lift. The old and the new museums attract millions of visitors every year from all over the world. Also, the impression has increased that one is in the center of a world power.

December 31, 1989

The Year of Liberation 1989

The liberation of Eastern Europe from Communist dictatorship was like opening a big prison. It should never be forgotten that gaining freedom was the highest aspiration and greatest good to achieve in the extensive democracy movement of this eventful year.

EPILOGUE

(The dates of entries for references to passages in the text that are relevant to the topics discussed are given in parentheses.)

The entries in this Diary begin in 1961, the year when the Berlin Wall was erected, and they end in 1989 with the fall of the Berlin Wall. Events of the 1990s are also included in the following final reflections. It has been pointed out in the Foreword that the attention of what was written down was drawn to the following subjects: 1) The civil rights movement in the United States; 2) The European integration and questions of European security; 3) Space travel and exploration; and 4) The emerging common world civilization. Consciously, also my own immigration experience to the United States was recorded. Summing-up, a number of conclusions can be drawn from these observations.

After the fall of the Berlin Wall, German reunification was approached immediately. In a series of negotiations, the domestic and foreign policy conditions for unification were laid down. In the so-called "Two-plus-Four" Talks (the two German States, plus the United States, the USSR, Great Britain, and France) the foreign policy issues of German unification were discussed. Decisive for reunification was the State Treaty on creating a common currency as well as a common economic and social order, on which the Federal Republic of Germany and the German Democratic Republic had agreed. The Treaty was signed in Bonn on May 18 and went into effect on July 1, 1990. Thereby, the German Democratic Republic accepted the free, democratic form of government under the "Grundgesetz," the basic constitutional law of the Federal Republic. The German Democratic Republic was dissolved on October 3, 1990, and, at the same time, the German unification completed.

The Civil Rights Movement in the United States

To assume that the racial issue in America has been completely solved would mean to expect too much. The misery of the ghettos in the inner cities still persists and the evil spirit of racial prejudices has not been totally overcome. But on the other hand, it would mean to close one's eyes if one would not acknowledge the great progress that has been made since the civil rights legislation of 1964. The Civil Rights Act of July 3, 1964 guaranteed the African American minority as well as minorities in general legal equality in American society. Racial discrimination as it was still practiced at the beginning of the 1960s belongs definitely to the past. Racial conflicts have decidedly been defused since the end of the 1970s. In the meantime, a considerable, well educated African American middle class has been formed, whose members can be seen in all professions and positions. The racial issue in America has not been solved completely but mastered to a large extent. I pointed out in 1964 that the America of the future can only be imagined as an integrated society (07-25-64). This holds true even more so at the beginning of the 21st century.

The European Integration

By my encounter with America, it had become clear to me early on that Europe would inevitably fall behind if it should not be possible to realize the European integration (06-23-61). European integration has been a slow, step-by-step process that also had its setbacks.

The first impetus to European integration was given by Robert Schuman, who, as French foreign minister, established the European Coal and Steel Community (ECSC) in 1951. The ECSC consisted of six member states: France, the Federal Republic of Germany, Italy, and the three Benelux States—Belgium, the Netherlands, and Luxembourg. German-French cooperation was essential for the further development of European integration. By the Treaties of Rome in March of 1957, the ECSC was changed into the European Economic Community (EEC), also called the Common Market, and by merging with the European Atomic Energy Community formed the European Community (EC). In July 1959, Great Britain, Denmark, Norway, Portugal, and the neutral countries Austria, Sweden, and Switzerland united to establish the European Free Trade Association (EFTA) with the headquarters in Geneva. As a result, next to the EEC, a separate free trade zone was created in Western Europe. But the center of gravity for the development of European integration lay in the EC. From 1973 to 1986 the number of member states in the EC increased from 6 to 12. Great Britain joining the EC in 1973 was of historic significance (01-02-73). In the same year, Ireland and Denmark joined the EC; 1981 Greece became a member; Portugal and Spain followed in 1986. Thereby, the European Community reached the total number of 12 member states.

At the beginning of the 1990s, two essential steps were taken for the realization of European integration. By the Treaty of Maastricht in 1991, the EC was changed into the European Union (EU). The Maastricht Treaty went into effect on November 1, 1993. It stipulated the European economic union and a common European currency. In 1995, Finland, Austria, and Sweden were admitted to the EU, whereby the number of its member states increased to 15. The Schengener Agreement abolished, starting in March 1996, border controls in most EU countries. Extraordinary political will of cooperation was shown in introducing the common European currency. The wish of many years of having a common currency (07-beginning-77) was fulfilled by introducing the Euro on January 1, 2002.

The European integration is still facing big tasks ahead. It is about interior consolidation and at the same time exterior expansion. In regard to interior consolidation, the European Parliament as legislative body and the European Court of Justice should be strengthened so that their transnational, federal authority becomes more effective. In regard to exterior expansion, a number of associated countries in Central and Eastern Europe are waiting to be admitted to the EU. Among them are the three Baltic States—Lithuania, Latvia, and Estonia—, Poland, the Czech Republic, Slovania, Hungary, Romania, and Bulgaria. How large and effective will this new, united Europe be?

European Security—Breakup of the Soviet Union

During the decades of the Cold War, Western Europe was exposed to a dual danger: On the one hand, there was the danger from outside of being overrun by the Communist East; and on the other hand, the danger from inside of being undermined by Eurocommunism. The helplessness and powerlessness of the free Europe were painfully felt when the Berlin Wall was erected in 1961, and when Czechoslovakia was invaded in August, 1968 (08-21-68). The Warsaw Pact States were far superior to the West in conventional weapons. The defense of Western Europe depended to a large extent, within the framework of NATO, on the nuclear protection by the United States.

The social upheavals, wild demonstrations and strikes in Western Europe in the 1960s and '70s destabilized the Western democratic governments. Especially alarming were the Italian parliamentary elections of June 1976, for Communism was standing at the door (06-15 and 23-76). A Communist government in Italy could have been a great worry to the Atlantic Alliance. The East had intended to dissolve NATO and to disconnect Western Europe from America. Following that, Moscow would have had an easy going in getting the whole of Europe under its sphere of influence. It did not happen. As a collective defense alliance, NATO proved to be very steadfast.

Having her SS-20 intermediate-range missiles targeted at Western Europe, the Soviet Union could have put Western Europe under pressure. The Council of NATO Ministers demonstrated, above all upon insistence by Margaret Thatcher, strength of purpose, when it decided on December 12, 1979 to go ahead to upgrade nuclear armament in Western Europe (12-22-79). Moscow was obviously convinced that the Western democracies would not be able to endure the resistance of the peace movement against the deployment of the Pershing II missiles (10-11 and 25-81). A gigantic struggle for the soul of Europe ensued, which finally ended in favor of the West.

The Berlin Wall was not only the horrifying reality of the divided city but also the symbol of the divided Germany and the divided Europe. Until late into the 1980s, it had not been possible to imagine when and how the tragedy of the divided Europe would one day end. During the decades of the Cold War, one continuously lived in the not unfounded fear that a nuclear war could break out. The great historic turning point came toward the end of the 1980s and at the beginning of the '90s, when the liberation movements in Eastern Europe tore down the Iron Curtain and brought the Cold War to an end.

The monumental sculpture "Breakthrough," which Edwina Sandys created from large slabs of the dismantled Berlin Wall, stands on the campus of Westminster College in Fulton, Missouri (12-beginning-89). It has many-sided meanings. The breakthrough in bringing down the Berlin Wall and ending the Cold War took place on several levels over a number of years. The human rights catalogue of the final accords of the Helsinki Agreement of 1975 proved to be a time fuse (03-beginning-77). The voices demanding more freedom could not be silenced anymore. Lech Walesa and the independent Solidarity Trade Union gave the impetus to overcome Communism in Poland. The historic first pastoral pilgrimage of John Paul II to his homeland Poland in June of 1979 had its effect throughout the entire East (06-10-79). The meeting of Ronald Reagan with Mikhail Gorbachev in Geneva in November, 1985, was the great historic moment for ending the Cold War. From Geneva, a direct way led, despite the misunderstandings in Reykjavik in October of 1986, to the summit meeting in Washington at the beginning of December, 1987, when the INF Treaty was signed (12-08-87). That was a milestone in nuclear disarmament, for an entire class of nuclear weapons was eliminated by the two superpowers. Intermediate-range missiles were dismantled on both sides of the Iron Curtain, whereby the danger of a nuclear war was substantially reduced.

The fall of the Berlin Wall was the bursting of the dam that could not be stopped anymore. In 1990-91, the democracy movement took hold of all the countries in the East Bloc from the Baltic to the Black Sea; it also spilled over into the Soviet Union. With "Perestroika" and "Glasnost," Gorbachev had encouraged restructuring and the liberation movement, but he could not control anymore the forces he had unleashed. In the second half of 1991, the events that led to the break-up of the Soviet Union followed in rapid succession. In the first free election on June 13, 1991, Boris Yeltsin was elected with a vast majority president of the Russian Republic, by far the largest Republic of the Soviet Union. On August 19, 1991, hard-core Communists carried out a coup. When Gorbachev was put under house arrest on the Crimea by the insurgents, the world held its breath. It was feared that the Soviet Union could fall back to the dark age of Stalinism. At that moment, Boris Yeltsin stood up in front of the Duma Building in Moscow, rallied the resistance to the insurgents, confronted the advancing tanks, and persuaded the troops to withdraw. The coup collapsed as fast as it had been instigated.

After the coup, Gorbachev remained isolated in the Kremlin, while power shifted more and more to Boris Yeltsin. Tendencies to separate from the Soviet Union were let to take their course. After the referendum of December 2, 1991, in which 92% of the Ukrainian electorate had voted for independence, the Ukraine separated from the Soviet Union. At the conference on December 21, 1991, in Alma-Ata, the capital of Kazakhstan, the Soviet Union under the leadership of Boris Yeltsin was, after 75 years in existence, dissolved. On December 25, Gorbachev resigned as president of a state that actually did not exist anymore. The Soviet Union had imploded, collapsing under its own weight. The former republics of the Soviet Union joined Russia in forming the loosely binding Commonwealth of Independent States.

With the end of Communism in Eastern Europe and in Russia, a new world situation has emerged which has also profoundly changed the question of security in Europe. When Poland, the Czech Republic, and Hungary were admitted to NATO in 1999, the three most important countries in Eastern Central Europe, committed to the principles of democracy, were integrated into the Western Defense Alliance. There was no danger anymore that Western Europe would be overrun from the East. But different questions of security have arisen. Nonetheless, as before, the North Atlantic Defense Alliance remains the best guarantee for European security. However, the European Union should do more for its own protection and speak with one voice more effectively in foreign politics.

Space Travel and Exploration

The development of manned and unmanned space travel and exploration was the exciting, fascinating event of the second half of the 20th century. Manned space travel began with Yuri Gagarin, who, as the first human, orbited Earth on April 12, 1961. John Glenn, Jr., followed, when he, as the first American astronaut, orbited Earth on February 20, 1962 (04-15-61). The goal of NASA's Apollo Program in the 1960s was to land on the Moon. Exciting and full of suspense was the moment when on December 24, 1968, Apollo 8 entered the far side of the Moon, losing radio contact with Earth, and then reappeared on the television screen (12-24-68). Fascinating was the image of the rising Earth in space seen from the Moon. The climax of the Apollo Program was reached when Apollo 11 landed on the Moon on July 20, 1969 (07-20-69). When Neil Armstrong, as the first human, set his foot on the surface of the Moon, the entire human race identified itself with him. One had the feeling of experiencing the beginning of a new age. There was jubilation and a whirl of excitement broke loose. The lunar landing was the most significant exploratory enterprise of the 20th century. The door was flung wide open for future manned space travels. The series of manned lunar landings was concluded with the flight of Apollo 17 at the beginning of December, 1972.

After completion of the Apollo Program, NASA was at first preoccupied with building the first American space station Skylab, which, however, was soon discontinued at the beginning of February 1974. Thereafter, NASA devoted its efforts to the Space Shuttle Program. Space shuttles provided carriers for space flights, which landed like an airplane on a runway and could be reused several times. On April 14, 1981, the first space shuttle Columbia made a picture book landing, gliding down on the runway of the Edwards Air Force Base in the Mojave Desert in Southern California (04-14-81). After landing, the Columbia was mounted on a Boeing 747 and flown back to Cape Canaveral, where it was prepared in the Kennedy Space Center for its next flight into space. The space shuttle proved to be an outstanding vehicle for supply delivery to the space station and other missions in space. The repair work by the space shuttle Endeavour of the space telescope Hubble at the beginning of December 1993 was a spectacular feat.

The Soviet Space agency put the space station MIR into orbit in 1986. In its 15 years of operation, MIR was a considerable success. In August 1999 MIR was put out of operation. When its orbit was finally lowered in March 2001, it burned out entering the atmosphere, while some smoldering parts splashed into the South Pacific. MIR was replaced by the International Space Station (ISS). The United States and Russia have cooperated in operating MIR as well as in building the new ISS. On October 31, 2000, a Soyuz spacecraft was launched from the Russian Baikonur cosmodrome in Kazakhstan, carrying two Russian cosmonauts and one American astronaut to the International Space Station. From then on, the ISS has been permanently occupied, orbiting Earth every 90 minutes. 16 nations are participating in the construction of the International Space Station.

Unmanned space exploration has been no less fascinating. When on October 4, 1957, the Soviet Union put the satellite Sputnik into orbit around Earth, it started a fierce competition between the United States and the Soviet Union in space exploration and for the control of space technology. While Russia landed probes on Venus, America remained focused on the exploration of the planet Mars. After a year long journey through space, the American space probe Viking 1 had a soft landing on Mars on July 20, 1976. The pictures sent back to Earth showed for the first time a landscape similar to that on Earth (07-20-76). This impression got even stronger when on July 4, 1997, the space probe Pathfinder landed on Mars. At that Mars landing, it was possible to set a robot in motion from Earth on another planet. The robot carried out mineral tests on rock samples. The wider panoramic view of the Martian landscape showed sand dunes, boulders, large rocks, hills and mountain ranges, as they can be seen on Earth. Time and again, the precision by which the team of scientists at the Jet Propulsion Laboratory in Pasadena, California, had planned and carried out this Mars mission, was astonishing.

At the same time, space probes traveled for many years through the outer solar system, flying by and exploring the planets Jupiter, Saturn, Uranus and Neptune. When after a 12 year journey through space, the end of August, 1989, the space probe Voyager 2 was approaching the planet Neptune, a veritable Neptune fever broke out (08-26-89). It was an exciting moment to experience how Voyager 2 reached the outer fringe of the solar system and was still capable of transmitting clear pictures back to Earth. Flying closely by Neptune, new moons and rings were discovered.

Space exploration did not only increase our knowledge of the solar system by leaps and bounds but it has also essentially changed the image of our planet Earth.

A Common World Civilization

After World War II great efforts were made, following a strong inner need, to promote understanding among peoples and to work for peace. It was a deep-felt need to reach out beyond one's own borders to get to know and understand other countries and different civilizations. Much good will has been spent on this endeavor. The many foreign studies programs of colleges and universities have been a significant part of this endeavor; also the many city partnerships across Europe and across the Atlantic have contributed to it. Private foundations and government programs made the exchange of students, teachers, scholars and artists possible. Especially intensive have been the efforts toward promoting better mutual understanding between America and Europe. The Fulbright Program has made an essential contribution to the transatlantic exchange of persons.

After having spent six months on research in the United States in 1961, moving from the East coast to California and back, I became keenly aware of a new international development—people from countries around the world, of different races and cultures coming together engaged in a dialogue. As I noted about these newly established international ties: "This is not just a fashion or ephemeral phase of our time, but is more akin to a tidal wave that will mold and shape mankind into a new form and way of existence" (09-17-61).

I saw great hope for the future in that development. Actually, international interaction has come about to an extent that would have been unimaginable at the beginning of the 1960s. Technology moved ahead of this development and has profoundly changed the modern way of living. Air travel, television and the Internet have brought the world closer together. Most effective were the revolutionary innovations in digital information technologies, initiated in Silicon Valley (12-24-86). Also, space exploration has created a new feeling of mankind belonging together as a whole.

Following the Western, American-European model, a common world civilization has originated, for which English has become the common language of communication. Besides the advantages of this new development, also drawbacks have shown up from early on. After flying from New York to Paris early June 1974, it came to my attention that the newly built Charles de Gaulle Airport in Paris was surprisingly similar to the John F. Kennedy Airport in New York. Air travel is only one example of an increasingly spreading conformity, which can be seen on highways, in the entertainment industry, and in supermarkets. Department stores in malls and shopping centers offer the same brand name articles worldwide. Globalization in its many fold structures is irreversible, a development that cannot be stopped anymore. Great efforts are needed to ease the tensions that have arisen and to create a common world in a humane spirit.

The Immigration Experience

Immigration is an elemental American experience shared by the vast majority of the American population. Although each immigration is an individual matter, it also includes elements of a collective experience. Thus, my own immigration experience has passed through stages which are also typical for the immigration to the United States in general. The decision to immigrate to America caused an immediate split of misunderstandings with family and friends in the home country (07-beginning-69). How could you leave such a beautiful place like Innsbruck and go to America? There were many answers to that question. First of all, my wife and I liked Notre Dame and felt attracted to America. When the University of Notre Dame offered me a professorship with tenure, we seized the opportunity to move here for good. Distancing or alienation from our home country has increased over the years. Not that we lost our love of our home country Austria, but we got out of touch with reality, while an idealized image of our old homeland took hold of our imagination.

This has been a common experience of immigration from Europe to America. A further consequence of immigration is the loss of one's native language. The ability to use one's own native language diminishes in the course of several years. In the inevitable pull of English, we noticed already after the first year living in America that our ability of expression or finding the right word in German was slowing down. Although we spoke German at home, our children who learned English fast in school conversed in English with each other (06-26-68). As a matter of fact, use of the native language diminishes in the second generation after immigration and disappears completely in the third generation. The decisive reorientation to American reality came at the moment of naturalization as U.S. citizen (06-29-82). However, complete adaptation to the American way of life may take years if not decades.

The stream of people from Europe has historically been the largest and culturally forming immigration to North America. According to a tabulation compiled for the Bicentennial in 1976, 46.7 million people immigrated to the United States from 1820-1974. Of these, 35.8 million came from Europe (01-18-76). To what extent are Americans aware of their European origin? The U.S. census 1980 not only registered foreign-born citizens and residents, but for the first time also ancestry awareness that may go back for several generations. Out of a total U.S. population of 226 million, about 215 million indicated that they were of European origin. That included single and multiple ancestry groups, meaning that a person could identify with one or more ethnic groups. There were nearly 50 European ethnic groups to choose from. The large ancestry groups with 900,000 or more persons showed the following data:

English (49.5 million); German (49.2 m); Irish (40.2 m); French (12.8 m); Italian (12.1 m); Scottish (10.0 m); Polish (8.2 m); Dutch (6.3 m); Swedish (4.3 m); Norwegian (3.4 m); Russian (2.7 m); Czech (1.8 m); Hungarian (1.7 m); Welsh (1.6 m); Danish (1.5 m); Portuguese (1.0 m); Swiss (981 thousand); Greek (959 thousand); Austrian (948 thousand).

[These data on foreign ancestry were provided to me by courtesy of the Bureau of the Census, U.S. Department of Commerce, Washington, D.C., in 1986.]

The records of the Ellis Island Immigration Museum indicate that the ties of Americans to families in Europe are of a more recent date. About 40% of the

American population can trace their origin to ancestors who had immigrated through Ellis Island (07-04-86). Newly updated records show that from 1892 to 1954 nearly 23 million people were processed at Ellis Island, most of whom had come from Europe.

The above quoted figures demonstrate that the awareness of European ancestry is astonishingly widespread among the American population. But the cultural ties with Europe go deeper than the immigration statistics would show. Americans consider it as a matter of course that they partake of the European cultural heritage. It is assumed quite naturally that it is also their heritage. Several entries in the diary refer to this natural attitude and desire for European culture (02-25-79 and 11-28-87). Works of the visual arts from Europe as well as literary manuscripts, first editions, and valuable collections, which were primarily acquired by private foundations, are being preserved in America with great care and touching dedication. At the many music schools of colleges and universities classical music is being cultivated more than one would generally expect. Liberal Arts colleges, whose tradition goes back to colonial times, have made the most essential contribution to the understanding of European art and literature in America.

The tales and novels of Henry James clearly show that Europe or the Old World has an illusory effect on the American psyche. The many Americans who go to Europe every year follow for the most part their ideal of the Old World. They are driven by the desire to see the great works of art in museums, they look for the idyllic, fairy tale landscape, stroll through the picturesque old cities and are guided through castles and palaces. The Jason figure of Thomas Wolfe pursues this journey through the historic cities and museums of the Old World—Bonn, Frankfurt, the Alte Pinakothek in Munich and the Kunsthistorisches Museum in Vienna—with a passion that cannot be explained by a tourist's interest alone. Wolfe saw the passionate desire of the traveling American in Europe related to the Jason myth and called it "blazoned with the Jason fire."

But will these strong bonds with Europe persist? In recent decades, a remarkable turning point in American immigration history has occurred. The predominant European immigration has been replaced by the immigration from Asia and Latin America. The U.S. census 2000 shows a considerable demographic shift in the ethnic-racial composition of the American population. The results of the census 2000 were made public on March 12,

2001. According to the tabulation of *The New York Times* of March 13, 2001, of a total U.S. population of 281.4 million 69.1% (194 m) were white, 12.1% (34 m) black, 12.5% (35 m) Hispanic, and 3.6% (10 m) Asian. While the portion of the white population decreased by 5% since the census 1990, that of the Hispanic increased by 3% and of the Asian by 0.8%. The portion of the African-American population remained the same. Surprising is the increase of the Hispanic population from 22.4 million in 1990 to 35 million in 2000. The American Population will soon reach the 300 million mark. Demographic calculations predict that in the coming decades the white and the non-white population in America will more and more balance each other. To a certain extent, the attitude toward Europe will inevitably change. But in my opinion, this change will not be far-reaching. American history is too closely connected with Europe that a fundamental change could take place.

The Atlantic Community

During World War II and in the following conflict with Communism, America and Europe have grown together to a "Schicksalsgemeinschaft," a community of fate. The reconstruction of the war-ravaged Europe was started by the European Recovery Program or Marshall Plan (06-05-87), which created the prerequisites for the closely interwoven economic cooperation across the Atlantic. As collective defense organization, NATO strengthened the Atlantic Alliance (05-29-89). The gigantic confrontation with Communism in the second half of the 20th century ended in favor of the West.

The Atlantic Community has been a new historical development after World War II. For nearly 200 years, since the Declaration of Independence in 1776, America and Europe held politically opposite views. It was the struggle of democracy and freedom against monarchy, tyranny and dictatorship. Before an Atlantic partnership could be formed, the idea of democracy had to be accepted in Europe and America had to overcome 150 years of isolation. The image of America in Europe has been highly ambivalent for centuries. It was more based on myth, utopia, and negative prejudices than reality. Only the extensive research in American history, literature, intellectual and social history in recent decades has led to a more accurate image of America in Europe. But the endeavors to overcome the deep-seated prejudices may still take some time.

As a number of passages in the diary point out, a far-reaching convergence or mutual adaptation in lifestyle, living standard and consumer goods has come about between America and Europe. This also holds true of the mutual understanding of liberal democracy. There will always be differences of opinion and tensions between America and Europe. But these differences should not obscure the fact that what unites America and Europe is stronger than what sets them apart. What unites America and Europe are a common history, the great European immigration to America, and a common cultural heritage. However, what binds America and Europe together even stronger are shared values: The respect for the dignity of the human person, the protection of civil liberties, and the prerogative of the parliamentary democratic form of government.

Has the puzzle America been solved? Not really, for one lifetime would not be enough for the task. But the many observations in this diary about America and transatlantic relations that span over four decades try to enlighten many of the puzzling questions. I hope that this volume will contribute to a better understanding of America and American-European relations.

INDEX OF NAMES

Adams, Samuel, 217
Adenauer, Konrad, 75, 382
Adorno, Theodor, 335
Agnew, Spiro T., 103, 173, 189, 190, 212
Aldrin, Edwin, Jr., 130
Alfonso XIII, Juan Carlos, King of Spain, 226
Alvarado, Juan Bautista, 41
Amann, Jacob, 58
Anders, William A., 113, 411
Anderson, John, 290, 295
Andreotti, Giulio, 254, 255, 257
Andrews, Julie, 391
Andropov, Yuri, 334
Aquino, Benigno, 363
Aquino, Corazon, 362, 363
Armstrong, Neil A., 130, 131, 440
Assad, Hefez al-, 352

Bach, Johann Sebastian, 348-49, 388
Baker, Howard, 207, 399
Bakhtian, Shapour, 268
Bartholdi, F.A., 370
Bayh, Birch, 228
Becket, Saint Thomas à, 144
Beethoven, Ludwig van, 371, 388
Begin, Menachem, 253, 261, 270
Bellow, Saul, 216-17

Bentsen, Lloyd, 401, 405
Berlin, Irving, 398-99
Berlinguer, Enrico, 232, 257
Bernstein, Leonard, 365, 388
Biddle, Nicholas, 23
Billington, Ray Allen, 158
Bodmer, Karl, 104
Böll, Heinrich, 175, 352-53
Bologna, Giovanni, 29
Bolzius, Johann Martin, 123, 124
Bork, Robert, 190
Borman, Frank, 113, 411
Brademas, John, 176, 270, 299
Brady, James, 305
Brahms, Johannes, 325
Brandt, Willy, 133, 134, 135, 136, 140, 145, 162, 169, 177, 178, 186, 199
Branigin, Roger D., 95
Braun, Suso, 77-78
Brecht, Bertolt, 335
Brezhnev, Leonid, 211, 273, 304, 312, 315, 334, 426
Brinkley, David, 109, 315
Brooke, Edward, 103, 104
Brown, Jerry, 236
Brunelleschi, Filippo, 255
Buback, Siegfried, 246
Buck, Pearl S., 165

449

Buffalo Bill, see Cody, William F.
Bundy, Francois, 74
Burger, Warren, 302, 369
Bush, George, 160, 161, 295, 297, 327, 395, 404, 405, 406, 407, 409, 410, 412-13, 415, 416, 420, 421, 422, 426, 427
Bush, George W., 372, 378, 408
Byrd, Robert C., 63
Byrne, Jane, 299

Cabrillo, Juan Rodriguez, 37
Carrington, Lord Peter, 317
Carson, Johnny, 129
Carter, Jimmy, 228, 230-31, 233, 236, 240, 241, 242, 243, 245, 247, 248, 254, 257, 261, 262, 263, 264, 265, 266, 268, 270, 273, 274, 280, 282, 287, 288, 289, 290, 291, 298, 299, 302, 310
Castro, Fidel, 24, 293
Ceausescu, Nicolae, 431, 432
Cernan, Eugene, 126, 178,
Chagall, Marc, 349
Charlemagne, Emperor, 259
Chateaubriand, Francois, 56
Chaucer, Geoffrey, 37
Chernenko, Konstantin, 348
Chiang Kai-shek, 157
Chirac, Jacques, 398
Chopin, Frédéric, 382
Chou En-lai, 165
Christopher, Warren, 268, 302
Churchill, Winston, 347, 382, 430, 431
Cimabue, 255
Clemens, Samuel ("Mark Twain"), 183, 277
Clinton, Bill, 383, 408

Cody, William F. ("Buffalo Bill"), 104-05
Collins, Michael, 130
Colombo, Emilio, 145
Conant, James B., 383
Conrads, Heinz, 129
Cooper, James Fenimore, 12, 25, 66
Cooper, Judge William, 66
Cornwallis, Lord Charles, 311
Coronado, Francisco Vasquez de, 33
Cox, Archibald, 188, 190
Crane, Hart, 20
Crawford, William R., 24
Crippen, Robert, 306
Cronkite, Walter, 345
Cunningham, Walter, 109

Daley, Richard, 233
Dante Alighieri, 144
Davis, Jefferson, 25
Dean, John, 186
Dearborn, Henry, 43
De Gaulle, Charles, 73, 75, 76, 91, 96-97, 117, 118, 120, 125, 146-47, 161
Dobrynin, Anatoly, 135
Dole, Robert, 236, 395
Domingo, Placido, 391
Donner, George, 277
Donner, Jacob, 277
Douglas, William O., 29
Dreiser, Theodore, 214
Dürer, Albrecht, 296
Dubcek, Alexander, 429
Dukakis, Michael S., 221, 395, 401, 402, 403, 405, 407
Dyck, Anthonis van, 57

Eagleton, Thomas F., 172, 173
Ehrlichman, John D., 186, 214
Eisele, Donn, 109

Eisenhower, Dwight D., 119-20, 215, 412
Eliot, T.S., 144
Elizabeth II, Queen of England, 91, 381
Ervin, Samuel J., Jr., 186, 187, 207
Escalante, Silvestre Valez de, 34

Falkland, Viscount, 317
Farrell, James T., 214
Fermi, Enrico, 85
Ferolli, Beatrice, 216
Fiedler, Arthur, 68
Figl, Leopold, 294
Fischer, Foreign Minister of the German Democratic Republic, 341
Ford, Gerald R., 190, 208, 209, 210, 211, 212, 215, 220, 225, 228, 229, 231, 234, 236, 240, 242, 310
Foster, Stephen, 57
Francis of Assisi, 255
Francke, August Hermann, 123, 124
Franco, Francisco, 226
Franklin, Benjamin, 23, 37
Frémont, John Charles, 34
Fulbright, J. William ("Fulbright Program"), 11, 12, 29, 90, 210, 442

Gagarin, Yuri, 23, 440
Gage, Thomas, 217
Gainsborough, Thomas, 37
Garrity, W. Arthur, Jr., 221
Genscher, Hans-Dietrich, 425
George II, King of England, 123
Gershwin, George, 68
Giotto, 255
Gipp, George, 396
Giscard d'Estaing, Valery, 199, 200, 231-32, 254, 306

Glenn, John, Jr., 23, 52, 210, 440
Goethe, Johann Wolfgang von, 183, 259, 260, 325
Goldwater, Barry, 61, 62, 70, 103, 265, 266
Gorbachev, Mikhail, 313, 348, 357, 358, 360, 373-74, 379, 380, 384, 389, 390, 393, 399, 400, 401, 407, 409, 410, 412, 418, 421-22, 439
Gore, Albert, 395
Graham, Billy, 44
Grant, Ulysses, 64
Grasse, Count de, 311
Gromyko, Andrei, 157, 326, 345, 346

Haig, Alexander, 302, 318, 320, 322
Haldeman, H.R., 186, 214
Hancock, John, 217
Harris, Fred, 228
Harvard, John, 31
Hasley, Louis, 280
Hawgood, John A., 40, 157-58
Hawthorne, Nathaniel, 11, 68, 69
Hayakawa, Samuel I., 240
Haydn, Joseph, 325, 365, 371
Heath, Edward, 161
Hemingway, Ernest, 320
Hensley, John, 431
Hesburgh, Theodore M., 61, 62, 196
Hesse, Hermann, 255
Holt, Harold E., 86
Honecker, Erich, 340, 385, 426
Hope, Bob, 359
Horowitz, Vladimir, 382
Humboldt, Alexander von, 34, 38
Humboldt, Wilhelm von, 38
Humphrey, Hubert H., 73, 74, 95, 98, 107-08, 110, 111, 112, 126, 167, 168, 233

Hunt, Richard Morris, 297
Huntington, Henry Edwards ("Huntington Library"), 12, 31, 37, 40, 158
Hussein, King of Jordan, 120

Jackson, Henry, 167, 228, 230, 231
Jackson, Jesse, 395, 401, 402
James, Henry, 143, 151, 445
Jan III Sobieski, King of Poland, 331
Jefferson, Thomas, 43, 113
John XXIII, Pope, 261
John Paul I, Pope, 261, 262
John Paul II, Pope, 38, 263, 267, 272, 279-80, 307, 321, 326, 330-31, 333, 366, 385-86, 439
Johnson, Lyndon B., 46, 59, 60, 65, 67, 72, 73, 74, 75, 82, 83, 86, 88, 89, 90, 92-93, 96, 98, 109, 110, 115, 116, 149, 177, 401
Jones, Maldwyn Allen, 219
Juan Carlos I, King of Spain, 226

Kafka, Franz, 20, 235, 330
Karajan, Herbert von, 150
Karmal, Babrak, 284
Kennedy, David M., 162
Kennedy, Edward, 100, 290, 295, 297
Kennedy, John F., 24, 45, 46, 65, 67, 71, 74, 90, 92, 99, 110, 113, 117, 121, 131, 338, 364, 401, 413
Kennedy, Richard S., 67
Kennedy, Robert, 91-92, 95-96, 98, 99, 230
Kerner, Otto, 89
Key, Francis Scott, 235
Khomeini, Ayatollah, 268
Khrushchev, Nikita, 46, 413
Kiesinger, Kurt Georg, 86, 133

King, Martin Luther, Jr., 46, 93, 94, 99, 360
Kirchschläger, Rudolf, 336
Kirk, Grayson, 62
Kissinger, Henry, 135, 163, 166, 170-71, 176, 189, 191, 220, 224, 229, 249, 254, 274, 381
Kleindienst, Richard, 186
Kohl, Helmut, 329, 332, 341, 350, 379, 416, 418, 429
Kosygin, Aleksey, 145
Kreisky, Bruno, 139-40, 170, 245, 258
Krenz, Egon, 426

Lafayette, Marquis de, 428
La Salle, Robert Cavelier, Sieur de, 43, 65
Laszlo, Stefan, 375
Le Duc Tho, 176
Lenin, Vladimir, 400, 401
Leonov, Aleksey, 223
Lessing, Gotthold Ephraim, 259
Lincoln, Abraham, 56
Lindbergh, Charles, 23
Liszt, Franz, 382
Lodge, Cabot, 61
Longfellow, Henry Wadsworth, 11
Louis XIV, King of France, 43
Louis Philippe, Duke of Orleans, King of France, 57
Lovell, James A., Jr., 113, 147-48, 411
Luciani, Cardinal Albino, 261
Lugar, Richard, 240, 361, 362
Luther, Martin, 325, 329

Maazel, Lorin, 321, 345
Madeira, Jean (Browning), 58
Makarios, Archbishop of Cyprus, 205

Mann, Thomas, 143, 195-96, 335
Mansfield, Michael (Mike) J., 148, 149, 166, 195
Mao Tse-tung, 165
Marcos, Ferdinand, 362, 363
Maritain, Jacques, 212-13
Mark Twain, see Samuel Clemens
Marquette, Jacques, 65
Marshall, George C. ("Marshall Plan"), 245, 382-83, 384, 446
Marshall, John, 372
Marx, Karl, 325
Maximilian, Prince of Wied-Neuwied, 104
Maximus V Hakim, Patriarch, 98
McCarthy, Eugene J., 90, 91-92, 95-96, 98, 107
McGovern, George, 65, 167, 168, 172, 173, 177
Meany, George, 108
Mehta, Zubin, 371
Melville, Herman, 12, 64, 66, 67, 70, 320
Menon, Krishna, 45
Menotti, Gian Carlo, 48
Mertensotto, Leon, 133
Metternich, Clemens von, 224
Metzenbaum, Howard M., 240
Meyer, Cardinal Albert, 62
Michelangelo Buonarroti, 71, 225
Miller, Arthur, 20, 48, 172, 183-84
Minelli, Liza, 325
Miscamble, Wilson D., 248
Mitchell, John M., 214
Mitterand, Francois, 199, 306, 311, 327, 350, 398, 370, 421
Mohr, Nicolaus, 158
Mondale, Walter, 236, 247, 297, 343

Monnet, Jean, 382
Montana, Joe, 316
Montgomery, Horace, 25, 95
Moro, Aldo, 257, 258, 337
Morris, Edmund, 305, 313, 321, 351, 375
Mother Teresa of Culcutta, 356
Moynihan, Daniel P., 240
Mozart, Wolfgang Amadeus, 150, 250, 382, 388
Musil, Robert, 258
Muskie, Edmund, 108, 109, 167, 168, 298

Nagy, Imre, 418, 419
Nicolet, Jean, 65
Nixon, Richard, 90, 91, 92, 98, 102-03, 109, 110, 111, 112, 115, 116, 117, 120, 125, 132, 138, 155, 157, 162, 163, 165, 166, 168, 169, 170, 173, 174, 177, 181, 186, 187, 189, 190, 191, 194, 195, 196, 197, 198, 199, 200, 202, 206, 207, 208, 212, 310, 338, 399
Norman, Jesse, 421
Norris, Frank, 12, 31, 214, 228, 229

Ogden, Peter Skene, 34
Oglethorpe, James E., 123, 124
O'Neill, Thomas P. ("Tip"), 364, 394

Pahlavi, Shah Reza, 266, 268, 282
Palme, Olof, 363
Parsons, Sir Anthony, 319
Paul VI, Pope, 86, 220, 225, 227, 246, 256, 260, 261
Pei, I. Ming, 421
Penn, William, 30
Percy, Charles H., 343

Perez de Cuellar, Javier, 320, 385
Pershing, John J., 283
Podgorny, Nikolai, 198
Pompidou, Georges, 136, 161, 198
Popieluszko, Jerzy, 342, 343

Qaddafi, Muammar, 364
Quayle, Dan, 404, 405, 406

Raab, Julius, 294
Raffaello Santi, 325
Rahner, Karl, 335, 336
Ramos, Fidel, 362
Reagan, Ronald, 82, 228, 229, 231, 236, 290, 295, 297, 298, 299, 300, 302, 303, 304, 305, 307-08, 309, 311, 312, 313, 315, 321, 322, 336, 338, 343, 346, 350, 351, 352, 356, 357, 358, 360, 361, 362, 363, 366, 369, 370, 373, 374, 375, 378, 381, 384, 385, 386, 389, 390, 391, 393, 394, 395-96, 399, 400, 405, 409, 410, 412, 416, 439
Reeves, Paschal, 67, 95
Rehnquist, William H., 369, 371, 372, 412
Reinhardt, Max, 133
Rembrandt (Harmenszoon) van Rijn, 30
Revere, Paul, 217
Richardson, Elliot L., 190
Riemenschneider, Tilman, 323
Ritter, Cardinal Joseph, 62
Rockefeller, David, 196
Rockefeller, Nelson, 61, 82, 90, 92, 103, 196, 209, 212
Rockne, Knute, 395-96, 397
Rockwell, Norman, 405, 406
Rodino, Peter W., 200

Rogers, William, 180
Roosevelt, Franklin Delano, 109, 215, 261, 347, 412
Rumor, Mariano, 145
Rusk, Dean, 45, 90

Sadat, Anwar, 220, 224, 253, 261, 262, 270, 310, 311
Sagan, Carl, 300
Sakharov, Andrei, 243
Sandys, Edwina, 430-31, 438
Scalia, Antonin, 369, 372
Scheel, Walteer, 222
Schiller, Friedrich, 244
Schirra, Walter, 109
Schlesinger, James R., 216
Schleyer, Hans-Martin, 251, 252
Schmidt, Helmut, 211, 311, 315, 329, 332
Schmitt, Harrison, 178
Schubert, Franz, 382
Schuman, Robert, 382, 436
¬Schumann, Robert, 382
Schuschnigg, Kurt, 252
Scowcroft, Brent, 420, 426
Semenov, Vladimir, 141
Semper, Gottfried, 347
Senghor, Léopold Sédar, 249
Serra, Junipero, 38
Seton, Elizabeth, 225
Shevardnadze, Eduard, 374, 380, 387, 426
Shriver, Robert Sargent, Jr., 173
Shultz, George P., 322, 345, 346, 359, 366, 373, 374, 375, 380, 386, 387, 388, 390, 391, 395
Siegel, Irving H., 89
Sirica, John J., 206, 214

Smith, Gerard C., 141
Solzhenitsyn, Aleksandr (Alexander), 195, 197, 334
Sousa, John Philip, 68
Spaak, Paul Henri, 382
Spasowski, Romuald, 314
Spellman, Cardinal Francis Joseph, 85-86
Spengler, Oswald, 226
Spiller, Robert E., 12, 21, 22
Stafford, Thomas, 126, 223
Stalin, Josef, 364
Stassen, Harold E., 61
Steinbeck, John, 320, 377-78
Stoph, Willi, 140
Strauss, Richard, 142, 150, 348
Suarez, Adolfo, 249
Sutter, John August, 40, 41, 43

Teng Hsiao-p'ing, 266, 267, 268
Thatcher, Margaret, 283-84, 304, 315, 317, 322, 438
Thieu, Nguyen Van, 218
Thomas Aquinas, 212
Tisserant, Cardinal Eugene, 62
Tito, Josip, 288, 289, 292-93
Tocqueville, Alexis de, 25
Toynbee, Arnold J., 24, 225-226
Tramin, Peter von, 216
Tresp, Lothar L., 121, 123, 124
Trudeau, Pierre, 319
Truman, Harry S., 383, 430

Udall, Morris, 228, 230, 236
Urlsperger, Samuel, 124

Van Buren, Martin, 409
Vance, Cyrus, 254, 292, 298
Vanderbilt, George W., 296

Verdi, Giuseppe, 371
Verne, Jules, 113
Vorster, Johannes, 247

Wagner, Richard, 325, 329, 388
Walesa, Lech, 301, 314, 428, 439
Wallace, George C., 59, 60, 61, 103, 107, 110, 111, 112, 167, 168, 169, 228, 231, 233
Walters, Barbara, 304
Washington, George, 69, 235, 212, 247, 311, 412
Weber, Carl Maria von, 347
Weigel, George, 267, 272, 307, 343
Weinberger, Caspar, 322, 366
Welsh, Matthew, 60, 61
Whitman, Walt, 20
Wilder, Thorton, 320
Wilson, Harold, 86
Winthrop, John, 221
Wojtyla, Cardinal Karol, 263
Wolfe, Thomas, 12, 20, 67, 296, 320, 445
Wright, James (Jim) C., Jr., 394

Yeltsin, Boris, 414, 439
Young, Brigham, 35
Young, John, 126, 306

Zorin, Valerian, 45
Zweig, Stefan, 203